For Mary & Frank

♡ Carla

THE PATH TO HEALING

CARLA BLOWEY

Dreaming Kevin
PUBLISHING
MONTROSE, COLORADO

ISBN 10: 0692260560
ISBN 13: 978-0-692-26056-2

Cover Design by Paul Frocchi, www.stillsthatmove.com
Illustrations by Kevin Blowey, Amber Blowey Higgs, Dillon Curry, Kyle Gladding, and Mitchell Davis
"Keven" © 2004 and "Kevin" © 2010 by Jason Blowey
All photos, artwork, and book format are the property of Carla Frocchi Blowey

Together Forever, copyright 1984 Shining Star Music, (ASCAP) Words & Music by Michael McLean, used by permission

Published by: Dreaming Kevin Publishing, Montrose, CO

Printed in the United States of America
Published August, 2014

For Amber

With Love, Mom

"Oh! Call my brother back to me!
I cannot play alone;
The Summer comes with flower and bee
Where is my brother gone?"

Felecia Dorothea Browne Hemans

Contents

Part III ~ The Search for Meaning

Part IV ~ Reunion

Part V ~ Afterglow 2014

Author's Note

The telling of my story will not make you a believer of my experience.
I only ask that you consider this: let my words strike a chord of truth
within you, so that you may hear your own sacred notes.
And then, embark upon your own journey,
and listen to the many ways in which
God speaks to you.

PART I

The Nightmare

1
In that Moment

Breathless, I climbed the last ladder stretching to the top story and pulled myself over to the wood floor. I scrambled about in the shadows and regained my footing to find yet another obstacle in my way. Stepping toward the closed door, I gripped the knob and abruptly pushed it opened. Horrified, I came face to face with the Blonde Woman from the cult. Locking her eyes with mine, she bore a hole through my soul with her cold stare. In disbelief, I stood frozen in the doorway, stunned that she had found the children and me.

Emerging from the dark her flaxen hair seemed to illuminate the space above her, revealing the wooden rafters in the attic. She stood erect in the shadows like a sentry on duty with her right forearm raised about waist high. In her hand she grasped a long silver blade that pointed upwards. Unyielding in her mission she summoned its power to intercept my path. Stunned, I sensed Kevin dangling from the rafters below her feet. Her relentless stare pierced through my heart, confirming her message. She had come for my son. In defense, I covered my eyes to break the spell while a desperate cry of denial came from deep within me. Peering through my trembling fingers, I exposed myself again. With one more look, she commanded the door shut, leaving me trapped on the other side. Screaming like a mad woman, I beat my fists upon the heavy attic door that separated my son from me.

I rolled my head from side to side trying to shake away the image of the Blonde Woman. My arms thrashed about, as the bed covers slid from around my neck exposing my drenched skin to the chilly morning air. I gasped; my heart was pounding so fast it felt as though I had been buried beneath a stack of blankets during the night. My eyes opened wide with fear and then squeezed shut from the glaring hallway light. Squinting this time, I detected a slight movement in the shadows before me. Startled, I rose up on my elbows and craned my neck forward to see the blurry outline of my husband's broad shoulders as he slid his arms into a button down shirt.

It was morning! I took a deep breath dropping my head back on the pillow, ever so thankful to be in my own bed again. Smoothing back the damp curls from my forehead, I rubbed my eyes to focus. "Stann," I mumbled, "I had this terrible nightmare about the kids; somebody was trying to take them away from me. I was running with them on the street, and..."

Everything seemed so clear just moments ago, and now as I tried to relay the dream it sounded crazy. Nothing I said seemed to convey where I had just been! I tried to say more, but all I could see were the Blonde Woman's eyes staring at me from the shadows. I lay there confused while Stann finished dressing for school. He was accustomed to listening to me ramble about my previous night's dreams. Frowning, he shrugged away his discomfort about this latest dream. Shaking his head he said in an almost disgusted tone, "Carla, I can't believe you dream that stuff."

I ignored yet another typical remark expressing his discomfort with my dream world. Suddenly, it dawned on me that if Stann was up, then the children were not far behind, and that meant I had better get moving. Christmas vacation was over and everyone would soon be on their way to school. We had transferred Amber to another elementary school in town just before the holidays, so I would be driving her there. The car pool with Kevin's preschool buddies would arrive first, then we would be on our way. I did not have time this morning to lie in bed and think about that awful nightmare.

Kneeling under the window above our bed, I peered through the closed vinyl blinds. The sky was overcast this January morning predicting another frigid day. Smoke curls wrapped around the chimneystacks disappearing into the gray morning light. The street lamp dimmed slightly; its timer confused by the cloudy dawn.

I pulled on a pair of jeans and a sweatshirt and attempted to calm down my unruly curls. My ear tuned in to the sound of an argument brewing in the hallway between the kids. I headed out squeezing past them on the way to the bathroom.

4

"Kevin, you have to make your bed first before you can watch television!" Amber ordered, shaking her finger at him.

"I don't have to! You're not the boss of me!" he shot back. Hot on his heels she followed him to the kitchen hoping to gain support from Daddy.

Stann gently diffused the quarrel with some light humor and refocused the kids on breakfast. Stann's mellow personality endeared him to almost everyone, especially his children. He was an outstanding athlete, but his masculinity never outweighed the love he showered on his kids. Eating breakfast with daddy became the children's special time with him to talk about the day ahead.

Our combined kitchen and dining area had sliding glass doors that led to a covered patio and backyard. The dining area opened left to the hallway and straight to the living room. The open concept allowed easy conversation between the two areas despite the limited space in our home. Showered and dressed, I hurried about clearing the dishes. I overheard Stann and Kevin talking at the table.

"Daddy, I don't want to go to preschool," Kevin announced quietly. He dropped his sandy blonde head and looked down at his cereal bowl, pushing the spoon aside.

"Oh sure you do Kevin. Everyone will be there. Kyle and Michael will be back from vacation too," Stann said sounding upbeat and lowering his head to look at Kevin. "Hey Sport, you need to eat so you can be ready to go." Patting him on the shoulders, Stann left the table.

I turned around to look at Kevin from where I stood at the kitchen sink. I was very surprised to hear Kevin say he did not want to go to school. He loved Miss Sharon, the directress at the Montessori school and never wanted to miss a day with his long time buddies, Kyle and Michael. I was stunned by this admission and said dramatically, "What? You don't want to go to preschool. I can't believe it!"

For the first time that morning, I really looked at him. Typically, he was dressed in jeans and a favorite T-shirt, covered by a red and black sweater. His size six pants were rolled up at the cuff waiting for an overdue growth spurt. His sandy blonde hair parted at the cowlick portraying another strong gene inherited from daddy. Neither of our children resembled my Italian heritage. My only claim was that Kevin and I shared the same brown eyes. However, this morning, those bright eyes were downcast and sad. He shook his head and said, "I just don't want to go today."

Kevin was usually very even-tempered and laid back like his daddy. He had a more sensitive, intuitive nature though, and I usually trusted his sense of what he wanted. I knew from experience that I should pay attention, particularly because it came on so suddenly. I moved to the table leaning on my elbows across from him. Speaking softly I said,

5

"Kevin, you like going to school. All the kids will be there, and you haven't seen them since before Christmas vacation."

He shook his head sadly again looking down at the soggy bowl of Cheerios. "Mommy, I just don't want to go today."

I didn't want to push him, hoping he would elaborate a little more on his own later. "He's probably just tired from last night," I thought to myself. I smiled, remembering the fun filled day we had with our friends making Italian sausage. The children had played merrily throughout the house, while eight adults set to work forming a comical crew of mixers and wrappers. The assembly line stretched across Dave and Kathy's kitchen counter and into the dining room as we transformed their home into a mini meat factory. The mountains of ground pork became a playground for us to laugh and catch up with each other after the long Christmas break. The eight children wasted no time in reconnecting. At one point, I found them barricaded behind the basement door laughing hysterically, their hot sweaty faces poking out from beneath the pile. It was a wonderful day, but we were all a little worn out and tired for that first day back to school.

Despite my prodding, Kevin continued to stare out the sliding glass doors as if preoccupied. I looked up to see Stann as he thrust an arm into his winter denim jacket, preparing to leave for his teaching job at the middle school. We would see him again at dinner, after basketball practice. He kissed Amber, wishing her a good day at the new school. Stann returned to the table and kissed Kevin on the forehead saying goodbye to him too. Curiously, Kevin remained seated, still in a pensive state. He did not initiate their usual boisterous exchange of wrestling and hand play.

Shortly after, Michael arrived for the car pool. Kevin's mood brightened at seeing one of his favorite friends. They watched cartoons on television until their ride came a little while later. Kyle, his other buddy, would also accompany them to school. Today, their driver was Kyle's new sitter instead of his father. I walked them out to the driveway, and Michael climbed into the mini-pickup truck first, next to Kyle. I remember thinking that I did not like the set up because there would be two in a seat belt; it wouldn't be safe. Kevin hesitated, not wanting to get in. Again, I was struck by his unusual behavior, but I encouraged him to have a good time. Puzzled, I waved goodbye as they drove off.

A few minutes later, Amber and I were in the car talking about what she might expect in her new third grade class. Her pretty green eyes reflected some anxiety at the prospect of starting over in another school. The new teacher, Mary Ann, was one of our closest friends (and another sausage maker). We hoped Mary Ann would get her back on track with math and reading. She worried most though about making new friends. I assured her that things would be great at her new school and that she was lucky to have one of our dear friends as her teacher. She was still nervous despite what I said, but once Mary Ann greeted her, she settled in quickly without a hitch.

Driving home, I finally took a deep breath from the busy activities of the early morning. "What next?" I thought. "I've only got a couple of hours before I pick up Kevin. I need to exercise, strip the sheets on Kevin's bed, start laundry, and take my film in to be developed."

After a quick change of clothes, I headed down to the workout room in the basement. Climbing on my exercise bike, I began pushing the pedals round and round mulling over why I had been in such a melancholy mood throughout the holidays. I had several worries on my mind throughout the month. It was a strange feeling and I could not shake it.

Obviously, the changes we were making for Amber were certain to cause some worry for her as well as ourselves. We were confident that this would be an opportunity for her to regain her self-confidence in school. We would get her through that just fine.

I thought about how different the holidays were without my mom since her death five years ago. Her absence in my life was particularly painful, and I often felt alone. In time though, I successfully grieved her death and moved on with loving memories. I had done the grieving thing. No, my mood was not about my mother's absence. I was over that.

I cranked up the volume on the cassette player and pedaled faster. All right now I reasoned, we had a wonderful Christmas together, just the four of us. Reminiscing, I reminded myself of the cozy Christmas Eve and Christmas morning with our little family. During the day, Stann played with the children while I busily worked in the kitchen preparing my mother's traditional Italian specialties. I smiled, picturing the kid's wrinkled noses turned up at the strong smell of that "stinky cheese" soup and lasagna with more "gross" cheese.

We dressed up for Christmas Eve Mass in clothes that I had coordinated in my favorite color, purple. We looked so fine that I took an entire roll of snapshots of us posing in front of the tree. Later nestled together on the couch, we shared hot chocolate and marshmallows while I read the Nativity story to the kids. The kids put out cookies and milk for Santa, and of course, carrots and water for the reindeer to complete the Christmas Eve ritual. They were so excited that it took them some time to settle down for the night.

When they were finally asleep, Stann and I made a beeline downstairs to the storage room where all their gifts were hidden. Stann had already put together Kevin's bike a few nights before, so we wheeled it into the living room. For weeks, I had searched for just the right size bike for Kevin since he had conquered two wheeling some time ago. He would be so surprised to get a cool bike.

Afterward, we barricaded the hallway with a chair and a note from Santa instructing them to wake up their parents before going into the living room. The diversion worked long enough for us to put Stann in place with the video camera. They rounded the corner wide-eyed with delight at the array of presents beneath the tree. Amber loved her new Cabbage Patch doll chosen especially for its resemblance to her –thick blonde hair, green eyes and chubby cheeks! I chuckled remembering Kevin as he approached his new bike with hands on his hips. Quietly, nodding his head in an affirmation of our choice, he said, "Yep, it's just what I need." After all the presents were opened, Stann cooked the most delicious pancakes for a leisurely breakfast.

The morning flew by, and soon and it was time to drive up to Grandma and Grandpa Blowey's house in Grand Junction to spend the afternoon with them. Stann's sister and her three boys would be there as well. I wished we had not committed to any specific time. Honestly, I was content to seclude ourselves from the holiday frenzy and just stay home.

Christmas came early to Grandma's house too, and the second round proved to be just as exciting. Shiny paper and colored bows were quickly strewn across the living room floor as the children tore open their gifts. We had a fun visit, and the kids spent the afternoon playing games with their cousins.

After Christmas, we spent some of the holiday vacation at home. While I worked, Stann enjoyed his time off from teaching with the kids. It had stopped snowing, and our sidewalk was cleared for Kevin to practice riding his new bike. Amber played with Barbies and her new games. A few days later, we left for Denver to visit my dad and my brother. It was an uneventful trip, except for more snow and hazardous driving conditions both ways. Our Christmas vacation ended with sledding at the park, watching videos, playing games, and making sausage with our friends. Who could ask for more?

I glanced at the timer on the bike. "Thank God. It's time to get off this thing," I said aloud. Onto the floor exercises and I would be done with this work out. I sang along with the music as loudly as I could, puffing and groaning through the leg lifts. My thoughts drifted to what was in store for the rest of the week.

Work. My mood took a slight dip as I thought about my hairdressing job. Tomorrow, I intended to tell Pati, my boss, that I could no longer work Saturdays. Stann and I discussed it over the holidays and agreed that if my schedule could not change I would resign.

For the past year I had been struggling with my work schedule. I had successfully built my clientele to a comfortable number and decided during the summer to cut back on my hours at the end of the year. I hated working Saturdays and ten-hour days. My schedule had become so restrictive that it allowed little time on the weekends with the family. Left behind, I would watch them go off to the movies or to the park, while I felt as if I had a ball and chain around my ankle. I dragged myself to work, resenting every minute.

I had become intimidated by the expectations of my employer as well as my own expectations of what I should be doing. I was caught between meeting her business goals and meeting the needs of my family. Complicating matters was my eleven-year friendship with Pati and the loyalty and love I felt for her.

I chose this career because of the flexibility it would afford my family life, but the longer I worked the more rigid my schedule became. I had lost control of my career and had lost valuable time with my family. It was not worth the money to sacrifice precious moments with them and to endure the guilt and stress any longer. I just wanted to be with my kids and my husband. I missed them. I dreaded going to work tomorrow. My mood plunged.

"For crying out loud, Carla, life is good", I thought. I had to shake this foreboding sense! "Once I get back into an exercise routine my mood will be better", I said out loud. I clicked the off switch on the cassette player and raced up the basement stairs to the kitchen. As I walked across the room, an eerie feeling came over me. Looming from the back of my mind, the Blonde Woman from the nightmare appeared again. I shivered at her menacing image. Now, in the quiet of the house that stupid nightmare was flashing in my head. I did not want to think about it. I didn't have time.

At a quarter past eleven, I left to pick up the boys at preschool. In good weather, the drive was less than ten minutes through downtown traffic. Uncertain of the condition of the country roads since the holidays, I took my time getting there. The quaint white schoolhouse was at the end of a tree lined gravel driveway. It was in a lovely rural setting with all the country amenities, horses in the field, rabbits in the barn, and the boys' favorite, Nana the dog.

I parked the Wagoneer and went inside to get them. No sooner had I stepped in, Kevin flew past me running out the door to the car. He didn't even say goodbye to Miss Sharon or any of the kids. He never acted like that when I came for him. Confused, I shrugged to her over the crowd of children and waved goodbye.

Outside, Michael and Kyle piled into the warm car. I usually had Michael sit in the front seat since he was the first one to be dropped off at day care, but Kevin was already sitting there. The other two boys climbed in the back, and they all giggled and talked while I drove out to the main road, still wondering what the rush was all about to get the front seat.

I loved to hear them kibbutz about their morning at school. Everything was always a joke with these boys, and they played it to the hilt. When their conversation quieted, Kevin proudly announced to the boys that his Daddy would let him take karate classes. Impressed by the news, they began a spontaneous demonstration of hand chopping movements and sounds imitating the Ninja Turtles.

"Mom, when does my class start?" Kevin asked.

I replied, "Well Kev, we don't know for sure that you can take karate. Dr. Winkler has to check your feet and tell us whether it is okay. We'll ask him at your appointment on Friday."

He immediately countered with, "Well Dad said I could take karate when I'm six!" Laughing I agreed, and I reminded him that he would not be six until the summer. He frowned at the idea of having to wait so long.

A few minutes later we arrived at the child care home where Michael and Kevin attended. Saying goodbye to the boys, Michael wobbled down the sidewalk like a duck in his snow gear. Bella appeared at the door, and they both waved back to us. Staring through the foggy car window, Kevin watched pensively as Michael disappeared into the house.

Then turning to face me he quietly said, "Mommy I want to go to Bella's today." The tone of his voice was serious, and those dark brown eyes seemed focused on something far away. "Boy, what is going on with him today?" I thought. I cocked my head sideways searching his face for a clue. "Well, you'll see the kids tomorrow when I go to work and you'll have all day to play with them. Okay?" I promised.

He gazed silently out the window a few moments longer. Then he climbed into the back seat to sit with Kyle. I drove off relieved to hear them whispering and giggling.

"Mom, we want to play today," Kevin announced loudly from behind me. "Can Kyle come to our house, please?" he begged, half giggling, half-serious.

Kyle chimed in with, "Please Carla, I really want to come home with you today".

Oh were they persistent! While they begged me to say yes, I was thinking about how I would get out of this one. Usually, Kyle spent at least one day of the week at our house while his mom was at the vocational school. Our friends were going through an unpleasant divorce, and our house was a port in the storm for Kyle. His mom and I had talked the night before about the new sitter and the changes in car-pooling. I knew that if I changed the routine his father would be upset. Anticipating the boys wanting to be together despite the changes, we had planned on a day for them to play later in the week. I promised her my support in whatever she needed to make things comfortable for Kyle.

As young mothers, we spent many afternoons laughing about our boys latest antics while they laughed and played together. Although two distinct little guys in personality and physical stature, they were as close as friends could be. Kyle was lean, and tall and Kevin was short and stocky. Kyle tended to be a little more serious while Kevin was the joker. Kyle loved coming to our house, and he was always a delight to have. The boys played so well together that often times I never knew they were around. They were definitely "buds" as they called themselves, bonded from birth.

I took a deep breath and sighed, "Guys, I don't think today is a good time because it's the first day for Kyle's new sitter. I think his mom would want him to stay there." Their protest was loud and gaining, and I had to stand my ground. "You guys can play on Friday for the whole day! I promise."

They both looked at me as though I had said no until the end of time. Big tears rolled down Kyle's ruddy cheeks. Kevin was clearly dejected and somber, his dark brown eyes searching me for a reason. I felt lousy. At that moment, I was very mad at Kyle's dad for making things so complicated for the boys. I expected them to be disappointed, but this was disheartening.

I turned the car into the narrow driveway and pulled up to the porch of their townhouse. The sitter, a young woman in her early twenties came out to greet us as I got out. I thanked her for driving in the morning and jabbered on about something unimportant, anything to overlook the boys' unmistakable disappointment at not being able to play together. I had shattered their plans of an adventurous afternoon of playing super heroes.

Kevin and Kyle barely looked at each other as they mumbled their good byes. I opened the car door for Kyle to get out and reminded him that he could come over on Friday. He trudged up the porch steps and stood beside the sitter looking as though I had abandoned him.

I climbed behind the wheel and waved goodbye, driving to the end of the road and turning onto the alley behind the greenhouse and past the hospital. Feeling bad, I tried to cheer up Kevin. "Hey, Kev, you'll get to see Kyle at preschool again, and then, on Friday you can play together. Okay?" Kevin was hardly ever mad at me, but today I knew I had blown it. He remained solemn the rest of the way home.

Heading south of town the view of the San Juan Mountains was obscured by the overcast skies. On most days, the majestic snow covered peaks were visible from anywhere in the valley. We had so much precipitation this winter that as soon as we shoveled the sidewalk it was covered with more. By noon the dismal weather had not improved, and it seemed colder than usual. I thought about ignoring my errands for the day.

Once inside the house, I warmed a bowl of chicken noodle soup and made a plain baloney sandwich for Kevin, just the way he liked it. I had a salad keeping my New Year's resolution. Afterwards he played in the living room while I made some phone calls. I mentioned to him that we would be going out again to run errands. He flatly declared he did not want to go anywhere. I felt even worse that I had thwarted his plans. The weather was so cold it actually seemed like a good idea to stay home. We didn't need to pick up Amber from school until 3:30 pm. I wondered how she was doing and hoped things were going well for her.

Time passed so quickly that afternoon. Kevin seemed content in the basement playroom, while I watched my soap opera program upstairs. When I went downstairs to put another load of laundry in the washer, I peeked in on him. There he was all curled up in his new blue beanbag chair watching a movie about whales. I reminded him to come up stairs when it was over, as we would be leaving shortly to get Amber. Really, though, I did not want him to spend the day in front of the television. I planned to read a story with him.

Sometime later, he came upstairs to join me. I asked him what book he wanted me to read to him. My kids loved to be read to and had memorized all their books cover to cover. He chose a book we had just read the night before. I suggested another one, and he agreed. We snuggled up together at the end of the couch. Soon, the clock said 3:15 and it was time to get Amber. I was so glad then that we did not go anywhere that afternoon. It was a good idea to stay close at home. Quite suddenly, in the tenderness of that moment, I felt a little sad again. I pulled Kevin closer to me brushing his hair against my cheek.

Then, I asked Kevin to get his coat, and obediently he took off to his room. Rising from the couch, I thought about how quickly the day had passed, and that, Kevin had never asked to ride his new bike. Of course, I thought, he had realized it was too cold. Mulling over that idea I faced the hallway, surprised to see Kevin standing there with something in his hands. He was holding onto a plastic hanger with an orange shoestring attached at the handle.

Kevin began to speak very fast as if telling me about his latest invention were an urgent matter. "Mommy! Look! This is what the guys use for the horses, and..." His voice trailed off while my perspective of him narrowed to just his face, blurring everything else. I could see only his features indicating that he was speaking, but I never heard what he said. In the next moment, I felt as though I had just awakened from a daydream. Feeling groggy, I shook my head to clear my sight.

The next thing I knew, we were in the car on our way to pick up Amber. Our first stop was at the old school where we picked up her friend, then, we headed over to Johnson Elementary to wait for Amber. She was to meet me at the corner of the four-way crosswalk, so I parked directly across the street. Curiously, since then, Kevin was in a very goofy mood and made us laugh with his silly antics. Whew! He was finally acting like himself.

At 3:30 p.m. I spotted Amber through the foggy windshield and jumped out to meet her. She looked so fragile standing on the corner in

12

the freezing cold, that it touched my heart. I hoped she had a fun first day and made some new friends. I greeted her with a big hug and excitedly asked about her day as we crossed the street. Once we got in the warm car, she told us that it went well. Kevin, now back to his old self, was so excited to see Amber. He had been saving her snack and teased her with it while she talked. By now his silliness was in full force, and he made the girls giggle so much that I put off talking about school any further.

About ten minutes later, we pulled up to the gymnastic hall. The girls tumbled out of the car still laughing with Kevin. They said goodbye and ran into the fairground building for their class.

Heading east on Main Street the last full rays of daylight were hidden behind me in the dismal clouds. Continuing south past the four way stop, I drove by the parkway where we had been sledding this past weekend. Tufts of brown grass poked through the flattened course where an exuberant crowd of kids and parents had worn a path. We had so much fun riding together on the plastic saucers that Santa brought for the children. Smiling, I continued towards our final destination.

The subdivision where we had lived for the past six years was about twenty years old with several models of houses occupied by families and retired people. Our three-bedroom ranch style house had a basement and average size yard. It was squeezed between a pair of larger bi-level models making it seem smaller. The streets were lined with mature aspen and cottonwood trees whose branches bore the weight of a harsh winter. Buried beneath the blankets of snow were neatly trimmed lawns and sleeping flowerbeds. I noticed only a few children walking home from school, bundled in their coats against the cold. It was a stark contrast from warmer days when our neighborhood bustled with the sounds of kids playing outdoors.

I eased the Jeep Wagoneer into the garage and pondered leaving the keys in the ignition since we would be leaving again shortly to pick up Amber. I left them there, but it was not out of habit. I looked over at Kevin sitting in the passenger seat expecting him to get out. He had already opened the door but stopped when something caught his attention. He pulled out a paperback book from the pocket in the door. His serious manner had returned and in a concerned tone he said, "This is Amber's book. She needs this book Mom. I'll bring it in for her."

Puzzled by his emphasis about a simple book I paused, and then said, "Kevin, that's really nice of you to do that for her. Would you put it in her room?" He nodded his sandy blond head in agreement and climbed down from the seat. I noticed it was the book Grandma had given her for Christmas. When we left their house that evening, I accidentally dropped it in the snow as I got in the car. I retrieved it from the snow bank placing it in the door pocket to dry. It had been there ever since.

Kevin opened the screen door and stepped inside the kitchen heading towards Amber's room. I followed and quickly took off my coat, leaving it on the dining room chair. The bleak afternoon sky cast long shadows through the sliding glass door. In the short time we were gone the house had grown dark. I flipped on the lights and began making dinner. "Mommy?" Kevin called to me from the hallway, "Would you read me a story again?"

Glancing over my shoulder, I noticed he was wearing his coat. "Sure," I said. "Just let me finish getting dinner ready before we leave again. Pick out the book you want me to read." Seeming a little anxious, he sighed and went back to his room. Turning my attention again to the mound of meat, I hastily measured a cup of breadcrumbs and dumped it into the mixing bowl.

"Mommy, can I ride my bike?" he asked quietly, his voice coming from behind me again. Startled by his sudden reappearance I spun around. To my surprise, he was standing by the table still wearing his blue and gray winter jacket. I paused to look at him, this time more closely.

My hesitation in answering was not about giving him permission to leave; I knew he was capable of riding alone. It was more about the hint of resignation I sensed in his voice, as if riding his bike were the only thing left to do. I moved over to him and routinely placed my palm on his forehead to check for fever. Normal. There were no obvious signs of illness except for his changing disposition. I gave up trying to figure him out today. I decided he just needed to do something while he waited for me.

"Okay, just for a little bit. It's cold out there," I consented. I helped him get the zipper on his coat started making sure he pulled it all the way up to his chin. I glanced down at the floor where his maroon colored knit hat lay next to the hutch. Thinking to myself I said, "He should have a hat on. But, not mittens, he won't be able to hold onto the handlebars...it's so cold...he's only going up to the corner anyway. He won't stay out there long."

"You're ready to go!" I said, as I peeked at him under the brim of the knit hat and kissed him on the cheek.

The thick fringe of long lashes framed his downcast eyes as they blinked against the top of his full cheeks. His dark brown eyes glanced up at me once, and he nodded without a word. Then, plodding across the kitchen, he went out to the garage closing the door behind him.

I stood up from my crouched position on the floor feeling more confused. "I'll go out to check on him in a minute," I told myself. Then, rushing about, I slapped the ground turkey meat together and molded a loaf in a pan placing it in the oven on 350 degrees. It would be baked when we returned, and I could boil the potatoes later. Stann had basketball practice until five p.m. and we would eat dinner as soon as we were all home. I moved to the sink and began cleaning up my sticky hands from the meat grease.

In that moment, a peculiar feeling came over me. Instinctively I turned my head to the right as if to see something. At that very same time, I also had the thought that I should find Kevin. I walked away from the sink, quickly drying my hands with a towel. Moving a few steps toward the dining area I intended to pick up my coat at the table. Instead, I continued walking towards the front door. In crossing that threshold between the two places, I felt a shift in my perception, as if the floor had disappeared beneath me. In the distance, I heard yelling. It was coming from beyond the door.

Kevin's out there! My pace quickened as the panic rose within me. Lunging to the door, I gripped the doorknob unable to turn it in my trembling hands. In desperation, I flung it opened looking to the left of the storm door window. Kevin was lying in the street at the foot of our neighbor's driveway.

I pushed the glass door open and screamed hysterically, "Kevin!" Half running, half trudging through the foot high snow, I crossed the yard to the mailbox. My blue leather loafers now packed in snow offered no footing, as I slid into the white truck parked along the curb. Catching my balance, I stumbled the last few yards to the edge of the driveway. I threw myself on top of his motionless body and cried out, "Oh my God! Kevin! Kevin! Mommy's here! Mommy's here!"

Frantic, I unzipped his coat and listened for a heartbeat through his sweater. My trembling fingers felt a faint pulse on his neck. "Oh, God... he's cold! He's cold, keep him warm, keep him warm...don't move him," I directed myself. Lying on top of him I cupped my arms around his body to contain his warmth with mine. I pressed my face upon his cold cheek crying, "Kevin honey, Mommy's here, Mommy's here!"

He failed to respond. "Wake up!" I screamed into his pale face. Raising only my head, I released a desperate cry for help that came from the depths of my soul. Its dire call echoed in the hush of the still, snow-covered street.

Suddenly, there was a spontaneous shift in my senses and everything around me moved in slow motion. I rose slightly, surveying the street, my head swaying left and right, as if moving independently from my brain. A man's face materialized to my right. I heard him yell, "I don't know where to go!" Doubling over he grabbed his head with his hands.

I shouted back, "Go call somebody! Go call somebody!" He wasn't moving. "Go in my house now!" I screamed at him. Slow motion, another shift. Outside of my body now, I watched myself mouth a command, pointing my index finger towards my home. He ran across my yard and disappeared through the door.

15

"Kevin! Kevin! Oh God! There is blood! He's bleeding...he's hurt!" I sobbed! His sandy head was framed in a halo of blood melting the packed snow beneath him. My hand shook as I carefully lifted the knit hat that rested low on his eyebrows. Turning his face slightly towards me I examined him further. Horrified by the gruesome sight, I felt my throat constrict. The whole right side of his head was flattened...his right eye was closed and displaced down to his cheek... the left eye was open and crossed inward.

A foreign sound from deep inside me began to wail, "Oh God, somebody please help me!" My unanswered plea echoed throughout the deserted neighborhood as I wept over my baby's lifeless body.

I shook from the freezing cold, unable to move my body except to raise my head and scan the desolate street. Once more, another shift, much slower. I saw a woman waving to me from a few houses further down. What was she saying? "Help me please!" I begged looking down at Kevin's still body. Another motion beside me, "Help is coming!" she yelled, hurling Kevin's bike onto the sidewalk. "No! Leave it alone!" I cried out, somehow knowing that nothing should be moved. Suddenly, more faces appeared and I sensed a hum of conversation around me. Then, from behind, a voice cried out in distress: "I didn't see him! I didn't know he was there!"

Lucidness returned as I spun around to the voice. Our eyes locked together, suspended in a moment that would bond us to each other for eternity. The thick wire frame glasses he wore magnified the growing panic and guilt reflected in his blue eyes. Recognition flooded my senses. It was the man...the one whom I had sent in my house to get help.

"It...it was you?" I asked bewildered. Instantly, my imagination formed a shocking picture of Kevin being crushed by the weight of a two-ton truck. The Driver stood there paralyzed by the burden of responsibility. Looking straight into his eyes again, I pleaded, "What did you do to him?" The implication of those words had sliced him to the core. He let out an excruciating wail that emanated through the growing crowd of onlookers. He clutched his head as he turned away to run from the searing truth.

Kevin's breathing became more shallow and slower. In my peripheral view another face appeared. "What should I do? Help me!" I cried, crouching over him to protect his head with my arms. "He's so hurt", I sobbed. I lifted up his limp head from the frozen ground ... blood and tissue were oozing out of his ears and his mouth...his upper teeth were shoved over to the middle of his tongue. Carefully, I scooped out the blood from his mouth so he could breathe. "Oh my God, how will we fix that?" I thought in a sudden jolt of clarity. His eyes, my Kevin's beautiful brown eyes, were wounded. How could he ever see with them again? Desperate for him to respond, I leaned down in his face, hoping he could see me through the opened left eye and know I was still there with him.

"Kevin!" I commanded, "Mommy's here, Mommy's here." Then, a choking, gurgling, sound came from his throat expelling more blood. His mangled body shuddered for the last time as he gasped for another breath. "It's too late!" I heard myself wailing. Draping my body over him, I cradled my sweet son to my breast and whispered, "I love you Kevin, don't go, don't leave me, Mommy's here! Mommy's here...Mommy's here...Mommy's here....." In that moment, Kevin died in my arms and with him went my life too.

* * * * * * *

The once silent and abandoned street became a frenzy of noise and commotion as paramedics and police arrived on the scene. Someone pulled me from Kevin to administer emergency first aid. There were faces all around me but I could barely hear their voices. Why don't they hear me? "Kevin's dead, leave him alone!" I screamed inside. Weightless and motionless, I watched from outside myself as I screamed at the paramedics. "Leave him alone! Please let him be!"

"I can't get a pulse," he called to his partner.

"Don't touch him anymore!" I shrieked. They shoved past me as they carried Kevin on a stretcher. I reached out to grab a hold, but he disappeared into the back of the ambulance. The paramedics climbed in continuing their lifesaving efforts. I darted toward the doors attempting to get in, only to be jerked back. Turning to the burly police officer I cried, "No!" Then, recognizing my friend, I begged to be taken along, "Please Gene, let me go, he needs me to be with him!"

"Carla, they have to do their job. They can't help him if you're there," he shouted back at me. Gene grabbed hold of my shoulders and forced me away from the ambulance, then, he climbed in. The doors slammed shut in my face, and the ambulance sped away with my Kevin, leaving me behind.

A woman's face appeared in the haze. "Where's Amber?" I heard her say. "What? Oh no! I have to get Amber at gymnastics. Where's my car?" Turning sharply, I met yet another face. "Where's my car? I have to be with Kevin! Where is Stann?" Distraught and confused I stood there helpless. Suddenly, I was lost on my own street.

Seconds later, a paramedic mouthed something to me. "Would you take me please?" I shouted back above the sirens. He nodded, pointing to his car parked across the street. The red-haired young man seeming older than his years jumped behind the wheel of the car as I climbed in too. Seated halfway on the passenger side, I saw my car parked in our garage. I knew my keys were in the ignition and that I should just drive myself, but my body would not respond to that logic.

"Come on go, go! Go fast! Go!" I slammed my hand on the dashboard and commanded: "Drive!" I sat forward while he sped away and within seconds, it was clear he had missed the turn. "Oh no, he's going the wrong way! This is the long way! He doesn't know the way!" I screamed inside.

The young man drove carefully while my foot pushed an imaginary gas pedal to make him go faster. It seemed like an eternity before we arrived as I sat trapped in agony. Finally, he pulled up to the curb several yards from the emergency room driveway. I jumped out of the car splashing in an ice puddle up to my ankles. I raced to the emergency room driveway and into the building, losing my balance as I stumbled up the handicap access ramp. Shoving my way through a crowd of people, I pushed through the Emergency Room doors.

"Let go of me!" I screamed angrily. "He's my Kevin. He's alone! Let go of me and let me in," I cried. Frantic, I fought to get past the swinging doors to find Kevin. Strong arms tried to restrain me, but I broke away frustrated and angry. Catching my breath, I looked wildly through the crowd to see Stann coming through a haze. "How did he get here?" I thought, becoming more distressed. In the next instant, I shuddered to realize I had to be the one to tell him. "Stann!" I screamed running down the handicap ramp to him. "Kevin's dead! They took him away from me. I tried to help him! My Kevin's dead!" Crying hysterically, I clutched his denim jacket falling into his arms.

Stann responded in total disbelief, unable to speak. Boldly he pushed us past the crowd towards the emergency room doors. Responding to the crisis at hand, the hospital personnel quickly diverted us to a small waiting room at the other end of the hall. "I can't see my Kevin!" I screamed, resisting their hold as they secluded us in the tiny room. I buried my face into the wall, scraping the narrow ridged paper with my bloodied nails. "Let me out of here! Stann, I tried to help him. I tried," I sobbed as grotesque groans grabbed at my throat.

Next, the door opened slightly and another staff person entered the small room seating herself across from Stann. "I want to see him now! What happened to him? How bad is he hurt?" Stann demanded rising from his chair. Glancing over at them I felt the floor shift beneath me. Closing my eyes, I fought off the dizziness as I braced myself against the wall. I opened them again only to face my daughter as she burst through the door.

"Daddy what's wrong? Where's Kevin?" she asked alarmed, climbing on to his lap. I sank into the chair beside them. How could we tell her Kevin was dead?

This time the room spun faster making me queasy. The air felt so close and heavy that I could not coordinate my thoughts with my body to move beyond my chair.

"We're doing everything we can. His chances are remote," she said from across the room.

"Remote? But… he's dead. Leave him alone please…you can't do anything."

"…Sign this please."

"I can't breathe. I have to get out of here. She's back! Why isn't she speaking?"

Looking down, she hid behind her glasses to shield me from the truth. "I'm sorry. We did everything we could," she said, looking up her face constrained.

Stung, I squinted back. *"But, I already knew that. I asked you to leave him alone."* Her pained expression faded from my view as I sank lower into the seat. The floor disappeared, and I clutched the arms of the chair to save myself.

Slowly I raised my head and looked past Stann's shoulder. Across the room sat two women friends from my church. In a moment of lucidness, I sensed in their grave expressions the purpose of their visit. "It's too late to pray. He's gone." I heard myself say inside. And then, I bowed my head giving them permission as Lay Ministers to perform the last rites.

Each time the door closed the stuffy waiting room became a jail cell restraining us from seeing our own son. We sat in stunned silence waiting to be freed from the shackles of hospital protocol. After what seemed an eternity a nurse ushered us out to the main lobby. Free at last, I felt a renewed sense of hope at being able to see Kevin. I was unprepared to face the sea of shocked and discouraged faces waiting on the other side of the door, faces that I knew. How did they get here? I became more confused and disoriented as they moved in closer. I felt trapped again. Their out stretched hands blocked our way to Kevin.

Frantic to keep up with the nurse, we pushed past the crowd. On reflex, I reached for Amber, but she slipped from my grip into someone else's arms. As we neared the emergency room where Kevin waited, I realized that Stann still did not know what had happened. "Oh my God. He can't see him like this," I thought, I bolted past the nurse in an effort to shield Stann from the horror.

I was too late, for Stann rushed by me, moving to Kevin's left side. "Hey…Sport," he cried, stroking Kevin's bare arms to waken him as he lay motionless on the gurney. Kevin's crushed head was wrapped like a mummy in white bandages, making his head appear larger than it was. He was naked with only a thin white sheet to cover him. Overcome with anguish, Stann lay his head on Kevin's shoulder pleading for him to

19

answer. I was in a frenzy, writhing in pain for my husband, crying for my son. "Get off me!" I screamed, yanking myself away from the technician. I resented his intrusion again as he held me up by the belt loops of my jeans.

"He's so cold!" I sobbed repeatedly rubbing his arms to get the circulation going. "He needs a blanket. Please put a blanket on him," I begged the nurse. Fully understanding my need to protect my child, she brought a white thermal blanket and spread it over Kevin's stiff, frigid form. Instinctively I took over, methodically tucking in the blanket all around making sure every part of him was snug. I smoothed the top of the covers as I had so often before kissing him good night. Only this time I kissed his bruised and twisted ankles as if to bless them in their pain.

"Can we come back?" I begged the nurse, recognizing her. She nodded yes, and I gave into Stann's strong arms that pulled me away from my baby. Clinging to each other we drifted into the crowd of grief stricken faces waiting in the lounge. We separated, and instinctively I moved toward Amber who was sitting with our friends. Overwhelmed by the sight of my frightened daughter I sat down and held her close. She immediately pulled back and made me face her.

"Mommy, I want to see Kevin," she said with tears in her eyes. Pleading for help I looked to the other mothers. They answered me with anguished faces, nodding their heads back and forth.

"Oh...honey." I stumbled for the right words, "He's hurt too bad."

"Mommy, I want to see Kevin!" she cried.

"Amber, I think it will scare you. I can't let you see him so hurt like this. I can't," I wept, tightening my hold.

There was another strange shift in my senses as if I had been spun around a hundred times. Suddenly, we were in a smaller room with our dear friends Dave, Mary Ann, Kathy, and David. The dim lighting from above gave off an eerie glow around the gurney casting harsh shadows about us. The heavy silence was shattered by gasps of disbelief.

Still hopeful, I searched this distended and gruesome form to find my baby's sweet face, any sign that would help me recognize my own child. His once agile body had been stripped of its youthful spirit and now laid stiffly before us. His head was wrapped with more white bandages covering the blood soaked ones beneath. His olive skin had turned a purple hue across his swollen cheeks.

My mind could not process the image that my eyes had clearly seen. I only knew that my Kevin needed more blankets. Why didn't the nurses know that?

Instead, they suggested that we go home for there was nothing more to do. My heart sank! Go home? The idea jarred the remaining bits of logic floating loose inside me, and I knew that Kevin could not come with us. Why couldn't I stay? *Just let me stay with him! He'll be here all alone with no one who knows him or loves him.*" I cried to myself. I could not leave him. I could not bear to leave my baby in that cold barren room. The nurses promised to take care of him, but how could they take care of him better than I? The remorse I felt at leaving him was more than my heart could bear.

Stann, Amber, and I huddled together in the back seat of Dave's car. He drove slowly down the front entrance driveway and turned into the parking lot. Powerless, I looked out the back window overwhelmed with guilt. The realization of what we were doing stabbed through my heart like a sword. In that moment, strangers were wheeling his body to the morgue. I had abandoned my child. *"Kevin, I'm sorry babe. I'm so sorry to leave you here,"* my heart cried. With that, my consciousness drifted away into the black of the night...

* * * * * * *

From somewhere outside myself, I watched the car park itself in our driveway. When the car door opened a sense of urgency seized my body and led me down the sidewalk toward our neighbor's driveway. I had to get to Kevin; he was lying in the street!

Running wildly, I stopped short catching my balance. The street lamp shone brightly on the white snow covered street, lighting the empty area at the foot of the driveway. There was a truck parked along the sidewalk in front of the neighbor's mailbox and other cars were now in the driveway. The anxiety rose higher in my chest while I searched the bare ground for the scene that was playing behind my eyes.

"Stann, he was right here!" I insisted pointing to the site that only I could see. However, as far as my husband could see there was absolutely no sign that any accident had occurred. I continued to examine the area for confirmation, babbling on about what I knew I had seen. Finally, under the glaring beacon of the street lamp, I spied one small drop of bright red blood glistening on the packed snow at the edge of the drive. My confusion escalated to absolute horror and I began to scream in hysteria. Stann grabbed me as I fell to the ground. "Carla, please let's go inside!" he pleaded almost carrying me back home.

I moved independently of my thoughts. It was as though I had stepped out of my own body. I was aware of voices around me, but they sounded so hollow and far away as pieces of conversation and images of faces floated by without a reference point. I did not have a grasp of the present hour nor could I distinguish the events that were happening in any particular sequence.

There were strange moments when I was jerked back into my body as if someone had shoved their hands against my chest forcing me backwards and off balance. Then I would regain my footing and realize I had not actually moved. My heart raced so fast that I could hardly catch my breath. My chest was filled with such deep anguish that there was no room left to inhale.

In the short time since we had returned, our house had filled to almost capacity. There was nowhere to turn without bumping into another body. Unbeknownst to me, Stann's sister Sandy, as well as our friends and neighbors began arriving before we came home from the hospital. Who had called them? How did they know? There were people huddled in groups everywhere I looked: sitting in my living room, standing in my hallway, leaning against my kitchen counter, answering my phone.

Their presence was out of place, and worse, their faces revealed the shock and disbelief I felt. When they embraced me, my own fears began to grow, and the pain intensified with each acknowledgement of our loss. I don't know whether I spoke or greeted them. They would just float by, out of view, and it did not seem to matter.

At times, I could hear Stann crying, but I had no sense of the direction from which it came. Although I knew I wanted to be with Stann I was incapable of making myself move toward him. I seemed to be wandering aimlessly but not going anywhere. When Stann seemed to be within my grasp he would disappear into someone else's arms. We could not be alone with each other for very long. We seemed to end up at opposite ends of the house with the crowd between. At one point, we were together for a brief time in Kevin's bedroom. Stann had sought refuge there and I found him sitting on the edge of the bed crying. Even in the privacy of Kevin's room, people were still coming in to see us. Our sorrow was shared by so many that it was impossible to grieve alone.

I left Stann in Kevin's room and continued down the hallway, pausing by the hutch in our kitchen. I picked up a plastic grocery bag its contents soft and heavy. I opened the bag and peered in. The stench from the closed bag made me wince, and I withdrew my head slightly. I reached in and to my shock pulled out Kevin's maroon knit hat. Startled by its reappearance, I clutched the moist cap in my hand. The woven fibers felt damp and sticky. Even my dulled senses could perceive it was soaked with blood.

My jaw clenched as I unfolded another piece of clothing. The odor was coming from his clothes. My poor baby had soiled his underwear, his body's natural response to the physical trauma he had suffered. He would have been so embarrassed. I closed my eyes. "Oh Kevin, what happened to you out there?" Someone appeared at my side and gently closed the bag, removing it from my sight. In the distance, I heard Stann say that the police wanted it back.

For the first time, I saw the dried blood caked under my fingernails staining my hands brown. Looking down I noticed more brown smudges on my red sweater and jeans and shoes. Puzzled, I said flatly,

22

"My shoes are wet. I need to change my socks and shoes. They're wet." Suddenly embarrassed by my appearance, I walked away intending to change my clothes. Instead, I slipped into oblivion for another uncharted stretch of time.

When I returned, the steady stream of visitors had ceased. The house was quieter now as family members and close friends milled about in hushed tones. It was then that Amber seemed to reappear looking frightened and sad. Looking for refuge, she held Kevin's baby blanket and Rocky the Cowboy, his Cabbage Patch doll. I had lost track of her in our own home. Wrapping ourselves in the blanket, we curled up in the corner of the sectional couch. I brushed my cheek against the blue cotton fabric smelling the familiar fragrance of soap and little boy. Sobbing, I held her tighter, so afraid that she would be gone too.

Pulling away she looked up at me with tear-filled eyes. "Mommy, if only I had stayed home from gymnastics I could have saved Kevin," she sobbed. I was shocked by her assumption.

"Oh honey, no, no, there was nothing you could have done," I cried, trying to reassure her.

"But, Mom, if I had been there I would have been riding my bike in front of him. I could have seen the truck and told him to stop," she pleaded, describing a valiant rescue. I could only envision both of my children struck down and lying dead in the street. What images could Amber imagine, if not to save him?

My little girl needed to rest, but how could I let her lay alone in the dark with these worries on her mind? Instead, we lay down together on my bed. I rocked us back and forth with my arms securely wrapped around her. She held Rocky, and now Benji, Kevin's stuffed dog, somehow knowing that they too missed the comfort of their master's arms. I smoothed the thick blonde hair away from her tear-stained face, kissing her forehead over and over until she succumbed to sleep.

The house echoed with an eerie sound of muffled sobs and voices through the poorly insulated walls. As I lay there, the images of the day flashed before me assaulting my visual senses. I felt ambushed by this mirage that appeared whether my eyes were opened or closed. I kept seeing Kevin's mangled body lying in the snow, and then close-ups of his disfigured face. His beautiful brown eyes, displaced and sightless, never knowing that I was there.

Suddenly, the Blonde Woman's eyes pierced through the darkness reminding me of our encounter. The memory of the nightmare induced a panic that gripped my chest causing my body to shake wildly. I cried out to the darkness, "Oh my God, the dream came true! They came to take him away from me!" Desperately, I held on to my daughter as if they were there again reaching across my chest to snatch her away.

The sound of grief stricken voices in the distance interrupted the trance, freeing me from its hold. I unwrapped myself from Amber and bolted from the bed. Dashing down the hall, I rounded the corner to the living room. There, I saw my father and my only brother holding Stann. Reaching out to them, I heard myself sobbing again in that distant, garbled tone. Without effort, I floated away into the fog....

2
The Fog of Grief

I spent the remaining hours of the night protecting my sleeping daughter as I lay beside her. In the next room, Stann lay alone on Kevin's unmade bed. His anguished cries were sequestered behind the closed door, but I could hear them through the wall between our rooms. It was an odd and unfamiliar sound for I had never heard my husband cry in the twelve years we were together. I wanted to be with him and feel him close to me, but this was not the time.

The sunrise soon cast its mourning light over the slumbering neighborhood. Pacing, I moved about my little house, waiting for the dawn to reveal the scene of the accident. When daylight came I made my break for the front door. Dressed in my bathrobe and blue loafers, I slipped out racing down the sidewalk to the neighbor's driveway.

I clutched my robe close to me shivering in the early morning freezing cold. Confusion and anxiety were mounting inside. Where was all the blood? Why did it look so different? In a frenzy I began searching the area for the clues to prove that I had really been here the day before. Suddenly, I felt a strong hold on my arm pulling me away. "Come back into the house Carla," Stann begged. His bloodshot eyes pleaded with me to come along. I began sobbing, pushing him away as I crumpled to the frozen ground. Before I knew it, he had whisked me back inside the confines of our home. I lay on my bed in a heap unable to move. What I wanted most was to get back outside. Why couldn't anyone understand that I had to find my Kevin?

I lay there wide-eyed for a long while, secretly devising a plan to get back outside unnoticed. Wiser, I made my second attempt. By now everyone had gathered in the kitchen for breakfast. I walked through the living room and quietly slipped out the front door.

Free at last, I began to search for my only clue, the drop of blood that I had seen last night. Hunched over on my hands and knees, I crawled on the snow packed street at the foot of the driveway probing every inch of the site. At last, I found my evidence glistening in the sunlight. A few tiny drops of blood were splattered on the sidewalk at the edge of the driveway and more out into the street. Yes! I had my proof. I had been here.

My satisfaction with this discovery was short-lived, for the reality of its meaning abruptly struck my chest like a brick and my heart sank to the pit of my stomach. My son's precious blood, was now frozen in the wintry landscape. No longer warm and life giving, it was encrusted in the top layer of the snow separated forever from his body. In time, it would be driven over and pushed deeper and deeper into the snow packed road. I wept as I clawed and scraped at the spots to preserve what was left of my Kevin.

My stiff and frozen hands clenched the crimson colored ice chips, drawing them to my broken heart. It was then I heard that strange, unfamiliar wail again. The noise came from deep inside my throat echoing from the depths of my soul as Stann once again carried me back home. Once inside, the chips had thawed to nothing more than pale red water. My Kevin's blood, his lifeline, had evaporated away forever.

Stann brought me to the privacy of our bedroom and stayed with me for a long while. Sitting on the edge of our bed, we held on tightly to each other crying for our son. In yet another emotional storm we had been swept away by massive waves of grief and crushed by its fierce tide. With each surge we were separated and then pulled under, left to crawl ashore alone. In time, our frenzied cries subsided, and we found solace in the steady rocking of our bodies.

My grieving husband braved the anxious crowd waiting in the kitchen leaving me alone to rest. My energy spent, I lay down at the end of the bed and closed my eyes. My head became very heavy as if it had grown twice its size, and my neck muscles were too sore to lift its weight. Soon, I felt myself drift away from the fading voices in the background.

With my closed eyes I peered through the thick haze focusing on a bright green grassy area. My attention moved immediately to the two figures in the middle of the scene. Upon closer inspection, I saw that it was Jesus sitting on a large rock! He was wearing a white robe that seemed to glow, and his face was so incredibly handsome and peaceful. And, to my surprise, the other figure was Kevin. There he was kneeling on the left side of Jesus' lap with his arm wrapped around his neck! He was very animated, and he waved his left hand to express himself as he spoke. Although I could not hear what Kevin said, I saw that his face was *alive* and full of excitement and joy! His beautiful brown eyes had that delightful twinkle! When Kevin and Jesus looked at each other, I felt the incredible bond of love between them.

My head jerked and I felt as though I had been dropped on the bed. Lifting myself up from the disheveled covers my eyes opened wide. Looking around I saw that I was indeed in my room and all traces of the bright green vista were gone. My mind was a scrambled mess. Where was I? Did I really just see my Kevin? He was so alive! Jesus? How could I have just seen Jesus? He looked so handsome. Was it just a dream?

Slowly, the confusion lifted and was replaced with the now familiar stabbing pain in my heart and the shudder of my body. The physical reminders were my only frame of reference to my locale. None of this made any sense, not the way I felt, not what I just saw, not this room, nothing at all. How could my Kevin be dead?

I cried out to the dead space, "Kevin! Why did you leave us? Why did you leave me behind?" My words hung in the air as I looked around the room expecting him to answer. "Oh my God what am I doing?" I sobbed. I feared I must be going crazy. I had to get out! Sliding across the bed, I watched myself get up, but I did not feel my feet touch the floor. I stepped out into the hall and wandered aimlessly toward the kitchen.

Dazed, I sat down at the table where someone immediately offered me a plate of food. In an automatic gesture, I took a small bite. Gagging on the sample, I spit into a napkin and wiped my tongue clean. Whatever it was tasted awful. The numerous potluck entrees did not complement each other, and the combination of smells began to nauseate me. I shoved the dish away and covered my mouth to stop from gagging.

Oblivious to the conversation around me and numb to the occasional hug or touch of my hand, I sat like an outsider in my own kitchen. The atmosphere of my home had changed drastically in one day. We had always enjoyed company, always making sure that our guests felt welcomed and at ease. In contrast, I was not even aware of their individual presence now for they all seemed to blend in sorrow. Their sadness was out of place in a home that I hoped was known for love and laughter. I was the stranger now in a house haunted with memories.

The smell of freshly mowed grass mixed with the aroma of hamburgers on the grill came to mind. Wiping the perspiration from my forehead, I sat on the step leading outside from the dining room, glad to be out of that stuffy kitchen. The shade from the big globe willow cooled off the covered patio enough to give us some relief from the heat inside.

Stann was flipping burgers at the barbecue and the kids were playing in the tree. They were busy rigging a rope to make a pulley on the lowest branch. Amber put rocks in the pail and then tied the rope to the handle, struggling to raise the heavy load upwards. Kevin stretched across the lowest limb, his bare arms barely reaching around the thick of it. Scooting further on the limb to lend a hand, he grabbed the rope and hoisted the bucket high enough to grab it. I smiled, delighted with their ingenuity.

I wiped the foggy glass for a clearer view. In one blink the backyard transformed to a snowy landscape and all traces of the memory buried beneath it. My father gently touched my shoulder bringing me back. Turning away from the patio door, I faced another reality more painful than I could have ever imagined.

Although I had seen little of him since their arrival last night, my father's quiet assistance and unyielding love had taken a priority over his own grief. His hazel eyes brimming with tears searched deeply into mine looking for a sign of recognition. Handing me a yellow legal pad, he said, "Honey... do you want to look over this list now?"

There were several pages filled with names of people who had called. I scanned the list wondering if I should return all the calls. What would I say? I don't know how to do this! Who can help me? Distraught, I flipped the pages searching line by line for the name of Mary, a therapist whom I had seen for grief counseling several years ago when my mother died. Suddenly, the image of the Blonde Woman's piercing eyes flashed upon the page I held. Shaken by the shift of reality, I looked away to protect myself. Instinctively, I knew that Mary would believe me.

Why wasn't Mary's name on the list? Discouraged, I assumed she probably had not heard yet. No. I couldn't be the one to tell her. I wrote down Mary's name and handed the pad back to my dad. Tearfully I begged, "Please Dad, find this woman for me and tell her what happened. I need to talk to her." Then drifting, I said, "Where is Stann?"

I needed to talk to Stann too. We seemed to keep passing each other but never connecting. Reluctantly, my dad replied only that Stann was outside talking to Officer Hill about the accident. I vaguely remembered some discussion that morning about Gene coming by. Officer Hill was the police officer I recognized when Kevin was being taken away in the ambulance. I was unaware that he had arrived, and I felt left out that no one had told me. Earlier Stann had urged me to remember what I could so that when the police interviewed me I could give them an accurate account of what I saw. That panicked feeling was back pounding loudly in my chest. What really happened out there before I arrived? I was certain I had seen a most horrific sight, but what was real?

After some time, Stann came back into the house looking troubled. I quizzed him immediately. "Who was it Stann? What happened to Kevin?" His bloodshot blue eyes looked so tired as he struggled to find the words.

"They still don't know anything. They haven't even taken his statement yet!" he said angrily. The police could not tell him much because the driver had been sedated since last evening. He wouldn't be giving a statement until this morning. The officer did say that the driver of the truck was somehow related to our neighbors but did not live in Montrose.

My heart sank at the disappointing news. We had been waiting for so long and now still nothing! And then, it dawned on me. "Sedated?" I said, my voice growing louder. "Stann, how could he possibly give a reliable statement if he were drugged? How much could he recall that wasn't affected by the drugs?" I cried out in anger.

Spurred by this sudden flash of rage, I left the conversation and moved to the living room. Pushing back the curtains of the picture window, I gazed out to the street. Squinting, I hadn't noticed the sun was shining today. The urge to bolt out of the house and go down the sidewalk hit me again. I didn't care who stopped me. I was going back out there. I had to see it again so I could help the police and tell them everything I knew.

"I was the one who was there! I know how hurt he was! He never touched Kevin to help him." I rambled aloud to myself.

The house was a buzz as everyone speculated on the identity of the Driver and why the investigation was moving so slowly. Stann was so overcome with emotion that he retreated to Kevin's room again. In a few moments I followed wanting to tell him what I could remember about the accident. I stopped short in the doorway. There he sat, alone on Kevin's bed, his sturdy shoulders hunched over in defeat. His eyes reflected such pain and sorrow as he watched the little boys playing on the floor. I could not bear to see the sadness on my husband's face. Instead, I looked away, knowing that if our eyes connected, our thoughts would mirror each other's pain.

Michael, and Stann's nephew, Dillon, were playing quietly with Kevin's toys. This scene made no more sense to me than watching my husband cry. It was unbelievable that Kevin's room and his toys were left unattended by him. These boys had been here a million times to play, but never without their buddy to lead them into action. It hurt my heart to see his things handled without his consent, and yet, I knew that Kevin had never denied them the freedom to play with his treasures. How much did they know? How much could they understand?

The morning stretched into late afternoon while we waited for news from the police. Other details and phone calls were being taken care of by our devoted friends. However, a request from the funeral home needed to be handled by us: they needed Kevin's clothes to dress him for the viewing.

In the privacy of our bedroom, we discussed his wardrobe as if we were packing a bag for an overnight stay with a friend. Stann suggested that Kevin could wear his favorite Batman T-shirt. I was appalled. That shirt was worn thin and the print was faded. It would look tacky and so inappropriate. I never let the children look ragged. I choked on a wave of mixed emotions stuck at the back of my throat rising fast like dam waters ready to burst after a rainy spring. What was he thinking? As I became more confused about our purpose, the swollen tide rose higher drowning out my criticism before I trampled on my husband's feelings.

We agreed on the Batman shirt to be worn under his Christmas Eve outfit. The purple golf shirt and the purple, blue and green cardigan sweater would go nicely with a pair of jeans. Returning from Kevin's room with the clothing Stann asked, "Are you sure this is what we want to send?" Then hesitating he added, "Because the funeral director said they would have to cut the clothes."

"Yes," I said, reaching deep into the closet for the green and white zippered sport bag to pack the clothes in. "They won't have to sew anything. These clothes fit him fine." And then, as an afterthought I said, "Why didn't they ask us for shoes and socks?"

A crack in the dam had been detected, and the waters of grief began to flow hard and fast as the image of Kevin's bruised and twisted ankles under the hospital blanket rushed by. Kneeling on the floor, I gathered all the clothes together and held them close.

Tenderly, I folded the tear-stained clothes; the jeans, the two shirts, and finally the sweater. I carefully stacked them inside the bag. Stann squatted beside me as he zipped up the nylon bag. We both held on to it tightly, neither one of us wanting to surrender its contents. I could not believe I was sending Kevin's clothes away so someone else could help him get dressed. "I don't want to do this!" I sobbed, clutching the bag away from him. "Tell them we want everything back, please." Dropping his head forward, he pressed his fist against his mouth. I wrapped my arms around his shoulders as we cried together, overcome with the reality of the task we had just completed.

"Will you be okay while I ask someone to take the bag the funeral home?" Stann said wiping his tear-stained face. I nodded yes, as the bag slipped from my hands. The bedroom door closed behind him, and I crawled back into the dark closet.

Hugging my knees, I sighed deeply as I rested my head against the wall. Camouflaged by my dresses and pants I hoped no one would ever find me again. What would it matter if I never came out? It was only the curious scraping sound echoing through the side window of the bedroom that was strong enough to draw me from my cave. Crawling out of the closet, I made my way past the bed to the window.

The view from our bedroom window was in direct line to the scene of the accident. To my dismay, I saw that there were several people talking and standing in the neighbor's driveway. Suddenly, I became worried that they were allowed to walk around the accident scene. *What if* there was something the police had missed in their investigation? Why hadn't they asked *me* anything yet? I had to get back out there so I could see it in the daylight. With that goal in mind, I boldly walked through the house defying the concerned stares of the people along the way.

Bravely I approached the driveway and came upon an older man who was shoveling snow out into the street. It struck me oddly. I immediately thought that all that shoveling came a bit too late. "If they had shoveled a path wider than a shovel's width and completely removed the snow from the driveway like the rest of us had done, then maybe, Kevin..." As if reading my thoughts, he stared at me coldly and did not say hello or speak to me. I continued a few more steps until I stood on the spot where Kevin had died less than twenty-four hours ago. The ground was spotless and all evidence of the bloodshed was gone.

Determined to see again, I closed my eyes allowing the images to come. I mapped out the scene in my head, moving in a complete circle as I faced each direction. I looked up and down the street several times. I placed the Driver's truck facing west in front of the driveway, but closer to the south side of the street, next to the red car that was always parked there. Facing east, two houses down on the south side, was the peach-colored house and parked away from the curb was the car with the flashers. A woman was waving to me. Kevin's red bike was about three or four feet out from the edge of the left lane driveway. Kevin was lying on the east side of the bike, but his body was on its side facing west. The old white truck with the side rails was parked even with the lamp post several yards west of the neighbor's driveway. Parked in the right lane of their driveway was an old, gray, mini pick-up truck. The street was vacant except for myself, and the man with the scraggly beard and wire framed glasses.

"Kevin, Boo Boo, why were you riding down here and not at the corner?" I sobbed.

Trying to make sense of my one-way conversation, Stann stood behind me straining to hear. This time he did not try to take me away before I could draw the map in my head. He was actually listening. Now that I had completed the task of reassembling the scene in my mind, I felt as though I had a reference point. Together we walked slowly back to the house our arms wrapped around each other in support.

The vigil continued as we waited for answers to the mystery of Kevin's death. Late that afternoon, Officer Hill returned with a brief and disappointing report about the lack of progress in the investigation. Any privacy in our home had vanished with the influx of people. There was nowhere that offered the seclusion Stann and I sought. In the end, a dozen loved ones were crammed into our small bedroom, their arms crossed in defense, moist eyes demanding answers. I sat in the middle of the bed feeling so embarrassed that are home could not offer more.

The twenty-year veteran officer was a husky man with flushed cheeks and blonde hair graying at the temples. A teddy bear at heart, Gene fought hard to set aside his emotion and personal concern for us because of our ten-year friendship, and tried to remain professional. However, technical the terms, they could not disguise the trauma we both had seen.

I withdrew even further, imagining the most horrific scenes of Kevin lying helpless under the wheel of a truck. It was then that I realized he had not been wearing his bike helmet. Shattered by another detail pointing to my guilt, I remembered my reasoning for not enforcing its use; the new helmet was too big and would have hindered his sight. Would a simple plastic helmet have protected him under the weight of a two-ton truck?

* * * * * * *

Later that evening when the others were settling in, I curled up beside my brother Paul on the pull out bed in the couch. We did not say much, but his arms protected me with brotherly love. Soon, he left me alone with my thoughts. Flashes of the nightmare returned...the children and me running down our street...opening the door to face the Blonde Woman hiding in the attic. What was real? The images of finding Kevin on the street became interspersed with flashes of the dream. Was I running away from this horror and yet, toward it simultaneously? Why had Kevin ridden his bike to the neighbor's driveway instead of to the corner, as he always did?

In a burst of clarity, I knew I had to write down as much of the dream as I remembered. I began recording the nightmare on a legal pad I found on the coffee table. I could hardly hold the pen and only got as far as writing the date.

"Hey, are you okay?" I heard a voice say softly. I looked up to see Mark, Stann's brother, who had arrived earlier in the day from California. Spontaneously, I blurted out, "Mark, I dreamed he would die."

He looked at me questioning. "Well, what did you dream?" he asked, uncertain where this was going.

"I dreamed that some people were trying to take the kids and I was running away and they caught us and she cut him down." It sounded crazy repeating it out loud.

"Sometimes our dreams are about our fears and maybe you just dreamed what you were most afraid of, maybe it doesn't mean anything..." he reasoned.

I interrupted him, "Mark, I dreamed this last night...it came true. They were trying to take him away from me."

"Carla these are just symbols of your fears," he rationalized. His voice faded away as I tuned him out. I knew I had chosen the wrong person to tell. He did not understand. Hurt from being dismissed and analyzed, I concentrated instead on recounting as much of the dream as possible.

Determined, I began to record the images that raced forward in sequence, but offered no details. Overwhelmed with emotion I struggled to maintain control of the pen as I was swept away in the flood of channeled images. My writing deteriorated to a childish scrawl as I came face to face with the Blonde Woman again. Trembling, I folded the paper and tucked it away in my notebook hoping to share it with Mary.

Dream Journal—

JAN 6TH I am walking on the our street with the kids. am very afraid because a cult is trying to take them away from me. I have them close to me. Next I am in a house on our street. There is a circle of black faced women. One of them next to me is trying to get to Amber. I feel her black hand come across my chest to grab her. I feel slap it away and scream you can't have her, we run and we run together to a house to be safe. In the house I know I am safe the kids are with me. I'm in the kitchen + I hear Kevin calling me to find him. There are no floors there only stairs going up + up I climb + climb these stairs calling to him listen to him call me. I'm at the top it is an attic I open the door — I am gripped w/ panic the cult lady is there w/ a chain saw she will cut Kevin down — he is hanging from a rafter. I scream for help she closes the door on my face —

I.C.#1

34

3

There are Things the Bereaved Must Do

Dream Journal: January 9, 1991
Kathy and I are tidying up my workstation so I can go home. A coat rack is next to the station, clients have left their purses on it. We said, "Oh well, too bad we're leaving". Pati opened the drawers in my station and when we looked in and saw the mess she said, "Oh tidy this up!" I said, "But it's not my fault!" Kathy puts things I don't need in the green and white zippered sport bag. She zips it up closed. We leave, and Nancy locks the door with her key.

     I do not remember going to sleep or where I slept that second night. I do know that I woke up. And when I did, every muscle and bone in my body ached so much that I lacked the strength to lift myself up. My neck and shoulders were twisted so tightly from holding on to people in desperation. My nerves were frazzled, and my body would shake uncontrollably. The constant attack of stabbing pains in my chest made my heart pound and my stomach churn. And, what was left of my mind was too scrambled to think straight let alone dream. No wonder I had dreamed about my workstation being untidy. My life had become a mess.

     I lay back hoping to regain enough energy to raise myself from the bed. Instead, my body began to shudder as I recalled seeing Kyle again when he and Nancy came to see us. It had been the first time since Monday afternoon. Kyle's big blue eyes brimming with tears reflected more than sorrow over losing his best buddy. My heart crumbled as his eyes cried out to me: "We tried to tell you! We just needed to play one more time..." But, how could I have known? Would he ever forgive me? Burying my face in the pillow, I cried for yesterday.

I hoped that once my cousins and two friends, Ann and Chris arrived I would feel a sense of order. I have no clear memory of meeting them. Perhaps the pain and sorrow in their faces were too much for my broken spirit to absorb. I do know that once we were together I felt a little more insulated. They brought with them their special gifts of compassion, love and humor to nurture me in my time of need.

By now the initial shock had lessened enough for us to comprehend that there were things that bereaved people were supposed to do. The funeral arrangements could not be put off any longer. I did not know where to begin nor could I comprehend its full impact. I was not clear on exactly what it would entail because I could not fathom planning a funeral for a child, let alone viewing my own son. Pati and Chris assured me of their help and that after meeting with Fr. Gary we would have a better idea of what we could do. Pati was the music director at our church and Chris was on the Liturgy committee, so I was grateful for their suggestions.

With that in mind I faced another dilemma. Although Stann was supportive of raising our children in the Catholic faith, he left the instruction up to me. He was unfamiliar with the Sacraments and rituals. At this point, a crash course would be futile. I struggled with how a Catholic funeral for our son could have any meaning for him.

In his favor was the affection he had for Fr. Gary. Stann had always come away touched by Gary's homilies. But, my worry for Stann was the fact that his father, a former Methodist lay minister, seemed uneasy with Catholic rituals. I had to dismiss that concern quickly, this was about what Stann needed not about making others comfortable with our faith life.

My head was swimming with so many worries that surely it would explode if I had another thought. There were bigger priorities now. It became even more complicated by the painful flashes of my sweet Kevin's crushed and bloodied face. My body's defense was to shut down thereby blocking out all the stimuli I could not process.

Sometime later, we met with Fr. Gary at the parish office to plan Kevin's funeral. Fr. Gary was a man in his mid-fifties; a tender and gentle human being who had blessed us with his homilies and presence in the parish. He was Stann's first real experience with a priest. Stann would occasionally accompany us to Mass and always came away feeling good because of Gary's simplicity in expressing the Word. I too had been blessed by the chance to know him as a person, unlike my childhood experiences with priests who seemed untouchable. I knew he would find a way to communicate God's promise of Everlasting Life to this vast mix of people coming together to celebrate the life of one of God's children.

There were so many decisions to make in such a short amount of time. And, none of them seemed to have much to do with Kevin. The familiar readings and rituals, while insightful and comforting, all seemed strangely out of place for a child's funeral. I accepted that there were guidelines and a certain sanctity required by the Church, but funerals were for the living to speak of the dead. There was nothing that spoke of Kevin, and this greatly disturbed me.

Following the meeting we returned home and invited anyone interested to discuss the music selections. I never remembered the names of any of the hymns, and neither did Kevin! Nor did he care! He always made up his own. I was content to sing my favorite pop tunes because they spoke of my love for my family. When Kathy suggested we listen to a tape of Christian music that her sister's friend had written and recorded, I could feel the resistance rising within me. I truly wanted to be open to everything so I agreed to listen.

Within moments, the soft melody began to capture our attention, and we quieted as the solo filled the room:

"Well it's hard to say goodbye and let go. And it's hard to see it end, when the memories we've just made may never happen again. But it's harder for time to ever erase the together times we've shared. So while we're apart remember all the love we've shared together. And for all that love, thank the Lord above, who showed us the way. That we can be together forever someday. We will be together forever...someday."

The medley became a lullaby rocking me back and forth as tears streamed down my face. I looked around the room. We all sat motionless; no one wanting their thoughts interrupted by another. The immediate impact of this song was enormous. It was clear to me that this song described our life together. With one look between Stann and me, it was unanimous.

Until now, we had been suspended by a dark mournful mood. This melody had stirred something deep within all of us, lifting us above the chaos to see clearer. Soon, we became animated with questions and ideas about the music and how it could be used. Quite unexpectedly a shift in perception had occurred, raising us from our emotions to our heads. While inconceivable at first, it now became possible to focus on the funeral as a means of expressing our love for Kevin and who we were as a family. There was now a goal to be met, and together we all assumed a role that was essential for its success. From that point on, it was a team effort and anyone that could be or wanted to be recruited was delegated a task.

Pulling away from our committed group, I felt assured that things would be taken care of for me. My attention span was unnaturally short, and I could not seem to find a balance. The future was incomprehensible and the past was too painful to contemplate, and when the reality of the present overwhelmed my senses, I retreated to the void.

****

I emerged from yet another lost block of time to discover that Stann and I were on the way to the mortuary for our first visit to see Kevin. The funeral home was an old two-story house, a mix of different architectural styles sitting on the corner of a busy intersection on Main Street. It had four miniature columns, two on either side of the door molded into the wall, reaching to the second story awning. Giant cottonwood trees that shaded the entire corner in the summertime bordered it. At first glance, the green shady trees disguised its purpose and the house blended in with the other older homes.

This afternoon, the white "estate" seemed rather ominous as the thick columns rising from behind the mounds of snow stood at attention in the crisp air. The one-hundred-year-old trees stripped of their green garments held the boundaries of the domain. This grand looking home was really a halfway house for the dead.

There was a significant sharpening of my awareness now as every detail of the viewing chapel seemed to stand out. My eyes were like the lens of a camera zooming in on the little nuances. The room was simply furnished with several rows of pews in the middle and a few stained glass windows on the right side. A stone wall decorated the opposite end of the room. There stood a small open casket, framed on both sides by several large floral arrangements. I tried to divert my eyes, but the tiny casket took precedence. My vision blurred with tears.

I flashed back five years ago to the product showroom of another funeral home: Reluctant, I walked clumsily amid the expertly designed caskets made of various wood and chrome; their lids opened to reveal plush satiny interiors to insulate cold stiff bodies. I tried to imagine what fabrics my mother, the expert seamstress, would have preferred to match her lavender dress. Giving up, I wondered what difference it would make now. My legs were swollen and my back sore from carrying so much baby in my belly. I could not walk among these deathbeds any longer. I was only a few feet from the door when I noticed a tiny white infant casket with blue satin interior displayed on a high shelf along the opposite wall. I began to tremble, suddenly afraid for my unborn baby. I leaned over clutching my hardened belly.

I blinked away the tears and pushed the memory to the furthest corner of my mind. My blurred eyes skimmed the tops of the pews as we walked slowly toward the front. The miniature coffin grew larger the closer we came. I kept my distance stopping a few feet away from it.

A small figure was lying down inside the padded coffin. Its hands were resting on its abdomen, and its legs were extended straight, disappearing into the closed end of the coffin. Its head rested awkwardly on the satin cushion. I imagined it should have been nestled snugly into the folds of the fluffy pillow, perhaps, resting on its side with hands tucked under its chin, deep in a dreamy slumber.

The dormant body was dressed neatly in blue denim jeans, a purple golf shirt, and a purple, blue, and green cardigan sweater. Peeking out from between the open collar was a white Batman shirt and a small gold cross. It appeared to be a little boy wearing my Kevin's clothes.

I further examined this stilted body for signs that would help me recognize him. All the familiars were there, his sandy blonde hair, his pudgy hands, his favorite T-shirt. If I moved closer, would I find any more distinguishing clues? I inched forward now standing a foot away from the casket.

This poor little boy looked as though his chest had been puffed up with a tire pump, making his arms and legs seem flat and extended. The shape of his face was restructured to assume a look that was once fresh and youthful but did not resemble the exuberant expression I knew. The once soft and supple skin was rubbery and discolored making the whole right side of his head seem artificial like a wax figure in a museum.

The rational part of me undoubtedly knew this little body was *supposed* to belong to my Kevin. But, the only apparent identifying clues were the familiar and well-worn clothing. Gently tucking the straw like hair behind his molded ear, I felt immediately repulsed and attracted to this ambiguous form. My thoughts began to wander...wasn't I supposed to cut Kevin's hair this week? His thick sandy mane had grown out quickly from the haircut I gave him just before Christmas...a sure sign that he was healthy and eating well.

* * * * * * *

Our family waited anxiously for us to return from the funeral home, worried about our reactions to seeing Kevin again. Stann and I were too overwhelmed to say much. It was much easier to change the subject or discuss plans for the funeral again.

Kathy, Michael's mother, had suggested a photo board displaying favorite pictures of Kevin at various ages. She volunteered to put it together if I were willing to look through the photo albums. It was then I remembered dropping off the rolls of film I shot during Christmas on

Monday. My brother Paul immediately offered to pick them up when he heard I wanted to include them in the collage.

I flipped through the first photo album. It was packed with pictures of every event Kevin experienced that I had been quick enough to get on film. One of my greatest joys was taking pictures of the kids. The fact that they were so photogenic was such a plus because as an amateur photographer I could never take a bad picture! I had stacks of photo albums. I had hoped that one day these albums would leave my care and go with the children. My solution was to get double prints of every roll so I could keep some too.

Kevin's life in pictures began with the fuzzy Polaroid shots taken in the hospital as a newborn bundled in a blanket lying in bed next to me. It ended in the second book with recent photos taken this past November of the kids goofing off. For the first time I realized that most of the photos were taken by me. Each photograph was a scene viewed through my mind's eye. Each picture told a story, and I could easily access my perceptions of the event as well as my feelings associated with it. It was as though my mind and the camera were one. These two photo albums held the story of Kevin's life through his mother's loving eye.

There was a level of excitement about seeing these photos that seemed bizarre. It was as though we were looking for proof that Kevin existed. When the developed rolls arrived, the last pictures held a surprise for us that no one expected. First, there was the fact that the two rolls practically chronicled our Christmas vacation. It was so eerie seeing the events that had just happened a couple of weeks ago...opening presents, sledding in the park, and feeding the birds. We were happy. We were together, and we looked normal. Secondly, and most intriguing, were the photos taken on Christmas Eve.

I had positioned us in front of the tree using the self-timer for a few family shots. I took several more of the children posing together. They were beautiful. Their sweet precious faces smiled back at me forever recorded in my mind's eye and on film. The most striking photograph was one in which Kevin and Amber were kneeling next to each other. Their hands were sandwiched together on Amber's lap, with her hand on top in a big sister fashion. They were both smiling and looking straight into the camera. Kevin's left hand was raised, signaling a thumbs up sign. I remembered that while I was focusing the lens he was getting my attention by saying "hey duuude" to me, a favorite expression of his. It was a sweet silly moment.

Now, the photograph took on a new meaning, as if there were something left unsaid. Someone suggested that perhaps he might be telling us with the thumbs up gesture that he would be okay. Our excitement quickly turned to wonder as we passed the photograph to one another. Was it really a sign? Or, were we so desperate for anything that might give us hope?

I wandered back to the living room to the stacks of photo albums. Something welled up in me, and I began to cry. Was it the harsh realization that this was the final roll of film? There would be no more pictures taken of our family together, ever again. I wanted to climb inside the pictures and travel back in time, away from the pain and hurt. Slumping over the pictures strewn across the carpet, I screamed inside, "No! It can't be true. I can't do this. I can't feel this way forever!"

* * * * * * *

After visiting with our family, Fr. Gary had sensed the need for a private healing service aside from the Rosary. I assumed this would also take place at the funeral home, but I was astonished to learn that he wanted to do a Communion prayer service in our home. Instinctively, Fr. Gary ministered to the spiritual need of our family rather than follow tradition.

Furthermore, at the suggestion of the funeral director, we were invited to move the service from our Catholic church to a larger Christian church nearby. Due to the numerous phone inquiries about the funeral, the director anticipated an unusually large number of people. This meant having to sacrifice a Communion liturgy at the service that would have been familiar to our family and uncomfortable for non-Catholics. How could we please everyone? Immediately, a flash of buried resentment toward my religion resurfaced.

Suddenly, I was angry that my son had been excluded from receiving Eucharist. Having not reached the age of reason nor the hunger to be fed, our little ones were denied the fullness of God because they weren't old enough. Why did we have to be a certain age to know God for goodness sake? The funeral service was for all the children, and I would not allow them to feel excluded by a rule that was now irrelevant.

It had been years since I had attended a Rosary, and I was still under the impression that we would be reciting prayers that evening. I remembered being ten-years-old and kneeling for the entire recitation of the Rosary at my grandmother's funeral. My knees ached from kneeling so long on the carpet, and my fashionable fishnet stockings were embedded in my skin causing red welts. How could I put Amber through this long and tedious ritual? This would be the first time she would see Kevin since she said goodbye to him at gymnastics two days ago. What could an endless repetition of prayers possibly mean to an eight-year-old?

In the last six years Amber had witnessed her grandmother's brave fight against cancer, the deterioration of her physical body, and inevitable death. The long awaited arrival of her baby brother only complicated matters. The loss of her beloved grandmother became

41

entangled with my grief and personal loss. Aside from caring for Kevin, the guilt and remorse over his handicap became unbearable for me. The stress of my mother's illness and death during my pregnancy, and then Kevin's birth had pushed me over the edge into a deep depression. Eventually, I sought grief counseling with Mary and it took me a year to get back on my feet again. Amber had been exposed to more than her share of pain and loss in her short life. I thought it was over.

Thus far, spending time at the home of her friends had distracted Amber. Anywhere away from her grief infested home must have felt like a refuge. In another hour it would be time for her to participate in the first observance of her brother's death. How could I explain these concerns of mine without confusing my daughter even more? Pulling her aside we settled down on the couch. I searched for the right words.

"Amber, honey...when we go to the funeral home to see Kevin, you may not recognize him...he was hurt very badly and they put makeup on his face to cover up his hurt." I choked back my sobs and I could not go on. Tears welled in her eyes as her sweet face begged for something to come out of my mouth that made sense to her. My crying had frightened both of us defeating the purpose of trying to prepare her. If I didn't believe this was Kevin, how could I convince her?

My effort to prepare Amber was futile. I returned to my room as the rest of the family readied to leave for the funeral home. Sitting at the antique vanity that my mother had given me as a young girl, I opened the bottom drawer. Tucked away behind some jewelry boxes I found the special keepsake I wanted to place in the casket.

The white silk rose was still wrapped in the zip lock baggie. I took a deep breath as my trembling fingers opened the plastic bag. I had placed this very rose in my mother's casket. We had ordered flowers for her funeral and signed a card, although it seemed presumptuous to sign for the baby since I was still pregnant. Instead, I placed this white silk rose with the pink and blue ribbons symbolizing the baby. I had kept it all these years as a keepsake for Kevin when he grew up. A simple gesture of love and remembrance that had now come full circle.

I sat in the front pew waiting for Amber to arrive with my friend Chris and her daughter. Stann bravely stood by the casket intending to greet everyone, but the task proved overwhelming and he accepted their consolation. It was far too painful to see Kevin hurt and broken. We could not comfort each other or the other family members. I was relieved that we had closed the viewing to the public. I felt trapped and defenseless as my consciousness began fading in and out again. Faintly, I heard the mournful sounds of crying and hushed tones in that now familiar hollow frequency. I could not distinguish whom they belonged to. I wondered what was taking Chris so long to arrive with Amber. I worried that I had not prepared her enough.

Seeing Amber's puzzled face as she walked up the aisle confirmed it. I rushed to meet her, blocking her view with my body until I could walk with her. As Chris and I approached the casket with our daughters, the two girlfriends bravely stepped forward, peering in at chin level. They spoke quietly to each other, commenting that it did not look like Kevin at all. Reaching in they touched his folded hands, only to flinch from the cold and hard skin. Subdued, they huddled with arms around each other; their heads pressed together side by side as they observed this strange view.

We pulled the girls away and returned to our seats waiting for the service to begin. But, curiosity tugged at my little girl and she asked to see her brother again. Gathering her courage, Amber approached the casket with me. The sight of Kevin in that monstrosity of a box had frightened her so. Her bottom lip trembled as she reached in to touch to touch him. Hesitating, she extended her index finger and gently pushed against his hand. Giant tears spilled from her eyes staining her cheeks as she quickly withdrew her hand, wiping it on her dress.

I could not withstand this constant attack of pain. It was torture to see my children separated by death. One was alive, and the other was dead and yet they were both in the same room! This was absolute insanity in its ugliest form. I could not subject my daughter to this madness any longer. Distancing ourselves from this lunacy seemed like the only sane thing to do. Backing away we returned to our seats in the front row. I held her close while the others passed in front of us to view this ghastly sight.

I am not sure of the events that transpired during the remainder of our time there. I retreated within myself, to a place that was timeless and space-less. I wasn't sure that anything I was experiencing was really happening, whether I was "out there" or "in" myself. There were images that leaped out and startled me; my frightened daughter standing before her brother's lifeless body, and seeing my strong husband's sturdy shoulders slump forward with an enormous burden of grief. There were other more comforting images; the red roses that Stann's brother, Mark, gave to us while he spoke of Kevin. All the while, I could feel Stann's trembling fingers entwined in mine as we prayed for the soul of Kevin Blowey and for the resurrection of his spirit. But, just where was my Kevin?

* * * * * * *

Afterward, an intimate crowd of family and close friends gathered back at our home for the healing service. My brother, Paul, assisted Fr. Gary with the preparations. In the far corner of my living room a small table with a cloth served as an altar. Resting in the middle of it was a gold plate of communion hosts and a goblet of wine. The sight of my brother playing substitute altar boy amused me. It was comical and out of place, yet it touched my heart to see my brother going beyond his comfort zone to participate. It certainly would have pleased my mom.

Passing through the kitchen, I overheard a conversation with my father-in-law as to the appropriateness of the Blowey family's participation in this Catholic affair. I shook my head in dismay hoping for Stann's sake this would not become an issue. I hoped his father, and anyone else who felt uncomfortable would be open to the healing aspects of this prayer service, rather than judge it by religious doctrine.

The lights dimmed and a hush came over the room. Fr. Gary had seated himself with his guitar in a chair next to the makeshift altar. We gave him our full attention as he began with a scripture reading. Then, in his quiet way he simply prayed that we touch one another with our love. He asked that Stann, Amber and I might draw on the support of our family and friends to get through this painful time in our lives. He spoke of Kevin's uniqueness and our need to honor him. While he sang and played his guitar the melody became a prayer that blessed our union with God and with each other.

Then, Fr. Gary invited us to receive a measure of healing in the body and blood of Jesus Christ. We stood single file, and I encouraged the children to move to the front of the line. The Father, the Son, and the Holy Spirit were truly present giving us nourishment for the day to come.

* * * * * * *

The mood of the evening became more relaxed and reflective than it had been earlier in the day. The intimacy of the service proved to dispel any apprehension that Stann's father, or anyone else might have had. We had conquered the first hurdle, successfully clearing it to come head onto the next. The funeral was supposed to bring a sense of closure to this phase of mourning. In less than three days we had endured the most difficult tasks assigned to the bereaved. It seemed as though we were bound to follow a detailed itinerary based on appropriateness and ritual. I grew weary of keeping up with the schedule for grieving and hoped that someone else was paying attention.

While people were helping themselves to the endless supply of food and drink, I eased back and separated from the crowd. Impressed by the impact of the service, I escaped to the privacy of my bedroom to gather my thoughts and rest a bit. A soft knock interrupted my solemn thoughts. The door opened and to my surprise Mary peeked into the room. I was so relieved and thankful that my dad had contacted her as I asked. For some time she had been leaving messages, but out of respect and privacy for me she did not include the fact that she had been my counselor. Whoever was taking the messages was unaware of Mary's importance to me so her calls were lost among the long list of papers.

She sat on the bed holding me, her petite frame strong as ever while we cried for my Kevin. Briefly, I told her in spurts what had happened.

"Carla, we are going to get you through this. I am here for you, and we will do it together. We have plenty of time for you to tell me everything. Let's just get you and Stann and Amber through tomorrow," Mary said, assuring me of her support.

"Mary," I hesitated. "There is one more thing." I looked straight into her eyes. Unflinching, I paused, forming my words carefully. "I dreamed it. I dreamed the night before that Kevin would die. They tried to take him away from me, and I couldn't stop her."

I registered within her dark eyes the recognition of knowing that I had been searching for these last two days. Finally, someone understood. She nodded her head in accord brushing back her long light brown hair and said, "You know, when we visited a month ago, I had this nagging feeling I would see you again, very soon. I had a feeling that we were going to be involved together again. I had no idea it would be this."

"Mary? What am I going to do without my Kevin?" I pleaded.

Her eyes filled with tears and I slumped over into her arms.

* * * * * * *

Our guests eventually found their way to their sleeping accommodations in the nooks and crannies of my home. Shortly after the service, Chris had taken Amber to her home to spend the night with them. I was relieved that she would be in a quiet and safe place with someone who loved her. I felt guilty about not being able to take care of my own daughter. I lacked the strength and clarity to do anything about it.

I settled under the covers, praying that I could go to sleep without Amber nearby. Instead, the scenes of her sweet brother laying stiff and cold in a coffin ambushed me. Would I ever be able to see Kevin again as I remembered him? I closed my eyes squeezing out the painful images to produce an array of brightly colored spots behind my lids. With each thought of Kevin the horrifying images returned even more strongly than before looming between the fading dots.

A noise echoing through the bedroom floor added to my frustration. Boomp...boomp...boomp. It had its own rhythm in a hollow sort of sound and became more pronounced the more I tried to ignore it. The incessant noise was driving me nuts! I threw back the covers, my feet hitting the floor with a thump and marched through the kitchen and down the stairs. I threw open the family room door. I stood there with my hands on my hips in the shadows of the bathroom night-light, ready to spit fire!

"Who in the hell is doing laundry and turned on that damned dryer at this hour of night!" I ranted.

I stormed down the short hall to the dark laundry room and shut the monstrous thing off. Satisfied, I came back to the family room and apologized for the inconvenience. My cousins were kneeling at attention on the floor.

"It was the dryer!" I hissed. Still raging, snapping my fingers and tapping my feet to the monotonous beat, I chanted "Boomp...boomp...boomp."

My cousins, Bunny and Laurene, were staring at me, their eyes as big as saucers. Suddenly, I got a glimpse of myself: a raving, spitfire, lunatic who slayed the noisy beast.

In the next moment we burst into laughter doubling over each other onto the floor! Wheezing and howling in hysterics we could hardly get a word in edgewise. Bunny staged several minutes of imitating me while Laurene and I gasped for air. Finally, one of us asked what guest felt the need to do laundry at that ungodly hour!

Quite seriously, Bunny gasped, "Oh my God, I think it was Stann!" Immediately, this proclamation sent us into another fit of hysterics. The thought of Stann deciding to do laundry was too much to imagine.

Our laughter gradually subsided, and we sat together on the floor. It was really the first time since they had arrived that we had spent any time together alone. Subdued again, reality had struck and a hush came over us. I realized that in my absence Stann had already begun to assume more household responsibilities. It was so painfully obvious that our laughter seemed out of place, and yet, it was unnatural for us to be together and not find the humor in it. We were caught against our will between two harsh realities.

I stayed a little while longer as we huddled together on the mattress talking quietly about the events of the evening. So much had happened in these last three days that it felt like a lifetime of experiences had been crammed into 72 hours. There was no respite from the onslaught of this tragedy, and no chance of a truce in sight with tomorrow's events on our minds. Sensing they were tired from the long day too, I left them to rest.

Feeling drained, I climbed the stairs as if my feet were made of lead. My mind took over. There was something very wrong with the fact that whether my eyes were open or closed, everywhere I looked I saw death and devastation. I felt displaced. I had searched this house for two days to find a space that felt comfortable. Somewhere that resembled the sense of the security I had taken for granted.

I did not feel comfortable in my own body. My strong and healthy frame was now fragile and weak. There was an excruciating pain from the gaping hole where my heart struggled to thrive. I clutched my throbbing chest to close the wound, but it was so wide my hands were not large enough to seal it back together. It grew wider and deeper with each agonizing cry, until finally the raw and vulnerable core of my soul was exposed. I mourned my baby. Where was my sweet Kevin?

I fled to the only place that held him suspended in my mind. I kneeled down pressing my hands against the firmly packed snow and ice, beseeching God to deliver my son to me. "Kevin!" I called out into the frigid night. "Where are you? Please come back to me!" I wept. My hands slid out from under me across the snowy site until I lay prostrate under the glaring street lamp. I felt his limp and broken body beneath mine. I wanted to take him back inside my womb where he would be warm and safe with me. "Oh dear God, it's my fault that I didn't take care of you. Oh, Kevin please come back to me!" I sobbed, as my husband lifted me from the icy ground.

Rescued from my grief, I was now tucked securely in Stann's warm arms on our bed. Burying my face in his chest, I stroked his moist cheeks. Together, we lay sobbing unable to make sense of the insanity our life had become. Our tearful dialogue was laced with topics from a television drama, the accident report, police investigation, lawyers and legal terms. It was frustrating to know so little about how Kevin died. What really happened out there? How could the driver not see him? What would this mean legally? I could not fathom the implication of needing a lawyer as people suggested. Did they think I was guilty of negligence? In a way maybe I was...if only I had paid attention to that Nightmare I could have saved Kevin.

Everything was out of control except the funeral arrangements. The day, the time, and the place were all written in stone. But, something very important was missing from the ceremony. How could there be a funeral *for* Kevin when there was nothing that *spoke* of *whom* he was and how much we love him?

"Well maybe we can have somebody read something, or Fr. Gary will say something about him for us," Stann suggested.

"Stann, no one can talk about him the way we can. *We're* the only ones who know him!" I insisted. "It has to come from us."

"You know I can't do that kind of stuff well," he said, knowing what I was implying before I even realized it myself. It scared the hell out of him to think about speaking about something so personal in front of a large crowd.

"It doesn't matter. We'll do it together. It's the only way the people will know our Kevin. They have to hear from us how much we love him and why." I had decided, and nothing would change my mind. I said, "Look, we just won't tell anyone until it's time to do it. I'm sure there will be those who would think we shouldn't, and they will try to persuade us not to do it."

I reached under my side of the bed for the journal notebook I kept there. I began to compose the eulogy, reading back to Stann every few sentences of what I had written. It was a joint effort, but I knew when it came time I would be the one reading it. It was not very long, and it was not complete, but considering the state we were in it would do. In addition, Kathy was putting together the picture board of Kevin to place in the entrance of the church. Stann proposed that we release balloons outside in the parking lot at the end of the service giving the children a part too.

I lay in bed reviewing the composition, satisfied with what we had done, but feeling like there was still something missing. By this time, Stann had dozed off. I closed my eyes hoping that I could go to sleep too and wake up in last December. Then a strange thing happened. I began to drift towards a distinct humming sound in the distance. There was music playing soft and low, and as I strained to distinguish the tune, its pitch grew louder in my ears. It was a sweet and gentle song and so familiar to me. Where had I heard that tune before?

I saw Kevin's face grinning at me as I glanced over to the passenger side of the car. I was singing along with the radio to one of my favorite songs. He had a good ear for music and quickly caught on singing out loud with me... "Turn on your Heart light!" we giggled. I explained to him that this was a song from one of our favorite movies.

"Mom, what does "heart light" mean?" Kevin inquired.

"Your heart light is love light shining from your heart every time you feel love or you give it away to someone," I answered.

"Oh, like when ET's heart lights up in the movie!" he exclaimed, his eyes twinkling with the memory.

Surprised at my words, I realized the lyrics also described Kevin. My thoughts wandered as I drove down Main Street. It was time to make my annual video of the kids. I decided to use this song to dub over Kevin's photos. I knew this song reminded me of him. Kevin had an immediate intimacy with people, and his gentle nature touched everyone he met. I made a mental note to jot it down in my day timer notebook. When we got home he wanted to watch the movie, so we spent that November afternoon snuggled on the couch. I did not remember until we were well into the movie that ET died....

I awakened to face the early morning shadows. This was the missing piece of closure that was needed for the service. I had to find a copy of this song before tomorrow evening.

4
"God's Mercies Are Not Spent"

My brother took on the task of finding a copy of Neil Diamond's song *Heartlight*. In our small town there were only three stores that sold music and none of them had it in stock. I was determined to have that song and on a hunch I suggested the radio station. They were very willing to help and loaned us a copy. I am sure Paul would have gone to Denver and back to find it. He would have done anything to make it happen knowing how important it was to me.

I contemplated the sacrifices and contributions that everyone was making. Our relatives and friends put aside time from their jobs and families to assist us in whatever way they could. Stann's buddies were so supportive by lending a hand wherever needed, and embracing him when they felt his grief. It was uncomfortable for most of the men to be that close to such raw emotion. But, as fathers they understood the meaning of their worst fear coming true. For the single men like my brother, its full impact would come years later when they held their first child.

It occurred to me that I was also surrounded by the most incredible women. I shared a unique bond with each of them. In most cases, their paths had never crossed until now, and the only thing they had in common was their love for me. Most people feel lucky enough to say they have one or two close friends. I was blessed to have ten times that many. Their presence was truly one of the greatest gifts in my life. I was overcome with a sense of gratitude and appreciation that I had never experienced before. I could not begin to understand how much their compassion and love would carry me in the years to come. But, I could not express much of what I was feeling for them right now.

The funeral service was scheduled for seven in the evening so as many people as possible could attend. It made for a long and tense day especially since everyone had something to do except me. I wandered aimlessly around the house, bumping into people at every turn. Finally, I retreated to my room and stared out the window at the street. To my surprise I saw my cousin, Bunny, outside. Wrapped in a black cardigan sweater, her arms were tightly crossed as she paced furiously back and forth at the edge of the neighbor's driveway. Her head shook back and forth, loosening the dark brown strands of curly hair caught in a bun at the crown. Curious, I went outside to meet her.

Caught off guard she looked up at me with tears streaming down her cheeks. She whispered, "I wanted to see where you were laying last night."

Embarrassed, I kneeled to caress the icy ground before us.

"I thought that if I came out here, I could know how you are feeling. But, I don't understand how this could have happened!" she cried hoarsely, flinging her arms about.

Finally, someone understood my need to be here. No one was trying to drag her back inside the house so maybe I wasn't so crazy after all. Quietly, I explained to her what I remembered of the accident, skipping over the most graphic parts. At last, I placed my hands on the invisible spot. "Bun, he was right here," I said, choking back the tears. She crumpled to the ground as she joined me in reverent silence. I left her there to contemplate the answers that eluded us.

Back inside things seemed to be moving along without any effort from me. It felt so uncomfortable to relinquish control of my life and allow someone else to make the decisions. It appeared that I even needed someone to tell me that I could use a little sprucing up. By chance I caught a glimpse of myself in the mirror. I looked an absolute wreck. I had not styled my hair or put on any make up for three days, definitely out of character for me. My shoulder length hair was an unruly mess of frizzy, permed curls and my face was pale with dark circles under my eyes. I was a hairdresser's nightmare.

Pati, my boss, and dear friend, had thoughtfully arranged an appointment with herself knowing that at some point I would be humiliated at the way I looked. I was so embarrassed. I did not want anyone to see me. Amber came along too, and one of the other hairdressers treated her to a shampoo and style.

It was our policy to offer complimentary services to clients during a death or illness in the family. Now, I was on the receiving end trapped under a drape and forced to sit in my own chair. The sticky plastic cape cinched tightly around my neck like a dog collar. I cast my eyes downward looking for lint and hair, anything to avoid looking at myself in the mirror. What difference did it make what I looked like? I did not recognize the woman in the mirror and neither would anyone else.

I concentrated instead on what Amber and Stann would wear for the service. As for myself and Amber, I always enjoyed color coordinating our outfits for special occasions and family portraits. This time I did not have a clue of what would complement a dark brown coffin. It turned out to be more of an issue for Stann than I realized. As a middle school teacher and coach, Stann's wardrobe consisted of golf shirts and slacks. He did not own a suit and was mortified to be without something appropriate for his son's funeral. His buddies made a grand effort to find a suit for him, and by today, they had found an almost perfect fit.

When we returned home from the salon, a project was under way to hem the pants of the borrowed suit without permanently altering them. The absurd scene in the laundry room involving my cousin Bunny and Stann was too funny to ignore. Her effort to hem the pants with masking tape and an iron made us laugh, and ultimately relieved Stann of his embarrassment. However bittersweet, the memory of her loving intentions lifted our spirits often in the years to come.

* * * * * * *

By early evening the last phases of the funeral arrangements were under way beginning with the final viewing of Kevin's body. Family members and close friends visited through out the afternoon to say their farewell. Most of them had gone onto the church when we arrived.

Holding hands, Stann, Amber and I quietly approached the open casket. Kevin's head rested on the white satin pillow in that same artificial pose. It was so unnatural for him to be this confined and inanimate. I had never seen this child motionless in his sleep. Even then, his lashes would flutter as he watched the dream screen behind his closed eyes, shifting under the covers to reach out for his night companion, Benji. I dreaded seeing his body separated from his spirit. Desperate for something to contradict what I saw, I searched his face for one movement that would tell me he was only sleeping.

The harsh reality of the present status of our family loomed before me. It was incomprehensible that we would never be together as a family again. The three of us had been left behind in this world, and Kevin was supposed to be in some heavenly state. *No! We just brought him home. He's just a baby. Boo Boo, we just said hello...*

"Mommy, why doesn't he look like Kevin?" Amber's voice quivered, interrupting my thoughts. She stepped back into my arms wanting to distance herself from him. A wave of despair swept over me

51

as I watched Amber's fearful expression. "Well, it's because he was so badly hurt, honey," I explained. *Please don't ask me how it happened.*

How frightening it must have been for Amber to see a child of her own size tucked into a giant wooden box! I realized that her last memory of Kevin would be this puffed up, bruised shell of a little boy. I held her closer to me, feeling guilty that we had subjected her to this horror. I felt her pull away and I panicked that she had read my mind. Instead, it was my father's nurturing arms that rescued Amber from this insanity. Gently he guided her outside to wait with him in the car.

Stann and I stood together in the silent chapel separated from our son by one precious breath. My heart ached to hold my Kevin. I wanted to climb inside the casket and cradle my baby in my arms. I wanted to breathe my breath into him so he would have life. *Please, wake up Boo Boo, so we can all live again.*

My desperate appeal went unanswered. His spirit had been released days ago. Resigned, I smoothed the purple and green cardigan sweater, and adjusted the collar of the golf shirt, careful to avoid the cold and artificial parts. The make up on his face was fading and I could see the bruises and reconstructive material. I felt nauseous at the thought of why it had been applied. I wondered why they didn't lay him with his left side facing out. Why didn't anyone think of that before?

Each attempt at separating from him was met with tears and more resistance. It was as if our feet were nailed to the ground and every effort to move from that spot set off spasms of pain surging through our bodies. "How can we walk away? How do we live without him?" we cried to each other.

Finally, Stann and I agreed that on the count of three we would release our hands from Kevin and walk away together. Counting slowly in unison we severed our physical ties to him forever. Tenderly, I whispered in his ear, "I love you Kev".

* * * * * * *

Dear God, How long have I been sitting here? Another shut down. The cobwebs had cleared enough to reveal a large room connected to a long hallway. We were in the church now. I remembered being here before for a preschool Kevin attended when he was three-years-old. I looked past the crowd gathering in the hallway. The memories came pushing through the clouds like a ray of sunshine on a stormy day...

I balanced the cumbersome video camera on my shoulder zooming in on Kevin and his classmate. Tired and impatient they fidgeted waiting for their cue to begin singing the program finale. The Christmas pageant had dragged on for over an hour. These two boys were tired of this Baby Jesus stuff! Their squirming was contagious. For Kevin, it started with the tapping of his feet, and a bend at the knees. It rose to his hips for a shake, and then a jerk at the shoulders, until his head bobbed in a frenzy. The temptation was too great, and neither boy could restrain the impulse to share this pent up energy and paw the other. The comical scene escalated; culminating in a contest of who could blow the hardest in the others face....

And then, the scene began to fade. The church hallway narrowed to a pinpoint, edging out the past. "My God," I whispered covering my eyes, "How did we get from preschool to a funeral in two and half years?"

The procession began with Ann and my three cousins who carried the baptismal cloth for the casket. Amber stood between us squeezing our hands, unsure of where she should be. The rest of the family; grandparents, aunts, uncles and cousins cushioned us from behind. The double doors swung open, and the thunderous pitch of over five hundred friends singing the opening song met us. With their support, we summoned our strength to follow the path that had been carved through the standing room only crowd. I heard Pati's emotion filled voice leading the congregation loud and strong.

I trembled as the music filled me to the depths of my anguished soul. The melody fastened to every cell in my body becoming a part of me forever. Months later I only had to hum the beginning notes to be taken back to this place in time.

The procession stopped at the altar. Kevin's' grown up buddies, now acting as pallbearers had preceded us with the casket. It was placed center aisle in front of the dais on the altar, the pews curving to a half circle on each side. It seemed larger and more menacing away from the funeral home. I was shocked to see the casket closed locking the body of my son inside. Mesmerized by its unwelcome presence, I could not take my eyes off it. It took up so much space that it crowded the entrance of the front pew where we sat. *I don't want it here! I don't want to sit in this pew beside it!* I could feel myself losing ground.

Fr. Gary began to speak, his voice booming through the microphone. Hearing Kevin's name echo from the walls of the church rattled me even more. I began to shake harder than ever tightening my grip on Stann's hand.

"I bless the body of our brother Kevin with water that recalls the day he was baptized. Just as Paul has written, when we were baptized in Christ Jesus we were baptized into his death. If we are united with Him by likeness in death so shall we be united with him by the likeness of His resurrection."

He continued, "When Kevin was baptized, he put on Christ." The four women painstakingly spread the white cloth across the top of the casket clothing him in Everlasting Life. Behind us the congregation's singing reverberated from the church walls to the center of my heart. Kevin's funeral had begun. I could not stop the course of fate.

We were swept along at a blurred pace like a movie video set on the fast forward mode. Occasionally the play button engaged allowing the video to run at its normal pace just long enough for me to catch up on the plot. I wished I could rewind it to the beginning of Kevin's life and rewrite the script.

We hoped that as people listened they would find something comforting in the service that reminded them of Kevin. Each song and all the scripture readings were specifically selected to exemplify a part of him, our time together, or a promise by God of his resurrection. Those loved ones who read or sang during the service transformed the written Word into something more meaningful for us by allowing their emotions to speak for them. Although I was familiar with all the readings it never occurred to me that I would be hearing them for the first time too.

In the distance Fr. Gary's voice came to full pitch now. "My soul is deprived of peace. I've forgotten what happiness is. God's mercies are not spent. Stann and Carla, you have to hang on to that. You might have to wait and be patient for God to reveal his faithfulness and love to you."

I looked up at Fr. Gary, fixated on his every word. Yes, yes, I nodded tearfully. I have forgotten so much. I have been deprived of the sense of peace that this child brought into my life. How long will I have to wait?

Fr. Gary's voice was softer now moving us to a more reflective mode. "The gospel spoke of the Lord welcoming the children. He compares the kingdom of God to the faith of a child." He remembered Kevin being a most precious child who, like Jesus, had an unquestioning faith and openness to all those he met, as he welcomed them to share in the kingdom of God.

I was too shocked to consider the comparison, for all I could see was Kevin sitting on Jesus' lap. Someone had pushed the stop button and replaced the video! Instead of the funeral I was watching my dream again in full color. My God, I saw them together! I really did see them. I felt their exchange of mutual love for one another radiating through the barrier of grief to touch me for one brief moment. It was real. And, my acceptance of it was the most lucid thing I had experienced since his death.

In that moment I experienced a truth that my body, my heart and my soul confirmed to my skeptical mind. Our time together here on earth was truly exceptional for *by knowing the goodness of Kevin we were shown the kingdom of God*. My heart was full with the knowledge that there was a place of peace. I wanted to go there now and be released from the pain and suffering. Suddenly, I felt very small and fragile, in awe of the wisdom that had been handed me so gently. A tiny voice whispered that there was more to know than I could have ever imagined.

Dropped back into the present moment I felt heavy again. The constant shift of my awareness from being lucid and aware to being completely absent was wearing me down. I longed for the service to be over. I looked up to see my father approach the lectern to read next.

My father's shoulders bore the weight of a lifetime laced with grief. Burying his grandson might be more than he could bear. In his career as an army medic he had seen more than his share of death and dying through two wars. Years later he returned to that role in caring for my mom during her lengthy illness with cancer, eventually burying her too. I had just regained my bearings and now the sheer anguish in his voice cut through my heart again.

The ominous message woven between the lines captured the attention of everyone. Magically, it was as if Kevin had penned this poem himself. He asked us not to grieve him but to laugh and talk of him as if he were right by our side. Did we not know he would come if only tears and grief were not a barrier?

"For I am loving you just as I always have...you were so good to me," my father sobbed. "Remember that I did not fear, it was just leaving you that was hard to face."

Oh Kevin! Is that why you went out alone? You were protecting me? I kissed you goodbye, and you wouldn't look at me because....

"We cannot see beyond, but this I know...I loved you so. T'was heaven here with you."

The open microphone magnified the resounding toll of grief as our companions received these tender words. I slumped over clutching my chest pleading for the pain to cease. "I cannot live without you! It can't be this way," I sobbed. I looked beside me to see Stann's weary and tear-stained face. Trembling, I turned his chin until his eyes met mine. We recognized that this simple poem truly expressed the essence of Kevin's loving and giving nature. United in our sorrow we held on to each other tightly giving each other what little strength we had left to approach the podium.

The assembly let out a collective gasp as we walked hand in hand up the steps. I shook so that I had to steady myself by holding onto the edge of the podium. Stann braced himself to acknowledge the crowd. Choking on his grief he began, "We came here to thank everybody for everything that you have been doing for us. All our friends and relatives have done so much for us. We can't begin to thank you for everything you've done."

"Thank God that we have friends like you," he said breaking down. "We have something that we want to share with you that we think is important." With tears in his eyes he turned his attention to me.

I concentrated on unfolding the wrinkled mess of paper I had clutched in my hands. Still trembling, the crackle of paper could be heard through the microphone. I raised my head, facing everyone for the first time. The stunning sight took me back. This unique perspective from the altar was absolutely breathtaking. An expectant crowd of people was sitting in a curved arrangement of pews that flowed from left to right in front of us.

I spoke. "I just wanted to see *all* of you first."

Beyond the altar filling the church to capacity was an incredible sea of faces floating before me. I studied every face in the room beginning far left, across the middle, to the far right, turning my head to include those on the ends of the half circle. Every expression was unique in its grief, yet their tears and sorrow blended into the next. In one sweeping look across the room I felt a connectedness, an at-one-ness with each person.

Embraced by their total love and compassion I felt lighter, floating somewhere outside myself. I was suspended in that moment of grace on a sea of love. I am certain that it was this energy that enabled me to speak. A few moments later I managed to find my voice, shocked to hear how unsteady and halting I sounded.

"Our Kevin was born during a dark time in our lives. My mother had just died after suffering a long bout with cancer. The news of my pregnancy was met with mixed emotions. I thought, My God, how can I have life growing in me, when my mother has death growing in her? I prayed that God would give her life too. When she died, our lives were filled with a darkness I had never seen before."

"Kevin's birthday, his birth day was the beginning of a new life for us. Out of the darkness came a little tiny light in the form of a beautiful baby boy! It was only a flicker at first, for we soon realized he had a birth defect. Kevin was born with clubbed feet. We thought we would never see our son walk, or run, or skip or ride a bike."

I continued, speaking faster, the pitch of my voice rising, "But, as we all know that was not meant to be! The doctors and the therapists gave him the opportunity to develop his physical skills with their professional guidance. And, our Kevin walked and ran and skipped and rode his way through life with a determination to embrace and experience all that came into his path! Out of the darkness, a darkness we did not want to know or understand, came our Kevin...our little Boo Boo Bear."

I paused to take a breath and pointedly said, "Kevin is our light to understanding love. He touched all of us with his love light; by the twinkle in his eye, with his sweet smile, his wonderful belly laugh and with a big hug around your neck. His touch, his love light is everlasting. We must always keep him in our hearts, not selfishly, but to share that love light with others. So they too, can know what love is."

I looked over their sad faces one last time wanting to remember this moment forever. Overwhelmed by the sheer magnitude of the intensity of their love I uttered a simple thank you.

56

We returned to our seats and held Amber very close between us. The music began, sending Pati's emotion-filled voice to blanket the sobs of the crowd. The assembly quietly joined in, only to raise their voices high in affirmation of God's promise that someday we would be together, forever.

* * * * * *

A tall lamp post illuminated the path leading to the church parking lot. A twinkling of tiny snowflakes drifted down from the black January sky. The delicate white flakes graced the baptismal cloth still covering the casket. I brushed them away smoothing the fabric that cloaked my son in Everlasting Life. The air was still and crisp, warmed only by the loving energy that radiated through the people joined for their final goodbye. Gathered tightly around the casket we held hands, grasping the ribbons swinging from the rainbow colored bouquet of balloons floating above.

The strains of the song "Heartlight" resounding over the crowd expressed the words that Kevin might say to us. "Turn on your heartlight. Let it shine wherever you go. Let it make a happy glow for all the world to see."

We sang along letting each word lift us higher, igniting the love light residing within our hearts. At the count of three we released the giant bouquet of balloons into the black void above. I raised my face to the night sky to see our goodbyes rising higher toward their heavenly destination. The falling snowflakes gently kissed our tear-stained faces as if all the angels in heaven had leaned down to express their gratitude for this gift of love; a precious boy named Kevin.

5

To Laugh One Last Time

Dream Journal: January 11, 1991
So many people in a room. Children playing, people talking. Kevin is beside me. I look up at the ceiling, and suddenly I see that it is caving in with water. It's as if it started as a small hole and stretched wider and wider as the water flooded through. People run in all directions. I turn quickly to get Kevin, but now he is lying down as I found him in the street. I pick him up and carry him through the falling water to the door.

      I yanked the covers back and sat up in my bed. The room was still dark, and the only sound was my heart thumping fast and loud inside my chest. I rubbed my face over and over to erase the scene before my eyes. I could not lay there another second and risk seeing it again. I had to get out of this room now. Still shaking I put on my blue terry cloth robe securing the belt tightly. I picked up my Walkman cassette player and the headphones and closed the door quietly behind me leaving Stann alone in a fitful sleep.

      In the hallway the doors to Amber and Kevin's room were closed, their current occupants tucked away for the night. I peeked around the corner of the hall; two more sleeping bodies in the living room and four more downstairs in the basement. The mayhem of the funeral reception was over. The memory diminished in the midst of the icy predawn slumber.

I needed to be alone. I wanted to find a familiar quiet place in my home but there was nowhere to hide. I walked into the kitchen lit only by the low watt bulb above the stove. The night shadows could not disguise the fact that my usually neat and tidy house was in such disarray.

Empty casserole dishes and pans were stacked on the counter waiting to be retrieved by their owners. An industrial size coffee pot sat on another cabinet, having perked endlessly for four days now. Towers of Styrofoam coffee cups stood at attention beside it. Against the stairway wall were grocery bags stuffed with staples like toilet paper, dish soap, and paper products. The table and chairs were pushed against the other wall to make more room for people to walk through. The dining table had become a catch all for everything from sympathy cards to stacks of dishes and pans.

Under normal circumstances I would have immediately begun to organize and sort through the mess. Now, it was just a passing thought, so immaterial because of the last few days. Choosing an empty spot, I crouched down on the floor in front of the corner cabinet between the oven and the dishwasher. My knees were tight against my chest, and my robe was taut around my legs wrapping me up in the quiet space I had created for myself. I put on the headphones holding them close to my ears and pushed play.

Gentle strains of the song "Heartlight" began to play softly in my head. The insulated ear cuffs blocked out the insanity of the present, giving me a sanctuary of solace. I closed my eyes swaying side to side, lost in its healing melody until I was lulled into a weightless sleep. There were no pictures or memories to haunt me only the soothing waves of music.

From far away the sensation of being moved interrupted the harmonious and fluid journey. I twitched, turning my back on the distraction. Moving towards the rhythmical path again I felt another interference.

"Carla," he said, then softly crying out, "Carla...let me have this. Don't do this to yourself, honey."

The music faded away as the headphones were pried from my ears. Paralyzed at the shock of being dragged back to reality I sat in my space. My father's teary bloodshot eyes came into view as he kneeled down in front of me. Suddenly, I connected with the fear reflected in his eyes. His daughter's sanity was truly in question. Exposed, I wiped my damp face with my hands and realized that I had been crying in my sleep. Stann appeared too, worried by my absence in our bed. Together, he and my father raised me to my feet. Slipping my arm from their grasp, I wandered away, through the messy and disorganized kitchen back to my asylum. Climbing beneath the covers I closed my eyes...

I am standing in a white kitchen looking at a white country style table and chairs set. There are two other sets. I am supposed to choose which one I like best. There is a smaller set to the left and further to the left of that is a full size dining room set. I really like the white one, but think the smaller one would be more convenient, but the larger one would seat more people. I can't make up my mind...

Outside the bathroom door I overheard voices and assumed that everyone was up for breakfast. Or was it lunchtime now? I had awakened and slipped into the shower unnoticed. I stood under the pulsating spray, turning the hot water on full stream until it ran cold. The images of the night before washed over me as I recounted the evening's events.

I was amazed at how much of the service I could remember though I felt so removed from my body. It seemed the only way to endure the pain. Yet, there were so many blessings throughout the evening. The greatest of these was the gift of touch. Before the balloons had a chance to sail away into the black cold night, our friends instantly huddled around, embracing us with loving and compassionate hugs. It was an incredible ending, and symbolic of the kind of support we could expect in the coming year.

After the service we returned home to a tidy house and enough food and drinks for a small army. I immediately noticed that my house had been cleaned. The carpet was vacuumed, the beds made, the bathroom smelled clean and fresh towels had been set out. I knew the ladies from the church were bringing food for the reception, but surely they wouldn't be cleaning! Who had done all this?

I was surprised to learn that a friend who owned a catering business and managed a housekeeping staff on a ranch had enlisted the help of several people. While we were at the mortuary, they came over to clean and set up the food donated by the parishioners from our church. I had never had such a treat as having my house cleaned. It made such a difference to me that our guests saw a clean and tidy home despite what was going on. Their generosity was another example of the compassion and assistance that would continue to bless us in the months to come.

Anyone driving by our house that night might have mistakenly assumed there was a party going on. I am sure the sound of laughter echoing through the front door was the last thing anyone expected to hear. But, as is typical of my mother's side of the family, my three cousins and my brother were in characteristic form. As a child I remembered the family gatherings at my grandmother's house lasting well beyond midnight when the laughter would vibrate through the ceiling of the third floor where all the cousins slept. Laughter is customary in our family and there has never been a funeral or wedding without it.

Our family had been through many trying times together, but this loss was unfathomable. This time, my cousins and my brother were there for me with our boisterous family humor and loving compassionate hearts. This was the only way we knew how to manage the pain as a group. I felt supported and taken care of, and I was so grateful they were with us. I know that visitors were taken aback by our openness to laugh and cry in front of everyone. Something had to alleviate the pain, even for just a couple of hours because the thought of looking ahead to the rest of my life was too much to consider. I believe our willingness to share our tears with laughter became the first step in our healing.

While I showered there was a discussion about getting me out of the house. My cousins had devised a plan to take me on a long ride for the day. It would be months before we would all be together again at the family reunion. I didn't know it would be the last time for many weeks before I would summon the courage to venture out without Stann and Amber. We accepted it as a well-deserved reprieve from the chaos, the significance of our excursion yet to be revealed.

I hesitated though, because of my concern for Amber. Adults would surround her after she had spent last evening with all the kids. It was my first grasp of the reality her life had become. She was an only child now. What would she do without her brother and playmate? Who would she play house with or ride bikes? What was she feeling and thinking about all this?

Again, I contemplated the night before and how strange it must have seemed to an eight-year old to have a party in honor of a loved one, and then not have that someone there. Puzzled that there were so many people in and out of our house, Amber asked me why they all had to come at once and why they kept coming back!

The truth was that even Stann and I were overwhelmed with the way people responded to her. Friends, acquaintances, and teachers brought her special presents and flowers. Their outpouring of concern and love was amazing and yet in her naiveté she couldn't fully appreciate it. In her world you were supposed to get presents for your birthday and Christmas and silly holidays, not because somebody died.

My mind had wandered again on Amber's behalf, but Stann assured me she would be fine. I hoped that Stann's nephews would come over later to be company for her. Still, it wasn't the same as being able to take off with Kevin to the backyard and roll around in the snow. Perhaps it would also give Stann a chance to connect with his family as they would be leaving soon too. Stann had always been the strong and steady one in their family, supporting the others through their trials and ignoring his own. Their support meant so much to him now that things were reversed.

Truthfully, I thought that I should not be leaving to go anywhere. I could justify it only by reasoning that this trip was my cousin's first visit to my home, and for what? They spent a fortune coming here for a damned funeral. I owed it to them to see something more than a mortuary and a church.

In a strange way I seemed to take charge of the excursion. It was the first thing I had a command of in the past five days. However brief, this sudden change back to a part of myself that felt in control was familiar and my body relished it. It was a feeling I would yearn for when I found myself in the depths of grief. In the distant future, having control over where I went and how far, seemed to be more about escaping responsibility than about maintaining control. When I was on vacation, meaning anywhere away from the hell I faced in Montrose, I thought I was free.

And so, we took off for the day with me as tour guide and photographer. Ann volunteered to drive since she knew the area from having lived here before. We headed south, far away from the madhouse. The intensity of the last few days fed the uneasiness among us as we sat crammed in the close quarters of my Jeep Wagoneer. Kevin's death had altered the lives of so many people, and here we were playing tourist.

Approaching the curve at the top of the hill I pointed out the spectacular view of the reservoir nestled in the foothills of the San Juan Mountains. The massive rugged mountains capped with snowy peaks became the backdrop for the frozen lake. The air was crisp and clean and the blue sky was clear of any winter storm clouds. Nature with all her untold wonders, and mysteries continued to evolve, radiating her timeless beauty. It was a glorious postcard day in Colorado.

We lamented the striking contrast of what we left behind in Montrose. How was it possible for Mother Nature to remain untouched and unaffected by our Kevin's death? How could life dare to continue without Kevin? The dissimilarity of the two was my first confrontation with one of life's unyielding truths...the world had not stopped because one of its beloved had died. Life had gone on without us this week. In spite of her beauty I was insulted that Mother Nature would be so ungracious to continue without skipping a beat.

Safely tucked inside the car accompanied only by our somber thoughts, we continued to our next destination. My cousin Regina, the Mistress of Song and Dance in our family, had a quick wit, a sharp memory and an excellent rhythm. Quite frankly, we never knew when she would break into a spontaneous verse or dance. So really it should have been no surprise to us that a song came forth at our next stop. As if we had not had enough food to choose from at home, she wanted to stop at the bakery in Ridgway. Ann kept the car running for the heater while we waited for Regina to return with something tasty to eat. A few minutes later we spotted Regina through the frosty car window dashing out of the bakery excitedly waving a paper bag! She hopped in the car fully energized by the successful find of a deliciously baked treasure.

"Guys! Guess what they had?" she exclaimed out of breath her eyes as big as saucers. Our interest piqued as we drooled in anticipation of opening the bakery bag that held this special treat.

"Showt-nen bread! I didn't even know there was such a thing!" she drawled. Removing the thick heavy cookies from the wax paper, she waved them in the air. Before we even had a chance to register the contents of the bag, she broke into a rousing rendition of the old classic song named for the bread!

Disguising her Philadelphia accent with a thick southern accent, she sang loudly, "Mama's little baby loves showtnen showtnen... mama's little baby loves showtnen bread!"

The four of us burst into hysterics over her impromptu delivery. Our encouragement pushed her to center stage for several more verses while we howled with laughter. We were an audience hungry for laughter and normalcy. Her comical antics proved to be the icebreaker needed to lighten our heavy spirits. We had been blessed with the gift of laughter. This moment of hilarity enabled us to endure the prevailing heartache by briefly breaking through the chains of insanity that bound us so tightly.

The tone was set for the rest of the afternoon, and each stop provided an opportunity for us to play and sing. Our sightseeing trip was blessed by clear blue skies and fair weather. The remainder of the afternoon was spent relishing each other's company in the beauty of the Rockies. By late afternoon the temperature had dropped considerably. It was close to dusk, and we decided to return home so we could get a bite to eat before our next excursion to the salon where I worked.

Our conversation varied and remained steady for a while. The crisp air and the long ride had tired us enough to stay quiet the rest of the way home. I studied the passing scenery as my beloved mountains disappeared into the darkness and my thoughts with them. A stretch of time later, I overheard Laurene urging Bunny to tell us about the nightmare she had the night before Kevin died. I could have never imagined that what she would share about her dream would be so important to me.

Bunny explained that in real life, her daughter Katelyn was supposed to go on a Kindergarten field trip by bus that past Monday. She was nervous about the trip and did not want her to travel without her. She knew she was being overprotective so she didn't mention her fears to anyone. However, that Sunday evening before, Bunny had dreamed about Katelyn and the upcoming school trip.

In the dream she was told that instead of picking Katelyn up at school she had to go to the airport. She asked the other parents who were waiting where the children were. She was told the plane was a little unsteady (and she saw an image of a wobbly plane landing). They told her that three people got off the plane, and they were a little "banged up". Bunny feared that Katelyn was dead. What frightened her most upon wakening was that she knew what the feeling would be like had Katelyn really died.

"All day Monday I could not get that dream out of my head and I would shake when I thought about it. Then mom called and told me about Kevin. The very first thing I thought was that I knew exactly the feeling Carla had when she found Kevin dead."

We were stunned into silence. I am sure to the others the dream seemed misconstrued by her shock and grief. But, it was very clear to me that something strange was happening.

"I had a dream too." I quietly interjected.

Silence.

"The night before the accident I dreamed that he would die...they took him away from me and I couldn't save him." I began to shake my head in disbelief hearing my own words out loud. There was no turning back. I had blurted it out, so I went on to describe the dream. They were dumbfounded, unable to grasp the meaning of the two of us dreaming about the death of our children simultaneously. Bunny and I exchanged nervous looks. I knew we were just as frightened by this seeming coincidence, as when we had awakened from our nightmares. It was so unnerving that no one would talk about it anymore. I withdrew myself from the conversation and turned to look out the window into the night, lost.

I remember next that I was playing hairdresser at the salon, styling everyone's hair. It was the first time my cousins had seen where I worked, and I was proud to show them my station. We laughed and goofed off the rest of the night. We lost track of time until about midnight when Stann finally called looking for us. They did not want to go to bed without seeing the transformations.

I felt steady enough to drive us home so we piled back into the Jeep. It felt strange to be behind the wheel after having not driven for almost a week. I did not feel as though I had a grip on the wheel, or a feel for the car at all. I did a quick check of the instruments as everyone got in. Regina took the front seat again and leaned over to pick up a folded piece of notebook paper on the floor. Assuming it was trash, I told her to put it in the slot under the glove compartment. I would clean out the car later.

It was midnight when I paraded my rowdy, but fine looking clients into the living room for the family's approval. They were received with clapping and hooting and a few groans for our prolonged lateness. We relayed the events of the day, replaying the high points and singing along with our leader, Regina. One thing led to another and more giddiness erupted lasting at least another hour into the late night. Although I was tired, I did not want to miss out on the chance to be with everyone. I knew the laughter would be over tomorrow.

6
Now We are Three

Dream Journal: January 12, 1991
I am holding Kevin's head in my lap. His body is lying down beside me. I am stroking his hair. He is sleeping quietly. I relished this chance to touch my baby again and feel the sense of peace he had always brought to my heart. As I shielded my eyes to ward off the intrusive light, my moment with Kevin began to dissolve before my eyes. I awakened to begin another day with tears.

Fully awake now with barren arms, I could only grasp that my family would be leaving. Returning to their lives, they would be taking with them any sense of security I had felt this past week. True to their promise they took turns calling me throughout the next few months, but I longed for their companionship. Although I felt connected to Stann's family, still after almost twelve years, understandably I did not share the same kind of closeness with them as my cousins.

In the past when the girl cousins were together, frivolity and laughter seemed to rule and time was of no concern. We have made an art out of farewells, prolonging our fun until the last minute in the most imaginative ways. Today, the goodbye ritual was postponed by default. I only remember the hugging. Holding on until the very last moment of separation when their arms slipped away from my shivering body. We could not stretch the inevitable. I would have rather they left without a sound in the middle of the night.

By late Sunday afternoon the last of our family was on their way back to their homes across the country. Our dear friends picked up where our family left off. Dave and Mary Ann invited us, as well as Kathy and David, to their home for dinner that evening. Later they accompanied us back to our empty house. I remember feeling so relieved that we wouldn't have to face our home alone. They had sacrificed so much for us by putting their obligations on hold, rearranging their schedules and leaving their own families just to be with us. How would we ever thank them ?

The four children played quietly in Amber's room, now that Kevin's room had been closed off. Little Michael seemed so lost playing with the older girls. It was the first of many painful and uncomfortable occasions when he and the other children were forced to adapt to this new rule at the Blowey's.

Kathy and Mary Ann helped me organize the kitchen and storage room by putting away the army surplus of paper goods, soda, and boxed foods. I was embarrassed by the quantity, and never anticipated that we would indeed rely on it when I wasn't working. When the last of the items had been put away it was obvious they needed to take their families home and resume their routine again. There were not enough words to express how much we appreciated their love and support. All we could do was cry and hug them. Reluctant, we loosened our grip and said good bye.

For the first time in seven days we were alone. An eerie silence crept over the house making our tired voices seem much louder in its vacancy. The three of us sat in the corner of the couch with Amber nestled between us. We discussed with her when she wanted to go back to school. I did not say it, but I wanted her to stay home with us, never to be out of our sight again. But then, the thought her spending the day alone without her brother was too cruel to suggest.

We told her she could choose whatever was comfortable and there was no need to rush back to school until she was ready. We reminded her that Mary Ann would be there if she were frightened. Surprisingly, she chose to go to school for a few hours and come home at lunchtime. We agreed Amber could call us at any time and promised to pick her up immediately.

It was becoming quite late, and Amber needed to be in bed soon if indeed she went to school tomorrow. We tucked her in as she held Rocky and Benji tightly in her arms. She bravely blinked away the tears, not wanting to admit that she was too frightened to sleep alone. We sat beside her with assurances that we would stay as long as she needed us to. "Amber, honey, we will get through this together. We love you so much," I said.

Stann kissed her moist cheeks, tears streaming down his own face and abruptly left the room, closing the door behind him. How dare he leave us! I could not put my grief first and abandon her to the night. Her imagination was her worst enemy. Didn't he know how frightened she would be to lay in bed alone in the dark?

The dim bulb of the night-light allowed me to see her furrowed brow. I lay down pulling her trembling little body into my arms. I had not held her asleep since that first night of horror. My cousins and girlfriends had stepped in with nurturing arms as surrogate mothers. I must have seemed so strange and scary to Amber. What kind of mother did she think I was now? If I had failed to save her brother's life, how could I protect her too? I smoothed my daughter's thick blonde hair against the pillow, kissing her on the forehead. Turning her head toward me she whispered, "Mommy, why didn't God save Kevin?" I pulled her closer too ashamed to let her see the growing absence of faith in my tear-filled eyes.

* * * * * * *

Half asleep, I slid off the bed careful not to wake her. In the dim light I could see her brows frowning at something behind her eyes, a troubled sleep so far from peaceful. I slipped out of Amber's bedroom tiptoeing to the closed door in the hallway. "Was he asleep yet?" I naturally wondered and hesitated to open the door that I might startle him. A stabbing pain was all the reminding I needed.

I lay my head against the door to catch my breath and then went on to my own room. I was so tired that all I wanted was to be knocked unconscious. Crawling into bed, I collapsed into Stann's strong arms. He had not been asleep. I felt guilty that I had someone to comfort me through the long night while Amber slept alone.

We lay together crying, unable to comprehend what the rest of our life would be like or worse what tomorrow would bring. We were living our absolute worst nightmare. What was real? What parts of the insanity were the nightmare? When would we wake up to our real life?

Dozing off, my consciousness hung somewhere between that place of being sleepy but not quite awake. Time had slowed down enough to let me float freely above my pillow. There, a beautiful white bird flew into my dreamscape landing softly before me. Laying back, it stretched its wings wide, wider. Its neck extended and lengthened while the arch of the back bowed. With each stretch it became whiter, almost translucent. Until, illuminating the darkness, it transformed into a body of light in human form.

7
The Lost Message

Startled by the thought we had overslept and would be late for school, I sat up in bed pushing the blankets off me. Leaning forward I caught my head in my hands as I brushed the cobwebs of sleep away. I sensed it was time to get the kids up and moving for school. Was Stann in the shower yet? How late were we? Rubbing my eyes the sleepy haze began to lift. I tuned in listening for the typical sounds of our house like running water and soft morning voices. Instead, there was an unnatural stillness I couldn't explain away.

In the next moment, that panicked feeling I was now beginning to recognize rose in my chest as if a force had shoved me from behind knocking me off balance. Ambushed by the stab of fear, I began a mental checklist of where Stann, Amber, and Kevin should be. Of course, asleep in their beds, burrowed under the covers shrugging off the morning light. The force struck again, straight on, slamming into my chest and shoving me back to this painful reality. Its striking power disabled me, and I slumped over rubbing my forehead in defeat. In seconds the cruel reality settled in releasing the reservoir of tears that had been dammed away all night.

After some time Amber and Stann awakened. I remained in bed trying to shut out the uncharacteristic silence that emanated throughout the house. In self-defense I blotted out the rest of the morning. I know on some level of consciousness that Amber went to school and was obviously taken there by one of us. Neither of us can remember doing so, and Amber has no memory of her first day back to school.

What I do remember is the significance of how the events of that day ultimately altered the direction my life was headed. Pati and the girls from work called early that morning to check-in on us. Stann answered the phone while we sat at the dining room table perusing the pile of papers, cards and letters before us. When he finished talking with Pati he passed the phone to me. I appreciated so much that they would call and support us. But, as had happened so often over the past week, I was not able to convey those feelings, much less hold a conversation.

She chatted briefly at first. Finally getting to her point, she assured me that I could return to work whenever I felt ready to do so. My colleagues would be willing to take care of my clients until I came back. I said thank you and wished I could tell her when that would be.

And then, in a burst of emotion she blurted out, "And, the girls and I have talked about it and I want you to know that you never have to work another Saturday again!"

The phone slipped from my ear, cradled by my neck. My head dropped into my free hand. I pushed the stray hair from my face, not believing what I had heard. Some unknown entity residing deep within me began to scream. A foreign voice yelled out from the hollows of my mind, "It's too late! Don't you understand? Without my Kevin, all the Saturdays until the end of time are worthless to me now! Is this what it takes for you to understand how important it was for me to be with my kids? I don't get a second chance. It's too late!"

The alien spokeswoman residing within me had no trouble shouting to my inner world about the injustice of it all. But, it was all suppressed at the back of my throat. Choking, I uttered a feeble okay, and that we would talk about it sometime. I hung up the receiver on the wall phone and then sat down at the end of the table crying into my folded arms.

"What did she say?" Stann asked looking over at me. "What happened?" he frowned, sensing there was more to our conversation.

I lifted my head up and stared blankly at him. "She said I never had to work Saturday's again." Tears welled up in his eyes. He knew what it meant to me.

"It doesn't matter now, does it? It's too late."

* * * * * * *

Staring blankly out the car window, I had forgotten where we were going. Whatever else we had to do that day seemed meaningless and out of reach. Echoes of this morning's phone conversation with Pati

70

haunted my mind. I could only shake my head in disbelief hoping I would wake up.

Only when Stann parked the car at the side entrance of the funeral home did I remember. We were supposed to pick up the death certificate today. I wondered why they could not mail the damn thing. I stayed in the car not wanting to see the viewing room so soon after the funeral. I felt bad that Stann had to go in alone to pick up the dreaded piece of paper, but, I could not bring myself to go in. Stann's sense of responsibility won over his reluctance to face any reminders of the viewing. His shoulders bore the weight of another burden that I could not share.

A few minutes later Stann returned to the car, visibly shaken and unable to speak. The anguish that consumed him had taken hold again. Handing the papers to me he drove on in silence to the dry cleaners. When we arrived Stann quickly grabbed the borrowed suit from the back seat and went inside while I waited in the car. I fidgeted in the passenger seat trying to get comfortable. Waiting alone only made me feel more trapped. I did not want to stay in the car anymore, but I did not have the strength to go in and face anyone.

Feeling agitated and more impatient, I stretched out leaning toward the dashboard. Looking down, I noticed a white sheet of paper rolled up in the slot below the glove compartment. For no particular reason, I reached for it and unfolded the sheet of notebook paper. I gasped as I recognized the folded paper that Regina had asked me about as we were leaving the salon that evening. This paper was the drawing Kevin had given me during the snowstorm on our way home from Denver just three days before the accident.

My eyes darted wildly across the page as I scanned the illustration. Suddenly, all my senses spontaneously came together tuning into a frequency much higher than I had ever experienced. My whole body vibrated with a deep sense of knowing and understanding of a great truth. It began in the pit of my stomach, rising to my heart and up into my chest, escaping through my throat in an anguished cry.

"He knew," I cried. "Oh my God... Kevin knew!" I sobbed as I hugged the drawing to my broken heart. My son had drawn a picture predicting his own death.

PART II

The Journey Begins

8
There are No Accidents

Dream Journal: January 15, 1991

I'm on a children's roller coaster with Amber, Kevin and Michael. Amber and I are in the front seat. The kids are laughing because I am too big for the ride. The ride is faster than I think it should be for children. At one point it jerks and I am hanging out over the seat bar. I am frightened for us, and I turn and look at the kids. They are not feeling well, they are sick to their stomachs. The ride stops on a rocky bank near a river. I help the children cross the rocks. I have a vision of a triangle, and then I see Stann at the funeral. Pain.

The lined loose-leaf paper had been folded into quarters concealing its contents for eleven days. Its omniscient message deciphered through the mind of a five-year-old and sketched with his hand, depicted an inner battle of conflict versus acceptance. In the first glance, I zeroed in on one simple and clear truth; my son knew he was leaving us. Kevin knew that he would die.

As I viewed the drawing, I experienced a tunnel vision effect. Everything in me and around me; every thought, every feeling, every view, was suspended outside this tunnel bringing a momentary understanding of a decree issued by something very powerful. My precious little boy had wrestled with this almighty power as he struggled with its command.

The immediate impact was like a rapid blow to the gut, forcing the air out of me, doubling me over in shock. In that pause came the realization of a truth that had been hidden deep within the cells of my body. A truth resonating throughout my fragile and broken frame.

Nonetheless, my intellect waged a ferocious battle with my senses denouncing all intuitive knowing as suspicious. My soul seemed not to stand a chance against this doubting force within my head. The more I searched the drawing delving for proof to argue against this innate knowledge, the more obvious it became that I could not explain this in terms my intellect would accept. Decree? By whom? Each question cast more fear and so the momentary understanding became clouded with more doubt.

The discovery of Kevin's drawing was not an accident, nor was it any coincidence. It had remained, in full view, in the car for over a week. Countless people had been in and out of the car in the past eleven days. It seemed an unnamed emissary was intent on capturing my full attention in the midst of my intense pain and confusion. However primitive the drawing, my son had left a powerful statement about his imminent death. It had been artfully designed to set me free.

I do not remember what happened after I found Kevin's drawing in the car that Monday morning. I only know that in the seven days after his death I felt as though I had been beaten up and left to live. All I really wanted was to die too. It was much later, when my emotions began to settle that significant details surfaced about the circumstances of how and when the drawing was created. The memories crashed forth like a raging tidal wave on the shores of my consciousness.

We left early that Friday morning, after spending the New Year holiday with my dad and brother in Denver. The weather report had predicted more snow throughout the Rocky Mountains so we chose the interstate for its accessibility to more towns. Driving west into the cloudy foothills, we immediately drove into the snowstorm that was headed for Denver. While the kids occupied themselves with their Christmas toys, I kept my eyes on the slow moving traffic and snow packed roads. I did not want a repeat of the near miss accident we escaped on our way to Denver.

With this recent memory in the back of our minds, Stann was even more cautious, keeping a reasonable braking distance behind the other cars. Visibility was poor with the snow blowing right into the windshield. Cars skidding on the icy highway caused us to swerve several times. Hours later we were all restless, but there was nowhere to pull over. Tired of being cooped up, the kids clowned around in the back seat raising the noise level a few more notches. Finally, I demanded they settle down and do something quiet together. They were making Daddy nervous to say nothing of what the noise was doing to me. I could not concentrate on the road and referee them too.

Amber pulled out crayons and paper from her backpack and shared them with Kevin. In a few minutes, they calmed down eager to begin drawing. Balancing a book on his lap with the sheet of paper on top, Kevin drew a small house and a figure below it. He made several attempts at drawing the roof, dissatisfied he turned the paper over and asked Amber to draw a house on the front side. Amber took his paper and drew a house with a door and two tiny windows. Then, giving it back to him she continued with her own picture. I watched their interaction and was pleased that she was being helpful. I then turned my attention back to the road.

A few minutes later, I turned back around surprised to note that Kevin was really struggling with his drawing. His wrinkled brow and tight jaw conveyed a mixture of intense concentration and frustration. Reasoning that these bumpy roads were not the steadiest of conditions to create artwork, I faced the front again saying nothing. From the back seat he called out, "Mommy, this is for you."

Reaching between the seats for the paper, I half-smiled as he handed it to me. It was clear by the look on his troubled face that he was upset. Glancing down at the paper, I was stunned when I looked at what he had drawn. The figures seemed so primitive and incomplete compared to the people figures he had drawn more recently. I knew at age five and a half he was capable of a more mature drawing than this. I scanned the pen drawing as he pointed out the figures from left to right at the bottom of the page; Amber, me, our house in the middle, and on the right side Stann and Kevin. His voice was urgent, as if he were trying to keep my attention, much like his tone on that fateful day when I experienced the tunnel vision as he explained the hanger device he made.

He explained that the circle above me was "a balloon with a face on it going up to the sky." Higher on the page, above the balloon, was the only full figure, and drawn next to it was a larger circle. Half listening to his explanation about the scene in the sky, I focused on the bottom half of the page.

"Kevin, why didn't you finish your picture? Look, you didn't finish drawing yourself," I said quizzing him. "And your face is marked out."

Clearly upset, he mumbled, "I can't do it Mommy," his dark eyes pleading with me to understand.

Puzzled, I continued, "And Kevin, why did you mark on Mommy's face too?"

He frowned again becoming even more agitated. Folding his arms on his chest, he looked down and said, "I just messed up Mommy. I just messed up. I can't do it."

Growing more concerned, I knew it was so unlike him to be worried about what I thought of his artwork. I thought I had always been rather supportive. Honestly, I had never seen him stress over a drawing before.

"Oh Kev, I really like your picture," I assured him. "I'll put it on my dresser. You can work on it later if you would like, when we get home. OK?"

He took it back and quickly drew the arms on Daddy as if that was the final touch. Looking more serious, he handed it back to me. "Mommy, I want you to keep this," he insisted. Smiling I reassured him, "Thanks Kev, I really like it". Then I placed it on the dashboard. By this time, Amber had completed her picture and presented a mountain with a big yellow sun and several colored stripes in the sky. It was as if she were unaware of the transaction that took place between Kevin and I.

It all came back to me in such clear detail. We had made it safely through the snowstorm and I never thought about any of it until now. Dear God, tell me! Why did we survive that perilous trip through two snowstorms to come home and see Kevin killed in his own neighborhood? Why didn't we just go off that curve and plunge to our deaths together?

Acknowledging my nightmare had been difficult enough for Stann. He had not been open to talking about it. Furthermore, what little time we had together was spent crying or tending to the funeral. And now, the suggestion that our son knew he was leaving us was too much to consider. As I relayed my memory to Stann, he became confused and upset with my frantic rambling. I could not blame him for being cross, he didn't have all the information and I sounded like a raving idiot.

Mary was the only one who knew all the details of the nightmare, and I needed her to encourage Stann to listen to me. I called her and told her about the drawing and she came to our house almost immediately. When she arrived, I had calmed down enough to explain what I remembered to both of them.

The three of us stood together closely examining the drawing I had placed in the middle of the dining table. Stann leaned forward, palms pressed against the dark pine table searching and not quite believing. Mary unconsciously chewed her thumbnail, intuitively connecting my recollections with the symbolic images in Kevin's drawing. Hands on hips, I anxiously paced the kitchen floor behind them, desperate for their confirmation. Impatient with their silence, I wandered back to the table to reassure myself of the drawing's existence. No matter how shocking it was to see, I kept touching it, tracing my finger over our blackened faces to erase the sense of doubt I feared from them.

Just what did I see? I saw that Kevin was in no further need of a body. Hence, the pen scratched form below his head. The balloon symbolized his spirit rising, transformed into the whole body that was drawn in the sky, the *only* whole body depicted on the page. Our blackened faces must relate to both of us being there when he died, unable to see one another. On an intuitive level, I knew the drawing was finished. I just did not see it as completed because the truth was too much to comprehend.

Kevin's drawing was even more perplexing when factored in with my own experience of dreaming a nightmare predicting his death. In these past few days, every waking moment seemed to be clouded by that horrible dream. Repeatedly, I would see myself fighting off the cult woman with the black hand, and then running with the children until we were finally safe at home, only to be ambushed by the Blonde Woman in the attic. I felt that door slam in my face a hundred times, shutting me out from being able to save him. Why would God allow these evil women to kill my son?

Why did I not take it more seriously? I chastised myself for not paying closer attention and shoving it to the back of my mind every time it came into view that day. How selfish of me to ignore the warning just because it frightened me. I could have done something to save him! But, how could I have known that it was not just another bad dream?

I could not take my eyes away from Kevin's drawing. In a strange way it was a piece of him, something as physical as the lock of hair I had saved from his last haircut. I could touch something that he had created especially for me. Knowing that it expressed his thoughts and feelings about the most significant event in his life was absolutely awesome. I grieved for my little boy who had contemplated this extraordinary knowledge. The struggle must have been unbearable. How could he have known? *Who was my son?*

9
The Dream Class

Dream Journal: January 18, 1991

Kevin is at a day care I don't like, but I have to investigate a few things. He and I sit on this long couch to watch a movie on a panel with the other moms and kids. We have to take our shoes off. We are in a basement. I don't like any of the other moms, and I feel sorry for the kids. It's naptime, and the children must lie down. The childcare person is mean and only wants to spend her time sleeping. I must get Kevin and me out of there. But first, I watch something on television. A man dressed up as a woman walks across a college campus. As he gets to the steps of the building to go down, the camera gives a close up. He looks weird. I am frightened, and I must get us out of there.

I get to Kevin, and he is undressed, the girls tell me the mean lady made them go potty on Kevin's face. I am so upset! I pick him up and put on one white sock with blue stripes and one black sock, then his shoes, and a sweater that is not his. I look in a pile of clothes and there is his leather jacket. We put that on and we are leaving quietly down the hall. He peeks into the mean lady's room and accidentally wakes her up. She screams that we can't leave! As we run down the hall to the stairs Kevin picks up a black pot of spaghetti sauce. We run down the stairs...I've got to get my shoes...one more level to go...Kevin spills the pot, and all the sauce is on the landing by the door. The mean lady screams in a witch voice "Did you spill on my steps! I'll get you!" Now I'm on the bottom

stairs almost to my shoes. I'm screaming "RUN KEVIN! RUN KEVIN!"
I want him to get away! "RUN KEVIN!" I wake up screaming "Run
Kevin!"

I kicked myself free from the twisted bed covers, my feet hitting the floor in hot pursuit. I lunged through Kevin's door searching the shadows for his sleeping form. The unmade bed was empty. Out of breath, I collapsed to the floor crying, "He's not here. She took him! Oh God...he's really dead." The sound of my own voice confirming this truth rattled my soul and crushed my heart. I ran back to my room and grabbed my dream journal from the nightstand.

I stumbled back down the hall to the living room, falling in a crumpled heap in the corner of the couch. Sobbing, I scratched the pen into the paper of my dream journal recording yet another horrific nightmare. The reality of what I had written became clearer as I bore harder on the pen, demanding that my baby be given back to me. I wrote my Kevin's name in desperation and growing anger, for all that I could see now was his name on a page. I beat my clenched fists on my chest to pound away this mysterious and abominable force that was making me hurt so badly.

"How could this be happening to *me*? Take it out!" I wailed. "I cannot stand this pain for the rest of my life! Do something God! Please make this go away and give me back Kevin...don't you know how bad this hurts? I just want my baby... I want my Kevin."

I lay there exhausted, curled up in a tight ball in the corner of the couch. Eventually, my body gave up the fight and succumbed to sleep, drifting away to the beach...

I am at the beach getting in the water with all my clothes on. Many people are swimming with me. Next Stann and I are in the beach house. A car is inside the house. We are sitting in the back seat with a male friend (?) Regina and Laurene say goodbye to us. As Regina leaves, she turns around and aims a gun at us, (it is only Stann and I now). She shoots into the car and misses. We get out and wrestle the gun from her. She has another and another, there were three guns. We get them all away from her.

When I awakened again, I wished my cousin had a better aim and more guns to finish off the job. It was easy to recognize my cousin as an aspect of myself that wanted to end the madness. It was the only solution to relieve me of my pain. In less than a week and a half, I had become a crazed zombie with no sense of direction or purpose, or concept of reality. I felt absolutely psychotic, certain that Stann would commit me to the care center at the hospital. Dying in that near miss accident in the snowstorm,

83

or being shot dead was definitely the preferred choice over living inside my head.

Only sweet Amber made sense as we clung to her in fear and sorrow. Very little of life mattered anymore. We were fighting a lonely and uphill battle without any strategy or reserve. Neither Stann nor I was capable of leading each other to neutral ground. This terrorist called grief, wreaking havoc and fear among us had invaded our life.

* * * * * * *

The next day I received a phone call from a woman confirming my place in a class I had signed up for a few weeks before Christmas. I had completely forgotten about it and was caught off guard when she asked whether I would be attending. What had I signed up for? Embarrassed, I mumbled something about not realizing it was time for the Dream Class. Then, to my surprise a voice in me declared that I would be there this coming Sunday afternoon.

Shaking my head, I tried to figure out what had just transpired. I was in no shape to go anywhere let alone sit in a class. What was I thinking? I stopped short. "Carla!" I shook myself to attention. "This is the Dream Class you have been wanting to take for so long." I clasped my hand over my mouth in surprise, sensing the timing of the call. I could talk to Diana, the instructor, about the nightmare! For the first time since Kevin died, I became hopeful. This random phone call had actually opened the door that would allow me to enter the darkest shadows of myself.

* * * * * * *

I sat sideways in the kitchen chair with my back pressed stiffly against the wall. Chris and Pati had stopped by that afternoon to visit. Chris was a close friend as dear to me as my cousins and Ann. Our five year friendship had grown after the loss of my mother and through Chris' recent bout with breast cancer. We shared not only our Italian roots and young motherhood but an uncanny understanding of each other. As soon as they arrived, I relayed the story of finding Kevin's drawing. Seated across from me, they studied the drawing captivated by its mysterious appearance yet uncertain how they should respond to it. As I divulged its history, their expressions changed from disbelief to awe. Their eyes filled with tears acknowledging its importance to me.

"Kevin knew he was leaving us," I said quietly, gently smoothing the paper with my hand. "It seems we both knew," I added.

Confused, they looked straight at me, unsure of what to say next. Chris reached across the table for my hand and asked, "Do you mean the dream you told me about last week...the one about the women taking Kevin from you?"

Stunned, I choked back the tears and said, "I told you about her?"

She nodded yes, her dark brown eyes spilling with tears. "It was when I came over to see you that second night. You weren't making much sense, but I knew that, whatever it was about, something had frightened you."

I wiped away the tears and pushed my bangs off my forehead. I squeezed the side of my temples to think more clearly. I trusted these two women with everything I had. We had just been through the most traumatic week ever in our relationship together. Should I expose myself any further? I closed my eyes shaking my head; hoping I could get out of the conversation. Something within me gave in, and I began to relay the horrible images of the nightmare to them. Astonished by the seeming evil tone of the nightmare, Pati asked what I thought it meant.

"I don't know," I said as the tears flowed again. "I am going to Diana's dream class on Sunday to find out."

* * * * * * *

I parked my red Ford Tempo in front of the Parish Center leaving the keys in the ignition with the engine running. Secluded behind the foggy windows I sat there motionless in the driver's seat feeling like the car had driven itself across town with me as its unconscious passenger. Chastising myself, I thought I should not have come alone. I should have come with Chris as she suggested.

Even with the heater on high blasting warm air on my face, my body shook inside my ski jacket. I pulled the zipper closed to my neck hoping to contain the uncontrollable shaking. I gathered my courage and entered the building. The tears began to flow as soon as I stood in the darkened hallway. I was a mess, paralyzed by fear and embarrassment.

The class had already begun, so I stood outside the door peering through the window. After these last few nights of dreaming I was convinced I needed to be here. The *Day Care Dream* was just another version of my attempt to save Kevin from the evil clutches of the cult women. Intricately woven into the dream was my desire to save Kevin and the very real struggles of loss and grief complicating my life.

Finally, I mustered up enough strength to dash in and take a seat in the last row. I stared straight ahead praying that I had become invisible or that no one had noticed me. Diana was well into the lecture so I immediately busied myself with taking notes. I could not concentrate but went through the motions of transcribing what I heard. I just kept hoping that she would be willing to talk to me after class.

As a child and into my adulthood, I had endured years of nightmares and remarkably vivid dreams. Whenever I would try to talk about them with my family or friends, I got the same response: "You are crazy! It was just a dream. Forget about it". Their discomfort made me feel different. I always thought there must be something weird about me since no one else seemed to be having these unusual kinds of dreams. As a little girl I had recurring dreams about falling into a pit of snakes, or running through a burning Indian camp with an arrow stuck in my back. I was so frightened by the dark that I would spend the time before I went to sleep praying that I would not dream or imagining something pleasant.

It was not until after I was a married that I realized there was some order to this chaos occurring in my sleep state. On one occasion when we were visiting Stann's family in Denver, I casually mentioned a dream about my mother and Kevin. I immediately sensed that Stann's oldest brother Martin was intrigued. We struck a common ground, and he offered to lend me a couple of books about Edgar Cayce and dreaming for further study.

That conversation was a turning point because he was influential in giving me the affirmation that my dreams were an important piece in understanding the conscious and unconscious self. Amused, I realized just how unconscious I had been. It also gave me the courage to look at the disturbing dreams as a tool to overcome my fears.

Over the next five years I kept a journal and studied my own dream process. The Edgar Cayce work was fascinating reading and I devoured everything I could find. Martin was always available by phone or when we visited and we would have lively discussions. This workshop with Diana was the opportunity I had been waiting for to expand my knowledge and learn from someone who was right here in town.

Diana was an extremely attractive woman, petite and blonde with classic European looks. She had a broad smile, and her face just beamed when she connected with people. Although her manner was quiet and unassuming, she was an intensely compassionate, intuitive woman with incredible spiritual insight. In signing up for the class I hoped to learn everything I could about dream interpretation. Today however, my sole purpose was to tell her about the nightmare and get some answers.

Soon, Diana concluded her lecture, and Chris immediately came over and hugged me, sensing how difficult it was for me to wait. She agreed to follow me home when I was through. Several people were waiting to talk to Diana so I held back until almost everyone was gone. When it was finally my turn I approached her timidly, mumbling something about needing her help with a dream. As the images of the children and me running away from the cult women flashed before me tears welled in my eyes. She immediately suggested we move to another room for more privacy.

Diana led me to the library and seated us in chairs across from each other, waiting patiently for me to begin. I struggled to keep my emotions under control. Breaking down, I relayed my story beginning with the nightmare and ending with Kevin's death. When I finished I realized that Diana had been crying too. Overcome with emotion she folded her hands over her heart and cried out, "Oh, *where* was God?"

We sat together for a long time talking quietly about the dream. Diana assured me that there was meaning to be found amid the frightening images, but she declined any interpretation until she had time to examine it alone. She promised to call me promptly with any information she might have. She was very concerned about our family and what kind of support we had in the meantime. I immediately sensed she wasn't taking this information lightly and that her intuitions were running high.

Through more tears I thanked her for listening, and she hugged me tightly. I left feeling as though I had made a major breakthrough, and yet I did not have any more information than when I arrived. I had no idea what she was thinking or what resources she would use, but I did know I trusted her. I knew I had made a valuable connection with someone who validated my experience without judgment.

Though I knew pursuing an interpretation was the right thing to do, there was a part of me that felt pushed by an unknown force. In coming there today I had taken a huge step toward something, but it felt as if I had stepped off the ship's plank and plunged into the ocean. I could not explain the resistance I felt inside.

In retrospect, even meeting with Diana seemed like a setup, as if I were expected to be there. It was as though someone were keeping track of my whereabouts, creating opportunities for me to connect with the right people. All I knew was that I wanted to escape the nightmare my life had become.

10
Messengers of Destiny

Dream Journal: January 20, 1991

A swimming pool, lots of people swimming. The swimming instructor wants to teach me how to dive. I think this is absurd. I already know. To please him I climb a very high diving platform. He meets me there and instructs me to dive. I turn to look out into the pool. Instead of one diving platform, there are several white ones each lower than the one I am on and lower than the next. They look like very wide steps. He expects me to dive into the pool and land in a very narrow area of the water. I refuse.

Patience has never been one of my virtues. Agreeing to wait for word from Diana was a critical step in trust for me. Even so, I had lost any concept of time, so what difference did a couple of days, or even a week matter? My moments were spent enduring an unceasing pain that could only be alleviated by someone who had the power to return my son to me. Why was that not happening?

I do not know what it was like for Stann during that time. I was consumed with my own grief and watching him and Amber mourn compounded it. It was absolutely excruciating to look into their eyes and see a pain and sadness I felt very responsible for. I cannot imagine what it was like for him to tend to the everyday responsibilities of our home, his job, our finances, and the family. For the first time in my life, I was absolutely useless. I was unable to follow through with even the simplest of tasks like taking a shower and brushing my teeth. An immense sense of guilt began to descend on me as he took on what were once my responsibilities.

The thought of being separated from Stann and Amber was so frightening that I dreaded them leaving every day. They were out of my reach. I could not monitor their safety and no one could guarantee it. After the first week and a half, Stann returned to work. Mary counseled him on the pitfalls of going back too soon but his sense of responsibility overruled his need to grieve. Many of the teachers were not only his peers, but longtime friends as well, and knowing he had their support was comforting.

I was grateful that Amber had our friend Mary Ann for her teacher, at least she was with someone who loved her. Other friends were taking turns picking Amber up from school and bringing her home. Her classmates from the old school were having her over to play just as before. Even so, I still imagined my little girl feeling frightened and alone sitting by herself on the school playground.

Again and again, so many special people came to our rescue. Casseroles and groceries appeared daily gathering in the freezer for a time when we might think about eating. Stann's sister checked in with us as well as his parents. My cousins and long distance friends took turns calling me every few days. My closest girlfriends even volunteered to stay with me the first week that Stann returned to teach school.

It was reassuring to have someone in the house with me for a part of the day and I was grateful for their concern. On the other hand it was embarrassing to have to be taken care of and monitored. It occurred to me much later they feared I would do something drastic if I were left alone. I would have never thought that *not* wanting to be alive without my son was now considered an extreme thought.

It was with Mary though that I felt completely safe. She packed a strong and energetic spirit in her petite frame giving her the stamina needed to walk this journey with me. She expressed a gentle compassion in her brown eyes, as I would admit the fears that were running rampant in my head. Understanding my vulnerability she agreed to meet with me at home for a while and we kept in contact daily on the phone.

As each day blended into the next my anxiety deepened while my mind manufactured an ever-growing list of things I was now to blame for. The position of parental responsibility for my children's welfare was now a burden to be reckoned. Topping the list was the first line of defense; *protect your children at all costs.* I had failed and everybody knew it.

The truth was that in my heart I believed it was my fault. I was the one to blame. If only I had said, "No! You can't ride your bike". If only I had said, "Yes, I'll read that story right now. Let's forget about dinner". If only I had gone outside with him. *If only* I had said "No", Kevin would be alive. I had let him down. My vow as his mother was to love him and keep him safe always. I had failed him. What kind of mother was I? What kind of mother did Stann think I was? He must think it is my fault too.

I knew they were all thinking it, or why else would Stann pursue retaining a lawyer. Our friends and family said we should have some legal representation when the police returned to question me. We must need a lawyer because they think I was the negligent one and not the Driver. As my fears grew and my depression deepened it seemed that their insistence meant something more. I was slipping away.

* * * * * * *

I debated picking up the phone as it rang for the third time. I had been screening calls through the answering machine because I lacked the energy and focus to carry on a conversation. On the fourth ring, I lifted the receiver before the machine could click on. I heard Diana's soft voice ask for me. I breathed a deep sigh of relief, and then the anxiety quickly rose in my chest as I braced myself for the conversation.

Rifling through the desk drawer I grabbed some scratch paper and a pen preparing to take notes on anything she said. I sat cross-legged on the kitchen floor unable to get in a comfortable position, until finally I settled on my knees hunched over the paper. We chatted briefly about how I was coping, but we both knew the purpose of her call and she got right to the point.

Diana began by saying that since we last met on Sunday she had spent some time in prayer hoping to find God somewhere in the midst of this nightmare. She explained further by saying that our dreams are communications from God to us about things that need our attention and nurturing to further our emotional, physical, and spiritual welfare. She believed there was a message for me despite the horrifying characters and frightening images. She was certain that God had not abandoned me.

I accepted that our dreams came from a higher level of consciousness within ourselves. I had never considered that they would come from God. I agreed that my dreams commented on aspects of my life needing my attention. However, I had never given my nightmares the same credence. They were so bizarre, never making any sense that I attributed many of them to a flaw or quirk in my personality.

Diana's sense of the nightmare was that it was actually a message from God sent in the form of Heavenly bodies. The circle of dark faced women were actually divine energies, not evil or cult figures as I had described them. She explained that in its fearfulness, my ego had actually masked their real identities by making their faces appear dark or shadowed, giving them a hideous form. I had identified the Blonde

90

Woman with the sword by her light hair. This indicated that she was a feminine energy sent to deliver a message about an event that was destined to occur. They were divine energies calling Kevin back home.

I held the receiver away from my mouth and laid my forehead on the kitchen floor rocking back and forth. I felt light headed and sick to my stomach. I knew that if I moved one inch from this spot I would surely throw up.

"I knew that God had to be somewhere in this dream Carla, and I believe these were actually Angels and not beings of an evil nature", she continued.

Crying I choked on my words, "Diana, why would God give me a nightmare? It was horrible! Why not just tell me in a way that I could understand so that I could save him?"

"Carla, God did not give you a nightmare. He sent you a clear message about your destiny. Your conscious mind could not handle the truth and therefore your fears masked the messengers and interpreted the message in the only way you could understand, by hiding it in the dark. What mother wouldn't fight for her child to live?" she exclaimed.

"Diana, why *my* Kevin? Are you saying he was *supposed* to die?" I demanded to know.

"There is a saying in scripture that says: when God shuts the door, no man can open it," she paused. "Yes, I think this is about Kevin's destiny, and yours. You are being asked to unmask the illusion of death."

I kept shaking my head in disbelief! How could this be true? How could it be a five-year-old child's destiny to be run over by a damned truck? Death is death! It means he's gone and I'll never see him again. What kind of an illusion is that?

Diana wanted to examine more of the dream symbols with me. She encouraged me to continue coming to the dream class and offered to meet privately whenever I felt up to it. I thanked her for all her help and half-heartedly promised to continue the class. After she hung up I let the phone slip from my fingers, as the dial tone echoed from the kitchen walls. I lay on the floor in a fetal position crying for a very long time. Just as I had refused to dive into the pool in last night's dream, I held steadfast to reason and logic. Yet, deep inside, my instincts were tugging at me to surrender and take the plunge to accept what I knew to be true.

11
Remembering

Dream Journal: January 23, 1991

My mom and I are looking at a photo of me in my wedding dress. The dress is white, off the shoulders and silk ruffles...the view is from above, and the train of the dress is placed gently at my side. There are pink flowers cascading from the train. Mom and I notice there were no close ups taken, and we want to know why.

So many people in one room. All my family is here for my wedding procession. The colors change from white to darker tones, and now the procession is really for Kevin's funeral. All my family is scattered and not sitting together. Calling out to each other during the service. My area of the church has to be moved upstairs. So we all end up sitting in another room at the top of the stairs. We can't hear the service nor do we know whether it's started, but we see people through the door still coming to fill seats. I want to be in the front, and I tell my family to come with me. I send my brother Paul first, and he walks ahead leading us through the middle of the church.

The church is empty, and the casket is in a small room with a few chairs. The service is over, we've missed it! My Dad appears and asks where we were. I'm furious! How could they go on without me! I turn to go back in the small room. The casket is gone. In its place, is a round table with a white tablecloth placed over it. Above the table is an arch. The arch has been burnt and is still glowing red and orange. In the center of the table is a white round plate for Eucharist. Placed on the dish are white chips of different sizes that have been burnt. The outer edges of some are glowing red and orange, but they are all still white. I'm confused because I'm expecting Kevin's casket to be there...but I realize it is his cremation remains. I am so confused because I think it might be communion hosts instead...I stand there crying and sobbing, so confused...I need my mom.

A moment before I had felt my mother's presence beside me. In the next, my heart was crying at the sight of my baby's smoldering cremation remains. I was trapped in this poor excuse for reality called my life and I could not escape it even in my sleep. If there were ever a more urgent time when I needed my mother, it was now. I needed her to tell me it was just a horrible dream. I needed my mother's reassurance and love. I could no longer mother myself as I had been doing these past five years since her death. Now, I felt that she had deserted me not once, but twice.

In the previous four years before Kevin's birth, she had bravely battled breast cancer, ovarian cancer, and then colon cancer. She died when I was nine months pregnant with Kevin. Despite the arsenal of chemicals, the cancer had advanced rapidly. My parents had shortened their annual fall vacation returning home to yet another barrage of consultations, tests, and treatments. Anticipating my mother's report, I was excited to share the news of my second pregnancy when I answered the phone that November evening.

"So, what did the doctor say," I urged, confronting her tendency to shield me from her illness.

"There's nothing more they can do," she said without emotion. My heart sank. I was unprepared to hear the acceptance of defeat in her voice.

As much as I had prayed for God to let her live, sadly, I knew then that she would not survive my pregnancy. From that point on, it was an unspoken knowing between us that in its extreme sadness could never be addressed aloud. Even so, I concentrated on the hope that a miracle would occur and ignored the truth nagging away at my heart.

There were angry times when I wanted to yell that if she really wanted to live and see this baby she should have taken better care of herself in the first place. I wanted her to *make* herself well. I wanted her to change her diet, be more active, or pray harder. Maybe, *she* was not trying hard enough? On the other hand, were we not praying hard enough for her? Why would God allow this malignancy to ravage her body when surely she deserved better for having served Him all of her life. I questioned this God who seemed cruel and vengeful, dispersing random healing, and unfair punishments.

It seemed that I spent so much energy praying for her health that I thought little of my own. I had so many things to worry about during

93

those last few months of her life that I hardly had the time to get excited about my pregnancy. I was making monthly trips to Denver to visit her while attempting to keep our home balloon delivery service open, and still be a mom to my two and a half year old daughter. When I did have a moment to ponder who this baby would be, I wrestled with how I would fit this second child into my life. We would be four instead of three. How could I divide my love and attention for this new child? How could I possibly love another child as much as my adorable Amber?

Intuitively, I felt deeply connected with this life within me despite the chaos that was happening around me. Everything about this pregnancy was different from my first. I had severe morning sickness for the first five months, and I carried him much higher reducing my mobility. There was an expectancy about the pregnancy that kept me aware of the baby's existence. When I would allow myself to be excited, the prospect of another personality was intriguing and mysterious. I would reassure the baby that when the time came I would be ready. I asked the baby to please be patient and allow me to do what I needed to do for my mother.

My mother and I did not speak of these things though, nor did we speak about her impending death. She was always guarded with me because I was pregnant, and I towards her because she was dying. As the last few weeks grew shorter, Mom allowed herself to speculate on my due date even hinting with anticipation that she might still be here. I took this as a sign of hope, and I went to great measures to establish a plan for her and my father to come as soon as I began my labor. I had it all arranged for them to fly on a commuter plane to Montrose with her I.V. pole, and a cooler to hold the numerous bags of fluids she needed. It was quite involved but definitely possible, if only she would hold on until then.

Instead, my mother labored first and the commuter plane took my curious little girl and me over the mountains to be with her. I arrived at her bedside early in the evening after all the relatives had gone to dinner. I knew my way around the hospital ward after having spent so much time there. I was shocked though when I realized that I had actually passed right by her room. I did not recognize her. It had only been a month since I had been home, and she looked as though she had aged twenty years.

Her face was drawn, and the sockets of her eyes were deep and hollow. Her voice was high and shrill because of the oxygen tube in her nose. There was little evidence of the vivacious woman I had known all my life. When I entered the room, she recognized me immediately. Her reaction was a mix of delight in seeing me, and an incredible sorrow in knowing that she couldn't conceal the truth from me anymore.

The next two days was a remarkable testimony of her undying love for her family and friends. My dad, my brother, his fiancée, and I all took turns staying with her as family members arrived from back east to say goodbye. With all the laughing, and crying and storytelling it certainly did not seem as though she were leaving anytime soon.

I regret not having the private time I wanted with her. My desire to accommodate others to have time with her too kept me from asking for it. There were a couple of moments where we connected despite the constant crowd of visitors in her room. At one point we talked briefly about the baby's birth. Sitting up in her bed, she abruptly announced to everyone that it should be a girl because of the multitude of baby girl clothing on hand. Laughter broke out among the family because everyone knew my mom's obsession with her granddaughter's wardrobe. Amber was better dressed than Stann and I could ever have hoped for because of my mom's delight in shopping for her only grandchild.

As the laughter subsided, she gazed down at her hands. Without looking up she said quietly, "It will be a boy though."

I held her hand to my moist face and sobbed. "Mom, I need you to be there with me! Please wait!"

Slowly the tears rolled down her sunken cheeks. Nodding her tired head she said, "I'll be there with you. I promise."

I dropped my head in defeat knowing she was still trying to protect me. I took her hand and placed it on my swollen belly. At that moment the baby kicked into her palm. It was the closest she would get to touch her grandchild in this life.

A few hours later she succumbed to a coma and spent her last day laboring to hold onto the breath of life. Her tired body ravaged by the drugs meant to keep her comfortable, began to shut down. Her breathing became shallower, and with each breath the effort to lift her chest became a greater challenge.

I wished that I could turn her bed around to the window so the warm sun could kiss her face. I marveled at the softness of her tanned skin while I stroked her hollow cheeks. I chuckled to myself remembering that no matter how sick she was when she came into the hospital she always found a way to get outside to the sun deck and see the mountains. She had the healthiest looking tan of all the cancer patients on the ward. That day, the last of May, would have been one of those wonderful Colorado mornings in the sun.

My energetic, spirited mother now lay motionless unable to support her head or adjust her blankets. I tidied the bed covers knowing she would have wanted to appear neat and in order even in her passing. I was glad that we had changed her sheets and sponge bathed her the night before. I was humbled by the opportunity to make this small difference in her final hours.

I had never watched anyone die before. It seemed to take such a long time for the organs to shut down. I was amazed at how diligent the process was, and yet so slow and arduous. There was a protocol to honor.

How much longer could she endure that torturous raspy breathing? Why was she holding on when letting go would feel so much better? My God, anything would be better than being stuck between pain and freedom.

I leaned over kissing her soft cheek whispering that I loved her. I knew now that I had to let her go.

"Mom, I know you're going to a place that's so beautiful...please let go," I whispered.

She moved her head ever so slowly towards her left side and opened her eyes, staring deep into mine.

"Mom! You heard me", I nodded back to her. "I know you heard me. It's okay! It's going to be so beautiful there...please let go... I love you". I whispered through my tears laying my head on her shoulder.

My father slipped in quietly moving to the left side of her bed. He cupped her chin in his hand and kissed her forehead. The raspy guttural sounds rose from deep within her chest echoing in the silent room. She let out a labored breath and closed her eyes. I closed my eyes too. Rocking slowly at her bedside, I sensed the warm presence of someone leaning over my right shoulder. I turned around to accept the comfort offered as my tears began to flow. I was startled to see that no one was there except the morning sun shining brightly beside me.

The week of the funeral and the remaining two weeks of my pregnancy was a blur. It seemed that I would never stop crying. I felt so lost and alone. The only thing that I could see clearly was the unnerving image of my mom's bulging eyes and hollow face staring at me in the middle of the night.

Just as promised she was with me when Kevin finally came into this world. My labor went quickly and with experience on my side this time, it was quite uneventful. When the time came to push life into the world, when it hurt so bad that I couldn't breathe, when I moaned that I could not push any harder, I cried out for my mother to help me. I pushed so hard that I felt as if I were floating in a pocket of black silence. It was there that I heard her voice urging me on. I could never have known how truly present she would be in that moment.

12
Spiritually Handicapped

Dream Journal January 24, 1991
It was my job to pick up Kevin's body at the funeral home. There is a viewing in progress when I arrive. I'm led to the back, down a hallway. One side is windows and on the other side are floor to ceiling shelves. Each shelf has a drawer. In the drawers are dead bodies, waiting for their viewing time. I am led quickly past these, but I get a glimpse of Kevin's baby blanket in one of the drawers. I panic and cry out for him.

Whatever healing powers my mother's presence offered in those few moments was quickly lost in the wake of Kevin's birth. Our attention took a turn from mourning a death, to grieving a new life handicapped by physical limitations. Unknown to us, this baby had been growing for nine months with bilateral clubbed feet.

Within the first minute there were complications with his breathing. As I lay trembling from the strain of the delivery, I was aware of a figure dashing into the room toward the baby's warming table. Stann stepped back from the commotion of doctors and nurses huddled around the baby. His face paled in fear and confusion, as he stood alone behind them. My heart was seized with panic as I heard someone across the room whisper that the baby had clubbed feet. Not having any idea what that was, I immediately assumed he was born with no feet at all! I pleaded for information, but no one would answer me. The breathing matter was the priority and while it seemed to correct itself they wanted to do some tests immediately.

Before they took my baby away, the delivery nurse wrapped him in thermal blankets laying him beside me on the table. Flat on my back, I turned my head to see my precious baby. Finally! We were face to face after having shared the same body for nine months. Since the beginning of this pregnancy I could not imagine what my life would be like with a second child. How I could possibly share the love I had with my firstborn with another. I thought I had given all my love to Amber. I was afraid I would not have enough left over for another.

I cannot find the words to explain the knowing that pulsed through me. Not enough love? Impossible! Looking into my son's dark eyes I realized that not having enough love was the impossibility. There is always *enough* love. In that moment, I knew it was possible to love them both equally. With one look into his beautiful dark eyes my heart cried, "Oh baby! I can't imagine what my life would be life without you." I kissed his sweet round face so bruised and squashed from the passage through the birth canal. Pulling the bundle closer to me, I breathed the smell of his unwashed newborn skin, rubbing his thick dark hair against my cheek. A wave of emotions both familiar and profound swept me away. I began to cry at the wonder of this perfect little being. I sensed that I had known him forever. It was as though we had been reunited.

Stripped of any defenses that could guard the most delicate and vulnerable parts of myself, my instincts took over. From deep within my gut I felt a rising sensation that stung my heart. The foreboding sense that I would lose him was so clear and distinct that it seized my soul. Fear rushed in, and I wept, "*No!* I will never let him go." I held him close shielding him from the nurse, the intrusive tests, and the world. I began to love him and protect him with an intensity I had never known was possible.

The unspoken message of my impending loss echoed deep inside me, captivating me in fear. The sense of knowing flowed from my gut, expanding into feelings that filled my heart with intense emotions. This *knowing* love and fear within seconds of each other, was not something that my naive self could process. This mysterious connection was unsettling. The irrational thoughts about my assumed responsibility for Kevin's birth defect only intensified my fear.

Left alone in my hospital room, Stann and I cried in each other's arms. This birth had an outcome that was already determined and far different from what we could have imagined. He was supposed to be protected inside me! I sobbed that during my pregnancy I must have done something to harm him. I thought I had done all the right things, eaten all the right foods, and read all the right books. How could this have happened to my baby?

Our imagination ran wild the longer Kevin was kept away from us. My fears breathed a life of their own. I needed him back in my arms. More than an hour had passed when the obstetrics nurse finally handed him to me. Our family doctor and the pediatrician reported that he was doing well, and they explained what to expect in the next few hours. Oblivious to them, I quickly unwrapped him. I had worked myself into a frenzy imagining that his legs might look like baseball bats with stumps for feet. I was unprepared for what I saw. Although he had feet, they were twisted and turned in so far that his big toes touched his calves.

Now that I had seen what my body had done to him I became consumed with guilt and remorse. No amount of explanations, reassurances or suggestions from the doctors would relieve my burden. I could not fathom how this deformity would be fixed. How would he ever walk on his own? Surely, he would be crippled for the rest of his life.

Only two hours had passed since his greatly anticipated arrival. It seemed that the shock would last for an eternity. In all the commotion of his birth our baby had not been named. Yesterday we had narrowed the choices to two names, *Kevin* and *Ryan*. I was clear in my desire to name him Kevin. It was Stann's middle name. As a child, Stann had never liked his first name and really wanted to be called Kevin. Loving Stann as much as I did, I knew that the name Kevin, meaning "kind and gentle," suited Stann more than he realized. If there were traits, I would love for our son to have it would be those that Stann so genuinely possessed.

Stann wanted to wait until the birth to decide, hoping to get a better idea after seeing the baby. Now he felt as if he had cursed the baby by presuming that he should be his namesake. It was obvious to me that this little guy should be named Kevin. Again, my instincts guided us and we named our son Kevin Ryan Blowey.

Adjusting to a newborn under normal circumstances was a challenge. Our first few hours became a battle to hold on to reality. Stann and I were still in shock over Kevin's birth defect. The next morning the orthopedic surgeon visited with me to explain the situation. At that time he ruled out any genetic factor since we had no known history of clubbed feet on either side of our families. He surmised that because Kevin was a large baby there was not enough room inside me for him to stretch out as he grew, thus creating the curved in shape to his feet. He believed the prognosis was good, and with casting, Kevin's feet would stretch back into their normal position. He warned us that it would be a long process. If the casting failed then surgery was a possibility later. He added with a note of encouragement that of all the birth defects a child could have, clubbed feet had one of the best recovery rates.

At the mere suggestion that my womb was not an adequate size to harbor my baby, I was overcome with new guilt. Leaving me in my room, the doctor went onto the nursery to apply the first set of casts to

Kevin's feet. I remember sitting up in the bed, in a daze, trying to make sense of this information. Then I heard the shrill cry of a newborn coming from the nursery.

I only heard Kevin cry once after the delivery but I knew this was *my* baby's cry. The piercing wail signaled to me he was in pain, and I had to be with him immediately. Encumbered by the episiotomy, I hobbled out of my room and down the hall to the nursery. I stopped at an open window where I recognized the orthopedic doctor leaning over the counter. Holding my sore stomach, I leaned through the opening and gently placed my hand on Kevin's beet red face. "Kevin, baby, Mommy's here!" I called to him. I broke down at the sight of his crippled feet being forced and stretched against their will into the cast material. A nurse tugged on my arm and forced me to turn away from the window. The next thing I remember I was back in my bed cradling Kevin in my arms, nursing away the trauma. Exhausted, we both fell asleep.

Within the next twenty-four hours my fears increased as I anticipated being released from the hospital. I dreaded going home because I would be alone with no help during the day. Kevin was almost two weeks overdue. Stann had used the time between his school break and his summer job, so he could not be there as we had planned. My dear friend, Ann (and Amber's second mother), pitched in by keeping Amber with her most days. Without her help I do not know how I would have coped.

Over the next nine months I became obsessed with my responsibility for Kevin's foot deformity. It was my body that was supposed to protect my son. I had failed him before he even had a chance to breathe. I questioned whether I had inadvertently done something to harm him, such as taking too many medications or not enough vitamins. I even convinced myself that I might have sat too much, reasoning that my posture did not allow him the room he needed to stretch and grow!

I struggled with this self-imposed guilt and the abandonment I felt by both my mother and God. The growing pressures of parenting a baby and a preschooler, while operating our home business was mounting as Stann spent more time working to support us. While it was necessary, it left me alone to deal with the children's schedules, the business, and the weekly doctor appointments to change Kevin's casts. If I wasn't crying, I was angry!

It did not seem as if we could get a break. What kind of God was this? Who was this unmerciful God who allowed my innocent baby to be born with deformed feet. For that matter where was my God? I had put my faith and trust in him as I was told to do. I prayed that my mother would be healed and that my baby would be healthy. Was that too much to ask? I was angry with God for abandoning my baby and me. I resented that He was screwing with our lives! More so, I was angry that in her death my mom had deserted me. How dare she die at a time when I needed her.

The post-partum depression and grief were intertwined so tightly that it was difficult to distinguish between the two. Why had I been given a life to grow within me when my mother had death growing inside her? Often, I wished that God had given her the life instead of giving it to me. I thought that somehow God had confused his timing. It made perfect sense to me that I could have a baby anytime in my life. Why couldn't God see that I needed her to live?

The unresolved grief, the challenges of Kevin's handicap, caring for two little ones and our household, the business, and emotionally supporting my father in his grief finally took its toll on me. One day in desperation, I opened the phone book searching the yellow pages for a counselor. I was surprised to find a number of listings for counselors in our small town. I was too embarrassed to ask anyone for a referral so I ran my finger down the list looking for a name to catch my attention. Nothing appealed to me until I came across the name of a practice called Rainbow Counseling. I immediately dialed the number and made an appointment. It was time for this emotional storm to end.

Soon I realized that God had not abandoned me. What were the chances of finding a woman counselor, only three years older than myself, who had a baby girl just two months younger than Kevin, and, whose name was Mary, the very name of the mother I grieved?

Mary and I immediately bonded as working mothers faced with the challenges of raising our babies. It was easy to share my concerns about Kevin's handicap with someone who understood the heart connection between a mother and her baby. There were many occasions when our babies crawled on the floor together as we marveled at their unique personalities. Mary was instrumental in helping me to find normalcy again while I explored the grief issues surrounding my mother's death.

Although it seemed my mother's dying was painful, there was a comfort in knowing she was free from the cancer that had plagued her for four years. Dying at the age of 55 seemed too soon, yet I admitted she had lived a very full life. As an Army wife of a First Sergeant, her duty was to raise her children and manage the household when we moved from post to post. She could turn any Army housing into a home with her nurturing touch and hilarious sense of humor. In their retirement, my parents looked forward to traveling to Europe again to revisit their favorite places. Although I still felt the loss and abandonment of my mother as if I were a young child, her absence forced me to become even more self-reliant and independent. I no longer had access to her sage advice by picking up the phone and dialing home on a whim.

As I matured I began to question the black and white terms in which life and death seemed to be defined for me. I could not imagine that my mother was relaxing on a fluffy cloud playing a harp as a parade of archangels and saints passed her by! That made for television image felt contrived and limited. It was ludicrous to me that all we could anticipate in our deaths was floating around from cloud to cloud as we earnestly prayed for the poor souls on earth.

My first dream experiences with my mother proved to me that she was indeed *somewhere*. There were no pearly gates or gold lined streets in this dream, only confusion and apprehension about her surroundings. She was still in her nightgown rushing through stores at the mall exclaiming she had to see everything! However, a month later, my dream journal reports a second dream, where I was with her in a big hospital room with lots of people. This time she was very calm looking healthy, not thin, and gaunt like when she died. We were walking together, and I was crying, "Don't go, please don't leave us! I need you so much." She turned to me and firmly said, "I have to die so that you all can get on with your lives." Shocked by her words, I cried, "No! Please don't leave me. I need you!" Then, I lost her in the crowd.

I awakened with a profound knowing that truly we had just been together. As I remembered more details of the dream, it was like recovering a memory of an event that had occurred just the night before. It was that clear. Each dream thereafter revealed a bit more about her adjustment to the afterlife and my acceptance of her death. In one dream I was amused when she told me *they* had important work for her to do and that she was quite busy. Seeing her alive and well in my dreams helped to blot out the image of her drawn face and sunken eyes.

More important, I was actually experiencing her presence. It was just as real as when she was physically alive. She was standing before me. When she hugged me, I could feel her soft skin against my cheek and her curly gray hair tickling my nose! There was joy and delight as we were reunited in laughter. I was fully awake and conscious in those dreams, and no one could convince me otherwise. However, I dare not speak of it for fear that another's skepticism would diminish those encounters as figments of a foolish and over active imagination.

My search to find meaning in my mother's death began with those dream experiences. They were first hand proof to me that life did indeed continue. I had the experience but not the language or the education to explain it. I had no one to share it with. The truth was that my dreams frightened and intimidated people. As a child no one wanted to hear about my night time adventures of falling into snake pits, or floating above my body as I slept in my bed, or running through burned out Indian camps, or dreaming about places before I had been there. I learned very early not to share these nocturnal experiences with too many people.

The acceptance and the openness I received from Mary during my grief counseling enabled me to trust my own process and explore beyond my limited beliefs. Over the next five years I began to accept and come to terms with my grief by first examining my belief system. I began to redefine life and accept that our consciousness is what lives forever. With or without the body, before our physical birth and after our physical death we do exist. Death was merely a transition stage into the next life, and that consciousness never ceased. As this concept became clearer and I found the words to describe my experiences it was confirmed for me. Gradually, I came to a place of acceptance about my mother's death. I could see the blessings and feel a sense of peace in it.

In resolving some of my grief about my mother, I cleared the way for defining my real fears and concerns about Kevin. I was then able to address the guilt I felt about Kevin's handicap and the immediate stresses for the upcoming surgery to correct the clubbed feet. Our baby, on the other hand displayed none of the fears or anxieties about his birth defect. People seemed to be drawn to his gentle spirit and to the openness in which he received them. No one noticed the casts on his legs. We joked halfheartedly that perhaps we were the ones with the handicap.

I remember an occasion a couple of weeks after he was born that hinted of something exceptional about him. One day Kevin and I had the afternoon alone. Stann was at his summer job. Ann had picked up Amber to spend the day with the children in her day care . It gave me a much-needed rest with Kevin.

Even as an amateur photographer I always had film in my camera. That day I took advantage of the quiet time to take some shots of Kevin alone. I propped up Kevin's fat little self in the corner pillow of the couch while he patiently allowed me to primp and pose him. Framing his chunky little body in the viewfinder, his dark hair and eyes and olive skin were a stunning contrast against his bright blue T-shirt, diapers, and the thigh-high casts. He looked absolutely adorable! He was so calm and settled; so mature looking for being only two weeks old.

After a couple of shots I kneeled beside him to focus on his profile. Just as I was ready to snap the picture, he turned his head slowly towards me. As his face filled the viewfinder, I was struck by the intense look in his eyes. I lowered the camera from my face, and our eyes locked together in a mesmerizing stare. His dark eyes seemed to penetrate to the core of my soul engulfing me with complete and total love. Again, I was overwhelmed with this sense of having known him forever. Tears welled up in my eyes, and I felt a lump in my throat. Seizing the moment, I snapped the photo without thinking to focus it again. Later, when the film was developed that picture was totally focused.

It seemed as though the birth of Kevin had awakened within me a place that had been asleep until then. A very powerful connection of a psychic and spiritual nature had occurred between us at his birth, creating a bond that was unlike anything I had ever experienced with another human being. It was a profound moment that I could not articulate easily because the emotions were so powerful.

I would not speak of it openly for fear that another's skepticism would cause me to doubt my inner knowing. I considered that perhaps this unique bond was more about the fact that I had just suffered the death of my mother and was clinging to anything that represented life. I felt extremely guilty, and responsible for Kevin's birth defect and my maternal and protective instincts had completely taken over. In retrospect, I believe I suppressed the awakening for several months because it did not fit into my belief system. The grief and depression had side tracked me, but the feelings never waned, and the connection grew stronger with each day that passed.

Kevin's surgery was successful and within a couple months, after the final casts were removed, his legs and feet became strong enough to support him. He walked, and he walked and he walked. It was a glorious occasion! It marked the beginning of a time when our little family was free of the chains of grief and the torment of guilt. We found a new sense of order and peace in our lives. We were blessed with a bright future and looked forward to the adventure of raising our children and growing old together.

My personal journey of self-discovery continued too as I ascertained just how limited my thinking had been. I subscribed to the belief that our consciousness was like a river of awareness that was connected to other streams flowing in and out of each other, eventually spilling into its collective destination the ocean, only to move out again with the tides. Once I grasped the idea that life does not end with physical death, I became more open to other concepts.

I still had my Catholic foundation and believed in Jesus as the Risen Christ and that Eucharist and the Holy Spirit had the power to transform our lives. The difference was that I began trusting my intuition more and developing a relationship with God that helped deepen my faith. God, in His infinite wisdom, had given us such a wonderful gift in free will. With power of choice there was always a positive in everything that seemed negative.

In the beginning, I resisted the concept that at the soul level, we choose our handicaps or illnesses as a means to support what we need to learn most. I clung to the belief that unfair punishment was the result of our transgressions. As his mother and protector I could not grasp why my innocent child was being punished for something, I might have unknowingly done. I could not figure out what sin I had committed that would produce this consequence, and why God would also punish my child.

When I became aware of the "blame game" and how long I had played it, I could reconcile my guilt about Kevin's birth defect. I did not create the birth defect. I did not choose it for him. If I believe that we are conscious and have free will before we come into the body, choice must be an option then too. Was it not possible that with free will we could choose the kind of body that would benefit our soul's growth, and in turn teach the most? I had never entertained the thought there was a partnership between God and the self in determining our life's plan. I believed everything was mandated and decided by God, and we played the cards we were dealt. The twist was that we dealt our own cards and God trusted us to play the hand with our soul's best interests at stake.

Everything about Kevin's personality defied that birth defect as if it did not exist; therefore, he was not affected by it. When at six months he decided it was time to stand, he pulled himself up to the edge of the couch and stood on his crippled feet proving to us that the affliction was indeed an illusion. The more I recognized Kevin as a *conscious being*, the more feasible it was for me to accept that he and God might have agreed on his handicap to further his souls' growth and ours. We were chosen to be his parents. It was an extraordinary sign of the great love they had for us.

Slowly, I accepted that Kevin's birth defect did not define who he was nor limited him in any way. It was really a lesson about my spiritual handicaps. If I believed that God gave Kevin and Amber the gift of choice to be in my life then I also had to believe that I had made a choice to be in theirs. When faced with that revelation I began to view my children as the teachers and myself as their student. They seemed wiser and more perceptive than I.

The next five years was filled with books, workshops and classes that enabled me to consider the limitless possibilities of the human spirit. Most exciting were the discussions about the Edgar Cayce readings and dreams. I was like a sponge, absorbing everything I could and squeezed out whatever did not resonate with me. I was given plenty of opportunities to practice what I learned. More often than not, I slipped back into the old beliefs and denied that I had any choice in shifting my perspective to perceive life another way. It was an exciting time of growth, and learning and I was eager to discuss these discoveries with others on the path of self-discovery.

It was immediately apparent to me though that not everybody shared my thirst to know God as Truth and Love or wanted to explore their dream world. I know I made people uncomfortable when I talked about a God who could not conceive of punishing us if we believed he was an All-Loving, only-good God. Perhaps, I would question, it was the self that sabotaged our efforts to receive God's love and guidance. The former illusions I had about God's love were embarrassing when I considered how much I had tried to control the way that God could love me.

With this newfound awareness, I became more conscious of my intuition as a signal from God to pay attention. He really wanted me to know about myself. He wanted me to choose more consciously. I began to place more faith in God and His love for me. With that came a trust that my family would be taken care of too.

Now, everything that I had studied and experienced seemed absolutely meaningless. It did not explain to me why *my* Kevin was dead. I could not conceive of the fact that Kevin would choose to leave us now or ever, and for that matter that I would agree to his leaving or the method! Free will no longer made sense. Who the hell was in charge if God could not or would not override our poor choices? I did not give a flip about personal growth and spiritual development if it meant giving up my baby. Furthermore, Angels wielding chain saws in the name of God's will seemed even more preposterous.

The chilling contrast between my mother's death and Kevin's death did not allow for comparison. Kevin died because of another human being's actions, not a disease or illness or truck. I believed his presence on that sidewalk was never given a second thought, but ignored and run over because of haste and neglect. My precious little boy was only five years old, not fifty-five.

He was just beginning to live! Kevin was my explorer who had packed so much adventure into his five-and-a-half years. He was going to karate lessons in the spring and entering kindergarten this fall. This winter he and Amber were going to take skiing lessons so that we could begin skiing as a family. There were swimming lessons and sunny afternoons at the lake. There were Saturday bike rides through the park now that he could successfully navigate a two-wheeler. There were plans to play with Kyle when they would magically turn into Super Heroes saving our back yard from imminent disaster. There was so much to do and all the time in the world to do it.

Until, now. There was no time left. In the moment of Kevin's death our lives were changed forever. In that instant, our family as we knew it, ceased to exist. We were silenced with one blow of circumstance. There were no more tomorrows for the family of four that played and laughed and danced and loved together. There would never be another sweet hello or tender kiss, loving hug or rambunctious laugh. I would never hear his deep voice say, "I love you too, Mom!" Never, again.

The reality of "nevers" was so incomprehensible that I lost any grip I might have had on my sanity. All I could perceive was that my entire body was in excruciating pain. It longed to touch my Kevin, to feel his cheek brush gently against mine, to hold him close to my breast and smell his tousled hair or feel his arms wrap so tightly around my neck.

I rejected everything I had learned. I could not integrate these facts into my world for it would mean an acceptance of something that I could not, I would not, believe to be true. I fought to wake up from this unbearable nightmare masquerading as my life.

13
"Where were You, God?"

Dream Journal: January 24, 1991
Stann and I drive up to a house expecting to get there before Kevin. He was dropped off by the parents of a child he played with. I enter the house and realize he has been left alone. I climb the stairs to the first level. Kevin comes down the stairs, crying, that he was left alone and that nobody stayed with him. I carry him and sit at the bottom of the steps, holding him close knowing he is scared at being left alone.

Our home had become a refuge harboring our lost and vulnerable family from a world we could no longer trust to keep us safe. Secluding ourselves seemed to be the only feasible answer. My only exception was in allowing Stann and Amber to go to school. It was a struggle for us to go our separate ways for even a day.

I drove Amber to and from school every day, for several weeks. Saying goodbye was painful for I dreaded returning to our empty home. One morning I drove aimlessly around town, until I found myself parked in front of our church parish center. Dazed, I walked inside and joined a small group of parishioners praying with Fr. Gary. I looked across the room to see Chris with her head bowed, eyebrows raised as she stared wide-eyed at me in astonishment. I do not know who was more surprised –Chris, because she had never seen me attend a daily communion service –or me, because I did not know why I was there.

In truth, I had been led there by an unseen, yet powerful energy, pushing me toward a place that would offer nourishment, warmth, and comfort. Each time I received Eucharist, I experienced a reunion with my God that restored my faith until the next wave of grief threatened to separate us. I understood now why the Church required our young children to wait for Eucharist until they were older. I always thought our children were being denied an opportunity for communion with God. I had it all wrong. In their innocence they had not yet separated themselves from God. They were not hungry. Perhaps, their dilemma was more about retaining their memory of Him.

Soon, it became my ritual to attend a communion service at least once a week. I would meet Chris, who had become my bodyguard, shielding me from well-meaning intruders until I could recreate my social and personal boundaries again. I had become so self-conscious I could barely receive their kind words. In time, I allowed the intimacy of the small, dedicated group to support me. Embraced by my faith community's compassion, they reminded me that God's mercies were not spent. It was there that my soul was fed with the body of Christ, filling me with hope, if only for a brief time.

On those mornings I felt grounded long enough to return home. However, once there I was faced with the dilemma of what to do with the rest of my time. A carton of thank you cards collected dust next to the heating vent, and the pile of unopened mail and unpaid bills sat at the end of the dining room table in the kitchen. I knew they needed my attention just as much as the unmade beds, the ten loads of laundry, the grimy bathtub, and the empty refrigerator. It was obvious what should be done, but when Stann asked how I spent my day, I could not account for my time. I could not explain to him why the vacuum, still plugged in, was left in the middle of the living room floor, and, why I still had not showered and changed my clothes by four o'clock in the afternoon.

It felt as though a powerful force had dropped me into a deep black hole. Each day merged into the next with no clear beginning or ending. A month ago the pages of my engagement book were dotted with social commitments, activities and play dates, juggled with work schedules and pick up times. My hairdressing appointments required another calendar of their own overflowing into my family commitments. The new year would have been more of the same with blank squares waiting to be filled. My life had been manageable, flexible and predictable. Now, calendars had lost all meaning. They were only an attempt to direct events and manipulate their outcome. Appointments, schedules and commitments were insignificant. Daily life was now surviving the twists, turns and traps of grief.

In truth, it was the closed bedroom door in the middle of the hallway that seized my attention, drawing me to it like a magnet each day.

In the first couple of months, the door to Kevin's room remained closed to visitors. It was a dense and heavy barrier to a place filled with books, toys, games and memories. The door was always closed unless one of us privately summoned the courage to open it and enter its sacred space. During the day while I was home alone, the door could pull me to its threshold from anywhere else in the house. At the oddest moments, I would find myself standing in the hallway with my hand grasping the doorknob.

Was it curiosity or fear that brought me there that morning? The simple act of placing my hand on the doorknob triggered memories of the Blonde Woman in the attic, and scenes of Kevin laying helpless in the street. The desire to wake up from the nightmare and prove it all wrong pushed me through the door to consciousness.

I shut my eyes to squeeze out the raw images and took a deep breath to gather all my strength and energy to open the door. A cold draft passed over my face as I stepped inside the room. I paused to listen for an invitation to proceed further, but there was only the rustling of my footstep as it crushed the fibers of the carpet.

I leaned against the narrow wall to steady myself. The daylight from the window above his bed shined brightly into the darkened hallway making me squint. My eyes adjusted to the glare as the shadows of a room abruptly abandoned by its owner came into focus. The bed was stripped bare; a set of light blue sheets and a Disney design bedspread lay in a heap at the foot of the bed. A messy array of favorite toys and new Christmas gifts was piled on the makeshift shelves of wood and concrete blocks. The toy box lid was ajar spilling its contents of trucks, balls and stuffed animals onto the floor.

I moved hesitantly across the room and sat down on the edge of the unmade bed next to the pile of bed covers. The late morning sun shining through the blinds cast its rays upon the familiar objects, giving me a sense of reassurance. From the bed, I viewed the room in its entirety. I recognized everything. There were action figures and guns, the shiny Batmobile, a new punching bag, and a box of Legos. Toys and keepsakes too numerous to name lay dormant waiting to receive orders from their Leader.

I took another breath, recalling that even at such a young age Kevin showed signs of good leadership. He freely shared himself as well as his possessions with his friends. During the funeral week, I felt that it was important for the children to have access to Kevin's room and his playthings as they always had when visiting. The suddenness of his death was cruel enough. If I needed to touch his stuffed animals to feel closer to him, wouldn't they?

In the first few days, I sensed that certain toys now belonged in the care of his sister or his friends. Amber had already claimed Benji, the stuffed dog who now held permanent residence on her bed in the arms of her Cabbage Patch dolls. Stann and I discussed giving Michael the Batman action figures, and the light up sword would go to Kyle. Although he agreed, I know it caught him off guard that I would consider giving away anything of Kevin's at the time. He went along, not truly understanding my instincts. Not even I understood why I should disperse those particular items then, nor did I miss them. Now though, seeing his personal things disturbed and moved was upsetting. I felt compelled to put everything back in its proper place so they could be retrieved more easily when he was ready to play.

My attention shifted to something else that appeared oddly out of place. Directly across the room the opened closet doors displayed a row of boys jeans, shirts and sweaters all draped loosely on their hangers. Several small boxes were stacked on the shelf above the clothes rack. A long blue box with compartments sat below it, stuffed with smaller toys and two pairs of shoes. In front of the organizer lay a pair of worn tan-colored work boots laced with yellow strings. I moved across the floor and kneeled down in the closet opening. I picked up one of the boots, rolling it tenderly over and over in my hands.

The boot leather was softened enough to show creases on the top where it had molded to the stride and shape of the foot. The writing on the inside had faded away. I ran my fingers along the worn lines of tread, wondering how many bad guys Kevin had chased away wearing these shoes.

Shoes…to anyone else these were just a simple pair of shoes serving a purpose to protect and support the feet of the owner. But to me, they represented a culmination of five-and-a -half years of casts, surgery, therapy and orthotic inserts. They allowed my baby to walk. They boldly stated Kevin's ability to run, skip and jump without limitations! Kevin had moved with such passion and enthusiasm, courageously conquering every obstacle as he quieted our fears.

As I clutched the boot to my breast the anger boiled inside me. We worked so hard to help make this happen for him, and now, *this* is what we get in return? *What was I saying? I did whatever I could because I loved my baby!*

"So, what is this God? What's the point?" I challenged Him to answer.

Desperate for an explanation I looked around the room dismayed to see nothing had changed. Shaking the boot in the air I sobbed, "Are you telling me he doesn't need this boot? He doesn't need any of this?"

"Goddamit! We did everything you asked of us!" I screamed. Standing up and shaking my fists to the ceiling I pleaded louder, "We loved him as you asked us to love your children!"

I stood in the middle of the room my arms flailing about me, slicing through the stillness to cut through whatever protected my Father from me.

"I prayed to you! I thought you would protect my children!"

My knees buckled and I folded to the floor. Alone, I waited for my God to apologize for His sin and beg my forgiveness. The only response to my furious command was a deafening silence that stabbed at my heart. A strange guttural noise, almost animal like came from deep within me. A sound that vibrated through every cell, every tissue, every muscle and every bone in my body screamed out in agony, *"Where were you God? How could you have left him alone?"*

Beaten, I crawled onto the bed and pulled the covers around me creating a cocoon of shelter from the torturous stillness. Abandoned by my God and with no mother to comfort me, I lay there in a fetal position holding my aching womb. My grieving heart longed to lie beside my baby and tuck him close inside. Instead, all I had left were my son's shoes.

14

The Mad Woman in the Mirror

The loving support of our friends continued while they became witnesses to the effects of our loss and daily suffering. For those who were parents, Carla and Stann now became synonymous with their own fears. We were living every parent's fear of losing a child. The Bloweys personified the realities of a nightmare come true. No one had any idea how close to the truth it would turn out to be.

Mary's presence as our counselor had become crucial in those beginning weeks. First, we depended on Mary's professional skills to provide some structure to the family grieving process. Second, it reestablished a bond of trust between Mary and me. She was acquainted with my history of loss on a level that no one else had ever been. In our sessions, I shared an agony that none of my friends, not even my husband, could bear to hear no matter how open their hearts were.

I trusted Mary's instincts as well as her insights. I was grateful for her guidance in helping me to regain a healthier sense of control in my life. In retrospect, I admire Mary's ability to stay the course given her own maternal feelings. It was perplexing to consider the coincidence that just five years before we began our counseling relationship with our babies in tow.

Three weeks had passed since Kevin died, but it felt as though it were only three seconds since I had kissed him goodbye and sent him off to ride his bike. By this time, we were no closer to an explanation of the details of the accident and no one was asking for my statement. The officer at the scene kept in touch with us, but there was nothing to report until the driver entered a plea at the court hearing next month. It marked our initiation to the lengthy and tedious legal process that would eventually cripple our faith in the justice system and the integrity of its leaders.

We were also disappointed by the response of our neighbors. It had been almost a month since Kevin died. The neighbors whose driveway had claimed his last moments had yet to address us personally. In that time, we had received only a sympathy card. In the beginning we dismissed it, assuming their focus was appropriately with the family member who had driven the truck. In addition, we reasoned that since the accident was still under investigation, perhaps they were advised legally to avoid any conversation with us.

Over the years I had known my neighbor as an acquaintance when our paths crossed for different social events. We rarely saw them in the neighborhood except to wave hello in the driveway. Even so, in a holiday gesture, I sent the children over with a plate of Christmas cookies and a card. They thanked the children, but they did not extend themselves further. Was it too much to ask for a response after Kevin's death?

As the weeks went on, we became more sensitive to the issue. It seemed as though they were blatantly ignoring us whenever we were in our front yards at the same time. Equally distressing was that they still had not made any attempt to shovel their sidewalk adequately, as most of the neighborhood had always done. It was not uncommon living in our southwest climate for children or adults to ride their bikes year-round when the snow was cleared. We felt strongly that had the sidewalk been cleared to allow more than a shovels width of a path, that perhaps Kevin might have had a better chance of navigating past the truck. Given his determination and self-confidence there was no doubt that he thought he could do it.

Admittedly, our speculation was fueled by emotion, confusion and disbelief. The more time that passed without any interaction from them, the more assumptions we made about their lack of empathy or concern. We tried to hide the hurt and rejection we felt by rationalizing their behavior and hoping for the best.

Another issue that surfaced strongly for me was that I no longer wanted people in my house. I began to feel suffocated by the daily visits from family and friends. Although I appreciated their efforts and sacrifices for us, I felt as if our life were an open book. Out of concern for our well-being, people were naturally discussing our progress or lack of it. It made me extremely uncomfortable to know we were being discussed one way or the other. Again, the atmosphere was charged with emotion and it was so easy for others to make assumptions about us as well.

One evening my in-laws called to say they were coming over to visit, and Stann invited them to stay for dinner. It had been a difficult day and the thought of preparing food for nine people let alone consuming it, repulsed me. I could hardly choke down a bagel without gagging and a full meal was nearly impossible. The half dozen entrees stored in the freezer could collect ice crystals till the next world war for all I cared about eating.

The two of us were alone when they arrived. Amber had gone shopping with our houseguest, a close girlfriend of mine from Arizona who had come to stay with me for the week. I quickly retreated to my bedroom to hide. The sounds of their conversations and the general noise in the kitchen seemed to penetrate the door interrupting my efforts to sleep. Finally, I dozed off still aware of the noise but too fatigued to fight it.

Somewhere in that place between wakefulness and sleep, I dreamed that I heard Amber and Kevin talking in the hallway. In my view from the bed I saw only the closed door but I heard their voices beyond it. I *sensed* Amber rushing to her room with Kevin on her heels as if she were hiding something from his curious self. I tried to wake myself so I could mediate the quarrel that was brewing. As my grogginess lifted, the raised voices in the hall drifted into my daydream becoming more distinct.

They were not the typical sounds of my home, and I realized it was not Kevin's voice at all. It was Kevin's five-year-old cousin following Amber down the hall, as he quizzed her about the package she had brought home from the store. The sound of his voice screeching through the door made my heart stop beating. The harsh reality of my child's absence could not be daydreamed away.

The sudden dismay amplified a thunderous roar of anger deep inside, raising me to a sitting position on the bed. Hunched over I caught my breath. Looking up, I faced my reflection in the mirror. Behind the numerous framed photographs of our family adorning my dresser, I was stunned to see a mad woman looking back at me. Her bloodshot eyes darted about behind the disheveled curly locks of long dark hair as she rose from the bed to meet me. She screamed out in a furious rage, and with one sweeping motion of her mighty arms, leveled the objects on the dresser top to nothing. All the precious knick-knacks and numerous picture frames went sailing across the room crashing against the closed door. Then, she collapsed to the floor in utter exhaustion.

Next, I remember looking up from a kneeling position to see several shocked and puzzled faces crowding the doorway peering down in disbelief. Stann stepped over the broken pieces to restrain me, tears in his eyes. I broke away from his grip and kneeled amid the rubble of broken glass. Horrified, I saw my damaged treasures strewn across the carpet. The china saucer plate that Amber purchased with her own money at a garage sale last summer was shattered. The potpourri jar that Kevin made me for Mother's Day was emptied. The contents scattered among the fragments of glass and china. Whimpering like a wounded animal, I gathered as much of the lavender potpourri I could salvage. Filling the decorated baby food jar only three quarters full, I secured it with the lace cover and ribbon. I knew I could not restore the china dish any more than I could reunite the broken family depicted in the shattered frames.

Someone brought a trash basket to the doorway and Stann began cleaning up the broken glass. Sobbing I lay across the bed clutching my Mother's Day gift, painfully aware that it was the last one I would ever receive.

"Mommy?" I heard a whisper in my ear, "Are you okay?"

Startled, I turned to face my daughter. Her eyes were wide with fear, and her round cheeks stained with tears. My explosive display of anger had frightened her, and still she came to comfort me patting me gently on the shoulder. I took her into my weak arms and apologized for breaking her precious gift to me. I tried to assure her that I was all right. Again, she asked me whether I was really okay. There was nothing I could say that would convince her that I was myself. If I did not recognize myself how could she?

Stann climbed onto the bed wrapping his arms tightly around the both of us. We lay together in our cocoon crying for a very long time. In that moment an exceptional bond formed. We discovered that we were much stronger when joined by our love for each other. Ironically, my angry explosion allowed us to find one another in the midst of our fear. In the years to come the power of our love for each other would always protect us from the destructiveness of our fear and anger. Despite the different paths we would choose on this journey we would know this deep and unbreakable bond.

The tenderness of our touch had soothed Amber enough to leave us alone. Assuring her that I was feeling better, we encouraged her to play with her cousins who along with the rest of the visitors, were waiting for some indication that we were all right. Stann left me alone in our room knowing I was not about to show myself in this wretched condition. The humiliation of having to explain myself to his family was more than I could handle then. I wanted everyone out of the house. As much as he wanted to abide by my wishes I knew he could never tell his family that we needed our privacy.

Instead, he wisely admitted that this situation was beyond his control. He called Mary, and she suggested that my girlfriends bring me to her office immediately where I could talk more freely. I agreed and was thankful for the escape. I walked swiftly through my kitchen feeling like a spectacle, hoping that whoever was looking at me would be gone when I returned.

The safety of Mary's office allowed me to process the evening's events without the fear of judgment or humiliation. The degree of this spontaneous and explosive display of anger was uncharacteristic of me in that I had never left behind a visible path of destruction. My usual emotional outbursts seemed so far away these last few weeks. I had become totally out of touch with any gut level reactions. Something as simple as hearing my nephew's voice had triggered a fiery rage in me that I had never felt before. I had frightened my husband and daughter beyond their imagination. In actuality no one was more frightened than I.

Every reference point I might have depended on was now distorted through a warped lens of grief. It boiled down to the enormous loss of control we felt about everything in our lives. There were so many people involved in our personal affairs. We were so disconnected and ill-functioning that we lost sight of our needs and desires and allowed others to interpret them for us. In an effort to accept help we had lost our boundaries. That night I realized I had to redefine what was appropriate help, and equally important, whom I could comfortably accept it from. In that, I began to regain a small measure of control. I recognized that I could give myself permission to say "no" based on what I felt, not what I should do. It was a turning point that allowed me to set boundaries that were flexible enough to survive the beginning stages of my grief journey.

15
The Street Lamp

There was a growing concern among our inner circle of friends that with too much free time on my hands I might withdraw even further. Perhaps my going back to work might be a distraction from the day to day pain and loneliness. In their minds, the most logical thing to do was to distract me from the troublesome thoughts and images by keeping me busy. No one could understand that the source of the pain was buried so deep within in my heart that no amount of activity could make it go away. Keeping busy and going to work had become society's remedy for grief; a method used to bandage the burning pain without ever having to cleanse the wound.

While I spun my cocoon of shelter, Stann and Amber were out there unprotected. I worried about Stann as he went through the motions of teaching math to a class of fidgety seventh graders. I knew he would rather be home grieving privately. It was not his style to appear unsettled or out of control. I also had deep concerns for Amber as she adjusted to new classmates. Were they being kind to her? Did she have a friend to eat lunch with and play with at a recess? Should we have transferred her back to her old school where it was familiar and comfortable? The anxiety over their well-being grew out of proportion as I became obsessed with their safety. It was not uncommon for me to show up at either of their schools unexpectedly.

True to form, my analytical self chimed along with everyone else's concerns for me. I could see that it was not fair for Stann to be the only one working full time. He too was having difficulty sleeping. Without the rest he needed, the responsibilities at work and his fear for Amber and me weighed heavily on his mind. In addition, our bank account was dwindling and we needed my income to help pay off the growing pile of late bills. I do not know how he made it through those weeks carrying so much of the burden on his weary shoulders.

The *shoulds* blared even louder when I considered the salon was less one full time hairdresser. I had no right to burden my co-workers with my client load any longer. I reasoned that I should have returned two weeks before, instead of inconveniencing Stann, my boss, the other stylists, and all the clients. I should be doing better than this. What was wrong with me? Of course, I should go back to work.

My inner voice screamed to protect me from the giant wave of shoulds bearing down on my conscience. I was scared to death to leave the shelter of my home and face public sympathy and scrutiny. I no longer trusted or felt safe in the world. It was far too risky when I considered what I would have to do. Part of my success as a hairdresser depended on my ability to make the client feel comfortable in my chair. Now I could hardly carry a conversation without drifting off or losing interest. My self-confidence was shattered. How could I hold it together and do a job that was worthy of my reputation?

In the end, the guilt I felt squelched my inner voice, suppressing its desperate attempt to be acknowledged. I went back to work. I was unaware that I had failed my first test for setting boundaries. It was a choice that would plague me for many years.

* * * * * * *

It was no coincidence that I came down with the flu on Monday just days before my first day back at work. By now, the emotional and mental strains had taken a physical toll on the three of us. The stress had weakened our immune systems so much that we were more susceptible than normal to colds and flu. I insisted that Amber stay home from school a day or two, but Stann continued going to work despite his discomfort. It was a pattern that continued with him for several years.

Wrapped in my terry cloth bathrobe with a heavy blanket on top, my shivering, feverish body lay in the corner of our sectional couch. A full-blown headache deepened the furrows of my brow and every shudder caused my skin to crawl. My feeble attempt with a meditation failed. I yearned for sleep but settled on finding a distraction.

In a half-hearted effort, I picked up a paperback book from the pinewood coffee table. The collection of grief pamphlets and books had

119

grown into a large pile. Several people had given me books pertaining to death and loss hoping I would find some comfort. I had no interest in reading anything that mirrored my miserable life nor did I have the energy to sift through the stack. It was quite uncharacteristic of me to refuse a good book. Today in desperation to lull myself to sleep, I thought I might doze off by reading something boring.

I raised my throbbing head off the pillow and squinted at the book I had selected. I focused on a picture of a seaplane soaring over a cobalt blue blanket of water. Embossed in white on the front cover was the title, *One*. With a second look, I recognized the name of the author, Richard Bach. It was a book that Mary loaned to me suggesting that its adventure would be an alternative to all the grief books. It might serve to challenge my thinking rather than burden me with the present reality.

During the time I was grieving my mother, Mary had given me another book, *Illusions,* by the same author. *Illusions,* was the forerunner to shattering some of the perceptions I held about death, dying and the afterlife. I had been set free from the conservative mode of thinking encouraged by my Italian, Catholic, upbringing. It was the beginning of my search for spirituality.

Disheartened over the fact that none of the metaphysical or spiritual concepts made sense anymore, my studies seemed a lifetime away. Depending on my mood, I vacillated between rejecting it all, to considering some of it feasible. Only the mystics and saints really explored their spirituality to such extremes. And, besides, I snickered, they all went crazy! What could this author say to me now?

Scanning the first couple of pages, my interest piqued when I recognized Bach's familiar style of writing. I delved into the first chapter and quickly learned the premise of this book was to explore parallel lifetimes occurring simultaneously, contradicting the concept of linear time. The main characters transcended a time warp only to be circling above the sea in a two-seater airplane. In the water below, they discover unique patterns of light beckoning them to fly on special pathways designed to offer an alternate perspective to their past or futures lives.

By the second chapter, my body succumbed to chills and I nestled beneath the blanket against the thick cushions. I rubbed my dry eyes and considered this idea of alternate lifetimes. I certainly felt as though I were in a time warp. I mulled over the possibility of several Carlas living out the fantasies of her youth; the angst-ridden artist, the enthusiastic kindergarten teacher, or the independent photographer. I tried to imagine what the patterns of light would be like beneath my ocean. Would I choose this route again given the same outcome? Could I consider a lifetime without my precious family? What pattern was I in now? The sheer magnitude of the subject made my eyelids heavy, and soon I drifted off to sleep; the open book clutched in my hand.

I felt my body floating without effort, high above an ocean of liquid light. Its languid waves rising with each gentle surge of energy creating another wave grander than before. There, I see my new friend, another bereaved mom, floating beside me. She too grieves the death of her son, gone for almost two years. I feel comforted by her companionship because she understands my loss. In the absence of words, I communicate with her. I tell her to find a pattern in the waves to slip into. Confident, she dives into the water of light and locates her child. The crest of the waves sparkle with a multitude of colors I have never seen before. Encouraged, I search the swells looking for my pattern among the legions of liquid ribbons swirling before me. The closer I am to the surface the more turbulent the waves. Finally, I decide to jump in the water and I am submerged in a pattern of fiery orange hues. Its oppressive heat closes in on me. I struggle to keep from falling to the bottom flapping my arms about me...

Snuggled beneath my blanket, I awakened drenched in sweat and gasping for air. My limbs were limp, too weak to stretch as I fought to pull myself up from the depths of an infernal prison. I had been abruptly dropped back into my body. Despite my discomfort, I was getting used to this pattern of waking up now. I knew I had to write down the details of the dream before they faded away. I scribbled a brief entry in my journal making a note to analyze its meaning with Diana when I met with her later in the week.

I felt more rested after an afternoon of sleep and continued reading the book with heightened interest late into the evening. As the main characters reviewed their past and explored their future lives, I contemplated how I would survive my present one. What could I have done differently to save my son from this untimely and violent death? If only I had simply said no to his request to go outside, or even delayed his departure by a few minutes it would have changed everything. Why didn't I pay attention to that wicked nightmare and see that it was really a warning? Maybe the dream was given to me to change a destiny gone awry. Maybe, Kevin was actually depending on me to rescue him.

Was it really his destiny to die as Diana had interpreted the dream? Had I failed him by not choosing to act on the information given to me because of my fear? What good was this prophetic dream stuff anyway if I had to dissect the meaning instead of getting a clear enough message to act on it? Disillusioned, I decided that this whole concept of free will was really a set up if there were such a thing as destiny. Was God just humoring His people by letting us think we really had a choice in anything important like living or dying?

My mind grew weary of these endless questions and assumptions. Apparently, God did not think I was worthy enough to know much or why else would He not answer me? I gave up, drained of any energy to sustain the intellectual fight. My family had been asleep for several hours when I drifted off, heading toward yet another dreamscape...

It didn't seem so high up until my attention focused on a white ball emanating a powerful beam of light over the darkness around me. As I hovered closer, it became more distinct and I recognized it as a street lamp shining in the night sky. Its strong rays encompassed a small area around the lamp post. Floating down to get a closer look, I hung on the periphery of the circle. Focusing my eyes beyond the circumference of the light I was surprised to see that at this level whatever direction I looked to was lit up. When my gaze moved to the next shadow, the light was there exposing the still and undisturbed neighborhood. I was keenly aware that I was at the scene of Kevin's accident. Every aspect of my neighborhood was exactly the same, just as I knew it in my waking life.

I expected to feel goose bumps as I passed over the frigid and snowy landscape confirming my whereabouts. It seemed as though I were in a pocket of insulation protecting me from the night cold. I turned my gaze to a shadow within the circle of light and moved closer to inspect its source. I felt as though I were about a foot or two above the snow covered street. A large red spot about three feet in diameter came into view. It was melting a hole in the snow, exposing the black tar of the street beneath it. Police and ambulance sirens echoed past the boundaries of the silvery rays glowing around the scarlet impression forcing me awake.

My head landed on the pillow like the thud of a bowling ball released too soon on the alley. I pulled myself up to a kneeling position and tore back the mini blinds covering the window above our bed to see the flashing red lights passing by our house. Instead, the street light shown like a beacon on the empty snow covered road. It was dead quiet.

* * * * * * *

I recovered from my bout with the flu in a couple of days, and braced myself to return to work. Stann was encouraged by this step hoping it would be an answer to the loneliness. Mary was supportive of my efforts, but was honest enough to admit it seemed too soon. I promised to take it slow, after all I was only starting with one day a week. In my heart, I was more concerned that my first day back would also be the one month anniversary of Kevin's death. The truth was I really wanted to postpone my return, but was embarrassed to say so. I thought everyone would think I was dwelling unnecessarily on the date. How could it be one month since he died, when my heart, my soul, my body and my mind felt as though it were one second?

My anxiety was high that morning as I readied myself for the day. I was becoming used to the stomach distress and uncontrollable shaking so I dismissed those as any further symptoms of the virus. I had never been this nervous or felt so physically out of control. I absolutely dreaded walking into the salon feeling this way. I finally arrived later than my usual time that morning. It would be a short day as I planned to be finished in time to pick up Amber after school.

My wonderful co-workers greeted me with open arms and tear-filled eyes. The mood of the shop was somber, so unlike our lively mornings filled with music and coffee talk around the reception desk. I sensed that no one knew what to say to me. My mournful presence affected the otherwise friendly ambience. I felt out of place and withdrew to my station in the center of the room.

Routinely, I unwound the long cords of my professional curling irons placing them in the steel holders on the counter and turned them on for the day. I checked the drawer for sterilized combs and brushes. How long had it been since I had cleaned them? I opened the cabinet above my head next to the mirror, and shook the bottles of styling aids. I was surprised I had so much product left after a busy season. I wondered which clients I had scheduled that week of Christmas?

My thoughts drifted to the last time I worked at my station. I could only remember the night I spent with my cousins styling their hair during the week of the funeral. The salon was filled with laughter. We had found a moment of normalcy and fun in the midst of the crises. It was a reprieve from the sorrow, a connection to what was familiar and warm. The setting was the same, but today I was lost without their support. Shaking my head, I closed the doors and stepped back to scrutinize the readiness of my station.

My right shoulder brushed against the picture frame hanging on the wallpapered partition that divided the three stations. On reflex, I glanced at the photographs of my darling children and handsome husband that filled the frame. Clients would compliment me on our beautiful family. Brimming with pride, I would share funny stories about my children's antics. Giant tears welled up in my eyes and before I could lock the floodgates they spilled over to my flushed cheeks. There would be no more silly tales chronicling the life of Kevin and Amber. What would I say when people asked about him?

Hastily, I swiped the tears away before anyone would notice. Bending down to the lower cabinets, I pretended to straighten the towels stored there. A knife had pierced my heart in one quick slice, slaying me to my knees.

Shortly after, my first appointment arrived and any reserve of false calm I might have had was gone. In my favor, the first client was a man given to few words and a simple hairstyle. I could feel my mouth forming some sort of a greeting but I never heard it nor do I remember any further conversation. Some strange defense mechanism took over cushioning me in a blanket like fog. Every few moments, I blinked hard to clear up the blurred vision so I might clip the hairs instead of my index finger. My fingers were gripped around the handles as if it were my first day in beauty school. Fortunately, experience had my scissors programmed to do their job and they snipped away.

I purposefully turned my back to the reception area so no one would detect my struggle but it also forced me to view my former life depicted on the wall. I tried to concentrate on just the client's head, blotting out the scene around me. The heartache was overwhelming, and the anxiety grew. My stomach was churning, and I felt as if I would surely throw up on this poor unsuspecting man. The recognition of yet another truth had hit me below the belt.

Seething with buried resentment, I remembered the issues the tragedy had put on hold. The profession I had worked so hard to be successful in had actually robbed me of precious time with my family. Only now, there was no second chance, and no tomorrows to compensate for lost time. I had invested long weekday hours and Saturdays to build my clientele, and in turn make a profit for the salon. It was worth little now. I had sacrificed priceless time with them to gain just another client. One more appointment on my books translated to more money in my pocket and one less hour with my family. I had all the clients I could ever need and a lifetime of Saturdays to work, but I would never have another Kevin. It was all for nothing.

A tremendous wave of guilt caught me off guard, and its forceful current pulled me under. I had compromised my values in the name of making a living. How many other women in the world had made the same choices? It was not uncommon, but all the mothers I knew seemed to get chance after chance to balance their lives. They got to keep their children. Why did I have to lose my son? Why was I the only one who felt punished? Didn't it count that I was trying to make it right by cutting back my schedule?

I had not reconciled the previous issues of guilt and resentment, and they would fester and boil for many years. I would never recover the passion or respect I once held for my career. Any success or achievements in the business paled in comparison with my failure as a mother. I had made a huge mistake in coming back to work now or ever. Its time was past, and my life was over.

I do not remember if I had any more clients after that. I came home in the early afternoon for a break and never went back that day.

Relieved to be out from under the caring but watchful eye of my co-workers I could not wait to get back to the shelter of my home. However, once there I paced like an animal from room to room trying to escape from the master called guilt.

My heart was riddled with remorse over choices that I believed were in the best interests of my family. I resented every moment that cosmetology school or my career had taken me away from my family. I wasted half of my time with Kevin and Amber serving my need to be fulfilled with a career. I could not believe that each agonizing moment without my Kevin now totaled an entire month in calendar terms.

Why did I have to feel this emptiness when my real life had been so full? Would I still have this gaping hole in my chest forty years from now? *Stuff it! Shove it deep down inside.* My inner critic prodded. Frantic, I broke away from the irrational thoughts that chained me and tore out the front door, down the driveway. The crisp clean air was just what I needed to clear my head and calm me down. "I'll walk to the mailbox and check the mail," I thought, disguising my desperate intent to reclaim my real life. The neighbors would have to drag me away from their damned property.

Some days I would boldly make way down the sidewalk to the scene of the accident, just a stone's throw beyond our mailbox. I would stand at the edge of the neighbor's driveway and close my eyes, earnestly praying that when I opened them Kevin would be riding home to meet me as we had planned. If I did it enough times I might rise from the depths of hell to awaken from the nightmare, and all would be right again in my world. Continually my efforts failed. Disappointment and despair would prevail bringing me to my knees on the cold hard packed snow. It would take every ounce of remaining strength to pull myself away from the site.

In the past few days the temperature had been a few degrees warmer bringing a welcomed break from the arctic like weather we experienced all winter. The bright sunshine, clear skies, and crisp air was more like our Colorado weather, seducing the residents out of their cozy homes. The concrete had warmed just enough to begin melting the drifts of snow packed along the sidewalk.

As I walked along the sidewalk in front of our home toward the mailbox, I noticed a thin stream of rusty brown water traveling past me in the street gutter. I turned my attention up ahead where our mailbox stood beside the street lamp defining the border between the neighbor's property and ours. The old white truck, the one I slid into as I rounded the corner that day, was now parked across the street giving me a clear view of the scene of the accident.

I heaved a sigh of relief; thankful no one was outside this afternoon. Assured that my grief would go unnoticed, I approached the mailbox to survey the place where I had last held my son. Had it really

125

been a month ago? Any visitor passing by would have no clue of the events that had occurred just weeks ago. How could it look so tranquil and untouched when my mind's eye saw only chaos and death?

Choking back tears, I turned away, praying as I had so often before that the scene would change when I got there. My stride quickened and I cast my eyes down at the sidewalk where a safe path had been cleared by the sun. Warmed by the rays, tiny drops of melted ice glistened on the sidewalk. Again, I noticed the stream of rusty colored water running by in the gutter. Its color captured my attention, and I assumed it was the melted snow from a parked car. Intrigued, I moved a few steps closer to the edge. I knelt down to let the cold water run over my fingertips. Now, closer to its source, the stream grew wider, and the hue a brighter red.

A stabbing pain pierced my heart, and I gasped in disbelief. It could not be! Repulsed, I scrambled back wiping my hands frantically across the thighs of my jeans. Rising, I stumbled to the edge of the neighbor's driveway a yard or more away.

The preceding days of generous warmth and sunshine induced an early thaw of the crusty surface of gravel and snow. A path of well-worn tire tracks leading to the entrance of the driveway, had created ruts and holes exposing the pavement. There, preserved in ice, was the precious blood of my child.

Reeling, I fell forward. My head snapped back crying out in agony. "They left him here!" I screamed, my voice cracking in a high pitch. Hunched over, I lay my forehead upon the icy grave asking God's forgiveness for this violation of my child's life. I dug my bare fingers around the jagged mound of ice trying to lift it from the pavement. Small fragments chipped off the edge slicing my fingertips. Desperately, I scooped up as much of the sacred bloody crystals that would fit in my hands.

I had to free Kevin from this improper burial! We cremated his remains, and yet the very substance of his existence was still separated from his body. His blood had been dismissed as a mess. Was the only solution to bury it beneath the snow? Did they think it would magically disappear if it were hidden deep enough? Sickened by an even more appalling thought, I realized that perhaps, for a day or two, our neighbors had been driving repeatedly over the melting bloody mess.

I ran half-crazed to our garage with the bloody chips clenched inside my hands. I grabbed a shovel from the wall and sprinted back to the street. With all my strength and fury I hoisted the shovel above my head and began smashing it against the ground breaking up the tomb of ice. Again, I crushed its head against the ground with such savage force that the metal edges bent inward and the handle cracked. Particles of ice and gravel split off the main mass revealing the manhole cover hidden

126

beneath the surface. With each blow a fierce growling noise emitted from deep within my throat, a primal sound that was part human, part animal.

The ground began to spin faster and faster and I was released from my body. My consciousness was aware of the grim scene below but my emotions were detached from the event as I floated freely above the street. In retrospect, I suppose it was a self-defense mechanism triggered to save me from my own violence.

In the hazy blur I was aware of two perspectives, one in front of my eyes and the other above the entire scene. I saw a woman approach me to help. From above, I watched her back away from the mad woman swinging a shovel as it sliced through the air. Stann suddenly appeared before me, his face wracked with confusion and fear mouthing words I could not hear. And then, from above, I saw him embrace his wife, shielding her from the horrible surroundings. I was back, holding on to the only person in the whole world who could understand the anguish in my heart.

Tucked away inside the safety of our home, I lay in a fetal position on the bed. My frozen, cracked hands shook as I warmed them to my chest. My white cotton blouse bore the blood of our child, stained post-mortem. The unrelenting clang of a shovel beating against the pavement echoed beyond my bedroom window. The last tangible proof of Kevin's existence was simply being thrown away. His life-blood had been reduced to rusty chunks of ice heaved into a dumpster. Stann had been left alone to dispose of the final remains of our beloved son.

* * * * * * *

Early the next morning a huge tractor appeared in front of the neighbor's house. I stood by the mailbox watching the black tires rolling back and forth over the pavement, breaking up the stubborn slabs of ice. Its massive jaws chewed up the chunks of gravel and ice grinding them into the ground.

The driver halted the truck and hopped out to greet me. Over the roar of the vehicle he said, "Ma'am, I surely am sorry about this," shaking his head in disbelief.

My arms were crossed tightly across my chest protecting my fragile heart. My lower lip quivered as I nodded my head.

"Don't worry ma'am," he gently assured me, "I'll take care of this for you, okay?"

Solemn, I whispered a thank you. Returning to my bedroom I watched from the window until he completed the dismal task.

Later that evening as I tucked Amber into bed, she remembered something important she had wanted to tell me earlier that morning. I was emotionally exhausted and hoped she would be brief. "Hmm, what was that?" I said, half-listening as I folded back the covers.

"Mom, I had this dream about Kevin last night," she said, her eyes opened wide. She had caught my attention. Curious and more attentive now, I urged her to tell me about it.

"I was sleeping in my bed, in my own room. Kevin was standing right next to my bed, where you are right now, looking at me. He was rubbing my face softly, like this," she said, smoothing her fingertips in a circle across her cheek.

"I was half-awake and half-asleep, but I could see that he had on white clothes. They were angel clothes," she said, nodding her head in awe, as she propped up on one elbow.

"Did he say anything to you?" I said, taking her hand, as my excitement grew.

"No, he didn't. I felt a little scared when I woke up. But then, I remembered that he looked perfect", she said smiling. "Do you think it was just a dream?"

"Oh honey," I answered, the tears spilling down my cheeks into her hair as I hugged her tightly. "It wasn't just a dream. I believe Kevin was really here with you, and me, too."

16
Lanterns of Love

Dream Journal: February 1991
Driving in our Jeep Wagoneer with lots of things piled up in the back. It is just Amber, Stann and I, and we are on the road to Mother Cabrini Shrine at Look Out Mountain. It is dark, and it is nighttime. We stop, and I get out to look for the road, but it is too dark. The snow around us lights up the surrounding area, but not the road.

In only one month, our small home had seen more visitors than in all the occasions we had ever entertained. There had been a steady flow of friends and family frequenting our home with offerings of food and assistance. I was in awe of the number of people who responded to our crisis and the creative and loving ways in which they extended themselves to us. Whether by thought or by deed or by prayer, our community embraced us.

Prayer groups from the various churches in town were praying daily for us. Catholic masses were being said as far away as Philadelphia and prayer chains were initiated in Oklahoma. Each day the mail carrier delivered a stack of letters and condolence cards. Some people wrote to share their stories of loss and how their faith in God had sustained them. There were heart-wrenching notes from bereaved parents offering their assistance when we were ready to accept it. And, most surprising were the condolence letters from strangers who had heard about the accident from a relative or friend.

We could not fathom the extent which our tragedy had affected our family, our friends, our acquaintances and our town. It was like the rippling effect of a stone being tossed into a placid pond. We were so touched by tender notes of sympathy and promises of prayer. So many parents felt compelled to assure us that we were not alone. It became apparent that they were just as unprepared as we were for this unscheduled trip to hell.

Traveling an obscure and rocky road, we zig-zagged around a mountain landscaped with grief. There were no guideposts to indicate where we were or mile markers to gauge how far we came. We maneuvered the treacherous hairpin curves of sorrow with fear and trepidation, ever watchful that around the next bend, might be an avalanche of more emotion. The darkness was impenetrable. This forbidding road led to a remote and unknown destination beyond our grasp.

The only visible sign of life was in the adjacent forest. There, in the darkness, glimmered tiny lanterns of light, placed by the grace of God. Hearing the call, they radiated compassion and love, illuminating a path for a family who had lost its way.

PART III

The Search for Meaning

17
Carving a Path to the Dream Time

Dream Journal: February 10, 1991
Walking with Amber to her new school. It is in downtown Denver. We are in a dark alley with stores on either side. She wants to stop at a candy store, but I say no, because this area is dangerous and we must hurry back to her old school. The stores are now boarded up and one of the walls has reddish orange paint on it.

The one month anniversary of Kevin's death was a painful awakening to what our life had become. Peering through the haze of sadness, we were unable to discern which direction to go until that traumatic day. It was a significant turning point that enabled us to change the perceptions we held about the grieving process for bereaved parents. In the depths of our grief, we experienced parts of ourselves that I never imagined existed. We saw the extreme side of anger and rage, as well as despair and sadness. I never thought twice about the way our society responded to grieving parents until I became one.

Complicating matters was the issue of living next door to the scene of the accident as well as the proximity of the Neighbors. It was inconceivable to us that another human being could be as insensitive as our neighbors had presented themselves. In the midst of the outpouring of love and compassion we had received from the community, the Neighbors *lack* of

133

response was shocking. For whatever reasons, in their controlled silence they ignored our pain and suffering. Our bewilderment at being shunned by this family grew into resentment. We felt victimized by their absence of human decency to acknowledge our innocent child's spattered blood in their own driveway.

Our only comfort was that with the sale of their house they would soon be moving away. We carried our disappointment and anger toward them for a very long time. I did not yet understand their place in my life as teachers. It was many years later when I realized that my *expectations* of them were causing my pain. Until I accepted that, given their level of awareness, they could not respond any other way.

In my confusion, all the events of the past month seemed grossly out of place. In the time span of only thirty days, we had survived the most horrifying experience of our lives only to relive it again and again. The shock of seeing Kevin's blood apart from his body, in the exact place I had cradled his crushed head, was the proof my doubting mind seemed to need. I had indeed witnessed his death. Sadly within two hours of his departure, the evidence had been buried. No trace of life to be found except a few drops of blood on the sidewalk. Now only a manhole cover marked the place, stained forever with his blood.

Given the chaos that erupted on that cold winter day, I am sure for decency's sake cleaning it up was the right thing to do. I wondered, whether things might have seemed more real if the scene were left undisturbed until I had returned home from the hospital. Would I have accepted it more readily? On the other hand, would I have been deprived of the proof I sought? Why did I need so much proof and Stann did not?

Stann and I instinctively chose different ways to cope with our grief from the moment Kevin died. He began to internalize his emotions, which protected him from sharing the feelings of weakness and vulnerability that made him feel out of control. Initially his focus moved outward to the things he could control, like gathering details about the accident, and following the legal process. Later, he pursued almost constant activity, whether it was fulfilling household duties and work related obligations, or strenuous physical workouts.

It became his sole responsibility to take care of the family and a part of him was angry about it. We had always shared those responsibilities. One evening we were discussing several pressing issues at once. I vaguely recall asking if he had taken care of a particular item. He exploded with anger. Standing in a fury, he flipped the edge of the solid pine coffee table, spilling books and a large plant to the floor.

"I don't even remember what I did ten minutes ago, let alone what I'm supposed to do tomorrow!" he yelled, and then stormed from the room.

I sat wide-eyed and speechless in the corner of the couch. I had never seen Stann erupt in such a way that he would mishandle himself. For him, his loss of control was unacceptable and he was careful not to ever expose himself to me. He reserved those outbursts for the punching bag in the garage, late in the evening after Amber was safely in bed. I can still hear the impact of his gloved fist hitting the leather, splitting the air, blow after blow.

Seeking the solitude he desperately needed, Stann would retreat to his weight lifting room in the basement. It was there that he could release his pent-up emotions and stifled energy. One Sunday afternoon, I stood in the hallway unnoticed, as he squatted to pick up the bar. Admiring his taut muscular body, drenched with perspiration, I envied the way he had always disciplined himself in his workouts. Today, I sensed that grief had taken hold, and that his self-control was suffering a major defeat.

I held my breath, as he moved through the arduous positions of a military press. Feet placed a shoulders width apart, his gloved hands gripped the cold bar, shaking the metal plates at the end. Breathing deeply and holding twice his own body weight, Stann easily lifted the bar to his thigh as if he were picking up a broomstick. A whoosh of air released itself, making room for the crucial next breath to raise it to his chest. His blues eyes narrowed, focusing on an imaginary point across the room. Sucking in more air and with a snap of the wrist, he snatched the bar to his chest. Balancing the weights, Stann's face contorted as his emotions boiled over into the beads of sweat pouring down his cheeks.

Blowing hard and fast to maintain his momentum, he consolidated every ounce of energy and strength for the final press. With one last burst of air, his trembling arms raised the steel rod of grief above his head and away from his broken heart. Each push was fueled by more anger and more pain, as he pressed again and again in retaliation until his weakened muscles succumbed to the weight of sorrow. Releasing his hold, the metal plates clanked together as they crashed to the ground in despair. Dropping to one knee, he bent over laying his head on his arms, sobbing. Beaten by his own emotion, he let me wrap my arms around his shoulders to comfort him.

I often wondered if he thought his grief held less value than mine. It was most obvious when people would inquire how I was doing. Never comfortable expressing himself on sensitive issues, he protected himself by diverting the conversation to my needs. It was only later in the conversation that his wellbeing would be addressed. I cringed when I sensed how insignificant he must have felt. Perhaps he felt there was not enough room for both of us to have a break down. Or, maybe, he was afraid of what would happen if he did let go. Who would pick up the pieces? His only choice was to postpone his own grief until I became more stable.

Stann's quiet reserve and conservative Midwest upbringing, combined with society's expectations, greatly influenced the way he dealt with his grief. I was very grateful that Stann had found two male friends that he could talk with instead of me. One friend, a colleague and counselor, privately offered Stann the compassionate understanding and spiritual guidance he needed. Stann came to recognize that although our grieving styles were different, his way was just as valid as mine.

The other man, a bereaved parent himself, had been a distant acquaintance until our separate tragedies brought our two families together. In an ironic twist, he and his wife had also lost their ten-year-old son in a bike-truck accident a year and a half before. Their surviving daughter had been a student of Stann's and a sitter for our children. In a courageous act of strength, Linda and David reached out to comfort us shortly after Kevin died, and their teenage daughter took Amber under her wing, nurturing her like a big sister. We met with them often, exchanging stories about our boys and sharing the tears of our lost dreams. Being with them and confiding our fears helped us to realize that our grief and mourning were normal. Their family became role models for us as we moved deeper into our grief.

While Stann's struggle was evident on the outside, no one could know the conflict that was churning on the inside. Only Stann knew his internal process, giving him the privacy he needed and the control he wanted. It was only in our most private vulnerable moments together that he could expose his brokenness, allowing me to comfort him. I treasured those moments for in them I felt needed.

Our eleven-year relationship had nurtured a deep love, trust, and commitment. I never imagined those strong holds would be challenged. I was appalled when a well-meaning friend cautioned us that most marriages suffering the loss of a child ended in divorce. It never occurred to me that divorce could be the result of this nightmare. A seed of doubt had been planted and I began to fear a separation. I soon realized that in grief we saw sides of each other that most married couples never see.

Reality had taken a sharp turn presenting a world of bizarre images and unmapped emotions. Stann struggled to reach out to me in my torment and my guilt, desperately trying to hold on to the logical and reasonable woman he loved. He could not understand why I blamed myself for Kevin's death. It was so obvious to him that I was not responsible for making it happen. I, on the other hand, feared that he secretly blamed me because I had failed my responsibility to keep our son safe in my care. I did not want to believe that he could be so forgiving.

For Amber, life at home was no longer fun or comfortable. Kevin, her trusted companion and only sibling, was absent from their daily activities. Sitting alone in the corner of the sectional couch, she silently watched their favorite television shows. Rocky, the Cowboy, and Benjie, the dog, looked out of place among her own dolls and animals. Playing house became tiresome when Amber had to play all the characters. Even meal times were uncomfortable as she staked her seat at the end of the table so that we would sit on either side of her. And, most heartbreaking of all, she secretly wondered that, if she had died, would she have been missed as much as her brother?

Amber's loneliness was one of the most difficult and heart wrenching things to witness. I grieved the loss of innocence that had been snatched away from her. The security she depended on was gone now because her parents were too consumed with their own grief to be emotionally present for her. We were not prepared for the intensity of her grief nor the impact it would have on our future together. I did not know how intricately woven our pain had become. Our tapestry of grief had many loose threads, threatening to unravel at the slightest tug. Thankfully, her quiet cries for attention guided us away from ourselves and always back to her. If we had not had her well-being to focus on we might have given up completely.

Eventually Stann and I reached a higher level of trust. We soon realized that all we had was each other. There was no one else in the world that could remotely understand what we were going through. Joined in our sorrow we set out on parallel paths with very few crossroads along the way. Traveling the uphill path of grief, we never moved forward at the same pace, or grieved the same issues at the same time. One of us would be delayed by a rockslide of anguish and sorrow, and the other would be miles ahead having found a shortcut. It made us feel very isolated from each other. When we remembered to rely on our connection of love for one another, we became stronger and more united.

My thinking self was in a crises and my intuition was in overdrive. Any reasonable form of reference had been splintered, the pieces of my former reality floated around me, waiting to be retrieved from the tumultuous sea of grief. I could only accept what I could see and touch. My intuitive side saw beyond what I could feel. Which one could I trust? Something had snapped and I was caught between two worlds, with two different set of rules.

Ruled by my emotions and quick temper, I learned quickly as a child, that my outbursts of passion were not acceptable. To protect myself from others disapproval, I withdrew during times of stress, imprisoned by an intense dialogue with my inner critic. I would presume one right answer, and adjusted my feelings to fit the appropriate solution. When my system would backfire, the doubt would set in and the feelings would begin to churn. Cloaked in hostility or self-righteous anger, I suppressed them to maintain my disguise. All the emotion I kept locked inside would explode. Embarrassed by my failure to meet my expectations of staying in control, I would chastise myself and the cycle would continue.

What I feared most about myself had come true. I had lost complete control of my life and I did not know how to get it back. In this frightened state I did not recognize the buoy of hope that God had given me to survive.

The nighttime dream/vision of hovering over the spot of blood was the climax in the chain of incomprehensible events that had occurred in the last thirty days. Unaware of its message I simply wrote it down in my journal to examine later. The power of its presence prevailed, allowing me to discover the evidence I needed to face the raw, cruel truth of my reality. While my body *needed* that physical encounter as a confirmation, a part of me had already been there examining the proof from an emotional distance without judgment. I believe the dream was like a spiritual lifeline directing me to locate more than a bloody heartache beneath the transparent surface. I was being guided to break through the barrier of fear, to dig through the illusion of death, and free the message of life.

I became reconnected with a part of myself that had been forgotten. The seeds of knowing had been planted and left to push their way through the black soil of my unconscious. When I trusted my intuition to guide me I could see beyond the physical and glimpse another reality that held guidance and wisdom for me. I had immediate access to that place every time I went to sleep.

My dreamscape was planted with personal symbols and archetypes waiting to be harvested to feed my starving soul. This sacred garden had been with me all my life. Only now did I begin to appreciate its purpose. To survive this tragedy I would have to carve a path through this alternate reality. God had been speaking to me in my dreams. Dreaming Kevin was the path to my healing.

18
Inviting God into the Process

Dream Journal: February 10, 1991

I am in Kyle's house. I am supposed to be taking care of him now instead of his sitter. I am holding Kyle, but he is much younger. His father wants me to take care of Kyle, but then he changes his mind and wants his wife to do it. I am angry with him for jerking me around. Now, I am holding Kevin (a younger Kevin) and I am happy again. The house has turned into a restaurant with lots of people. His father is gone now. I am glad because he has been replaced by my favorite television star, and he is much nicer. I am so confused about where I am. I am very happy to be holding Kevin though and walk out of the restaurant to a patio.

Kevin's round belly naturally fit into the curve of my side as I balanced him on my hip. The softness of his cheek brushed against my neck as I cuddled him in my arms. Holding him tightly, I take us away from the crowded restaurant. I only want to be with Kevin, not all those people. The patio fades into the background as I walk away. I am dreaming again. "Go back with him Carla", I urged myself, "Don't wake up now."

Shutting out the morning light, I captured that final image of Kevin on my private screen. The more I concentrated on holding the picture the less distinct it became. Bits of scenery floated through my consciousness edging out my view of Kevin altogether.

139

The tears had begun to flow before my eyes were open to release them. I had finally slept after several nights of insomnia only to be awakened too soon. Eventually, exhaustion had taken over and I had rested enough to recuperate from the trauma of the street incident. I hoped that my normal sleep pattern might return, instead a new one had formed. Last night I had begun dreaming again. Rolling over to the side of the bed I reached down to retrieve my notebook and record another memory of Kevin.

A month ago I had relied on my camera to capture those precious moments of our life together. Frustrated not to be able to develop the film behind my eyes into photographs and videos, I had only a pen to transcribe the image on a page. Amazingly, in the four weeks since Kevin's death I had logged over thirty dreams. Even now, I am puzzled at my ability to recall them with such detail.

I was dreaming Kevin, and I longed for any connection that would put me in his presence again. I prayed to stay in the sleep cycle long enough to dream him. I would go anywhere if only to see my Kevin again. There was no doubt that whether asleep or awake the feelings of closeness felt the same. My heart rejoiced to hold my son close to me again until we were separated by the break of day. I recorded every dream about him to preserve each new encounter. Memory was all I had.

Going to sleep each night was like attending the sneak preview of a movie. Every aspect of my life was recorded on dream film for a private one time showing. The heavy curtains concealing my unconscious were wide open revealing the past, present and future of my life. Nighttime brought a strange dialogue and bizarre landscapes that commented on my feelings of loss and abandonment. All my fears, desires, and memories were intricately woven in the story line. I was the lead actor, and anyone who had ever crossed my path became a supporting character on my dream screen.

Many dreams commented on the sheer chaos of my waking life. The others, like hovering around the street lamp were more ominous. I had only enough energy to transcribe them for future reference, no matter what the content. I could not fathom when I would be able to review them with a rational mind to unlock their mysterious messages. How often had I been on the verge of discovering their healing messages only to ignore them? Or worse, what if I never dreamed Kevin again?

I decided then, that the key to unlocking these chaotic dreams was to continue educating myself about dream symbols. As terrified as I was of the Blonde Woman, I wanted to know why she came to me. Mary encouraged me to continue the dream class with Diana and learn as much as I could. Together the three of us might try to make sense of what was going on in both my worlds. I had no idea that my own dream journal would go deeper than any book could ever take me.

In our talks, Diana explained that her dream philosophy focused on the constant presence of God in our lives. She explained that our life long relationship with Him is about our journey toward wholeness. His presence is not always recognized in our daily routine. Understanding that, God uses our dreamtime to speak to us symbolically about our choices for achieving spiritual growth and healing. She asserted that by discovering our personal symbols and exploring archetypes, scripture, and mythology we could unlock the mysteries of our unconscious world and access our inner most thoughts. It would require that we question our motivations and why we react or respond the way we do. Ultimately, we can choose to recognize God as a positive loving force, unhindered by gender or judgment, guiding us toward our destiny.

At Diana's suggestion, I read several books by Carl Jung and John A. Sanford, two leading experts on dreams and healing. My first exposure to dream work was through the Edgar Cayce readings, and these two authors echoed Cayce's teaching that our dreams are reflections of the waking life as well as the unconscious. Like a child discovering ice cream for the first time, I was fascinated with all of them. These teachers challenged me to consider that in the context of symbols and archetypes my dreams confronted me with my most hidden desires and fears.

I was fascinated to learn that in all ancient cultures, dreams were highly valued for their guidance and direct connection to the spiritual world. With that I came to understand that God speaks to us on many levels. I was interested to learn that even Tertullian, an early Christian philosopher, believed "there are dreams which are due to the natural functioning of the soul, while others are sent by God".

Inviting God into the process was a new concept for me. The idea of God speaking with me was not something I had ever considered. However, if I truly believed that God resided within me then I had to accept that He would be in every part of me, even in my dreams. Unfortunately, my ego thought God and I spoke the same language. When in fact, I did not speak His language at all. My unconscious, the part of me that thinks in images was receiving important data from God and I could not understand it.

The Nightmare of the Blonde Woman was stocked with archetypal symbols, floating up from the pool of the collective unconscious. I learned that just as we have common body parts that make us human, so too are there elements of the psyche that are universal to us all. Just below the surface lay my personal unconscious consisting of forgotten or repressed memories. Beyond that, reaching to greater depth is the world of the collective unconscious. In my studies, I read that dreams can originate from the depths of the collective unconscious. My dream experiences were validated by the explanation that universal symbols, inherited patterns of behavior, myth, mystical experiences, psychic connections with others and encounters with the deceased or angelic entities were shared by all of mankind.

In a strange way it was as if interpreting the nightmare of Kevin's death was an assignment necessary to complete my mission for survival. Everything I believed to be true was now being tested as I read my own personal dictionary of symbols. I was not satisfied with my initial interpretation of the nightmare as evil, nor could I completely accept the simple explanation of Kevin's death being his destiny. I could only grasp that there was information to question. I was consumed with an intensity I had never experienced for anything else in my life. I would not rest until I had exhausted every possible alternative.

In doing so, I was unaware that I had made a very conscious choice about how I would survive. By making the commitment to examine the information given in the nightmare, I had actually taken another step on the path toward my spiritual healing and wholeness.

The dream of jumping into the reddish-orange patterns of the sea was symbolic of the current struggle in my unconscious. I needed rescuing from a situation that threatened my emotional stability, and yet, I had a burning desire to see what was beneath the surface. It was time to learn the language of the Spirit and discover what mysteries were hidden in my unconscious.

Becoming aware of my gut level responses would keep me connected to my intuition, a more accurate guide than my ego. Outbursts like my response to hearing my nephew tagging along after Amber when I expected to hear Kevin's voice were more than a response of angry disappointment. Clearing off my dresser was a symbolic gesture of making space for the way I needed to grieve by sweeping away the old patterns and starting clean. I had actually set a precedent for us and unknowingly paved the way for both Amber and Stann to discover their path too. I was taking the high road.

Equipped with my reference books on symbols, archetypes and mythology, I set to work on my assignment. First, I wrote several revisions of the Nightmare to include every detail that came to mind. In our counseling sessions, Mary provided a safe place to dialogue about my experience in the Nightmare. The subsequent drafts revealed more specifics that surprised us both.

For instance, I clearly saw the children standing to my right, and I was shielding them with my arm from the dark faced women. The Blonde Woman appeared earlier among the circle of women and spoke to me. The kitchen was bare, and I was standing by the counter. It is there that I heard Kevin calling for me to come find him.

Most intriguing, was the fact that the Blonde Woman was not really holding a chain saw, but a long blade. When she raised her arm, I saw a silver round-tipped blade and I had an instant "knowing" that she would cut him down. My personal dictionary defined it as a chain saw. When I sensed that Kevin was hanging from the rafters my mind could think of no other way she could cut through the wood. Another interesting point was that Kevin and I never saw each other. I hold only an image of him dangling below the right side of Blonde Woman.

I soon realized the power of my own language. If my ego could deceive me about seeing a chain saw, what else was it hiding?

19
The Halo Dream

Dream Journal: February 15, 1991

I am at the scene of the accident. Kevin is lying down on the street as I found him in real life. I am lying over him, but my perspective is as if I am standing up. Gently I pick him up into my arms, and he feels lighter. A golden light is glowing all around him and fills my view until it is all I see. I hold him to my breast and walk away leaving the other body in the street. But, I have Kevin in my arms. The cousins are playing together, and one of the boys is jealous that Kevin is back. I don't want him to look at Kevin that way, so I carry him away... I must give Kevin a haircut as I intended to do just before he died...we giggle as I style his hair a different way. I say, "Let's show everybody how handsome you look!" I carry him again and show my father. He looks at me strange and asks why I am carrying a dead Kevin. When my father looks at him, Kevin is stiff. But, when I look back at Kevin he looks at me and smiles. He's alive to me. Kevin and I know he is alive! I show him to a woman, and she looks at me as if I am strange. But, now Kevin is getting heavy and I can no longer hold him. I stumble and fall with him. We fall to the ground, and he lies there. I think he is probably dead just like everyone believes.

My worries about never dreaming Kevin again were unfounded. In the next few months, I would see him come to life on many different levels in an assortment of roles. He would appear in a memory to soothe

144

my broken heart, as a teacher for my own growth and healing and as a messenger to forewarn me of the journey ahead.

I was in awe of the affect this latest dream had on me. It was heaven to be able to hold him and carry his body away from the accident. It was as though I was given the chance to fulfill my desire to save him and lighten my guilt. The golden light filled the dream screen blocking out the physical aspects and horror of the accident. God was giving me an opportunity to see Kevin in a different light, the state of glory. I held on to this image whenever my body remembered the deep pain of experiencing Kevin's death.

However, in my enthusiasm to accept its message I failed to delve more deeply into the second half of the dream. At the time, I desperately needed confirmation of his continued existence. Perhaps, if I had pursued the dream one step further I might have heard its prophetic language. Although its meaning is clear now, I did not recognize it then. I was too focused on the way it validated my constant need to know that Kevin had survived his death. Breaking the dream apart and identifying my personal symbols helped to peel away the surface interpretation, which *seemed to be* about my not accepting Kevin as being dead.

The second part of the dream was a commentary on the obstacles I would face in the midst of that acceptance. On one level, the jealous boy and my father represented those who were suspicious of my spiritual experiences and who stood in authority or judgment of me. The jealous boy and my father also represented aspects of me too. Cutting Kevin's hair was symbolic of the sacrifices I would make to pursue my life's journey. I would need to forfeit my image, and restyle myself. In sharing what I learned, there would be those who would not see Kevin as clearly as I. There would be many moments of doubting what I saw and what I knew to be true. In those moments, I would stumble and fall from the weight of carrying my past beliefs and perceptions.

Sadly, I did not get the positive reaction I expected from most people when I would tell them about the Golden Light Dream. Instead, they were suspicious of my emotional state because I was too far out there. Even Chris, one of my most open-minded and spiritually supportive friends, feared that I was too far from my Catholic roots and on the edge of a breakdown.

The truth was that I too secretly feared I was going crazy. Teetering between the two worlds, I received a glimpse beyond the door that separates us from the physical. The path to wholeness involved sacrificing my entire belief system, and so it seemed my mind as well.

No matter how involved I became in the dream process, the Blonde Woman still haunted my days and nights. A simple trip to the grocery store took twice as long as I wandered the aisles aimlessly, forgotten list in hand. Her searing eyes intruded my thoughts, seizing my attention and consuming my life. Was it more than coincidence that I dreamed a nightmare about someone taking Kevin's life just twelve hours before he died? Was it really a prophetic message about my destiny *and* Kevin's destiny? Why would God send a messenger to me? What was I supposed to do with this piece of information? Did He really think I would sit back and let it happen? If this were a warning, then why didn't He give me the means to stop it? For that matter why didn't He intervene? In all my studies, would I ever know the answers?

The door to my unconscious was left wide open and what entered was a level of awareness that sharpened my intuitive abilities. Though everything seemed out of control, there was a synchronicity to these events that at a gut level I could not ignore. For example, my cousin, Bunny, and I had both dreamed of our children on the same night. Bunny dreamed about losing her own child too. In her dream, she *sensed* what it would feel like if her daughter had died. Bunny instantly connected with my real loss that, in turn moved her to make the trip to see me. The dream had shown Bunny and her sisters departing on a plane feeling very roughed up. Just a coincidence?

Was it also a coincidence that I sensed Kevin's distress that fateful morning? Or that I failed to pursue his feelings, unaware that he had already communicated his thoughts too me in a drawing three days before? No, it was not a *coincidence*. It was about being connected with people at an intuitive level and sensing their emotions, thoughts and needs. Bunny's dream experience was an example of the capacity of the unconscious to provide information through an uninterrupted stream of consciousness flowing from one individual to another. Slowly, I was beginning to accept that the coincidences surrounding Kevin's death seemed to point to an event that was waiting to happen.

When I began to acknowledge coincidence as a state of synchronicity, I was forced to consider that there are no accidents. I came to despise that cliché and resented its implication. I fancied myself as having more control in life. Though at this early juncture, my angry self would not grant Kevin's dying as a fulfillment of his destiny. There must be a mistake, and the clues were in the Nightmare.

Nonetheless, God responded loudly by sending me the assistance I needed most to discover what my ego would not accept. This part of the journey included companions who very gently embraced my fragile and broken spirit. They became allies and devils' advocates whose role was to stay anchored in their belief systems while allowing me just enough tether to explore beyond my own.

Immediately, my next supporter arrived by telephone call. On this occasion, my brother Paul called to tell me about a college course he was taking and that one of his assignments was the traditional research paper. I was proud of the way he had overcome so many personal obstacles this past year. I was hoping that Kevin's death would not deter him from moving forward in his studies.

Getting to the point he interjected, "I have an idea for my paper that I want to talk with you about. If you're not okay with it, then I won't do it."

I could not imagine how my approval of the theme for a simple English paper would matter. "What did you have in mind?" I asked, my curiosity rising.

"Well," he hesitated, "I was wondering...may I use your dream about Kevin dying in my paper? You have me interested in all this dream stuff so I thought I would research dream interpretation."

I was shocked. I appreciated his listening ear, but I never realized he was that interested. "Whew, uh, I guess so," I wavered. "What in the world would you write about it?"

"I was hoping you would tell me!" he laughed. "The paper has to be instructive as well as interesting. Do you have any suggestions for reading material?"

"Oh right, I just happened to have a stack of books you could use," I joked, thinking about the growing pile of resources beside my bed.

"So, you're okay with this? It won't be too hard on you?" he queried. I took a deep breath before I answered. I really did not know a great deal I reasoned. How much help could I be in my present state of mind? But then I mused, hadn't I just committed myself to learning all I could about dream work? Before I could give it more consideration, I blurted out yes.

The timeliness of his call served to bless our collaboration in so many ways. It strengthened our bond of trust, and it gave my brother a means of alleviating my grief. It also helped me to stay focused enough to lay the groundwork for one of the most profound experiences yet to come.

* * * * * * *

A few days later, my father invited us to spend the weekend with him in Denver hoping a change of scenery would give us a reprieve. Escaping the haunting memories in our home seemed like a good idea. I did not anticipate how difficult that trip would be for it was the first time we had left our home without Kevin.

His absence was painfully obvious when Amber climbed into the back seat alone. She hastily sat behind me arranging her backpack and pillow on *her* side, leaving Kevin's space free. As of late, her beautiful green eyes lacked their luster and twinkle. Today they expressed a loneliness felt only by her as she searched the unoccupied seat. Tears welled in my eyes as I witnessed the extent of her solitude. What we thought would be a simple escape turned out to be sheer anguish for

147

Amber as she struggled with the burden of being an only child. How does one learn to be alone after having shared a lifetime?

Within forty-five minutes we rounded the highway curve marking the site of our near miss accident during the holidays. Driving at night in blizzard like conditions, we narrowly missed hitting an oncoming car that had swerved into our lane. Now, I was disappointed at the thought that perhaps our family's destiny had been thwarted by Stann's excellent driving skills. Now without shame, I truly wished we would have crashed and plunged to our deaths as one. Was it a coincidence that we lived? Why did Kevin die a week later just fifty yards from his front door? It made no difference how it might have happened; we felt dead either way.

The remainder of the trip triggered more upsetting memories of our last Christmas at Pop's house. As soon as my father opened the door, I knew it had been a mistake to come back. Overcome with emotion, he choked back the tears unable to greet us in his normal fashion. My father could not hide his expectation of seeing both grandchildren. Amber and Kevin had always bounded through the door with a boisterous greeting, running into Pop's open arms for a hug. Now, with fear and hesitation, he embraced only Amber.

That Saturday evening we also visited with Stann's oldest brother. We talked about our struggles and he suggested doing a simple meditation to help ease our anxiety. While its calming effects were short lived, it did help me to fall into a deep sleep when we retired for the evening. At one point during the night, I was very much aware of hearing my own voice. I heard myself saying, "Wake up!" and I struggled to open my eyes. I sensed Kevin's presence right where he would have slept on his cot by the side of the bed and I kept telling myself to wake up.

The next morning as Amber and I were making the beds she said, "Mom, if Kevin were here he would want his cot to be near mine, right?"

I nodded to her, suddenly caught off guard, remembering that last night I sensed his presence in the room. Swallowing hard I replied, "Yes, he would probably want to be by you and the television so he could watch cartoons in the morning."

"You know what Mom?" she paused searching my face for an opening. "I thought Kevin was in the room with us last night...near my cot."

Stunned, I dropped to the bed and cocked my head sideways as if she had read my mind. "What do you remember?" I said.

"Just that it felt as if he were here and then I thought I heard talking," she shrugged.

"Amber," I whispered excitedly, reaching for her hand. "I felt the same thing. I think Kevin was here with us."

Her big green eyes blinked back the tears, relieved that I believed her. My heart was full with the confirmation that Kevin was near us. How strange that we would even feel Kevin's presence away from home. Although the mourning continued despite our whereabouts, Amber and I had sensed Kevin's presence. When I shared our story with Stann, he too admitted waking up in the middle of the night with the same suspicion. He dismissed it though. I would not believe that it was the strangeness of traveling without Kevin or that our desire to have him with us manufactured an illusion of his presence.

By Sunday evening, I yearned for the safety net of our home. I wanted to be secluded from any reminders that life continued for the rest of the world. I was sadly mistaken if I thought a trip over the mountains was an escape from the pain. We could not drive far enough to elude the throes of grief. Three days was too long to be away, and I wanted to get an early start back home. While I packed our suitcases to leave the next morning, Amber fluffed the blankets and tucked herself in on the cot. I zipped the suitcase closed and shoved it towards the wall.

Clutching Kevin's stuffed dog, Benjie, she asked, "Are you going downstairs now? Can I have the door open again?"

I moved to the side of her makeshift bed. Leaning over I kissed her cheek releasing the tears we both held. "Amber, would you like me to stay until you fall asleep?" She nodded yes, and hugged me tightly around the neck. Since the first night of our arrival I had been lying down with her at bedtime, just as I had at home every night. The spacious master bedroom in my dad's condominium held too many memories of adventures with Kevin for her imagination to bear alone.

I stretched out on the edge of the king size bed and pulled her cot close. Pushing her thick bangs off her forehead, I exposed a troubled brow. I blessed her there with a kiss good night, and prayed for a peaceful sleep. Within minutes, Amber dozed off turning on her side to nestle in for the evening. I crawled across the bed, pulling the covers down and slipped quietly underneath them. No sense in going downstairs, for the sooner I went to sleep the faster morning would come. Reaching above me to the headboard, I switched off the lamp and went to sleep…

I strolled down the right aisle of the movie theater toward the best seat in the house, mid row and center. No need to hurry, as I was the only patron for the evening show. Seated comfortably, I noticed before me an enormous white screen stretched across the length of the stage. Soon, the interior lamps dimmed enclosing me in total darkness. Immediately, I felt my consciousness lift up from the seat and move outward.

Without effort, I floated through the black void that was once the screen, to the threshold of a lush green vista of rolling grass and trees in bloom. I thought to step into the landscape, but sensed the shadowed chasm between was too wide to cross. Instead, the desire to see more provided an instant close-up of the scene. My attention moved to the foreground focusing on a figure standing alone. It was Kevin!

He stood there with his hands thrust in the pockets of his jeans, wearing a navy and white baseball jersey, with a red letter "A" on the left side. My Kevin was smiling at me! There was an incredible aura of calm about him as if he had never experienced a hint of pain since he last saw me. And, to my relief, our deep connection to one another had prevailed despite the separation. I sensed an exchange of love between Kevin and me that soothed my soul and brought me a moment of peace.

As my heart filled with joy, my sight broadened and revealed a brilliant glow of gold and white light. A full size halo shimmered around Kevin's figure as he maintained his pose amid its radiance. The energy that embraced him was a remarkable sight. My consciousness grew heavier as the desire to leap beyond the void to join him overcame me. A pulling sensation at the base of my head brought me back to my pillow with a thud. Instantly, the tears began to flow as I reached out across the night to hold my son.

It was not until later in the afternoon well into our trip home that I could find the words to record the dream in my journal. Although I was elated, I could not yet verbalize it to Stann. When I did, he seemed confused and distant. I was in awe of the glorious halo that surrounded Kevin illuminating him at its center. I had been gifted with his presence in an extraordinary manner unlike anything I had ever experienced. Each encounter before this had been precursors to this phenomenal experience, seeing the love exchanged between Kevin and Jesus as they sat together, and watching myself carry Kevin's Golden Light Body away from the accident.

Until now, the dreams of Kevin reflected my longing for the past and gave me opportunities to play out the memory of simply holding my baby and smelling his soft skin. The recent Golden Light Dream began in the past at the accident, moved away from the illusion to the present, showing the gift of perpetual glory, and ended with a summary of the spiritual road ahead. Now, to see Kevin again, whole, happy, beaming brightly was the ultimate experience of my life.

Even in my grief, the multiple levels of power to heal my misperception impressed me. We had finally connected in the Somewhere, that place between here and there that seemed unreachable. Its numinous quality depicted archetypes from the collective unconscious portraying a concept of a heavenly state that my ego could understand. Its simplicity astounded me.

20
Stolen Time

Dream Journal: February 25, 1991
I'm dodging people in a school hallway, trying to get somewhere. A young blonde woman sneaks up beside me and tries to take my watch right off my arm! I am appalled that she would have the nerve to steal it right off my arm. I fight her off, and although she doesn't fight back, her insistence on keeping the watch is strong. I'm so mad I scream obscenities and say, "Who do you think you are?" I am finally away from her...I walk into a mall store and notice all the clothing is dark and drab. I want a swimming suit. I notice a sale rack of children's clothes. I find a pair of yellow and orange flowered pants for Amber in a size ten, too big for her. I am irritated that I cannot buy anything for Kevin.

We had taken our first trip without Kevin, and no miracle had occurred in our absence. He was not waiting to greet us at the door. It was the first of many attempts to run away from home and stay in touch with the rest of the world. It felt like hell in either place.

Preoccupied, I unpacked my suitcase and sorted the clothes for the laundry. Amber and Stann had long since departed for school leaving me alone with my thoughts. What to do this week? Nothing that seemed worth my while.

I had scheduled appointments at work for three days a week in hopes of regaining my clientele and to help with our depleted finances.

151

Since my day revolved around Amber's activities, I could easily work around her needs. I dreaded adding two more days. It only meant gaining more appointments and having to see more people. The "should" of life pulled me down again and a feeling of uselessness swept over me for what my life had become. Days spent worrying about how to spend my time.

Disgusted, I slammed the dresser drawer shut shaking the picture frames and knick-knacks. That stupid Blonde Woman had shown up again last night in a more youthful disguise looking less than angelic. Only this time I was not afraid of her, I was damned pissed off. How dare she reappear and try to steal anything else of mine let alone my watch. Wasn't my son enough? I turned to the nightstand and picked up my notebook from the floor. I flopped down across the bed to peruse the meaning of her return.

I could read between the lines. Who did she think she was fooling? In my heart I believed she had stolen precious time from me, time that belonged to Kevin and me. I was appalled at her nerve to steal from me again. Yet, something about her insistence puzzled me. Whatever it meant at least I had put up a fight.

I positioned myself to write upon the pages, but the pen would not move. Since Kevin's death it had been difficult to put down a word of my thoughts unless it was about a dream or a few notes. I had always been able write about my feelings, but now it was too painful to seem them in print. My body sank deep into the bed, and soon I heard that familiar wailing sound moving through my heart and rising to my throat. Its pitch echoed across the empty house and returned twice as loud to frighten me. The shock of hearing my own pain was enough to reduce me to sobs. In defense, I began to write fast and furiously scratching the page with the tip of the pen…

"Will I always feel like I'm just waking up? I'm in another reality most of the time...as though I have one foot here and one foot there? Or, one big toe in this reality and the rest of me out there?

I am so sick of hearing how strong I am that I could scream! Why can't I see it or feel it...or know it? If people only knew the truth. I am not really here! Most of the time I just want to throw up my guts until there's nothing left inside...food makes me sick, deciding what to eat or cook is irritating...deciding on anything is a real pain.

There are fifty bejillion firsts to deal with and there won't be time left for the seconds. Something as simple as glancing into the back seat and seeing only one child becomes an "event" and another first to acknowledge. Every single aspect of our life is so different that I don't recognize us anymore.

And then, people say, "Oh Carla, you're doing so well. I know I wouldn't be able to function if it were me." I want to scream back at them, "I'm not! What makes you think I am? You see me only at that moment when I am struggling to hold myself together for YOU. You don't see me when I can't even finish loading the dishwasher or when I find his toys around the house. Or when I am driving and I forget where I am going...or when I am filled with so much despair that I lay paralyzed in his room. You don't see me as I really am...afraid of life."

I've decided that I am making a pact with Stann and Amber. If I should die an untimely death (Who am I kidding? What a screwed up word.) I promise that I will do everything un-humanely possible to communicate with them. There is no reason that our loved ones should be left to wonder and question. It's crap. If dying is a part of the living process then why should it be such a mystery? Why don't we promise to communicate with each other on levels that a human being can understand before we leave this messed up world, instead of using ominous symbols and guessing games?

Pearly gates or silver clouds, which do you prefer in heaven? Heaven? Oh forget it, we don't go to heaven until we get it right. But, does getting it right mean continued suffering and pain, or forgiving those that wouldn't or couldn't forgive you? Does getting it right mean starting over again, and again, and again... I don't get it."

The pages of my journal were splashed with confusion and anger. I thought I had integrated my Catholic roots with a more universal and conscious spirituality, and yet here I was criticizing what I had learned. Regardless of any debate I might be having in my head, my body solely yearned to see and feel Kevin again. That is all I wanted. And, the only way I could see him was in my dreams or in pictures.

A burst of energy lifted me off the bed and out to the living room. The two photo albums representing his life were now placed at our fingertips under the coffee table. Nestled into the end corner of the sectional couch I cradled my treasure. The only thing of any real value to me now. Turning the pages, I relished each pose that allowed me to stare into his deep brown eyes and see his glowing smile. I poured over the photo journal recorded on film by my mind's eye. As so often when he was alive, Kevin's exuberant demeanor struck me. He had a self-assured, confident look that seemed mature and wise beyond his age. I could always feel the love he felt for me reflected in his eyes.

And then...I gasped to see him again. There he was in a navy and blue baseball jersey with his hands thrust into the pockets of his jeans posing for me in front of the preschool back in September. Only the gray door of the building was visible behind him. I remembered thinking that day what a great picture it would be as I snapped the shot.

Instantly, I was in three places, focusing the camera to pull him into the center of the frame, hovering at the threshold longing to join him in the Halo, and peering through the wavy texture of the photograph as it came to life before my eyes. Placing my fingertips upon his face, I sobbed, "Oh Kevin, you knew I would find the picture." Amid the symbols of the tree of knowledge, the green vista of transition and the full halo was an image pulled from the banks of my memory. Its purpose was to give me a tangible piece of evidence that would begin to dispel the doubt as I grieved his physical absence. The *Somewhere* did exist beyond my dreams, and so did Kevin.

I received each dream as if it would be the last one, thankful to have the gift of peace, if only for a moment. I truly did not believe they would continue. Much to my surprise Kevin kept appearing in one manner or another to help me over the next eighteen months. Nevertheless, in my naiveté, I became disappointed that these powerful experiences did not alleviate the pain my body felt. I had the notion that I should be doing better because of them.

When I accepted the concept that we store every experience we have deep within the cells and tissues of our body, I began to understand why feelings of pain, anger, sadness and even joy are hard to let go of. My body was an example of how much trauma I had suffered from the accident. Things outside of myself triggered emotions that lay beneath the surface waiting to escape. The simple melody of a song or the smell of Kevin's clothing produced a stirring that was tantamount to a nuclear reaction within my body. Once the switch was on I could not prevent the wave of emotion no matter how much I tried to suppress it.

I also had a choice of what I did with it. I learned that honoring my body's responses to the most significant event in my life would be far healthier than rejecting or suppressing it. I had to give myself permission to feel to whatever depths of grief I wanted or needed to at the moment, without doubting its validity or letting others judge the period in which it should happen. Whenever frightening images snuck up to ambush me, I had the choice to dwell on what I saw or replace it with a positive recollection of Kevin. Meditation and relaxation methods were extremely helpful in calming the anxiety and creating a quiet time to let those positive images surface.

I relied on the Jesus Dream, the Golden Light Dream and the Halo Dream for reassurance of Kevin's well-being. I also hung his drawing in our kitchen. The drawing was like a love letter that had been lost in the mail only to be found when the Hero was lost at war. The photograph of Kevin in front of the preschool with his hands in his pockets had transcended time, coming alive in my dream. I placed it in a frame on the nightstand by my bed.

These private gestures were not about memorializing Kevin as some might have thought. It was about keeping myself sane and grounded by placing the proof before me despite what the rest of the world appeared to be. It took years of daily practice to disengage from the fearful images. It is the hardest discipline I have ever mastered. God in His ultimate desire to love me through this tragedy had given me yet another tool to manage the pain.

21
The Nightmare Revised

Dream Journal: March 1991 Revision

I am walking down our street with Amber and Kevin. I am very afraid because a cult is trying to take them away from me. I have them close so that I can protect them from the people that are trying to get them from me. Next, I am in a house on my street and there is a circle of dark faced women. Directly across from me, on the other side is another dark faced woman with blonde hair. Amber and Kevin are to my right and I have my arm across them. Suddenly, I feel a black hand come across my chest to grab Amber. I slap it away, screaming that she cannot have Amber. I am screaming obscenities to this woman. The kids and I run to a house to be safe. It is not my real house, but it is my house. In the house I know we are safe and the doors are locked, and I am safe because I know the kids are with me. Next, I am in the kitchen, standing by the counter. The kitchen is bare, and I am the only one there. I hear Kevin calling to me to come find him. He says, "Mommy come find me, I'm in the..." the rest is blank, I don't remember the word. I run to find him, and I realize that there are no floors and I must climb these ladders and stairs that go up. He is calling for me to come find him, and I climb in the direction of his voice. I am at the top; it is an attic. I open the door, and I am gripped with a panic. The cult lady with the light blonde hair is standing there with a chain saw, and she will cut Kevin down. He is hanging from the rafter to her right, but I can't see him. I turn to scream for help, and she shuts the door in my face. I am screaming what sounds like "yyynnaancee" as I beat the door. I look to the left, and there is a figure, to my right is the closed door.

My brother's research paper was due in less than six weeks. We spoke almost daily on the phone as he produced the beginnings of what would be a finely crafted paper. My singular task was to define the personal and archetypal symbols and provide a summary. I became so focused on our project that I never noticed the purple crocus pushing their hearty buds through the crusty snow.

It was an enormous undertaking that required assistance at my end from my three women companions; Mary, Chris and Diana. I appreciated their willingness to walk this journey with me and share their perspectives as the mystery unfolded. Diana had been right. Breaking down the dream lessened the fearful tone and allowed me to see it differently. My instincts were so sharp and my desire to know so strong that I could easily recognize when something resonated with me or not at all. I became consumed with this project to the point that little else mattered to me.

In the beginning, Stann was encouraged when I went back to work. He also supported me in whatever I needed to do in understanding my dream world. He never doubted the validity of the Nightmare for *me*, but when I shared my findings, he offered little feedback. He came to believe that my obsession contributed only to the intense guilt I already felt.

His discomfort came to a head one evening while I was explaining the significance of one of my dream symbols. Hiding behind the sports page, he would look up occasionally nodding as if he were paying attention. Feeling ignored, I asked him what he thought about my latest dream.

Tossing the newspaper aside he answered with an edge to his voice, "Why can't I dream Kevin? Why isn't he coming to me too? How come you're the only one who gets to dream about him?" He sounded jealous, as if to imply that Kevin had chosen me over him. I hesitated, realizing that it was really about his frustration in wanting that same connection.

"Stann you've never been a dreamer, and besides, you rarely remember your dreams anyway. Perhaps he will come to you in a different way. If you stay open to..." I reasoned.

"I am open!" he shot back angrily. "I just don't believe that God wanted him to be run over by a truck and die. Where is the sense in that dream?"

It became clear that he was overwhelmed by the Nightmare and its importance to me. I could not blame him or be angry because he had no reference point. My encounters with Kevin were not valid for him because Stann only trusted what he could see and touch. He wanted a personal experience with Kevin that equaled mine. While I came to find solace and comfort in the spiritual world, he struggled to connect with Kevin in the physical world. We pushed through the dark phases of grief, lost to each other for a time, as we drifted toward different paths.

No matter how much I uncovered about the Nightmare, its healing message was difficult to grasp. Mary had grown used to my frequent anxiety attacks, as I would question my worthiness to receive any spiritual gifts. Her gentle counsel gave me the courage to risk exploring more deeply with meditation and journaling. I discovered that relaxation exercises could help me remember more details.

I began to see that the people walking with me in the Nightmare appeared as cult figures for a reason. They were a personal symbol reflecting my fear around being tricked and controlled. To heighten my awareness and gain my trust, the cult had included me in their circle, now comprised of only dark faced women. Their identity was disguised, only this time a blonde woman emerged as the spokesperson. The Blonde Woman succeeded in distracting me from my children. She stood out from the rest because of her flowing light blonde hair and powerful ability to divert my attention. Absorbed in her deception, I let down my guard long enough to allow the dark handed woman a chance to reach for Amber. Why wouldn't I perceive them all as evil? Anyone that would take my children from me could not be good.

It was difficult to respect the Blonde Woman as an Angelic messenger or the other women as feminine earthly energies calling Kevin to return to a state of oneness. I associated them with deception and fear. Death was darkness, not a return to unity. However, the key to the Blonde Woman's identity was not in the shadows of her face, but in the lightness of her hair. Symbolically, the illumination of her hair defined her as a spiritual being. In fear, I masked her face with a shadow to shield my eyes from her true form. I would not believe that I was worthy enough to be in the presence of a Heavenly energy. In my humanness, I could not face the light of God.

In the Nightmare, I ran to the only place I knew we would be safe. If the confines of our home would secure us from harm, it was there I let my guard down. I had presumed that the cult wanted Amber, since she was the one the woman tried to grab. Even then, I underestimated the power that had been given to the Blonde Woman. Death was at my door, and the child they wanted would be claimed where I lived.

The actual events preceding the accident, showed that I had kept us close to home all day. I pushed the Nightmare to the back of my mind until it became a reality. As the dream foretold, I stood in my kitchen while Kevin psychically called out for me to come to him. Our spiritual connection with each other was so strong that I sensed the need for me to go to him. As I gripped the knob of the front door, I experienced the same panic I felt facing the Blonde Woman. Only this time I knew Kevin was on the other side, outside.

I had ascended the ladder to the attic, where the physical meets the spiritual. The Blonde Woman knew that I would come at the beckoning of my son. In her certainty and might, she raised her sword as an implement of authority that decreed the Word of God. Kevin's earthly life had completed its cycle. She did not grant me passage through the door to the next world as she had Kevin. Instead, I was left behind to open yet another door. My ascension would follow a different path. In that moment, our destiny was sealed, and the transmutation of Kevin's soul had begun.

My initial interpretation of the Nightmare had the threads of fear and evil woven through every scene. Because I feared the messenger, I missed the message. I surmised that God knew I would never willingly give back a gift that had been given in good faith. I was so deeply rooted in the physical world that I could not accept that God would call him home so soon. My ignorance certainly had protected me from a Truth I would have tried to stop. Did I really believe that we were partners with God in planning our life's mission? If I did then, who was I to interfere with any agreements made between the Father and His child Kevin?

Kevin's drawing of the house and my dream could not be reasoned away as coincidences. We had both been given the same message. Kevin's accuracy in drawing my own shadowed face was a chilling prediction of how dark the journey would be for me. While his own eyes were open, his mouth could not speak of what he knew.

And still, there were missing pieces to this spiritual puzzle. What was the Blonde Woman saying to me in the circle? It had upset me so much that I dropped my guard and let the black-handed woman grab Amber. What was Kevin saying when he called out to me? Why can't I remember where he told me to find him?

These questions remained for the next year and a half. I felt an overwhelming sense of responsibility with the knowledge given me but I did not know what to do with it. In my opinion, I had a right to know the whole plan. I thought myself to be a much better student when I was fully informed and certain of my goal. Still my doubting mind searched for more tangible proof. I became frustrated and angry to the point of rejecting it all. I did not want to believe it. I did not want to believe that my son was meant to die.

The more I struggled with the spiritual implications, the more obsessed I became with the details of the accident. At least in the physical world, there was something that everybody else could see that would affirm my old beliefs and feelings. Another human being, was responsible for my son's death, not a truck. Could we not all agree on that? Did I not have a right to be angry about it?

For some, the obvious seemed to be that the truck driver should step forward and accept the responsibility of carelessness. For others, the obvious lay in the unfortunate timing of being in the wrong place at the wrong time, and that no one should be held accountable. And, for still others, it was about a child's lack of safety experience and his trust that the world would provide it for him.

I found myself agreeing with all of them. My belief system told me that cause and effect equaled consequences. Stann and I were programmed to follow the expected course of pursuing justice. We presumed that fairness and truthfulness would prevail. In the end, we were swept away by our expectations and became victims of the justice system.

I felt very different and removed from any normalcy in the physical world. Stann did not recognize me, and friends and family wondered how much counseling I would need. For a while, he remained resistant to the idea that Kevin had a destiny other than the one he had mapped out for his son. Amber longed to be as important as her brother in my eyes. Friends and family members were too frightened to contemplate it or considered my instability as a temporary stage in the grief process that I would get over.

During my search, I discovered a piece of scripture referring to the symbolism of a shut door. In the *Dictionary of Scripture and Myth*, I was amazed to learn that a "shut door" symbolized the "termination of the cycle of life on the lower planes".

Luke 13:23-25, continues, "And someone said to Him, 'Lord are there just a few who are being saved?' And he said to them, 'Strive to enter by the narrow door; for many I tell you, will seek to enter and will not be able. Once the head of the house gets ups and shuts the door, and you begin to stand outside and knock on the door saying, Lord open up to us! Then he will answer and say to you, 'I do not know where you are from'."

The definition goes on to say: "Those who have not kept pace with the scheme will not gain entry (secure a place of fulfillment) unless the lower self avails itself of the advantages offered by the influence from On High, no grace is obtained. The insufficiently progressed souls shut out have to await further opportunities of improvement."

How does one become sufficiently progressed? Shall I spend the rest of my life grieving and concentrating on self-improvement and spiritual exercises to gain access through the door? Was Kevin's death deemed my once in a lifetime opportunity for improvement? What mysteries did Kevin know that I did not?

During this time I remember being home alone one evening while Stann was out. After Amber had gone to bed, I sat at the dining room table before a huge pile of bills overwhelmed at the thought of tackling the checkbook. The irony of not being coherent enough to balance a checkbook and yet interpret deep psychological and spiritual themes seemed ludicrous. My real life was about making a living and providing for the family, and doing the best we could to have fun and love each other through this life. I thought I knew how to do that. What I thought I knew was no longer real. What was the tradeoff for spiritual enlightenment?

Stretching my arms upward in despair with tears streaming down my face, I called to my Lord, "What do you want me to do with this? Please show me how to do this. It's not fair that you tell me this is Kevin's destiny without some explanation. What I am I supposed to do? You are expecting too much from me!" I cried as I pulled my hands away from His reach.

In my next session with Mary, I relayed my feeling of hopelessness about the Nightmare. Mary made us some herbal tea, and we settled into our favorite chairs at the old oak dining table. The weathered windowpanes began to fog slightly as the room warmed up from the heat of the wood stove. I stared at the steam rising from the mug dunking the tea bag up and down.

"Mary, What am I supposed to do now? I know something so profound, so powerful and I can't even share it with most people." I said dismayed. "Not even Stann. He doesn't really want to know any of it." I added, my fingers instinctively massaging my chest in a circular motion.

"I'm sure it frightens him to see you confused and hurting. He just wants you to be okay. He doesn't understand your need to follow this through." Mary said trying to reassure me.

"I know that. I really do, but nothing is ever going to be the same again." I said choking back the reality. "I don't know who I am." I whispered. "I only know that I'm not Kevin's mom anymore...that part of me died too."

Tears trickled down my flushed cheeks, like drops on the steamy windowpane. Mary reached across the table with a gentle touch to hold my hand.

"Carla, I believe with all my heart that you will come through this stronger and more whole. I know you won't let this go until you understand it completely and can live with it. But, you also have to figure out how you and Stann and Amber will get through this and live a life with joy again."

I knew that she was right. Until my memory improved there was nothing left to do with the nightmare. My limited understanding of the dream world told me that there were multiple levels of meaning in every dream. In grief and fear my conscious mind was blocking any acceptance of its meaning. How long would it take to grieve? How long would it take to release fear? The prospect of spending the next forty years in this body pursuing "opportunities to advance my soul" did not appeal to me. How could I survive in this world and yet prepare for the next?

I wanted out. I wanted to be in the Somewhere, free from pain and longing, free from struggle and fear, free to be with Kevin.

22
Ashes to the Wind

The brisk air stung my moist cheeks as I hiked the last set of steps leading up Mother Cabrini Shrine on Lookout Mountain. The spacious blue sky surrounding the hilltop allowed a clear view of the Denver skyline to the east. Facing west, the interstate highway wound its way through the foothills disappearing beyond the snow-covered peaks. I loved the peacefulness this mountain had offered to me during these five-and-half-years since my mother's death. In all her travels it was one of her favorite places. In my youth, we had often walked this mountain on a Sunday afternoon. When my children were big enough to make the trek, I brought them here hoping they could sense my mother's essence in the tranquility that graced its land.

Our small group gathered on the far hillside away from the curious crowd of Sunday visitors. The people joining us today; my father, Stann's brother and mine, as well as our friends Dave and Kathy from Montrose, brought comfort and support. They represented all our loved ones on either side of the mountains who were with us in spirit as we struggled through yet another ritual.

We moved in closer huddling around the stained glass jar containing the ashes of our beloved son. The bouquet of colored balloons twisted and bounced above us as if it were impatiently waiting its destination beyond the clouds. Each of us held a ribbon connecting our thoughts and prayers in unison as we silently blessed the body of Kevin

Ryan Blowey. After a few moments, we signaled our readiness to release him by letting go of the ribbons one by one. With a giant swoop, a gust of wind swept the bouquet of love up to the heavens. It rose quickly bobbing back and forth across the currents in anticipation of the Somewhere.

Shielding our eyes from the sun, we watched the balloons fly higher and higher until they became one colored dot among the clouds. Then, we invited each person to take a handful of Kevin's ashes to spread over the hilltop and observe a private moment of silence. While the others moved in different directions across the hillside Stann and I joined Amber, guiding her to an open area of brush a few feet away.

Removing the plastic bag from the colorful urn, Stann dug his hands deep into the ash allowing it to sift through his fingers. His strong hands shook as he tenderly turned some small fragments of bone over and over in his palm. Handing the bag to me, he wiped the tears from his eyes with a dusty finger. Following her daddy's lead, Amber grimaced as she quickly scooped the grayish white particles into her little hands. Her furrowed brow and teary eyes reflected the confusion she felt seeing this gravel like substance that was once her brother. I felt the same, my body stiffening at the touch of the coarse pebbles so unlike Kevin's soft supple skin.

We explained again, that spreading ashes was an important part of a funeral when there was no burial. I assured her that releasing the ashes to the earth would in turn help something else to grow. It was a feeble explanation, but it was all I could bring myself to say. I stepped out of her space to give her room and some quiet time before she released the ashes. Instead, she quickly tossed them into a thorny bush and brushed the chalky dust from her hands seeming repulsed. I wrapped my arms tightly around her trembling body and kissed her cheek in praise of her courage.

Stann moved further down the hill selecting a more private space. I left him alone knowing that he was uncomfortable with any public display of mourning. I would wait until later when he felt stronger to share that moment with me. I released Amber to the arms of my brother while I walked to the high chain linked fence lining the boundaries of the shrine property.

It seemed such a short time ago that I had stood there balancing my pregnant and clumsy frame on the slope to cast my mother's ashes. Then, I held Kevin's body within mine keeping him warm and protected until his birth. Clutching the gritty ashes to my heart, I remembered the body it was...vibrant, alive, joyful. I wanted no part of this dry coarse matter that left me feeling cold and detached. This was not my son. I raised my hand to the west and let the swirling current lift the ashes high across the peaceful countryside.

* * * * * * *

That evening back in my father's condo, I crawled into bed feeling exhausted. We had reached an important milestone in our acceptance to let go of Kevin's remains. In releasing his body to the earth we celebrated the transition of Kevin's soul to the Somewhere. I believed in the promise of Everlasting Life and knew that Kevin had been granted the presence of God wherever he might be.

I desperately wanted to know where that was and how one might get there. What happened between death and rebirth? What was it like for a child? Was he looking for us or did someone meet him? Was there darkness? Did he feel pain? There was so much to learn about the afterlife. I grew even more tired at the thought of how much I had to do to get my present life back in order.

Dream Journal: March 30, 1991
I am back in college again. I am aware that I am dreaming as I walk across the campus. Finding the classroom seems to be a problem, but I know all the students and I am sure I'll find it. I am irritated though that I have to go back to school. I watch some men play basketball in another room. They are being pushy, and I tell Thomas to please not act that way. I finally find the classroom and discover that I am 15 minutes early. I decide to walk around and find myself on the roof of the school building. It is open except for a waist high retaining wall around the perimeter. I am aware again that I am dreaming, everything is very lucid. I walk to the wall and look out to the sky. I am met by a beautiful formation of giant white birds flapping their wings gently in a wide circle. Their wings are stretched wide and overlapped as if they are holding hands. As they flap their wings, they disappear and become a glowing white circle of light. One of the birds comes to me at the edge of the wall. It is gigantic, about the size of a small dog. The bird looks at me and allows me to stroke its head and neck. Its feathers are a striking white, soft and clean. I notice now that the bird's right eye is bigger, and that side is facing me. The eye is so much bigger now and covers more of the side of his head. It is a beautiful clear blue. It's as if I can see right into it. The bird looks down and then directly at me. I walk along the wall petting him as we cross the roof from one side to the other.

I lay there motionless, not sure if I had returned or not. My opened eyes searched for a reference point in the dark shadows of the bedroom where there had been light just a moment ago. The giant bird's eye was so clear, captivating my attention, as if *my* eyes were inside the sphere surrounded by the blue perimeter. This time I never felt as though I were asleep. I was fully aware that I was dreaming. I knew I had experienced a lucid dream. I was called to wake up within the dream and witness it consciously. My dreamscape had become an advanced placement classroom in which to process higher learning at a quicker speed.

The Birds of Heaven, as I call them now, were spiritual beings who introduced themselves to me on the school rooftop, my highest point of awareness. They came to assure me of God's love and the purity of their intent to assist me. In releasing a part of my past with Kevin, I had signaled a readiness to begin my studies in the most complicated subjects of grief, anger and forgiveness. My teachers would come from all walks of life, in many different forms, often disguised or unknown to me. I was disappointed to learn there were no lectures to attend, or textbooks to buy. The tests were experiential, scheduled on Divine Time. I had only my dream journal as a study guide.

23
Unmasking the Illusions

Traveling the last stretch of highway into Santa Fe, the twinkling lights of the city illuminated the jagged outline of the Sangre de Cristo Mountains. The poor countryside of northern New Mexico with its tiny pink adobe homes contrasted with the more affluent appearance of this historic town. As we passed the popular style of Spanish pueblo and territorial dwellings lining the streets of Santa Fe, I wondered what Amber and Stann were doing at home in Montrose. I wanted to phone them as soon as we reached our motel room. I needed to hear their voices.

I was anxious about being away from them. It was the first time since Kevin died that we had been separated for more than a school day. Truthfully, I was scared to be away on my own. Not an easy admission on my part after having grown up as an army brat traveling much of Europe and the United States. Now, at thirty-three years of age, I could hardly navigate my way around Montrose let alone take a road trip with girlfriends.

A week ago, Chris had invited me to accompany her and two friends from church to a monastery in New Mexico. Privately, she was concerned that I might be straying too far my Catholic roots. She hoped a retreat setting would provide an occasion for me to rest and pray among friends. The four of us had been closely acquainted over the past few years and this weekend would provide an opportunity for us to share our stories, as we each sought healing for our individual pain and loss.

In the springtime, the New Mexico climate was much like southwestern Colorado, warm during the day and still cold at night. I noticed that even here the last of the snow had melted away, allowing the daffodils to unfold their petals to face the sun and rejoice in its warmth. Suddenly, it was spring. I had missed its grand entrance of warm winds and colorful blooms. Mother Nature had continued to cycle through her seasons bringing new life to the earth. I had been left behind, still in the past, seeking shelter on a cold overcast day in January. Would it still feel like winter ten years from now?

Six weeks had passed since I summarized the Nightmare. There were pieces missing and I could not accept its incompleteness. I thought that once I had analyzed the dream I would feel some sense of satisfaction in uncovering a part of the mystery. My need to know why Kevin died grew even stronger with each uncovered piece. I would not be satisfied until I knew why. Burdened by its ominous message, I put it aside hoping to gain new insights with time.

I continued to journal my nightly travels and examined the symbols and metaphors for meaning. The dreams were now processing the daily struggles of grief and loss that affected every aspect of our life. In many dreams, I was in an empty classroom, having missed the class or I was driving a car that would stall or shift out of gear. I dreamed of arriving late to work, only to screw up someone's hair and walk away. I dreamed of walking through new but empty houses or shopping for clothes and shoes that did not fit. I relived the accident scene in a hundred different ways. Many nights I would awaken to find myself wandering around the house or standing at Kevin's bedroom door.

The best dreams though, were of holding Kevin's sweet face in my hands. I savored every touch, every kiss and every look we exchanged. I missed him so much. I yearned to feel his arms around my neck hugging me tightly or lying close to him at bedtime to read Curious George. Five years was not long enough to accumulate the kind of memories I had planned for us. I had spent the last three years juggling my career, when I should have known there would only be one chance. I thought I could have it all, balancing family and my career. In the end, I had nothing but memories and a client list.

It was becoming more difficult to get through a full day at work with these guilt-ridden thoughts plaguing my mind. I had the support of my co-workers, and my clients had been very understanding. However, I was so embarrassed that my personal problems were affecting my performance and making clients uncomfortable. My grief was clearly visible and deeply felt by anyone who sat in my chair. My defenses would kick in whenever I had a new client or one I did not know well. I became very reserved and quiet keeping the conversation focused on their haircut and off of me. I prayed they would not ask me anything about myself or notice the picture frame of family photos. I dreaded hearing the question, "How many children do you have?" I did not know how to answer it.

Even though I booked my own appointments, I felt restricted because it determined when I could grieve. I could not schedule the waves of grief that snuck up on me. I remember one morning I was feeling very overwhelmed and did not want to go to work. I dreaded seeing the apprehensive look on everyone's face when I would walk in: Was she okay? Were things better today? My anxiety deepened and by the time I drove into the parking lot I was sobbing uncontrollably.

I laid my head down on the steering wheel wishing the car would magically drive me home. Paralyzed, I sat there crying for what seemed like an eternity. Suddenly, there was a knock at the window. One of the girls had seen me drive up and was worried when I did not come in on time. I was mortified to be found so vulnerable. Later, I was grateful for her concern and intervention. We both recognized that in my confusion, I might have been a danger if I had attempted to drive away unnoticed.

I did not want to be there anymore and preferred the seclusion of my home. The past few weeks had been unbearable and I was thankful for this escape. I had always been drawn to the beauty and mystique of New Mexico. I heard that it held something special for everyone who visited there. Now, I was on a road trip in search of the peace and quiet that eluded me at home.

* * * * * * *

Rolling over to my left side, I kicked back the covers to cool off. Chris, Kathy and Sharon had been asleep hours ago while I dozed off just long enough to be jerked awake by a restless tic. I was so uncomfortable without Stann lying beside me. I needed his reassuring touch when I awakened feeling lost or confused. After the long ride I was tired enough to reach the dreaming stage of sleep, but would have rather not gone there. I just wanted to sleep. Instead, I dreamed of overflowing toilets and showers stopped up with greasy rugs and blankets. Why couldn't I dream about clean water?

We are on a trip with our friends staying at a hotel. Stann and I are out by the pool. There are lifeguard towers with chairs. One of the towers has a round black charcoal barbecue grill on top. We are cooking hamburgers on it two at a time. Stann and I leave, but when we come back the grill has caught on fire. Flames are shooting up. The flames touch the electric wires that are now strung between the other towers causing sparks to fly out everywhere. No one is concerned except Stann and me. I run to the next tower and climb to the top throwing cups of water out to douse the flame. It doesn't work. I come down from the tower and meet

Sam the Life Guard. He tells me it's okay and not to worry. He hugs me and I think I could probably trust him.

I woke up feeling even more tired than before. Did I just climb a tower to save everyone from an electrical fire? Considering my effort to extinguish the flames and sparks with a measly cup of water, I proved that I did not know much about firefighting. Sinking deeper into the pillow, I wondered why I would trust a lifeguard who did not have enough sense to clear the pool and call the fire department. I dozed off again praying I would stay asleep.....

Sitting high in the lifeguard chair I can see the entire pool area. Stann, Dave and Kathy, and all the kids are swimming just below me. They are all having fun as the kids splash about jumping in and out of the water. Suddenly, I look again, and to my horror Kevin is lying down at the edge of the pool just as I found him in the street. Standing up, I scream to Stann and the others to help Kevin, but they don't notice him at all even though they are right there. Frantic, I climb down the tower steps calling for somebody to help him. In the next second I am there, kneeling, as I pick up Kevin in my arms. Cradling his head close to my breast, I keep crying "Kevin, Mommy's here!" over and over again. He never wakes up.....

"Not again!" I whispered, bending my arm across my face to cover my eyes and stop the tears. "Why can't I save him?" Startled by the vivid images of Kevin lying unresponsive in my arms, I sat up peering through the darkness. Realizing my roommates were still asleep, I got up quietly, and tiptoed to the privacy of the bathroom. Flipping on the light switch, I closed the door and leaned against it. The vanity lights flickered as I squinted to block the glaring bulbs. Relieved to find the toilet working and the floor clean of sewer water, I felt assured that at least I was not back in that dream. Not that the last one was any better.

"Oh, why couldn't I save Kevin like I did in the Golden Light dream?" I thought. If my dreams reflected my deepest desires, as well as my fears, then why couldn't my unconscious humor me with the happy-ending I wanted? Bending over the sink, I splashed cold water on my face. The running water flowed through my hands as I hung my head low. I just want to sleep for a few hours without a dream I thought. I knew that rest was all I would need .....

Stann and I are back at the pool. We are near some steps in front of the building. We see Sam the Lifeguard. I tell him the grill is still burning. "Don't be upset, it's okay," he said, reassuringly. So we decide to grill two more hamburgers.....

169

Stirring slightly, I reminded myself to go back to sleep. "At least the fire wasn't out of control...and besides, Sam said it was okay...I can sleep now...everything's all right," I reminded myself, dozing off. This time, I floated easily across the sea of my unconscious drifting toward yet another dreamscape.....

I lay back floating on the warm liquid surface absorbing the soft light on my face. Sighing, I said, "Oh, yes, I finally get to swim in the pool." The gentle waves of slumber had delivered my tired soul to peaceful waters.

Relaxing deeper into the water my heavy legs sank lower until my toes lightly touched the bottom. Rising, I stood waist high in the pool. There were many people floating around me now. I notice a woman with dark hair standing a few feet away, smiling at me. She is my Guide.

The soothing ripple of waves rolled in and out to the edge of the pool like a lagoon, while shimmering lights of rainbow colors danced playfully across the top. With one closer look, they become creatures of colorful light swimming beneath the surface. The current grows stronger as their speed accelerates through the water. Their fluid forms dive in and out of the sparkling water like dolphins emerging from the depths of Mother Earth's womb. I delight in their beauty and freedom to move so effortlessly.

The Woman Guide is standing beside me now. She turns to me and says, "Wait, and one will come to you."

Surprised, I answered, "There is one for me?" motioning to myself. Nodding yes, she smiles again, looking past me.

Glancing to my left, I think I see a baby swimming in the light filled water! Pointing to it, I lose track of its path beneath the rolling waves. Suddenly, the waves splash against my abdomen. Looking down, I see a baby girl emerging from the waters of life before me. In awe, I grasp the baby in my hands lifting her high in the air. Her dark brown wavy hair frames her sparkling eyes and happy face. "She's come to me!" I exclaim, pulling her naked little body to my breast. "She is mine."

The sounds of the motel shower running full force blasted through the wall. Slowly my consciousness stirred as the image of sparkling light-filled water and the vividly colored creatures from last night's dreaming stayed in focus. I was in awe of the beautiful waterscape of light and color still dancing before my eyes. And the baby! That beautiful baby girl with the dark brown hair came to *me*!

I rubbed my eyes to greet the morning light. I wondered how long I had actually slept last night. I stretched my arms above my head as more snippets of last night's dreams flashed by: swimming with the baby,

170

grilling the hamburgers, and running to save Kevin. As I played my dream video in reverse, I counted six separate dreams.

Each dream spoke of my present pain and the fears yet to overcome. Sam, my Lifeguard, assured me that I was protected. I accept Sam's declaration that everything is indeed okay. The firepower of the Holy Spirit could not be extinguished, and it would give me the energy I needed to go on. Finally, I am released to the warm water of the universal womb, the source of all existence flowing with potentialities. The twinkling light-filled waters had purified my soul with the promise of a new life.

* * * * * *

The two-story adobe building stretched across the monastery grounds, its bell tower visible between the pine trees. The monastery was well hidden below the sloping road bordered with tall evergreens. Tucked away, it seemed to beckon one to seek quiet and solitude in its natural rugged surroundings. In this short time, I had fallen in love with the smooth rounded lines and warm earth tones of New Mexico. As we approached the large wooden territorial style doors, I felt a quickening in my heart. What mysteries lay behind them for me? Would I find some measure of peace? The serene setting signaled an end to my inner chatter as the four of us walked quietly through the thick doors into the dimly lit entry.

We wandered into a small lecture room furnished with a variety of chairs facing a low podium. To the right we followed a long chilly hallway. The place seemed deserted until we encountered a woman who was a resident of the monastery. She informed us that we had arrived during the dinner hour, and that we were welcome to join them. Checking off our names, she accompanied us to our sleeping quarters at the end of the hall.

Our rooms were unadorned and simply furnished with two double beds, and a small bath. All the rooms opened to the same hallway, offering a view of the grounds through the large windows lining the outer wall. Anxious to explore the abbey, we quickly settled in. Soon, we headed back towards the lecture room on the opposite end of the long building.

There, we discovered another adjoining hall from the lecture room leading to a darkened chapel. A doorway to the left of the podium gained access to a narrow staircase leading to the second floor and the dining room. In addition, another door, farther to the left, led to a lounge area. It appeared to be a den with couches, chairs and reading material spread about. The large windows framing the two far walls made the room brighter and cheerier than the rest of the abbey.

I felt a sudden fatigue from our day of sightseeing and shopping in Santa Fe, I sat back on the couch beneath the window and briefly closed my eyes. Chris perused the pile of books on the coffee table, while the others visited with a young man from Ireland. I was distracted by their voices and joined the conversation instead.

The Irishman was a tall handsome man, perhaps in his mid-thirties, with dark hair and warm brown eyes. Disguised beneath his clothes was a once athletic frame, now bent and hunched at the shoulders. He was very congenial with a lively sense of humor. As he explained the itinerary for the weekend, he seemed very familiar with the program as if he had been here before. Slipping the metal crutches from his muscular hands he lowered himself to the couch to sit beside us. He was quite engaging, and soon the four of us were introducing ourselves to him.

While the others talked, Chris nudged me and said, "Carla, look at this book I found." She handed me a thin white book titled *Summerland*. I glanced at the cover, intrigued by an illustration of a blonde-haired, naked child, holding a dove. This simple drawing piqued my interest and I immediately began reading. Deep into the first few pages, I wandered away to another couch in a quieter part of the room.

It was a heart-rending tale of a child's journey through the dark valley of death accompanied by a band of angels. Upon her arrival she is embraced by a man and falls asleep in his arms Sometime later, she awakens and climbs onto his lap to sit. Her face brightens to see him again. Smiling down at her, He softly calls her by name. In that moment, their eyes meet, and she remembers that he is Jesus. On the last page was a striking illustration of this precious child sitting on the lap of Jesus. The exchange of unconditional love reflected in their eyes was not new to me. I had seen it before. I had seen my Kevin sitting on the lap of Christ.

"Are you okay?" said the Irishman sitting beside me. Startled, I looked up, wiping the tears from my cheeks. "Is there something you want to talk about?" he said in an overly helpful tone. I felt uncomfortable with his assumption that I would share my feelings with a stranger. Pointedly, I said, "Thank you, but I don't want to talk about it." I was immediately turned off by the Irishman's intrusion and made a mental note to stay clear of him. Thankfully, Chris was beside me now. I placed the booklet on the coffee table, and turned toward her, raising my eyebrows to signal for help. Chris told me the evening prayer service would begin shortly. Seeing an escape, we quickly moved toward the door to meet Kathy and Sharon in the chapel.

The altar stood in the center of the chapel, with four or five rows of hard backed chairs facing it on either side. These were reserved for the Benedictine monastic community during the Liturgy of the Hours, a prayer service conducted four times a day. The retreat participants sat separately in chairs arranged in rows several feet from the altar. We took our places in the back row.

As the evening prayer service began, my thoughts wandered back to the book. Since last night's dream of the water baby, and today's discovery of a book about a child's transition through death, it seemed that God was working overtime with me. What were the chances that a pastor in Norway grieving the death of a friend's child, and a bereaved mother in Colorado would share the same vision of a child's reunion with Christ? It was mind boggling to consider the depth of our connectedness as human beings. I took a deep breath and bowed my head, praying for courage to face whatever He wanted me to know.

I straightened my back against the padded chair, blinking hard to clear my thoughts. Opening my eyes, I noticed the Irishman seated in the front row of the right wing, deep in prayer. Propped beside him were the metal crutches. I felt a twinge of guilt at putting him off earlier. I did not intend to be rude. I was feeling vulnerable and needed to protect myself. Considering his story, I was sure it was a spontaneous need to reach out to another human being in pain.

In our brief introduction, we learned that he was the only survivor of a horrific plane crash. Left for dead, he had awakened among a pile of smoldering bodies retrieved from the crash. He had spent the last five years recovering physically, emotionally and mentally from the trauma. It struck me odd that in the ten minutes we had talked to him, he was so forthcoming with such intimate and painful details of his past. I, on the other hand, cringed at hearing my own voice say, "My son died." I could not imagine wanting to share any details of Kevin's gruesome accident now or ever.

Diverting my eyes, I shifted in the chair for a better view of the altar. We were seated too far in the back for my short attention span. Losing interest in the repetitive prayers and psalms, I attempted to hum along with the music. Listening closely for a note I could reach without embarrassment, I tuned into an unusual melody of notes playing under the liturgy music. It was unlike any song I had heard before. Soft angelic tones filled the chapel, blending in harmony, as if they had been rehearsed in the heavens a million times. It was a beautiful sound, rising and falling with intense emotion lifting my heart with unexpected joy.

I wanted to join in, but I could not distinguish the words or even the tune to harmonize. Craning my neck to find the source of this incredible sound, I realized it came from the mouths of the abbey community seated around the altar. Empowered by the Gifts of the Spirit, they sang a celestial rhapsody of spontaneous prayer in the mysterious language of the Gift of Tongues. Each note lifted our hearts, inviting us to seek a more intimate relationship with Jesus Christ. Moved beyond words, the four of us exchanged smiles as we experienced this phenomenon of the Spirit.

The service ended shortly after and we filed out of the chapel to the lecture room. We talked excitedly about this celestial choir with its spontaneous songs. I had never heard anyone speak in tongues. It was the most beautiful form of prayer I had ever experienced.

Later, too tired to record the day in my journal, I pulled the worn, gold cotton bedspread around my shoulders creating a cocoon for the night. Secluded behind the walls of the abbey, I sensed the tranquility I had been missing these past months. The angelic melody from tonight's service played softly in my head lulling me to sleep. For the first time since Kevin died, I slept peacefully through the night.

* * * * * * *

I awoke the next morning feeling more rested than I had been in weeks. My mind was clear and sharp and I looked forward to the day's events. The scheduled lectures and discussions were balanced with quiet time and prayer throughout the day. Between lectures, we took advantage of the good weather taking long walks around the grounds sharing our thoughts with each other.

The Irishman seemed attracted to our group of candid women, seeking us out during the breaks for more conversation. He introduced us to a middle-aged couple he was traveling with, who were friends of his from Texas. They were very nice and we spent some time visiting with them throughout the weekend. I kept my distance though, not wanting to expose myself. The Irishman shared more of his story, especially with Chris, who discovered that she knew about this particular plane crash from her years as a flight attendant.

I was amazed at the painstaking way he described the burning flesh and morbid cries of the dying passengers. With each memory, his emotions intensified as if it happened yesterday, instead of five years ago. There was a part of me that could identify with his seeming need to replay the scenes with such accuracy. I had spent these last few months rehashing every aspect of my trauma too. I supposed we both needed to hear our story enough times to believe it ourselves. In contrast, I was not comfortable meeting new people and discussing my loss.

I was most intrigued by the lectures on discernment; the ability to perceive the presence and the working of God in our lives through every day experience, scripture, visions and dreams. In becoming more aware of the many ways that God manifests His will in our lives, we can recognize what is truly God sent and what is not. In this fashion, He honors our free will by confronting us in familiar ways to get our attention. Soon enough those little coincidences or synchronistic occurrences will raise our consciousness to a level on which we can view our world from His perspective. Although I had been acquainted with this concept, I seemed to understand it more fully this time.

My dream experiences were affirmed again and again throughout the weekend, giving me a sense of acceptance. I recognized these were not considered the norm. I had come to accept that, at least for now, this was the most uncensored way in which God could reach me. I seemed to identify with this group of charismatic believers searching for God where we least expected to find Him.

A reconciliation service was scheduled for midday. Buried feelings of resentment surfaced in me as we moved once again to the chapel. I held with my church another fierce issue. I objected to the idea of seeking absolution for my sins from a priest who knew nothing about my motivation or desires. Why were we required to seek forgiveness from a stranger if the Church wanted us to have a personal relationship with Christ? I understood that priests were descendants of the Apostles, but in my view, present day priests held no more power to forgive than I.

As a child, I remember a nun telling my catechism class that God was just too busy to hear all our sins or prayers. In my innocence, I imagined God sitting behind a huge desk on his golden throne besieged by earthly requests, while Angels delivered messages and fielded phone calls. I would absently recite the penance prayers, my blue rosary beads dangling from my tightly folded hands. No matter how many prayers were assigned me in accordance with my misdeeds, I never felt forgiven. As I grew older I learned that the only way to feel forgiven was to make right what I had done wrong. The problem with that theory was the false sense of control it gave me in fixing mine, and everyone else's problems. I can see now it was the beginning of my "good girl" syndrome.

It had been several months since I felt good about anything, least of all myself, I mused, fidgeting in the cushioned chair. Looking around the room, I was surprised to see that the reconciliation service was far from the confessional experience of my youth. The dark, scary closet was replaced by the casual setting of the airy light filled chapel. Paired chairs were placed at intervals along the chapel walls designated as stations. The atmosphere was open and inviting, unlike the claustrophobic feeling of a confessional.

We were asked to reflect on something that had caused pain in our lives and seek reconciliation through prayer and spiritual guidance. I sat stiffly, caught off guard by the invitation. Mulling over the guilt I felt at compromising my family for my career, the anxiety grew inside me. While each of my companions made their way to one of the priests, I gathered my courage. After some time, I chose the younger priest closest to our row. It was the shortest route and I feared I would turn around if I had too much time to think about where I was headed.

175

As I seated myself across from the young priest, I was struck by the immediate intimacy that was created by placing two people face to face. By placing two chairs across from the other, we had created a confidential space with invisible walls that were honored and respected. I felt welcomed by his kind eyes and his openness to listen to me, a mere stranger. Overwhelmed by my unexpected need to share the burden I carried, the tears trickled down my cheeks.

Staring down, I folded my hands tightly and placed them on my lap to keep from shaking. The words would not come, only tears of sorrow and regret overflowing from the swollen river of my heart.

"Father, I am in so much pain. I thought I was doing the right thing. But now it all seems to have been for nothing," I sobbed.

"In my heart I wanted to be home with my children, but I had to make a living. I tried to make every moment with them count and still honor my commitment to my job. I enjoyed my career. I was going to cut back on the hours, but I felt obligated to finish the year." I explained, looking for understanding in his warm eyes. Choking on the guilt I had suppressed, my throat began to close up as the words fought their way through.

"Father, it doesn't matter now. I did not listen. I waited too long. I have all the time in the world, but now I don't have my son...he's dead," I wept into my hands. "How can God forgive me?" I pleaded.

Gently, he placed his hand on my shoulder. His warm touch seemed to ground me. "There is nothing God can forgive you for. In His eyes you have not done anything wrong. He knows you loved your children and did the very best you could at the time."

"God understands how hard it was for you," he said quietly. Then pausing he went on, "He wants you to forgive yourself."

The compassion in his voice touched my grieving heart. Sensing the depth of my inner struggle, he did not pretend that I could easily grant myself the forgiveness that God knew was unnecessary. Together we prayed that I would someday free myself of the chains of guilt that bound my soul so that I might receive the grace of peace God so wanted me to have.

* * * * * * *

Climbing the narrow stairs to the second floor, I walked down the dimly lit hallway to my appointment. I held the purple folder with Kevin's drawing safely tucked inside, close to my heart. I entered the first room on the right. It was small and sparsely furnished with a low couch and a few folding chairs. On Diana's advice, I had made an appointment with one of the priests for a spiritual consultation about my nightmare and Kevin's drawing. She had visited and studied at the monastery many times seeking rest and guidance. She was hopeful that I too might find some spiritual direction at the retreat.

Waiting anxiously, I sat on the couch. In a few minutes, a middle-aged man of slight build appeared in the shadows of the doorway. Standing up, I put out my hand and said, "Hello. I am your next appointment. My name is Carla."

Extending his hand to shake mine, he introduced himself too. "I'm Fr. Andrew," he said, motioning me to be seated across from him on the couch. As we settled into our seats, he smiled slightly, inviting me to begin. I was unaccustomed to these open invitations and intimate sittings among Catholics. I felt insecure and drained from the reconciliation service. I wished I had prepared myself more for this meeting. The tears welled in my eyes again. Where should I begin?

He waited patiently, his kind eyes supporting me until I composed myself to speak. Choosing my words carefully, I began to relay my story, beginning with the details of the dream and ending with the real life nightmare of Kevin's death.

"Fr. Andrew, I've done some work with the dream analyzing the symbols, but there is so much I don't understand," I said sadly.

"Even more confusing is this..." I added, pulling out the drawing from the purple folder. "We found this drawing a week after he was killed in the accident. He had drawn it for me a few days before he died."

He reached for the paper holding it arm's length in front of him. His expression instantly changed from indifference to curiosity as he became intrigued by the symbols.

"What do *you* see?" I asked, appealing to his intuition.

Scooting forward to the edge of his chair, he took a deep breath and sighed. Never taking his eyes from the drawing he said thoughtfully, "I sense that your son knew he was going home." Pointing to the top of the page he continued, "The circle and the whole figure of Kevin represent a return to oneness." A wave of sadness washed over me drenching me in tears.

He went on, his voice softer now, "I don't know why you were not allowed to see Kevin's accident, yet see so much in your dream. I do believe God is allowing you to see beyond the door, just as your son did in his drawing. For whatever reason, He wants you to unmask the perceptions you have of death. God is inviting you to see through the veil of illusion."

Touched by the certainty in his voice, I lowered my head nodding in agreement. He had affirmed much of what Diana had already told me. Only this time I wasn't suffering from shock. In that fleeting moment, the veil had been lifted and I was allowed to see my life's mission. The tightness in my belly confirmed what my heart did not want to remember.

Overwhelmed with sorrow and regret, I could not forgive myself for being a part of a plan that caused my family so much sadness and pain.

I felt even more conflicted than relieved. The guilt now encompassed a deep sense of responsibility to carry out a divine plan I could not remember saying yes to! Again, I was caught between opposing worlds. The spiritual world held the answers to this mystery cloaked behind the curtain of illusion. My son was so deeply connected with the spiritual world that he was able to translate his knowingness to the primitive symbols of the physical world. I had ignored the Nightmare, and then could not accept the interpretation I worked so hard to uncover.

My inner world held me captive with its concepts of blame and guilt. I could not have felt more responsible for Kevin's death than if I had driven over him myself. I took on more personal responsibility than I ever demanded of the truck driver. In my mind, I had failed as a mother in the worst way. I had sacrificed the needs of my family. If I had taken a stand instead of being the loyal employee, if I had said, "My family's needs are more important than how many clients I serve," would I have lost so much then? During the subsequent years of my grief journey, I vacillated between remembering, regret and resentment. I vowed never to let anyone or anything interfere with my love for Stann and Amber, not ever.

* * * * * * *

Dream Journal: April 28, 1991 Early morning.
Chris, Kathy, Sharon and I are walking around the outside of the monastery and then into the building. We walk down the hallways looking out the long windows. Next, it is morning and we are in the same room getting dressed, except that we are bare-breasted. I notice that Chris who has had a mastectomy, now has two breasts, but this does not seem unusual to me. We are all comfortable with being bare-breasted and begin to walk through the door. I am last in line. Just as I get to the door, I bend down and pick up a brown robe. I pull it over my head and cover my breasts proceeding through the door.

I showered and dressed quickly that morning, hoping to meet up with the Irishman before we left at noon. In haste, I gathered my toiletries from the bathroom, shoving them into the suitcase with my clothing. Checking the time, I remembered that breakfast was still being served. I hoped to catch up to the Irishman in the lounge. I grabbed my notebook and the purple folder heading full speed down the chilly hall.

The dramatic affects of last night's healing service lingered in my mind. It had been a long and emotionally exhausting day for all of us. In sharing insights about our personal losses, my women friends and I reached a new level of intimacy between us. If at that point, nothing more became of the weekend, I felt blessed by the opportunity to share my pain openly with them and to acknowledge theirs.

Last night, the four of us sat with the Irishman and his two friends, the married couple, in the front row closest to the altar. I was amused by how relaxed and comfortable we had become in our seats, no longer opting for the back row. We chatted quietly about what to expect from this charismatic service. Chris, Sharon, and Kathy were familiar with the practice of laying on hands. My only reference point were those evangelical revival shows on television. There always seemed to be an actor staged, ready to toss his crutches into the crowd at the moment the Spirit healed him. Tonight's atmosphere was much different than an auditorium of healed believers crying dramatically as they collapsed to the ground in praise. There was an air of reverence and anticipation for the presence of the Lord.

Pulling out of the conversation, I reflected on the day's events. I prayed that God would show me how to forgive myself. This self-imposed guilt threatened to cripple my ability to accept my own humanness and live more fully. Swallowing hard, I cleared my throat and joined the community in worship. The service had begun, signaling the turning point to my new life.

The familiar hum of celestial devotions invoking the Spirit emanated from the hearts of the monastic community. Each note of heavenly praise rose above the crowd, stronger and louder than before. Swept away by the rising tide of emotion swelling within me, I could scarcely catch my breath. I felt full, as if accommodating something inside of me. Above the harmonious blend, a voice whispered softly to me, "Trust, and you will receive". In that moment of grace, I remembered who I was. As the Holy Spirit descended upon me, I opened my heart. Filling my empty well to the brim, I drew into myself His strength and Love.

Buoyed by this incredible energy that lifted my soul and renewed my spirit, I opened my eyes to see this wonder. Before me, was the Irishman. Called by the Spirit to receive the Grace of God, he rose from his seat. Gripping the cuffed metal crutches to steady his broken body, he placed them one in front of the other as they squeaked from the strain. His legs once strong and sturdy, dragged slightly while his muscular arms bore the weight of his pain. The distance to the altar was only a few feet away, but for him the journey was long and the road was rough.

Standing before the priest, his broad shoulders slumped forward. Instinctively, I straightened my shoulders, as if to carry his pain too. And suddenly, in a moment of clarity, I realized why I was so uncomfortable with this innocent man. He mirrored my fear of what I might be five years from now...alone and broken, crippled by my guilt.

179

A wave of compassion carried me to his side. Joining his two friends, I placed my hand on his trembling shoulder. In turn, I felt the gentle touch of my friends from behind. As our energy pulsated from one to the other, I prayed that the Holy Spirit would mend our brokenness and lead us back to the path of wholeness.

This morning with complete resolve I entered the lecture room. Picking up the pace, I dodged my way through the maze of rockers and chairs. The breakfast crowd had begun to gather for this morning's presentation. I found the Irishman in the lounge visiting with his friends and a small group of people. Suddenly feeling self-conscious, I waved to get his attention.

"How are you this morning?" he smiled brightly, his Irish brogue rolling off his tongue.

"I'm good, thank you," I said feeling more relaxed than ever with him. I seated myself at the long table beside him.

Leaning my way, he said softly, "I want to thank you again for standing up for me last night. It meant a lot to me that you and your friends would come up."

"Well, you're quite welcome. It was a gift to me too," I said. Pausing, I smoothed my hand across the purple folder. "I have something I would like to share with you, if you don't mind."

Cocking his head to the side, he raised his thick eyebrows with interest waiting for me to continue. Clearing my throat, I began, "A few months ago my son was killed while riding his bike on the sidewalk near our home. He was only five-years-old...."

"I'm so sorry," he said, his dark eyes searching to know more as he touched my arm. I felt the anxiety rise in my chest as the words knotted up in the back of my throat. "A week later, I found a drawing he had made for me three days before he died. I would like to show it to you."

I slipped Kevin's drawing from the pocket of the purple folder and slid it onto the table in front of him. His eyes widened as he scanned the drawing skeptically. I went on determined in my plan, "I believe that... my son knew on some level he was leaving. He knew he was no longer in need of a body." I pointed to the shadowed figure at the bottom of the page. "I believe this balloon symbolizes his ascension. And, the full figure next to the circle in the sky represents his return to God."

I looked deeply into the Irishman's eyes. "I had to share this with you because the message is about hope. It's about God's promise that we will return to wholeness one day."

The Irishman's cheeks flushed and his eyes moistened with emotion. He took the sacred paper into his hands as if to memorize the page. Nodding his head deliberately, he asked, "What is your son's name?"

"Kevin," I said proudly, smiling at the sound of it.

Looking back to the drawing he whispered, "Thank you, Kevin." And then, turning to me he said, "I will always remember this. Thank you for sharing it with me."

Carefully, I tucked the paper back inside the folder, holding it close for safekeeping. I squeezed the Irishman's hand. We parted in tears, knowing that our paths would never cross again.

Across the room, Chris sat with the married couple, seated on the same couch where we had met their Irish friend two days ago. They motioned me to come over to them. Our conversations had been casual yet brief throughout the weekend. Through no fault of their own, I knew very little about them. I had become quite adept at keeping people at an arm's length.

"We just wanted to thank you all for last night. It meant a lot to him," the woman said. I nodded my head and smiled, feeling self-conscious again. Lowering her voice to a more serious tone, she said, "Your friend just told us that you lost your son recently."

Feeling vulnerable that my secret had been exposed, my head bobbed in acknowledgement. The sudden rush of heat to my cheeks exposed me further.

"We lost our son too," she volunteered quietly.

I sank into the couch beside her, my head bowed in recognition of her loss. Confident and at ease she began to talk about the death of her son. Humbled by her openness to share her pain, I listened as if each word were my own. In the years to come, I would call upon this moment whenever I was asked to tell my tale. I would remember how this mother modeled for me courage and grace in the midst of suffering. In sharing her story, she gave me an opportunity to listen with my heart, and she gave herself, the gift of perspective.

Raindrops splattered against the car window blurring the countryside of adobe homes and sagebrush. Tears trickled down my cheeks. I did not want to go home. I felt torn between my longing to see Stann and Amber again, and an overwhelming need to stay in the seclusion and safety of the monastery.

24
Forgiveness Class

Dream Journal: May 11, 1991

I'm in charge of a class for people who want to get well. The class is about forgiveness. There are many people in this group and I know some of them. A young man, and an older, bald-headed man, a married couple, two brothers, and a European woman who doesn't speak English very well, are all arguing among themselves. I finally get them quieted down enough to listen. We are seated at a round table. The European woman is on my right, the wife is directly across from me and Stann is to my left. I ask them to hold hands. I tell them it is important that we pray for forgiveness towards one another and to ourselves.

I had been expecting his call. His voice was low and calm, unlike the anguished cries and hysteria that I had remembered. He paused, and then, stumbling over his words, introduced himself. My heart skipped a beat as my hands tightened on the receiver. For weeks now, I had planned exactly what I would say to the Driver if we ever spoke again: "What happened out there? Please, tell me everything you saw. Did you see my Kevin?" But, when I heard his voice, my carefully rehearsed questions remained stuck in the back of my throat.

We had received a very carefully worded and remorseful letter from the Driver a few weeks before. He had expressed deep sorrow about the agony our family was going through. He said that he and his wife also

182

had children, and that they understood the love and joy children bring to our lives. He was greatly distressed over the tragedy, and in his words had sought counseling to "be able to live with himself."

Shortly after receiving his letter, we were shocked to learn that the Driver had entered a not guilty plea to the charge of "careless driving resulting in death." We were stunned and hurt. From the tone of the letter, we thought we had sensed a genuine grief and remorse. We recognized the courage it had taken to write to us. We never expected that he would plead not guilty, nor did we expect that five months of negotiations lay ahead of us. It seemed clear to us that the only appropriate response was to admit his responsibility.

Since we had received the letter, we had been asking the District Attorney to arrange a meeting between the Driver and us. The District Attorney had asked me pointedly what I thought it would accomplish. My response had been straightforward. I could not accept his plea. I did not understand his intent in declaring himself not guilty, after having expressed to us in the letter his deep sorrow. I had to look into the Driver's eyes again. Only then would I understand his motivation.

I had seen this man only once. In that painful moment, I had been able to read in his crazed eyes the depth of responsibility he felt. Like a valley separating two mountains, the gap between what I had seen that day and what he was saying now, seemed impossible to forge.

I had been struggling with my own involvement with this accident. Now, five months later, I still had not come to terms with the Nightmare or Kevin's drawing. The conflict between my instincts and what seemed rational had become a raging battle. I did not believe, not ever, that this man had intended to kill our son. However, a gnawing voice said he was not a pawn, and, that on a higher level he might have said yes, too. While I wanted to hear him tell me about that fateful day, I was more concerned about what I could see in his eyes. Was he as sorry as I for having participated in this mystery? Was he too struggling with the truth?

No matter what spiritual concepts I had been exploring, I still lived in a physical world. This was a world that reacted to injustice by establishing blame and responsibility and, ultimately, consequences. It was structured to insure that the defendant was given a fair chance to prove his innocence. The unique phrases and procedures of our legal system were confusing or open-ended. Once again, I had to learn another language. Sadly, I never realized that the terminology could be interpreted to serve any motive, not necessarily the truth.

It would be years before I would fully integrate the spiritual lessons of God's interpretation of justice. I would wrestle with a knowingness that was in sharp contrast to the perceptions I held within my belief system about truth and justice. I had wanted the Driver to simply accept responsibility for having caused Kevin's death. I asked for nothing more.

Now, hearing his voice I felt glued to the floor. In the silence of the kitchen, I could hear only my heart pounding wildly as I waited with expectation.

"Would it be possible to meet with you and your husband this Saturday?" he inquired.

I swallowed hard. We had scheduled Amber's birthday party for that day. I would not let anything interfere with our plans, especially not the man who I believed was responsible for making her birthday so sad. Taking my time to answer, I said firmly, "We're having a birthday party for our daughter that day. We're trying to make it special for her."

He interjected quickly, "Oh, I understand. You should do that for her," sounding as if he was truly concerned for Amber.

We agreed to meet the day after her party, at a park in our neighborhood. The conversation ended abruptly and I hung up the receiver. I felt relieved. Albeit short and tense, the initial steps had been taken. There would be a meeting, and there would be no lawyers to intercede. However, Amber's birthday would be our first priority.

* * * * * * *

The month of May was the beginning of a string of holidays, birthdays and family milestones that were now marked as firsts. My first Mother's Day card without both of the children's signatures was difficult to accept. Amber had selflessly penned her brother's name next to hers, making the letters much larger and darker than her own name. The sixth anniversary of my mother's death was a reminder of yet another loss. One I thought I had reconciled. Another date would have marked the fifth year of Kevin's successful operation to correct his clubbed feet. Amber's birthday was by far the most unbearable first occasion we had endured since Kevin had died.

I had always loved celebrating my children's birthdays. Their births were the two most important events in my life. Nothing surpassed the joy of being given these two delightful children. Their birthdays marked the passing of another year filled with the wonder of growth and independence, until now.

Amber's ninth birthday was our first confrontation with time's insistence to move forward and drag us along. As this year would pass, her memories would only include mom and dad. There was no sibling to share her third grade accomplishments, her joys, her laughter or her pain. Sadly, each birthday would take her farther away from the time she remembered with her brother.

Our only goal for her birthday was to cover Kevin's absence by letting her invite as many friends as she wanted to the party. By the end of the school year, she had made a few new friends and wanted to invite them too. When she handed me the final list, I was stunned to see she had invited fourteen friends! I was comforted by the fact that she felt close to that many peers.

We had set a precedent though for the next several years. In our desire to honor her birthday and celebrate our daughter, in the end, we over-compensated. We had become so aware of her aloneness during holidays and family gatherings that we actually had brought more attention to it. We had showered her with too many gifts and bigger parties, hoping she would not notice, if even for just a few minutes, that Kevin was not there.

As the guests arrived for the party, we routed them downstairs to the family room for the festivities. I noticed that they were unusually quiet and orderly. Until recently, most of them had experienced happy occasions in our home, free to roam and play. In the aftermath of Kevin's death, our home must have seemed scary and uninviting.

Soon, the number of guests and her responsibility as hostess overwhelmed Amber. Her moist green eyes perused the growing crowd of nine and ten-year-old girls as she anxiously looked to me for direction. Frustrated that even a birthday party now required careful scrutiny and attention, my heart cried out for normalcy. It was not fair that my little girl suppressed her joy at being one year older, because she felt stifled by our family's fear and grief. I cursed everything and everyone that had taken away her spontaneity and her childhood.

In that moment, I was angrier with the Driver than I had ever been. If only he would had looked behind the truck that day, used his side mirrors, or paid more attention to the going's on of the neighborhood. If only he would have been more careful, Kevin would be here with us, celebrating his sister's life. I hated what he had done to us.

I suppressed my anger and recognized that what Amber and the girls needed most, was permission from us to have fun. While Stann operated the video camera, I became more animated, joking with the girls as we played our first ice-breaker game. My Party Girl personality quickly surfaced on cue. As a shy teenager I would hide my insecurities with my other wise-cracking, spirited persona. Using humor and silliness to slay the beast of fear, my other self would take control long enough to allow me to slip into the shadows and regain my confidence.

Midway through the festivities Amber and her friends began to relax as they danced and laughed with each other. I was so relieved when they began to loosen up and be little girls again. They giggled when Stann demonstrated his version of the moonwalk and laughed out loud when he and I danced to the disco beat, exaggerating our steps. It became apparent that in our willingness to risk being silly we created an atmosphere of acceptance. However short-lived, it was okay to have fun in our mixed up world.

The next day, Mary, Stann and I, crossed the parkway intersection at the corner of our street. The bright blue sky intensified the snowcapped mountains to the south. The fresh smell of spring and a hint of lilac filled the air as we walked towards the playground.

After careful consideration, we invited Mary to join us in our meeting with the Driver. We really had no idea how we would react at seeing him, given our mistrust and confusion over his not guilty plea. I worried most about Stann and how he would be affected. He had kept a tight rein on his anger these last few weeks. I feared that one look at the Driver would unleash a fury of emotions unknown even to him. I hoped that Mary's presence would lend us the support we needed. I felt badly that the Driver and his wife had not been made aware of her presence. I did not want them to think we had stacked our side, I just had no way to contact them.

As we approached the playground, I was relieved to see that it was deserted. Claiming a table nearby, I suggested we sit as if we were conversing. I did not want to appear like watch dogs ready to attack an unsuspecting passerby. Taking my place, I looked up and down the familiar parkway dividing the two subdivisions. A row of backyards enclosed by cedar plank and chain link fences lined the green way several blocks long. Gray colored boulders dotted the blanket of grass shaded by young aspen and tall evergreen trees. The wooden jungle gym, still deserted, showed signs of wear and tear after years of constant play. Through the tear-streaked window of the past, the laughing faces of my children appeared as they dashed about the playground....

While Amber raced to the top of the old Ronald McDonald slide, Kevin pushed at her heels. "He's coming! Hurry Amber," he giggled. Hunched over, Stann lumbered across the sandy pit growling like a hungry bear. Glancing over her shoulder, Amber screamed in delight, as her blonde ponytail flipped behind her. Safely inside the metal enclosure serving as their hide out, they huddled together whispering in anticipation. Kevin's sandy colored hair soon emerged from the opening. His dark eyes twinkled with glee as he searched the gym for Stann. Unaware that Daddy Bear was waiting at the bottom of the slide, he reported to Amber that all was well.....

With trembling fingertips, I massaged the center of my chest to ease the pulsing anxiety. A lonely tear rolled down from the corner of my eye as the memory faded and the deserted playground reappeared. Rocking slowly, I wondered if we would ever play again.

186

There was nothing left to discuss as we sat there that day. Every possible scenario had been examined and considered. Nonetheless, our nervous chitchat continued in spurts as we faced the street, instead of one another. Our conversation halted as a red car slowly approached, parking at the curb. My heart dropped to the pit of my stomach.

Rising from my seat, my knees buckled as if the earth had moved beneath me. Stann stepped away from the weathered picnic table, planting his feet to steady himself. Both hands hung at his sides, his fingers stretching wide then closing in an airtight fist. Silenced by his clenched jaw and sealed lips, his blue eyes narrowed. It was impossible to reach my husband across the deep crevice of grief.

We met them halfway at the sidewalk, as if we were designated hosts for a tour. Seeming hesitant, they walked hand in hand from their car. I was immediately struck by the Driver's average height and slight build. He seemed much smaller than I remembered.

The introductions were brief and awkward, but a necessary protocol where confusion and mistrust reigned on both sides. Mustering all her strength to facilitate our foursome, Mary suggested we move to the picnic table. Leading us past the playground, her petite frame grew taller as she assumed her professional role. Once seated, Mary explained to the Driver and his wife that we had requested her presence at the meeting as our counselor, and as a mediator. In her compassionate way, she declared her support of all of our efforts to move toward an understanding of the accident as well as each other. Defining her role further, she offered her assistance to each of us.

While Mary talked, my gaze rested on the couple seated across from Stann and me. Too afraid to really look at the Driver, I focused on his wife instead. Blonde and fair-skinned, wearing large glasses, she might have been about thirty-years-old. I really did not pay much attention to what she looked like or what she was wearing. I was more curious at how normal and real they both seemed to be. A part of me felt relieved that they might be as ordinary as Stann and me.

Feeling bolder, I searched for signs that would identify him as the man I saw that cold January day. The scraggly brown beard was gone making him appear much younger than I remembered. I recalled the heavy denim jacket that made his shoulders seem much broader. Today, dressed in jeans and a plaid shirt, his slender build seemed to shrink each time he adjusted his seating.

By chance, our eyes met briefly, in painful recognition. The memory of that day stabbed at my heart and I could not hold my stare. Looking away, his mournful blue eyes filled with tears as he hid behind the wire-rimmed glasses.

They sat close together, their arms entwined, as she held his hands in hers. Strangely, I was impressed by their intimacy, and her open support

187

of him. While he made several attempts to speak, she leaned closer, gently stroking his arm. Finally, gathering enough courage he said, "I'm sure you want to know what happened that day." His eyes lowered, darting across the splintered table top, but never looking up.

I scooted closer to Stann, slipping my arm through his. His elbows locked close to his side anchoring all his emotions in place. I held on tight hoping to stop my body from shaking me right off the bench. We had waited so long for this moment, guarding ourselves from what we might not really want to hear. There was no going back. We listened quietly while the Driver began to tell his story.

Traveling from out of state, on a job related trip, he had been driving a company truck to transport heavy equipment. *I pictured the red and silver truck parked in the driveway, exhaust fumes billowing from behind. Attached to the bed of the truck was a white shell constructed of wood. It stood a foot above the cab and hung over the sides.*

He explained that on his way to the delivery, he wanted to stop in Montrose to visit his sister. She had delivered her first baby earlier that day. The Driver spoke of the excitement of sharing the news with his in-laws, our neighbors, as he headed down our street to their home. *My thoughts shifted to the day after the accident when we had learned about this baby. I was shocked that these two events were allowed to happen on the same day. I felt a deep sense of sorrow that this child's birth would always be equated with the loss of another child's life.*

He remembered parking the truck in the driveway and bounding the steps of the porch to the front door. He recalled standing there for a time ringing the bell. When no one answered, he walked around to the back yard to see if anyone was home....*just as Kevin was leaving his own home to ride his bike down the sidewalk towards the neighbor's driveway.*

From then on, he struggled to maintain control as the anguish rose in his voice. Scant details of his actions hung in the air for confirmation. "When I realized that no one was home I got back in the truck....and then," breaking down he motioned to me. "I saw.....you." He placed the palm of his hands upon his head trying to rub away the memory of our encounter. "I didn't know where to go," he cried.

Trembling, I reminded him, "I told you to go in my house and call for help." My voice sounded weak not at all like the command I had given that day.

Facing me again he nodded in agreement. "But I didn't know you didn't have 911 here. I couldn't get through," he lamented, pleading for us to understand.

Our tear-filled eyes stared expectantly at the Driver as we tried to envision his story. Hanging on to every word we waited to hear the most significant piece that might complete the puzzle. "I didn't see him until I was on the street." he protested. *My impatience grew, "Please tell me how*

it was that you couldn't see him?" I screamed from deep inside myself.
He claimed he looked before he backed out to the street. I countered with
tears, "You didn't look enough."

Burdened with remorse, he began to talk in circles doubting the worth of his existence. He wished he could change things and take away our pain. We assured him that we believed he did not intend to hurt our son. The fact remained that Kevin was killed when the truck the Driver was operating ran over him. We needed to hear an acceptance of responsibility. Drowning in his emotions, his wife became defensive protecting her husband from speaking his own truth. Each time he seemed on the verge of acknowledging his responsibility at the wheel, she hushed his cries. "We don't know God's will," she pleaded with him. "We don't know why God made this happen."

Her words stung. I was shocked that her interpretation of God's will meant that it absolved him of his accountability. How could she blame God for her husband's actions? Suddenly appalled by her ignorance, I confronted her.

"I can't listen to this anymore. I cannot agree with what you're telling him to believe. This is not about God's will. GOD did not *make* this happen," I charged. "This is about cause and effect. It's about what we do to one another without thinking twice, how our actions will affect someone else's life. It's about taking responsibility for one's actions," I concluded. They both looked at me as if I had two heads, unsure as to which one had spoken. Perplexed they stared blankly, seeming unable to grasp what I had said. Even I could not believe what I heard myself say given everything that I knew.

All along, I had felt shackled by my desire to respond appropriately and without blame. In my passion, I had said more than I should have. The questions remained, swirling and spinning inside me like a tornado. *"I didn't hear you say that you could have looked twice before you backed out. I didn't hear you say that you even touched my son. I haven't heard you say you are sorry. Aren't you going to apologize? Do you know the hell we live with every single day because you didn't look?"* *"Damn the nightmare, damn the drawing, DAMN destiny. YOU could have stopped it! It was up to you then because I failed to heed the warning. Don't you see that I am responsible too? How can I share with you what I've learned, when we can't even agree on the definition of God's will?"*

Caught between the two worlds again, I could not admit that God's will had prevailed. The frenzied dialogue inside my head raged on until my weary eyes met his again and truth prevailed. We both knew he couldn't say any of those things for the truth was too shocking to hear, too painful to witness, too real to live.

A sudden calm descended on me as if I had reached the eye of the tornado. It was then that I heard the quiet voice of reason. "You cannot

189

expect him to admit to something he truly believes he is not capable of having done. As a decent man he cannot fathom himself taking a life." In that moment, I sensed his vulnerability. Moved by the gentle nudge of the Spirit, I knew I had to forgive him his humanness. I did not know how.

The four of us stood again at the sidewalk, the final crossroad of our trek together. We had reached an impasse going our separate ways to begin rebuilding our shattered lives. The awkwardness had returned as our emotion-filled group attempted a polite goodbye.

In that last moment together, our eyes connected one final time. I refused to look away for I might miss the confirmation I sought. The thick lenses of his wire-framed glasses magnified his damp blue eyes. Reflected in them I saw a man wracked by intense guilt and the heartache of responsibility. Surrendering to our fragile and vulnerable humanness, I stepped forward. Embracing him, I whispered, "I am so sorry that we both had to be a part of this." He stiffened, unable to respond.

Just as he was unable to voice his truth, I was unable to voice my forgiveness. It is only now that I realize there were no words adequate enough to speak of such things. We parted then, our paths destined to cross again.

25

Nothing Matters Anymore

Dream Journal: May 30, 1991

There are people in my backyard. I notice that the Neighbor is talking to my friends. I march over to her and demand that she leave my yard. She insists that she is so sad and sorry, but she doesn't look it. I tell her that it's too late after she had been mean by ignoring us. I chase her out of my yard as she is mumbling poor excuses for her behavior. Next, I meet the Driver's wife and I tell her to take the Neighbor away, and for the both of them to get out of my life. Screaming, I chase after them with a hammer, fully intending to hurt them. Suddenly, there is a framed wall like a partition, with no dry wall on it. I beat the hammer along the bottom board between the two by fours yelling with each hit, "Nothing matters anymore!"

    At Mary's suggestion, I began taking daily walks for fresh air and exercise. On occasion, several girlfriends volunteered to walk with me, lending an ear as I vented my confusion and frustration. When I walked alone though, I would hide under the portable cassette headphones clamped to my ears. I had discovered a tape with lyrics that seemed to express my pain. It was as if the artist had been walking in my shoes.

    With each walk, the tears would begin to flow as soon I left my driveway. Pounding the pavement along the parkway encouraged the anger to surface, propelling me across the street, and down the country road. Determined to complete the three-mile loop, my pace quickened and more rational thoughts would come with the release of emotion. When I neared home again, my stride would slow to a crawl as I approached the manhole cover marking the scene of the accident.

The world had suddenly become a nasty and dishonest place and I resented having to face it every morning. Thankful for the chance to be alone, I began to appreciate those solitary walks for they gave me an opportunity to process my thoughts and feelings freely. During these healing walks I came to value Stann's need for a physical workout. Just as I found fleeting moments of clarity, I realized Stann might be experiencing similar moments of rational thinking too. Desperate to hold on to these snippets of insight I would write what I could remember in my journal.

One day I headed out the door determined to walk as far as my legs would carry me. Steaming with anger and frustration, my body felt like it would explode if I stayed inside the house a minute longer. My thoughts raced along with me, as I stomped down the sidewalk.

We had just received the disappointing news from the District Attorney that the Driver still intended to plead not guilty to the charges of "careless driving resulting in death." According to the District Attorney, the Driver did not believe he had behaved carelessly. There were no witnesses. He could freely claim that he had sufficiently looked before backing carefully out of the driveway. The legal team representing him seemed to be stressing semantics, asking us to accept that this man had backed cautiously and carefully over our son and his brand new bike.

Up until this point, Stann and I both felt that we had responded fairly and compassionately to the Driver. Stann too had sensed that this man was struggling with his conscience. In one of our late night talks he had declared, "I can't put myself in his shoes and imagine what it would be like to take another life. I can hardly believe that I am standing in my own shoes experiencing the loss of my child." Just as we understood the burden we had to live with, we recognized the Driver could not live untouched as well. For this reason we never felt a jail term or excessive sentencing would be appropriate and we told him so the day of our meeting in the park.

All we wanted was an admission of responsibility. I cannot explain why that was so important to us, except to say that, we had lost all our trust in what we thought our world was about. And, because we held certain expectations of fairness and justice we thought an admission of responsibility was the right thing to do. Grant us that and we did not care if we ever heard from or about him again. We just wanted it to end.

For myself, I had become entrenched in my dreams and the spiritual concepts I was just beginning to understand. I was being asked to take a huge leap of faith to trust what I could not touch. I needed something concrete, something that told me *why* we had to live without our Kevin. Above all, regardless of whether he was negligent or not, human decency should prevail. Admitting one's responsibility and accepting whatever the consequences might be seemed the very least that he could do. If our situation was reversed, would not the Driver and his wife expect the same?

Stann and I became enraged at the way the system seemed to work against exposing the truth. There would never be any mention of responsibility or consequences connected to this act of "not looking." Pursuing justice was not about examining the facts, but pointing out the incongruity of the language. It became a debate over the literal meaning of the charge "careless driving resulting in death".

What was there to debate? A five-year-old was run over by a two-ton truck driven by a thirty-year-old man! Would this collision have occurred if the Driver had been more aware of his surroundings? Didn't awareness equate with being careful? Perhaps, the real debate was about experience and thoughtlessness. Who had more life experience and the greater responsibility in the end?

We were confused and disappointed that the law could be so loosely interpreted as to dismiss our son's right as a citizen and in the end the value of his life. Little by little our faith diminished as we witnessed first-hand the manipulation and exploitation of our justice system. Life became more complicated than ever now that we were involved in the legal world. Its hidden agendas and distorted representations of the truth sickened me.

The anniversary of my mother's death only added to the burden. It not only marked the six years since her passing, it signaled the coming of Kevin's sixth birthday. One more of the many first anniversaries colliding one after another, within in just two months.

Overwhelmed by the hopelessness of it all I wanted to run away as far as possible. Rounding the corner at the top of the hill I pressed on faster, my head throbbing like a bell clanging wildly in a summer storm. The only way to end the madness and be free of the legal charade was to suggest that the District Attorney to drop the charges. How could we do that to Kevin? Why should we have to give anything to them? Hadn't we lost enough? We were the victims, damn it. The truth was owed to us and the Driver had the power to give at least that much to us.

Half walking, half racing, I pushed through the din of noise in my head. Disheartened, I cried out, "Nothing matters anymore!"

"I can't do this any longer," I cried. "It hurts to be here. It hurts to be left behind.....it hurts to hurt. Please God, let me out," I begged, staggering off the path. Blinded by another storm of grief, I collapsed on the grass bordering the playground. Hugging my knees close, I buried my face but my arms were not big enough to embrace myself. In anguish I called out for my mother.

"Oh Mom, I haven't the strength to do this on my own. Do you know how I can do it? Tell me please? Something has gone wrong. The world is turning the truth against us....how could I have been so wrong about the Driver?" I asked weakly. Looking up I hoped to see her beside me. Instead I saw the empty picnic table that marked the place of our meeting with the Driver. Its presence cast a dark cloud over my memories of playing here with the children. Closing my eyes again, I doubted that I had ever been there before.

"God, is this all there is to your world? Is it only going to be about deception and manipulation from now on? We have screwed up this world of yours. Your gift to us is a mess. I'm frightened for Stann and Amber and me to stay here." I sobbed uncontrollably.

"Mom, what am I teaching Amber except fear? What are the depths of our pain and why must we feel it? Without it, would joy and happiness in this life be so hard to recognize?" I cried, desperately needing her wisdom.

"Please, Mom? Tell God that I need to know what He wants of me. Is there a purpose for me?" I pleaded through the tears, unaware that He had already sent me the guidance I sought in another dream.

Dream Journal: May 17, 1991
The shop is different. Things are unorganized and clients are standing in the way, waiting for their appointments. I am trying to leave, but people keep interrupting me asking to be seen. There's a phone call from Bella, Kevin's day care mom. She tells me Kevin is very sick and has had an asthma attack. This is his second one since he's spent the night with her two nights in a row. I am shocked. I can't believe I've been at the shop that long and that Stann forgot to pick him up. She said Kevin was upset that he was being left and we were working too much. I tell her that I am coming to get him. I am so upset and start to leave, but a woman gets right in my face and demands to be taken care of now. I try to accommodate her with someone else, but she is acting belligerent and pushy. I know I have to take care of her because it's my job but I have to get to Kevin. The dream ends before I can get out of there and pick him up.

It was devastating to remember the dream about leaving Kevin at daycare because I was trapped at work. I realized that Kevin represented the frightened little girl inside of me who needed to be taken care of, and it represented too, the grief that was left unresolved because there was no time to deal with it. It became clear that God was asking me to walk away from the chaos and confusion to heal myself.

I wanted out, but the critical voice that resided so deeply within me, kept screaming about my responsibilities. My dream journal chronicled the growing frustrations and pressures of trying to deal with my family, the legal system, and my job. I could no longer ignore these messages. When I dreamt I had scheduled three clients at the same time, I knew I could no longer ignore the messages.

In the dream, I was dashing back and forth between the three clients as I cut their hair. I used a clippers on each one, chopping their hair in different lengths and then left them sitting in my chair. I ran out of the shop covering my bare breasts so no one would see me. In the end, I returned, screaming inside with frustration and anger. I recognized then, just how vulnerable and exposed I felt in having to deal with my grief publicly.

I had spent many counseling hours with Mary lamenting my decision. I was fearful that no one, not even Stann would understand my need to leave. Finally, I had come to a clear decision via my dreams. Mary pointedly said, "Carla, this has been a long time coming. You have found the courage to stand up for your needs. Not Pati's business needs, not your career standards, and not the clients' expectations. By doing this, you are gaining a more realistic sense of control in your life." I appreciated Mary's validation and her acceptance that my decision was Spirit guided.

I finally found the courage to discuss the idea with Stann that I wanted to take a sabbatical from my job for the summer months. I shared my hope that the three months would give me the time I needed to return healthier and more focused. Stann and Amber would be on vacation from school and it would give us all an opportunity to reconnect. I should not have been surprised that he wholeheartedly supported my decision.

Wrapping up my final day at work, I carried out the last box of hairdressing supplies to my car. I dropped the box in the trunk of my Ford Tempo and slammed it shut. I breathed a deep sigh of relief as I slid behind the wheel and turned on the ignition. After months of trying to maintain the facade, I was finally walking away.

Little did I know that God's insistence to clear my appointment book meant more than getting myself healthy and focused. Distracted by the legal questions, my workload, and the daily trials of grief, I had paid little attention to my health. I attributed the fatigue, loss of appetite and mood swings to symptoms of depression. I was shocked when I read the results of my home pregnancy test. Positive. Nothing in our lives had been normal for so long now, that only the inconceivable seemed normal. Nothing had gone according to my plan, so why should I be surprised by this?

It was one of my first lessons about the difference between desire and intention. Since Kevin's death, Amber had begged us to have another baby. She could not comprehend that the nine-year difference in age would provide a sibling not a playmate. Stann and I explained to Amber that we would be willing to have another baby when we were stronger and healthier. Definitely, not now. I grieved her aloneness and the thought that if Stann and I died, Amber would be without any immediate family. I wanted to give her a sibling to connect with in her adulthood. In my heart, I knew that I would eventually have another baby, but my intent had to be clear and not based on my fears.

I was so afraid. And the truth was, my track record wasn't so impressive. I did not believe I had done such a great job in protecting her brother from harm. I obviously had some gene that allowed for a birth defect. And, I could hardly take care of myself, my daughter or my husband, let alone another baby.

I understand now that my desire was to fill the excruciating void in our lives. My barren womb had come to symbolize a dark place. I questioned its ability to bear life. While I yearned to escape the blackness of grief by leaving my body, my true intention was to live.

With this pregnancy, God in his wisdom had given me a purpose, something tangible and with meaning. He was giving me another opportunity to recreate my own life while serving as a vessel to birth another. This child, this colorful being of light from the waters of the universal womb would bring love and joy, wisdom and courage. This child would teach us how to love again, and with time, how to play again.

* * * * * * *

Ironically, the date of Kevin's birthday had fallen on a Sunday, the actual day of his birth. Five years seemed so little time to share a life. Kevin's birthday had passed by without him. There were no candles to blow out nor presents to open, only videotapes to play back. From now on, Kevin's birthday would mark the years of our growth without him. We had survived almost six months without him, going through the motions of living. At times during those six months, it felt like only six seconds since we touched each other. When we longed to hold Kevin close the separation felt more like sixty years.

We spent Kevin's birthday decorating the little blue spruce tree in the park at the intersection of our street. The miniature evergreen had been planted there in Kevin's memory by the school administrators, a gesture initiated by our dear friends Dave and Mary Ann. Unknown to them was the fact that they had chosen the very place where we had played together so many times.

The five foot high blue spruce stood alone at the top of the tiny hill facing our street. Nourished by the sun, its roots had taken hold, showing no signs of shock from being replanted. Surrounding the base were clusters of pink and purple petunias, their wide blooms opened and colorful.

Tenderly, we wrapped the silver birthday banner round and round its young branches. Stann stretched up to tie the pinwheel that Amber had chosen for the top of the tree. I handed the plastic milk jug of holy water to Amber and she began watering the thirsty roots. On our last visit to the mountain shrine I had collected the water. It seemed fitting to bless this tree with the water that flowed beneath the mountain soil that was now mixed with our son's ashes.

Stepping away from the tree I admired our work. The pinwheel spun slowly in the breeze as the wind caught its tips. The blue needle branches rustled a gentle birthday greeting. "What are birthdays like in heaven?" I heard Amber say. Fighting back tears, I shook my head unable to reassure her that he would be having cake and ice cream. I had decided that birthdays probably did not mean anything once we were out of the body. Maybe, they celebrate re-births in heaven, since the soul is returning home to its spiritual body. I was comforted by my own definition, but knew it was not what Amber needed to hear.

I walked around the tree to honor it from all directions. Coming back to the front I faced east looking down our street. The tree stood in a direct line to the scene of the accident. I felt a sudden wave of nausea and fatigue. I turned my back choosing to fill my teary view with the precious little tree. The bittersweet feelings for the new baby inside me, filled my senses like the sickening smell of lilacs. I stepped toward Stann needing the comfort of his arms around me. We pulled Amber into our embrace, holding her tightly between us. I had three children now, one beside me, one lost to me, and one inside of me. "Please God", I begged, "tell me how to do this."

The week began with Kevin's birthday and ended with mine. I was not looking forward to being thirty-four or pregnant. Morning sickness had taken over my days and by evening I was ready for bed by eight p.m. Unfortunately our house was like an oven simmering in the heat as the still, hot air, added to my misery. I would sit in front of the oscillating fan or on the patio waiting until the house cooled off enough to sleep.

One evening in the middle of the week, I plopped down at the end of the couch like a baked potato. Pointing the channel changer at the television, I searched for a program to pass the time until I could go to bed. Stann perused the sports page at the other end of the couch while Amber played in her room. Oblivious to the programs, I clicked by the stations one by one and stopped at a commercial advertising a made for television movie.

Ironically, the movie was about the death of a child. Lured by the opening scenes implying the child's sudden death and her grieving parents desire to learn the truth, I put down the remote control. I hoped the movie would speak to my heart and give me something to relate to. Instead, I was disappointed when it turned out to be one of those "ghost comes back from the dead to avenge its death" movies. The special effects were interesting though. The girl appeared to her mother as bright spotlight and led her to the clues.

Stann had finished his paper and declined to stay and watch the movie with me. He returned about twenty minutes later, curious that I was still watching it.

"How's that movie of yours?" he interrupted half-sitting on the low back of the couch.

"Well, it's not what I thought it would be. The child turns out to be a ghost that gives the mother clues to find her murderer," I said, disgusted. I was glad he had distracted me and I clicked the off switch of the remote control.

"I just couldn't stand to watch it," he admitted.

"It was so unrealistic, Stann. Nothing like what I've experienced. And besides," I continued sarcastically, "I'm not impressed with their version of life after death." Without further discussion, we retired for the evening.

A cool breeze carried the smell of an impending summer storm, clearing the house with a breath of fresh air. In the distance, the night sky grumbled. The windows were opened wide and the drawn mini-blinds blocked the annoying light from the street lamp. Exhausted, I immediately fell asleep.

Startled by a crash above my head, I bolted up. Awakened from a deep sleep, I crunched up my nose, rubbing it hard to rouse myself. Stann had stirred slightly mumbling for me to shut the window. Shadows flickered around the room as the blinds banged against the screen. I noticed a ray of light shining to my left above the mirror on my dresser.

Having regained my bearings, I realized the wind had lifted the blinds allowing the street lamp to shine on the bedroom wall. I grabbed the blinds and closed the window halfway. I slipped back under the sheet and dozed off. A short time later, another forceful gust and the intruding light awakened me again. This time, I knelt under the window and lifted the blind. Ambushed by a bright light shining in my eyes, I abruptly dropped the blinds to the windowsill. Still groggy from the disruption, I raised a slot or two and peered through.

The street lamp illuminated the front yard and out into the street like a Hollywood movie set. It was as if the main scene had been highlighted against the dark night while the rest of the neighborhood stood asleep in the shadows. Hanging low above the houses, the moon cast an eerie bluish glow intensifying the surreal scene.

A gust of wind caught the blind again bringing me back to real time. Too tired to ponder the exact arrival of the coming storm, I closed the window a few more inches. Lying down for the third time, I dozed again for a few minutes only to be roused again by the wind and another flash of light. I sat up with one thought in mind, "Kevin wants me to sleep in his room."

I surrendered to my instincts. Carrying my pillow I went immediately to Kevin's room. The wind had also blown these blinds askew, leaving the slats in disarray. I closed them erasing the stripes of light stenciled upon the wall. Folding down the Mickey Mouse covers, I climbed in to Kevin's bed.

I had been here so many times before in the middle of the day. Overcome with despair, I would stare blankly at the four walls while entire afternoons would pass me by. Kevin's room remained intact, undisturbed by grieving visitors. Obscured by the darkness, his toys sat dormant on the dusty shelves, shirts and socks stuffed in the dresser drawers, the closet door closed to more memories.

I lay there praying hard, "I'm ready to come to you Kevin, I won't be afraid." The wind blew back the blinds, revealing the light. I knew then that I was ready too. Soon, I fell into a deep sleep....

I sat up straight, peering through the shadows to the end of Kevin's bed. I was in Kevin's room and everything was as it should be, seeming real and un-dreamlike. Without effort, I seemed to move forward until I was at the end of the bed. My eyes were clear and focused on a pinpoint of light blinking softly in the air before me. Multi-colored lights of the same size flickered around it, growing stronger as they blinked in harmony. I was mesmerized by the synchronistic display of light that reminded me of fireworks. Stann appeared beside me, "What's wrong?" he asked. Without looking away I smiled and calmly said, "Kevin is here. Look at the lights." I pointed in front of me as he turned to look.

Stann stood with me at the foot of the bed. I did not take my eyes away from the blinking lights. Suddenly, I was aware that I was dreaming. In that lucid moment Kevin's face appeared life size before me, framed by the multi-hued blinking lights. I was so excited to see him and delighted that he looked like himself. At once I noticed that he was not alone. A secondary image flashed showing a high wall to the left and a road behind him where shadowed figures stood together. There were others with him- their pulsating points of energy supporting his visit.

I was so overwhelmed by the happiness reflected on his face that I did not hear what he was saying to me. "Kevin, I love you!" I responded, my heart warmed by our reunion. Next, I became aware of moving across the room with him, our eyes still connected.

"Mommy, Please don't be sad," he said with concern, bestowing me with more love.

Touched by his compassion I cried, "Mommies are sad when their babies are gone." Moving closer, his eyes told me that he understood the pain and heartache of his absence. I felt the tickle of his hair brush against my face as he hugged me tightly. Then, in whispered tones I sang to my baby, swaying back and forth in rhythm. Stann appeared again, joining us in the middle of the room.

I woke up in Kevin's bed curled up on my right side, with my hands tucked under my chin. I stared wide-eyed and straight ahead. A moment ago I was standing right there in front of the dresser. "We were *together*," I reassured myself. "Kevin came to me in his room," I marveled as tears spilled over on the pillow. A damp chill filled the room as the wind carried raindrops to the window pane. I pushed the window closed above me. Pulling the covers to my neck, I lay down again in the same position as I had awakened. A sense of peace swept over me lulling me back to sleep.

26
Another Chance

Dream Journal: July 24, 1991

Amber, Stann and I visit Kyle at his home. He is not ready, so we visit with his father. Impatient, I go to Kyle's room and find him sitting on the top bunk getting dressed. Suddenly, I see that Kevin is there with him. He has been there all along playing with Kyle while we waited . I am so happy. I turn to look at Amber and Stann and they are happy too. I know at once that this is my chance to hug and touch him. As I realize that I am dreaming, Kevin says, "Mommy, I love you!" I reach out my hand to touch him. My hand is shaking, but I know that I must concentrate or I will lose my chance. I touch his face with my hand and kiss his sweet cheeks. Holding him close to me I say, "I love you, Kevin" Another chance. Yes.

The August sun dipped below the blue-green mountain peaks, extinguishing its blazing rays of fire. The night brought a short reprieve until the oppressive ball of heat returned at dawn. The watering hose slithered through the lawn like a snake as I pulled it across the sidewalk. Cranking the handle of the water spout shut, I stacked the slippery coils against the house. The remaining water trickled from the hose over my bare feet onto the sizzling cement.

I sat down on the porch step, while Amber rode her bike back and forth in front of the house. With Stann at football practice for the evening, Amber and I had spent a quiet dinner together. Afterward she had asked me to come outside with her while she rode her bike. Knowing that she was frightened and needed my support I reluctantly consented. It was nerve wracking to watch her. Every time a car turned the corner, my radar engaged and I would look to make sure she was out the way. Watering the flowers was my ploy to place me closer to the street, just in case.

I waved to Amber as she rode past me to meet her new friends next door. My presence seemed to reassure her as she steered into the Neighbor's driveway. I cringed at the sight of the tires circling the manhole cover where her brother had died. In late spring, the Neighbors had sold their house to a family with children close to Amber's age. We were relieved when they moved away and we were grateful to have more compassionate neighbors. The children became fast friends spending most of their summer vacation playing between the two houses.

Stann and I were amazed at Amber's courage to face the scene of the accident every time she visited them. We worried that the constant exposure would be hard on her, dredging up painful memories. Her need to play and connect with her peers was much stronger though, and proved to be a powerful component in her healing process. It was no coincidence that God had led her there with the promise of companionship and acceptance.

In the beginning we misunderstood Amber's need to play as a denial of what was happening around her. We worried when she did not cry or express herself about things we thought she should be upset about. While she romped and played with her friends, we discovered it was not denial. It was, instead, a keen sense of knowing when she needed to grieve.

In her counseling sessions with Mary, the issues around her grief became more defined. Stann and I were devastated to learn that she had been carrying feelings of guilt and responsibility over Kevin's death. She secretly grieved their last morning together because she had argued with him about making his bed. She too, shouldered the responsibility of being unable to save him. Amber believed that if she had been home, instead of at gymnastics, she would have been riding bikes with him.

I began to see similar signs of grief in all the children affected by the loss of their friend Kevin. Kyle, Michael, Stann's nephews, Kevin's classmates, and the many children who had spent hours playing at our house, were all struggling. They exhibited many of the same symptoms of grief that we did. Notably, some of them were frightened to sleep alone or were apprehensive about riding their own bikes as freely as they had before. At times, like Amber, they were overwhelmed by Kevin's absence in their play or uncomfortable with their parents mournful faces and confusing discussions about what was happening with the Bloweys.

Whether in our home or at school, they instinctively banded together for moments of relief in their playtime. I envied their ability to grieve in the moment and move on to the next with joy and laughter. In those moments I sensed Kevin's presence among the children, whispering in their ear to remember to play. I hoped they could hear him for the rest of their lives.

I would often dream of the children playing together, Kevin always right beside them. In the dreams, I seemed to be the only one aware that Kevin should be dead. The children seemed not to notice though as they carried on joyfully with him. I was particularly comforted by the dream of visiting Kyle and finding Kevin playing there with him. I believe God was assuring me that Kevin was with all the children as they grieved his loss. And, recently, in yet another shocking discovery, Kevin had given Amber a sign that he understood the loneliness she would endure.

One evening, Amber and I began our nightly bed time ritual for her. She was notorious for putting off going to bed, and now the delays were more exaggerated. I couldn't be upset though. I did not want to lay in the dark battling shadows of the past either. So, we would set the cassette player with a soothing instrumental piece and I would read a story to her.

That night Amber decided on a chapter book that Grandma had given her last Christmas. She pulled it from the book shelf and handing it to me said, "It's the book that Kevin saved for me." Settling under the covers, she waited for me to begin.

I looked at the book in astonishment. Its pages were wrinkled dry from when I had dropped it in the snow at Grandma's house on Christmas night. I had placed it in the door pocket and forgot about it, until Kevin had found it on the day he died. Remembering aloud, I repeated the story to Amber. I could see Kevin's face so clearly that day when, turning to me in the car he said, "This is Amber's book. She needs this book, Mom. I'll bring it in for her." He was so serious and focused. What was so special about this book?

Engulfed among the withered pages we read well past her bedtime that night. Written over thirty years ago, the story told of a young Indian girl and her little brother who were accidentally left behind as the white men on a ship took their tribe away. Two days later, the wild dogs killed her little brother and she was left alone on the island for many years before she was rescued. It is a powerful tale of her physical and emotional survival against the odds of nature and the inner strength that sustains her soul.

Was it any coincidence that Kevin had insisted on making sure that Amber had this particular book in her possession for a time when she would need its haunting message most?

Later that summer, Amber and I were busy cleaning out her room and packing toys in preparation for our move. With the move to a new house, Stann and I feared another loss for Amber over leaving her old neighborhood friends. We admitted to her that we felt the same way. Even though we were only moving five blocks to the adjacent neighborhood it seemed a million miles away from our real home, our real life.

I had encouraged her to sort through her things and decide what she wanted to take to the new house. Sitting among the boxes and trash bags, she reminisced about Kevin as she came across toys and stuffed animals. Laughing and crying seemed to come naturally to both of us that day.

I stretched my legs from their crossed position to take the pressure off my abdomen. My body was changing faster than I could come to terms with the reality of my pregnancy. It seemed my belly popped out overnight and I had grown out of my clothes by the first trimester. This not only amused Amber, but gave all of us proof that I was indeed pregnant.

We had kept the news to ourselves, except to share it with a few friends. It seemed the whole town knew everything about us, our private life had become so public. We needed time to adjust to this turn of events before we told anyone else. Stann and I had mixed feelings of joy and fear surrounding this child's birth. We remembered the joy of holding our two precious babies and wondering who they would become. Sadness had become a way of life for us and bringing a baby into that chaos was unthinkable.

I had decided not to return to my hairdressing job at the end of the summer. At only three months pregnant my body had slowed down considerably as the baby drew its nourishment from me. I knew I had to concentrate on my emotional, physical and spiritual health to provide a positive environment for this baby. The roller coaster of grief had jerked my whole being through twists and turns that left me reeling. Disoriented and nauseous, I lacked the stamina to stand on my feet for a ten hour work day, and endure the public scrutiny of my life.

Carefully Amber packed away her special Cabbage Patch dolls for the new baby. In her quiet way, she began to talk about the baby. She asked me where I thought babies really came from.

Hoping to skip over the facts of life I shrugged my shoulders and said, "From heaven of course, that's where we all come from." She shook her head in agreement while I went on. "I think that babies remember God more than adults do, because it hasn't been that long since they were with Him. As we grow older we seem to forget what it is like to be with Him. So, we spend the rest of our lives trying to remember. Sounds confusing, huh?" I knew I lost her when she crunched up her nose. My explanation was a bit too wordy for a nine-year-old. I tried another approach.

"You know what I believe Amber? I believe that since babies come from heaven, and Kevin is in heaven, the new baby and Kevin already know each other….."

"Oh yes, and they are talking to each other," Amber chimed in. "Kevin is probably telling the baby all about us: You are going to have a *great* big sister and two parents who love you," she laughed out loud, packing another doll away. I threw my head back and laughed too, wondering just what that rascal would say about us. I really did believe it. This baby would be no more a stranger to us than Amber and Kevin.

My dream about the baby rising from the waters of life meant more than I had dared to interpret. The fire of the Holy Spirit warmed my soul and lighted my way. But, deep down I did not feel worthy of being given another gift. I shuddered to think what was in store for us. All of my children had been born during the most crucial periods in my life. What would this colorful light-filled being teach us? How much would this child remember about God?

* * * * * * *

I shoved the stack of empty moving boxes from the middle of the kitchen floor against the stairway wall. Plopping my weary body onto the floor in their place, I leaned back against the refrigerator. Cabinet doors were open, their contents half emptied, utensils and cookware were strewn across the counters. Crumpled newspapers and plastic bubble wrap lay in a pile near the stove. There had been a hundred interruptions this morning and I had accomplished nothing except to alienate Amber and Stann from my presence.

Feeling crabby and uncomfortable, I had taken out my frustrations on the both of them. Poor Amber took the brunt of it when I yelled at her for something she didn't even know she was supposed to do. Realizing I had overreacted, I blamed my raging hormones for the outburst and I apologized to both of them. In defense they had wisely left the house for the remainder of the afternoon leaving me to my own miseries. As I sat alone in the midst of my mess, I broke down and cried out, "I don't want to do this. I don't want to move without my Kevin."

As was often the case during my grief journey I had failed to recognize that my edginess was attributed to more than just an imbalance in my hormones. I was upset because I was being forced to do something I did not want to do. My life was once again, out of my control. Angry, I lashed out at the Driver blaming him for the cause of my resentment. In a scathing tirade of accusations, I screamed out, "It's because of you, that I don't have my son. It's *your* fault that I have to leave my home without my Kevin. It is not fair that you deny your responsibility. It's not fair that we have to go through this trial."

The unleashed contempt I felt for him stoked the burning coals of rage inside of me. A few days before, the District Attorney had informed us that the Driver had rejected an offer to plead no contest with a deferred judgment. The terms were simple; no other traffic offenses for one year, a few hours of community service, and, at our suggestion, a donation to the handicapped children's fund in our school district. The Driver's rejection of what we considered reasonable terms was insulting. Had he changed so much since our meeting? Or was it all an act to get us to drop the charges? Had I deceived myself into thinking that I had really experienced that moment of truth with him?

The next step was a trial, and I would be called as a witness. But, a witness to what? I only knew that Kevin died in my arms without the chance to tell me what had happened to him or why he was leaving me. The volley between the prosecution and the defense had become a ridiculous debate over the words "careless" or "not careless". The loss of Kevin's life had faded into the background. He had become another name in a long list of victims who were identified only by their case number. Who would speak up for Kevin? It could only be me.

Standing up I kicked the empty boxes aside, repulsed by the reality they represented. Six years ago I had moved into this house pregnant with Kevin. Now, I was leaving this house, pregnant again, without him. Did anybody else think this was as bizarre as I thought it was? My mind could not comprehend it and my heart did not want to feel it.

Raking my fingers through my unruly bangs, I grabbed my hair as if to rip the thoughts from my scalp. The throbbing only grew louder pounding harder against the back of my eyes. I hated being trapped inside myself, forced to listen to the ranting of the mad woman. Why couldn't I just let it all go and forget about the Driver and the trial? Beaten again, I wandered aimlessly around the house until I finally stopped at Kevin's door. I stepped in. My gaze fell upon the cinder block shelves stacked with toys, books and preschool papers.

"Oh Kevin," I sobbed, "What do you want me to do with your things, honey? I don't want to pack your toys away. There will be no place we can come and feel close to you."

I kneeled down in front of the shelves with my arms crossed defiantly, determined not to move anything out of place. Red plastic baskets filled with art supplies, Happy Meal toys, and miniature cars, lined the bottom shelf. Trucks were parked in a makeshift garage below. The top shelf displayed a race car dashboard, a box of Lincoln logs, Legos, and a pile of preschool papers. I leaned in blowing away the thick layer of dust preserving their place in time. Very little had changed in Kevin's room, even after eight months.

I sighed in defeat, as flashbacks of Kevin played before me. There he lay, fast asleep in his crib tucked beneath the blue and white rocking horse quilt that Grandma Blowey had stitched. Yawning, he stretched wide, turning his head to face the wall. His tiny legs wrapped in plaster below the knee, poked out from the blanket. Oh dear God, how could I pack these memories away?

The flood of grief pushed forth a giant wave of tears. Compelled to touch something of Kevin's, I reached for the closest thing at hand, a pile of preschool papers. One by one I sifted through the drawings of Ninja Turtles, treasure maps and airplanes. My fingers gently pinched the pages as if they were vintage photographs. As I placed them in piles before me, I came across a familiar sheet of yellow legal paper. My heart jumped in recognition of the pencil drawing.

It was a drawing from last summer. Kevin and I had retreated to the living room away from the scorching July heat. We lay on our bellies stretched out on the beige carpet in front of the big box fan. The long flat blades pushed the still hot air around the room offering little relief. I ripped off a couple sheets of the yellow note pad and gave it to Kevin. He began drawing while I began writing a letter. Sometime later I looked over to see him propped up on his elbows studying the paper.

"What did you draw Kevin?" I asked, as I scooted over beside him.

"It's a picture of me." he said, handing it to me. I grinned at the self-portrait. A happy Kevin with outstretched arms beneath what looked like a wing shaped form.

Pointing to the figure at the bottom half of the page, he said, "This is me. I have these suitcases. I'm going in an airplane by myself." With his index finger he dotted the printed numbers going down the left hand column that he had circled. "Those people are waiting for me to get on."

"You're very grown up to be going on a plane by yourself," I said smiling. His sun-kissed face lit up as I turned the page over and began writing what he had just told me. My stint as a preschool teacher several years ago taught me to immediately record the children's stories about their drawings. They seemed to enjoy hearing their words read back to them later. I had accumulated more than enough samples of their drawings always tossing them into a keepsake box for later.

"Kevin," I prodded, "is there anything else you want me to write?" I knew from experience he had said all he wanted to but I always gave him a chance just in case there might be more. Still propped up on his elbows, he seemed reflective as he examined his art work. Taking the pen from my hand, Kevin added two circles, drawing them inside the eyes on his face. "There it's finished," he said approvingly as he surveyed it one last time. "You can keep it."

"Thanks, Boo Boo," I said amused.

I hugged him, and then, he left to play with Amber. I looked at the drawing again. The inked circles stood out from the rest of the pencil drawing, making the eyes appear brighter. I wondered if he had intended the circles to be glasses or pupils. While he talked, I remembered thinking how grown up he seemed about going on the airplane alone. Considering that Stann would be flying alone to California for his brother's wedding next month, I didn't think it too unusual that he would emulate his hero.

However, the circled numbers, those people who were waiting for him, intrigued me. Oddly he never mentioned Amber, Stann, myself or anyone we knew. Giving it no further thought, I kept the drawing and put it in the growing pile of treasured art work.

How long had this pile of papers been stacked on the toy shelf? My housekeeping skills were worse than I thought. Turning the page over I looked for the date: "July 3,1990". My stomach flip-flopped with a wave of nausea. I remembered then, that it had been drawn just ten days after his fifth birthday. The familiar chord of knowing struck loudly. *Kevin's drawing conveyed a Truth that he had known almost seven months before his death.* While Kevin lay beside me on the floor that day, he had been having a conversation with God.

Much wiser than his five years, Kevin had been consciously communicating with God in the language of the Spirit. Arms stretched wide, his heart open, Kevin had accepted God's invitation for his spiritual growth and ascension. This holy message had been filtered through his ego as he struggled to convert it into human terms. Kevin had illustrated his understanding of their agreement by drawing familiar symbols from his personal experiences. Going on an airplane alone was the best example he could come up with.

Staring at the drawing, I sat cross legged on the floor with the rest of Kevin's precious papers spread around me like a blanket. There were so many levels of information contained in this one drawing. In the coming months I would only begin to scratch the surface as I sought to interpret its message. I was in awe of the impact this must have had on my little boy. My wonder soon turned to sorrow as more details came into focus. Details that only I would recognize. Kevin had also forecast his own injuries.

First, I saw the eerie image of Kevin's crushed head superimposed on the yellow paper. To an outsider, it would appear as if his limited drawing skills had produced a lopsided head with goofy eyes and missing hair. But, *I saw* the misshapen head of my son, the head that I had cradled in my arms. It had been flattened on the right side by a truck tire. His right eye had been pushed in downward to his cheek bone, leaving the left eye wide open. The drawing showed his head separated from his body. I remembered my hands holding his broken and limp neck as I screamed for help. With symbolic sight I now saw that Kevin had existed in both worlds.

Kevin had been dreaming too. Consciously stepping into the spiritual world long enough to receive information and support from His Father, he would then translate it to paper. That yellow piece of paper, taken from a legal pad, symbolically represented a Holy agreement. Kevin knew that it would be safe in my hands, until the appropriate time came to reveal its message.

Now as we faced the trial, another point of supposed closure on our grief journey, this drawing claimed to be the first page of his journey home. Were there more? My instincts told me to look again. I dug deeper into the stack of artwork like a puppy looking for his favorite bone. I did not know what I was looking for but as I viewed each drawing, I felt an excitement that I had not experienced in a long while. At that moment they were separate pieces of artwork seemingly unconnected. Within weeks they would become the tangible proof God knew that I longed to see and to touch. If only I would pay attention.

* * * * * * *

Simmering hot days almost always gave way to cooler evenings in Colorado. Seeking relief from the stuffy house, I stood in the front doorway wishing for a breeze. I peered through the screen looking up to the mid-evening sky. A full moon glowed brightly, hanging low like a big white ball just above the street lamp. The light shone through the transparent clouds like a delicate veil draped over the moon. It reminded me of a night last autumn when the kids and I had run out to the front yard to see the full moon. They thought it looked like a giant beach ball. I was taken by its closeness, as if I could reach out and touch its face.

I stepped out to the lawn while the moon slipped in and out of the clouds, growing brighter as it rose higher into the blackness. Coming into view again, I noticed several bright rings around the perimeter pulsing like a halo. Mesmerized by the radiant aura, I walked down the sidewalk to the edge of the Neighbors' driveway. Moonlight distorted in the glow of the street lamp cast an eerie bluish glow onto the path.

I had paced this area so many times searching for pieces of my memory. I wanted so desperately to know those last moments of Kevin's life. Scrutinizing the Neighbors' driveway I wondered again if he had seen the truck backing out as he rode behind it? Why in the world did he take this path instead of cruising down to the corner like he had always done before?

Turning away from the driveway I stepped out three feet into the street. The buzzing street lamp vibrated in the cool air, like a swarm of bees inside a hive. I shivered at the sight of the manhole cover forever stained with Kevin's blood. My shoulders tightened as I recalled the knit cap soaked with blood, covering Kevin's crushed head. When I had lifted him from the ground, the melted snow beneath revealed a few squares of the manhole cover. It seemed like such an odd thing to remember.

As the moonlight filled the shadows around me, that familiar shift in my senses signaled me to pay attention. Suddenly, as if seeing the manhole cover for the first time, I noticed a deep crack circling the cover about five inches out from the perimeter. My gaze widened and I saw two more cracks stretching straight down from the bottom of the circle, and two more extending from either side of the circle. On a closer look, the cracks were actually black tar lines where the pavement had been repaired. It seemed to define the manhole cover. I had examined this spot a million times and yet tonight something was different. I had seen this design before. But where?

Confused, yet curious, I walked slowly across the damp grass, speculating on the origin of that simple pattern. By the time I reached the porch I knew where it had come from. I went directly to the stack of art papers in Kevin's room. Lying undisturbed on top of the pile was the airplane drawing. Kevin's self-portrait stared at me from the middle of the page; a circle for his head, two lines for legs stretching straight down from below the circle, and two more lines for arms, extending from either side.

Clutching the yellow paper, I ran out of the house and back to the street. The moon had concealed itself behind yet another curtain leaving the street lamp to illuminate the shadows of doubt. Catching my breath, I stopped beneath the hazy light and held the drawing at arm's length. Kevin's self-portrait matched the tar design around the manhole cover.

"Carla, what's wrong? What are you doing out here?" I heard Stann call out to me as he sprinted across the lawn. Slowing down he stepped off the curb to join me in the light. Sliding my purple frame glasses on top of my head, I stared wide-eyed at him, unable to speak. Touching my shoulder with his fingertips he nudged me gently to respond.

"Look at Kevin's drawing," I whispered, handing it to him. With his eyes fixed on me, he reached for the paper. I took a step backward.

"It's the one you just found," he noted with a quick glimpse. His face grew long and serious as if to brace himself for another revelation. He had been trying so hard to understand my intuitive world. Since I had found this drawing, Stann had become more open to the idea that Kevin knew he was leaving us. It was hard even for him to deny Kevin's own words.

"Stann," I hesitated. "I think the drawing is telling us something more. I have looked at this spot a million times and never noticed these black tar lines." Straining to see with my eyes, he followed my index finger as I traced the head, two arms, and two legs in the air.

"Are you saying he knew it would happen here?" he said in disbelief.

"Yes, and I can't explain my sense of this," I said exasperated. "But when I noticed the tar design, I knew I had seen it before. I had seen it in the drawing. I don't think it's any coincidence that they match."

Rubbing his forehead Stann mulled over this discovery. He agreed that Kevin's self-portrait held a striking similarity to the tar design. Standing beside him under the lamplight I explained that I also saw Kevin's disfigured, broken face in the misshapen head of the drawing.

"I can't expect you to believe me, because you don't know what Kevin looked like when I found him that day. It is so strange Stann. I am the one that had the Nightmare, I am the one that found him, and I am the one uncovering these drawings. Why?"

Looking away, I waved my arm over the street, my voice grew weary. "Maybe, that's why I've been so drawn to this place. Maybe, he's been calling me back here so I would make the connection to this drawing."

Stann took me in his arms and drew me close. "I don't know why this is happening to us. No one will believe it."

"I don't care about what other people believe. I know that Kevin was trying to tell us something important." I sobbed, laying my head upon his chest.

When I looked at the scene of the accident, I saw death. It was as real to me as anything I had ever experienced. I had touched it. But my son saw something there that I could not. Kevin saw beyond his death, and he had reached out to embrace it.

I broke away and kneeled in front of the manhole cover. I braced myself against the ground to combat a sudden wave of fatigue. I had grown tired of the mental gymnastics required to process these spiritual concepts. Smoothing my hand over the raised metal squares I prayed for the courage to face whatever was ahead.

A sliver of moonlight peeked out from behind a heavy cloud, a subtle reminder of its ominous presence. As I rose to my feet a cool breeze passed lightly across my shoulders. Inching backward to the curb I saw that the arms and legs had become less distinct bringing the metal lid into focus. In the obscure light it stared back at me like the encircled eyes of Kevin's self-portrait.

213

27
Forgotten Clues

Dream Journal: October 1, 1991
Mary and I are on the top floor of a house. It is open and spacious. We are discussing the trial and how I will respond. We each go to sleep in separate rooms. I wake up thinking that we have forgotten some clue. Going to the doorway of my room I find Mary at the door of her room. We talk about how we both realize we have forgotten a clue. She says there is a dummy figure outside dressed in Kevin's clothes. The light from the night is coming through the blinds. In a moment, we see a truck drive by. We can see it, but we are not looking out the window. We lay down on her bed and go to sleep. The next time I wake up my eyes stay closed as if I am too tired to open them. I walk back to my room. I only see where I am going by putting my hands out in front of me like a blind woman.

The answering machine clicked on, cutting the second ring short. I half listened as a monotone voice requested the caller to leave their name and number after the beep.

"Hi, it's me." Chris' voice came through loud and clear from the night stand beside our bed. Hiding her concern she paused, "Are you there?" Hesitating again, she coaxed, "Please, pick up, okay?"

Reaching from the middle of the bed I picked up the receiver, "I'm here."

215

"Hey, I thought you might be out somewhere," she replied sounding relieved. "What are you up to this morning?" We both knew she was well aware that I had been ignoring the phone.

"Nothing. Just lying here," I replied flatly.

"Hmm, you sound tired. Are you feeling okay today?" she asked, giving me an opening to talk.

I sighed deeply, rolling onto my back. "Yeah, I'm tired of this life."

Hearing the emptiness in my heart she softly responded, "I know how disappointed you must be about the trial. We all are."

"Well, he won. I'm sure he's not disappointed," I said with quiet sarcasm.

"Yes, but we know it won't be easy for him to walk away from the truth," she said trying to reassure me.

"It doesn't really matter," I said bleakly. "They believed him. They wouldn't let me tell the truth. They didn't really care about Kevin."

"You did everything you could...." Chris said, her voice fading as I checked out of our conversation. Sensing my preoccupation, she prodded, "Are you still there?"

No, I'm not. I don't want to be here anymore. What's the point? My inner critic began stirring the pot of guilt to a rolling boil.

"Yeah, well I failed him again," I said feeling my throat constrict. "I gotta go." I hung up the receiver before Chris could utter a goodbye. Turning over I wrapped the comforter tightly around me like a cocoon.

Secluded behind the closed blinds of our new home, I had not gotten out of bed since Amber and Stann left for school. Apathetic and unmotivated, I stared blankly at the newly framed photos covering my dresser, the only decorations in the otherwise bare room. It was almost eleven a.m. I knew I should eat something for the baby. In the last week I had lost my appetite, repulsed by the travesty of the trial.

Two days before the trial, we learned the original charges had been reduced to a simple traffic offense. Even more disturbing was that the autopsy, the only evidence proving Kevin's death, had been omitted. Our case had become nothing more than a formality. A sad yet unimportant statistic allowed to fall through the cracks of the system. The District Attorney's office had struggled to save face with our bereaved family by going on with the trial knowing full well there was nothing to prosecute. Someone had dropped the ball, and no one was willing to claim the error. I knew then that I might be the only voice for Kevin, when given the opportunity to sit on the witness stand. I believed until then, that my truth could make a difference.

Unfortunately, we were unprepared for the prosecution to fail miserably in its presentation of the case. Frustrated by the flat and dispassionate manner of the prosecutor, we felt cheated of any

216

representation. And, in a shocking turn of events, the prosecution dismissed the only other witness, the woman who had moved Kevin's bike after the accident. He claimed her testimony would be repetitious to mine. I would be the only witness for the prosecution.

In the end, I would be restricted from telling my truth. My testimony had become useless. I was forbidden to describe Kevin's injuries or even mention that a death had occurred that day. I was not allowed to express my observations of the Driver's emotional state after the accident. Since the Driver was no longer being prosecuted for "careless driving resulting in death," these facts became immaterial. The six person jury, seemed to be wondering along with the rest of us, "Careless driving regarding what?"

Stann felt powerless as he sat with our family and friends behind the flimsy spectator railing. They could only support me with their eyes as I was forced to answer the carefully worded questions posed by the defense attorney. I had been silenced. I became a puppet in their masquerade of justice.

Midway, the defense shifted their focus back to Kevin. A collective gasp of horror came from our restrained group as we listened to the Neighbor's son describe an erroneous portrayal of our innocent son. He depicted Kevin as a reckless, unsupervised child riding wildly up and down the street, defying both parked cars and traffic. Stunned, we sat there gagged by the court. I was prohibited to come to Kevin's defense. And, the prosecution did not invite me back to do so when I begged to set the story straight. The Neighbor's testimony remained unchallenged, and Kevin remained another faceless victim. It was one more betrayal by a system that had promised to seek truth and justice.

The final blow came when the Driver took the stand. The composed and confident young man in the witness box was different than the man we had met in the park. Careful not to look my way his eyes focused only on his attorney, as he sat straight across from me. The Driver delivered a very well-rehearsed account of his actions, eliminating any reasonable doubt that he might have been less than careful that day. His testimony was not in accordance with the emotion-filled details he had given us, nor what I had witnessed. It was the final betrayal. How could we tell our daughter that justice had prevailed?

A small intimate group of family and friends gathered at our new house after the trial. Our sparsely furnished living room offered little seating as people milled about, confused and angry. There were messages to return from anxious relatives and friends awaiting the verdict. Neither Stann nor I had the strength to deliver such disheartening news. I watched Stann move from room to room, seeking out a spot that felt familiar and comfortable. His tired blue eyes and furrowed brow reflected deep

217

disappointment and sorrow. In an uncharacteristic move, Stann had prepared a statement to read to the court, if, after a guilty verdict, the judge would invite us to speak. It lay crumpled on the coffee table, his grief unheard.

Amber sat quietly on the floor in front of the couch beside me as I rocked in the blue matching recliner. I had explained that things did not turn out as we had hoped; the driver did not admit responsibility for Kevin's death. How could her nine-year-old mind comprehend all the legal terms when we could barely understand them? The system had failed her brother by allowing his life to be misrepresented and his death to be dismissed as a non-event. This world and the ignorant people who seemed to have control of our lives sickened me.

"Mom," I heard Amber call out, bringing me back to the moment.

"What, honey?" I said, shifting in the recliner to face her. Her long blonde hair fell softly down her back as she hugged her knees close. Pressing her chin down on top of them she looked deep in thought.

"Mom, why don't people tell the truth?"

Tears welled in my eyes. I did not have the answer. Before I could respond, she spoke up.

"When you tell a lie, you can't get it out of your head. Someday you have to tell somebody," she declared. "Maybe that man will change his mind someday."

I sat speechless, shaking my head in disbelief. My daughter had blessed me. I grieved her loss of innocence and the lonely times ahead. But, in the midst of her pain she had gained a wisdom far beyond her youth. I could only hope to be as wise and as forgiving as Amber.

Empty days and sleepless nights spent rehashing the trial, had taken its toll on both Stann and me. The more we talked about it the more unreal it seemed. Neither of us imagined that this would be the outcome. It seemed so obvious that the essential issue was that an innocent child had lost his life. Why didn't they do more to protect his rights? Why didn't they seem to care?

Sequestered in our home, we had become more withdrawn and depressed unable to hold a conversation about anything other than the trial. Stann's enthusiasm for teaching and coaching diminished as he struggled to contain his anger and disappointment. Concerned for my welfare as well, he could hardly manage the long days away from home. Mary and Chris stayed in close contact with me when I allowed them the space. In the end, I could not get out of my own way.

Journal Notes: October 26, 1991

"I expected to feel better after I wrote that hateful letter to the Driver. We made our disgust and disappointment clear about what we thought of him, and that ignorant group of individuals representing him. How could anyone destroy the memory of a child to justify his innocence? Oh God, I feel worse. I never imagined I would ever feel such contempt for anyone.

I expected the Driver to react in a certain way that I deemed the right way. I expected that because I had been so *wronged* that I believed it was up to him to make it right. Did I unconsciously offer him an ultimatum that said, "I forgive you, IF you accept your responsibility?" Well, I still do forgive him his humanness, even though he hasn't expressed his responsibility. But, am I still giving him an ultimatum? Am I wrong to blame him and hold him responsible for his part? How much blame is enough? Or, will I go crazy thinking that it's all my fault, that I had all the control and I blew it? Am I really angry because he complied with this stupid destiny thing however unconscious he was? WHY does *he* get to be unconscious!

Am I holding on to this pain because I can't forgive myself? Is it because I really blame myself, and will continue to blame myself, until I think he's blamed himself more!? Am I expecting the Driver to assume more responsibility than he is capable of? Am I expecting more than is humanely possible of either of us? I know, I believe, that all this will affect his life. I know that he cannot really walk away unchanged. I just resent that my life is changed. It makes me angry. How can I make that anger dissolve? How can I turn it into a positive? Will the Driver ever be truly out of my thoughts?

Will I ever accept that Kevin's destiny was to leave us? Or was it just a possibility that came true because of circumstances that jelled together? Am I supposed to forgive Kevin for following his destiny or his fate? *Why did I say yes to this?* Or is all this just bullshit, and I'm in a deep coma in some hospital trying to wake up? I haven't evolved any more than the man in the moon."

I believe now, with all my being, that the trial would not have turned out any other way. We had missed an important clue. Still blinded by grief, we had dismissed the most profound pieces of evidence. Kevin had been trying to divert our attention, hoping we would focus on the real evidence. If only we had recognized the airplane drawing as proof beyond a reasonable doubt. Kevin had accepted his destiny. We could have released ourselves from the tangled web of the legal system without any further disillusionment. If only we had recognized that this Holy document was the only proof we would ever need, we would have freed ourselves, and the Driver too.

Instead, we clung to fear. The world we lived in expected the legal system to pursue retribution. Our belief system had become clouded by an unrealistic view of justice, and an unrealistic expectation of human behavior. The Driver's denial or at least the appearance of a denial went against everything I believed to be true about human nature. In my thinking, shirking responsibility was unthinkable and unacceptable. Until we changed our perceptions, the pain and suffering would continue and we would feel like victims again and again. At the time, we could not see outside of our "victim" perspective. We hurt so much. Later I came to accept that my intuitions about the Driver were right that day in the park. It would seem that he too felt victimized by the whole chain of events.

Over the next ten years, we learned that spiritual justice was far more valuable than any verdict delivered by a human court. It had been unfair of us to assign blame or responsibility, when we were not privy to another's agreements or conflicts with their God. And, just as important, when we as humans did not have the awareness of such spiritual agreements. All that mattered was how we chose to respond to adversity and in the end what we chose to do with it. Spiritual justice was about a forgiving God embracing His children despite their fears and mistakes, not judging them because of it.

In the months after the trial, Stann and I followed a very dark path of despair and hopelessness. Walking blindly through the shadows of fear and doubt we felt separated from God and from our own people. However, Kevin's drawings remained to be seen, beckoning us to look again.

I came to understand that Kevin's drawings were the same as my dreams. Each of them held a message that could be translated from personal symbols as well as archetypes from the collective unconscious. In his drawings, Kevin was inviting us to see past our fear of his death. In the Airplane drawing, the second circles drawn in pen around his eyes represented his spiritual eyes, the ones that reveled in his destiny to return home.

In the Ascension drawing, Kevin had spontaneously drawn his transition from this world to the next. With my new sight, I discovered that Kevin had drawn on both sides of the paper. The backside depicted a full figure and a house above him. When held up to the light the backside is visible creating another dimension to the drawing. The Father figure and the small figure from the back now appear as one. I remembered that the last things he drew were Daddy's arms, and then he gave me the paper. Could those have been the arms of his Father lifting him from his earthly body?

I also discovered that Kevin had actually left us a series of pictures detailing his inner journey. Page after page of spontaneous drawings depicted Kevin's conversations with God. Over a period of seven months, he had wrestled with his acceptance to honor the agreement he had made with his Father. It was never easy knowing that it meant he would have to leave us. Kevin's love for us was deep, and his faithfulness to his Father was true.

I became even more determined to interpret Kevin's drawings, just as I had immersed myself in the Nightmare. My personal library expanded from bereavement literature to include books about children's spontaneous drawings and their symbolic meanings. I was relieved to learn that in the world of archetypes and symbolism my son and I were considered normal.

With a renewed confidence, I began to share Kevin's drawings with art therapists and spiritual counselors. Again and again, they confirmed what I already knew. Was it any coincidence that the validity of Kevin's drawings would come only after his death?

As I examined the evidence, my skepticism began to wane lifting the dark clouds of doubt. In Kevin's drawings, I had been given a way to understand his link to the world of the Spirit. Reading Kevin's journal helped to soften my grief when my body yearned to hold my son.

And, most importantly, with time I could fully forgive the Driver and the Neighbors. I realized that they could not have responded any other way, not the day of the accident or thereafter. The power of destiny was much greater. I also accepted that in my humanness, I did not have to like it.

God's hope for me was to begin to trust without reservation, to have faith without proof. I wondered why it was easier for me to accept Kevin's drawings as sacred, rather than my Nightmare. Kevin's illustration of his spiritual understandings seemed less threatening than my nightmare and they seemed more complete. Perhaps, because he was far more trusting in his Father's will than I. The Nightmare still haunted me, and its incompleteness disturbed me more.

PART IV

Reunion

28
Endings and Beginnings

Dream Journal: January 8, 1992 Early morning
I am sitting at the dining room table eating lunch with Stann and Kevin. I have given Kevin a bowl of soup. The bowl is oversized and the soup is hot, so he is being careful. I am sitting next to him watching him eat. I realize that I have another chance to look at him. I marvel at the beauty of his face. I touch his right arm and stroke his hand. I smile at him, and Kevin smiles back his sweet face beaming.

The pointy needles of the blue spruce poked through my knit gloves jabbing at my fingertips. Pulling the glove off with my teeth, I unhooked the ornament from the snow-laden branch with bare fingers. Carefully, I wrapped the handmade decoration in tissue paper and placed it in the box at my feet. My heavy frame waddled to the back of the tree where I checked the rest of the branches for hidden ornaments.

Kevin's tree had been transformed into a glorious spectacle of lights and decorations this Christmas season. We asked Amber and her cousins, as well as Kevin's friends, to make a special ornament in memory of Kevin to hang on the tree. They fashioned the most beautiful keepsakes from pine cones, clay dough, and wood. Each day a different ornament appeared on the tree as the children came to the park to hang their mementos.

225

My eyes stung with tears as I remembered our valiant effort just two weeks before to light the tree. Initially, we had envisioned Kevin's tree decorated with hundreds of miniature lights. Knowing there was no electricity available in the park, we decided to use battery-operated lights instead. Stann wired the star he cut from scrap wood for Amber's ornament with battery lights. She had painted the star bright yellow and glued wooden block letters that spelled Kevin's name to the center. When he turned on the switch, the Lilliputian spruce became a blaze with a hundred twinkling lights.

The next morning we discovered that the batteries had only lasted through the night. Our spirits plunged when we realized that we would have to replace them each evening if we wanted the tree to stay lit through the holidays. Later that afternoon when we returned to the hill, Stann and I could not hide our disappointment and tears. This little tree was the one thing that had brought some joy to our hearts as we faced our first Christmas without Kevin. Our idea had been a bust. Braving the cold, we began removing the defective strings in silence.

"Hey there! What can we do to keep this tree lit?"

Startled, we looked up to see a middle-aged man trudging through the snow from behind the tree.

Rather bluntly, I cried out, "Do you have any electricity?" My sarcasm had gotten the best of me.

"Well, as a matter of fact I do," he proclaimed. "I'm Ed. I live in that house right behind the tree," he said jabbing the air with his thumb. Extending his other hand, he shook hands with Stann. "My wife and I saw it last night from our kitchen window. It was beautiful. What's this tree for anyway?" he asked.

We tearfully explained our story of Kevin's tragic death, the gift of the tree and our vision of lighting it in memory of him. We concluded with the present dilemma of the battery lights. Ed had been listening intently as we poured out our story.

With tears in his eyes, he finally spoke, "Please, let us help you light this tree. Our son was diagnosed with cancer as a child, and although he lived, we know a little bit about your pain." He went on motioning with both hands, "You take all this stuff back to the store and get some extension cords and some real lights. We'll hook it up to my house and we'll get this tree lit tonight," he said enthusiastically.

Overwhelmed with emotion, Stann put his arm around me and wiped his cheeks with his free hand. "You don't know how much this will mean to us, sir, we really appreciate your offer. But, we want to pay for the electricity we use."

"Absolutely not," he said firmly. "You better get moving while there is still daylight and the stores are open. See you in a little while."

Waving goodbye, he stomped through the snow and entered the gate of the chain link fence separating his yard from the park.

Excited about our good fortune, I talked non-stop all the way to the car. With little time to spare, we raced to the store and purchased a box of three hundred miniature lights and several extension cords. Within the hour, we met up with Ed again. He was real! This was really happening. Our excitement grew despite the long shadows of dusk and the near zero degree temperature. Together, we set to work, wrapping the new strings around the tree until it was covered from top to bottom. I replaced the ornaments while Stann and Ed used flashlights to hook up the extension cords down the hill and through his backyard.

By the light of his kitchen window, Ed positioned himself on the patio waiting for our signal. "Ready!" Stann hollered waving his arms. Instantly, the tree was aglow shining brightly on our tear-stained faces. Running back through the snow Ed joined us in a triumphant cry that echoed through the park. We laughed and cried, and hugged each other as the miniature lights twinkled before us. It was a spectacular and joyous sight. For the first time in a year my heart was full with hope.

As word spread of the little Christmas tree in the park, more ornaments appeared on its young branches. We were astonished at how many people, even strangers, felt compelled to visit the tree as they left offerings for Kevin and other children who had died. We realized then that Kevin's tree had a far greater purpose. A simple act of generosity and compassion by one couple had given us a ray of hope during a dark and mournful time. Kevin's tree had to be shared with other bereaved families so they too could honor the love light of their precious children.

I brushed the snow off the last ornament and placed it in the box. We had driven by last night for one more viewing. Our new friends were willing to keep the tree lit through New Year's and until the anniversary of Kevin's death. We were grateful for their kindness and understanding.

Stann had already wound the extension cords and stacked them in the Jeep Wagoneer. I fastened the lid on the box of sacred ornaments. They would be safe in our storage room until next year. Unknowingly, we had created a ritual that would signal the beginning of our holiday season. It felt strange to realize that we would be doing this again.

Clumsily, I carried the box on top of my belly, stomping through the crusty snow to meet Stann. Taking the box from me, he put it in the car and closed the hatch door. Then, arm and arm we hiked back to the small hill and stood in front of the bare tree.

"I'm glad we named it the Heartlight Tree," I said catching my breath. "Kevin is pleased too, I'm sure." Tears singed my frozen cheeks and my glasses began to cloud as I buried my face into my gloves. The burden of his long absence was too much to carry today.

"How can it be a year?" Stann whispered, pulling me closer to him.

Clinging to the past, we had spent the last year battling our darkest emotions and facing our worst fears. We experienced more pain, grief, and suffering than we could have ever imagined possible. It would take years of introspection and analysis to comprehend the extent of this mystery and its impact on our family. In the meantime, we had lost a year of our lives. And yet, somehow, we had survived.

A few weeks before Christmas, I encountered the power of my grief-stricken thoughts. One morning, after a particularly stressful night, I reluctantly drove Amber to school and then, continued on to do some errands. Dismayed that it had snowed hard the night before, I cursed the weather. I hated snow. I hated feeling cold. I hated everything about winter, especially Christmas. By the time I finished my errands the mad woman inside had once again taken control, unleashing a furious one-sided dialogue while I drove around town.

"I don't care what other people are planning for Christmas. I don't want to know how happy they are. Why can't we have a happy Christmas too? I want my life back!" the Mad Woman demanded pounding the dashboard. Stepping on the accelerator, I drove through the next intersection. Midway, I was shocked to see the Neighbor drive past me in the opposite lane.

At once, the Mad Woman went ballistic. Her wild eyes bore through the window. "How dare you look away and pretend I don't exist. I hope you have a rotten Christmas too!" the Mad Woman yelled at the foggy glass. She sped along as I gripped the wheel to gain control. "How could you hurt us like that? My kids brought Christmas cookies to your house. And you, *you* couldn't even come to my door and say you were sorry my son died? How would you feel if it were your son?" she screamed louder as I stepped on the brake skidding past the stop sign.

Next, I remember driving into the safety of our garage. I pulled down the visor, pushing the button to the automatic garage door. I collapsed on the steering wheel as I folded my arms over my head. The Mad Woman's voice blared on above my wails as the garage door sealed shut. I sat there defenseless, my pregnant belly held hostage in the driver's seat. Soon, the Mad Woman's rage subsided and my sobs diminished to a pathetic whimper. Draped like a dishrag over the steering wheel, my body had lost its will to fight. My consciousness began to fade until, I caught sight of the keys dangling from the steering column. And then, some thing, some force, some energy, pushed me out of the car. Horrified, I realized that I had left the ignition on while I sat in the car.

That day I had steered myself in a direction that may have brought more disaster. I knew I was not capable of consciously taking my own life. But, in my desire to be free of the heartache, I had set myself up to do so. While it might have looked as though I had tried to take my life and our unborn child with me, I had only been seeking a reprieve from the pain. Grief had literally knocked me unconscious. My body was tired and in my weakness I had lost my will to protect myself. I had lost any love for myself. The powerful force that rescued me that day, whether guardian angel, loving son, the hands of God or perhaps all three, must have loved me very much.

****

Dream Journal: February 10, 1992
I am on a journey, walking and crawling through caves and narrow passages. I wake up but easily slip back into the dream again. This time the journey starts over. There are two entrances to the caves. Some of our group goes to the other entrances. But I know the right way and Stann and I proceed on our own.

The one-year anniversary of Kevin's death was a culmination of unforeseen changes, unwanted challenges, and unexpected closures. The memory of our life as a family of four remained, keeping us connected to our past and bonded with each other. Equally important were our courageous attempts of reconciliation. Those small steps away from the past counted as giant steps of acceptance moving us forward on the journey.

Blessed by the kindness of strangers, the support of our loved ones, and the gentle mercies of God, we had survived. Many times, I prayed that God would recognize the depth of our pain and release us to the Somewhere. I did not want Amber and the new baby to grow up in a world of deception and illusion. What could we offer them here except pain and heartache?

It was during those times I would feel the strong arms of loved ones carrying us across the lonely plains of grief. Their unyielding compassion helped us regain our bearings whenever we lost our way. Gradually, they began to release their embrace knowing that someday we would have to stand alone. With loving support, they stood by us as we prepared to welcome another child into our lives.

Their desire for us to find happiness again drove an exuberant anticipation that became contagious. It was the dose of reassurance we needed to strengthen our confidence. Stann had worried about how he would feel towards another child and that he might hold unfair expectations. I worried if I was sane enough to be the mother of a newborn again. We both had been holding back our excitement for fear that even this would become another nightmare. It was the ultrasound that confirmed the reality of this baby's existence and helped calm those fears.

Stann and I watched in amazement as her tiny feet, with five toes each, kicked about inside me. Her heartbeat pounded loud and strong through the speakers as if to say, "Hello, Mommy and Daddy. I am really in here!"

One day I uncovered an old baby name book I had used for naming Amber. Browsing through the list, I read the names out loud matching them with our last name. When I came to the name "Megan" I heard the memory of Kevin's sweet voice saying it instead. I felt my heart skip as his voice triggered yet another memory. He would often tell me about a baby girl named Megan, at the child care home he attended. Once, he described in hushed tones how very, very tiny Baby Megan's hands were. Cupping his own hands together to show me, he spoke of her with such awe and wonder.

I believed my memory was not a coincidence but another heavenly message that our baby girl existed in the Somewhere and was already named. Amber and Stann happily agreed, and from then on we referred to the baby by her name and it made the approaching birth seem more real. By the time Megan was born, we felt as though we had known her for years.

In my quiet times when I knew Megan could hear only me, I promised to love her with all my heart and soul. I begged her to be patient with me while I gathered the courage to do so. I no longer feared birth defects or death. I was more afraid of life and my lack of control over it. Regardless of my fear about being worthy of this precious gift, I knew I could not fail this child. Once again, God had expressed his confidence in me by giving me what I needed most.

In the end it was Amber's enthusiasm that pushed us forward, forcing us to concede to our future. Her excitement grew when we began to include her in all the baby plans, from choosing the wallpaper to buying sleepers and equipment. She delighted in seeing my expanding belly contort out of shape as the baby kicked and stretched inside. I even brought her to my weekly checkup so she could hear the baby's heartbeat.

Although there was much emotion surrounding my two previous labors, physically they were uneventful. Our hard earned experience in the birthing department had prepared us well. This time I practiced my deep breathing and added meditation exercises. I was determined to be more emotionally stable. Stann and I also took a refresher course at the hospital and to our chagrin discovered we were the oldest parents there. It was quite awkward. We knew far too much about birth and death.

Following the advice of yet another dream, I decided to invite Mary to be my back up labor coach. In the dream I was alone and had started labor. Mary arrived and I told her the contractions had begun. She spread an Indian birthing blanket on the floor and told me to lie down on it. Then she said, "I'm supposed to be with you when you deliver." Mary had walked every step of this journey with me and it seemed fitting that she should be with us to welcome this new life too. She was honored when I told her that divine guidance had intervened once again. Having Mary beside me helped to bolster my motherly instincts and her positive outlook helped balance our fears.

Miss Megan as we have come to call her, arrived fashionably late, garnering as much attention as possible for her grand entrance into this world. I am certain that all the angels and saints held their breath as she descended at the speed of light into her body. Pure energy, she emitted love in its highest form reminding us that there was more to life than death and grieving.

Journal Notes: March 7, 1992

I know we have a long road ahead. But, for the time being I have savored every moment of joy possible since Megan's birth. It was so wonderful to feel pure love again. I never thought I would ever feel this way again.

At the hospital, the corridors of the obstetrics ward had emptied and our visitors had gone home to spread the news. Alone at last, we lay facing one another after so many months of sharing my body. I ran my fingertip lightly down her delicate nose and around her full lips. I nuzzled closer, my senses filled with the strong scent of birth still clinging to her skin. I was in awe of her goodness. Remembering the dream from Santa Fe, I bowed my head in thanksgiving for this precious gift from the universal waters of life.

Then, grinning to myself, I knew we shared a little secret that no one else could ever understand. Megan had just left Kevin's world, bringing with her all the peace and joy and love that abounds there. I reveled in the idea that only hours ago they had been together. It made me feel so close to Kevin and yet deeply connected to both of them. God's message was as clear. This love was so pure and good and it was what He wanted for us.

I have been hanging on to that promise for the past three weeks. I have suppressed my sadness and grief in an attempt to make this joy last forever. Reality will come crashing in soon enough.

231

29
To See Differently

Dream Journal: September 3, 1992
I walk into my church and I am carrying Megan in a baby carrier. A white wall about four feet high has replaced the crying room in the back of the church. It divides the rest of the church from this small space. I stop there and put the carrier down on a pew. I leave Megan in the carrier while I go to the restroom. It doesn't bother me to leave her alone in the church. When I return I notice the choir balcony is still above the crying room where it used to be. Many people are sitting there. I see that Stann and Amber are sitting in the middle of the church. I wonder why Stann didn't pick up Megan and take her with him to his seat. I look for Megan, but, to my surprise, Kevin is sitting in the pew, holding her in his arms. Oh, he looks so sweet! He is holding Megan so tenderly and I am touched by his gentleness. I notice he is wearing a blue windbreaker jacket and not the coat he wore when he died. It's the one he called his "coach jacket". I smile and say, "Oh Kevin, thank you so much for taking care of Megan! He smiles happily at me and hands Megan back to me. As I sit down I think that we should all be sitting together. I assume that Kevin will go sit with Stann and Amber, but I don't see where he goes. I realize then that the back of the church has become the front, everything is reversed and it is all white. Fr. Gary is at the altar before me. I am the only other person there.

Megan snuggled deeper into the folds of my terry cloth robe resting her little head on my bare breast. Her moist lips pressed against my skin, still sucking long after the milk was gone. Raising her to my shoulder, I shifted my hips to push the overstuffed rocker into a reclining position. I tucked the pink and cream-colored blanket around us, securing her place with me for the rest of the night. Closing my eyes, I sank deeper into the cushion recalling Kevin's sweet face as he held his baby sister.

Kevin's eyes sparkled with glee as he grinned at me. He held her like a long lost treasure wrapped snug and secure across his lap. My heart was full of gratitude for the gift of seeing my two children together for the first time. While I had been grieving the loss of one child, I had been handed the gift of another. The promise of the Santa Fe dream had come true. New life had come to me, and it was mine.

Megan had captured our hearts, gently leading us away from sadness to moments of joy again. Her striking dark blue eyes would dance with delight as she began to recognize our voices. Her full lips spread wide when she smiled at us, as if to say, "Yes, I know you too." Alert and happy she reminded us of a time not so long ago when we had shared such moments with Amber. As Megan's buoyant personality emerged, she seized every opportunity to gain our attention and pull us out of the past and into the present.

Stann, Amber and I immediately stepped forward to claim our relationship with this beautiful being. Amber would rush home from school to hold Megan in the big rocker while she watched afternoon cartoons. During the commercials she would talk to her sister rocking Megan and cooing softly, "Hey baby, hey baby girl." Stann's concerns about readily accepting Megan disappeared too. The first time he scooped her into his strong arms he remembered how unique each baby had been before. It wasn't long before he was babbling and cooing with her too.

I was relieved that my motherly instincts had taken over. My initial fears about being capable enough were put to rest for a while. During the day, I relished our quiet time together in the big blue rocker. Wrapped up in her comforter, Megan nursed contentedly in my arms while I would doze or read. When Stann and Amber returned from school I would relinquish my hold until another feeding. Each of us wanted our special time alone with Megan to smell her powdered skin and smooth her fine hair, all the while bathing in her peaceful glow.

Within a few weeks, the changes and adjustments of having a baby in the house became overwhelming. Our new home quickly filled with diapers, blankets and baby toys. Nighttime feedings and sleepless nights taxed our reserves leaving little time for socializing. We had taken Amber's independence as a nine-year-old for granted when Megan now demanded every minute of our attention.

Through all the work and all the joy, the pain of Kevin's absence remained. It was difficult for others to understand that Megan did not fill the void left by Kevin's death. We missed him more than ever as we recognized that each of Megan's milestones took us further away from the past. Emotionally and physically exhausted, I would lay awake in the middle of the night crying to have my former life back. Only now, I could not imagine my life without Miss Megan. Reality knocked again, forcing me to open yet another door. How could I reconcile my bittersweet feelings?

I discovered that these feelings were not uncommon for grieving mothers. My new friend Linda, the bereaved mom I met after Kevin's death, had expressed the same longing for her separated family after the birth of her son. We spent many long walks pushing the baby strollers as we shared our illusions about death and the grieving process. As bereaved parents, we mirrored the fear of parents everywhere. We were living their nightmare and we lived it alone.

At Linda's persuasion, I accepted her invitation to join a grief support group she had been attending. I trusted Linda and to my relief the support group welcomed me with open arms. At the first meeting, they embraced me with kindness and compassion allowing me to pour out my heart to them. I surprised myself with an unknown readiness to express how much it hurt.

The group was successful because of our willingness to share the broken parts of ourselves, parts that our friends and family could not face. We could accept one another's pain because it resonated so deeply with our own. None of us tired of hearing the details of another's grief no matter how many times we felt the need to repeat it. We recognized that we would not want anyone else to experience what we had to live, yet, it made us feel very lonely and singled out. It was with these women that I came to understand the healing value of sharing my story. In turn, I learned the difference between offering sympathy and being and empathetic listener. In doing so, I began to accept the healing power of a listening heart.

Many times I remembered the courage of the bereaved mother I met at the monastery. In her story, I also heard my own pain. She modeled for me the strength she had gained by risking her vulnerability to reach out to another. From her example, and from the women in my support group, I learned to risk expressing my truth in spite of my fear of rejection.

Several months after the retreat, I had my first opportunity to do the same with a newly bereaved couple. Looking into their mournful eyes, I recognized the sorrow and disbelief I had come to know, and I am sure I mirrored that for them. I knew they would ask us if it still hurt, if the pain ever goes away. How could I tell them that nine months later the pain was still strong enough to knock me off my feet at any given moment?

And what about their two surviving children playing quietly on the floor nearby? The oldest, a son no more than ten-years-old, held my attention. I knew that he had witnessed his brother's accident. I ached for this innocent child and the burden he carried. Would he ever be able to erase those painful images? At thirty-three I could hardly stand to close my eyes, how could he sleep at night? Would our surviving children grow up to live normal healthy lives despite this atrocity in their life?

My heart grieved for this newly bereaved family, because, while I could relate to the depth of their pain, I also knew it was only the beginning for them. It was a startling reminder. Somehow, through all the madness, our life had become tolerable for moments at a time and we had survived. I did not know how, or why, but it was true, and they needed to know it. I am not sure how my honesty affected them that day, I only know that it gave me the courage to reach out again and again to other bereaved families.

Eventually the weekly support group meetings became more than a place to talk about grief. It seemed a natural progression to explore the way death and grief had affected our spiritual lives. Our diverse backgrounds and religious upbringing contributed to lively discussions and soulful insights. I felt comfortable sharing my emerging spirituality with them. It was the only place I could talk without fear of rejection or scrutiny. Social outings and gatherings had become excruciatingly uncomfortable. I felt exposed and vulnerable anywhere else. The support group temporarily filled my need to connect with people, people who could truly understand how my life had changed.

However, the daily responsibilities of caring for a baby, and working hard to reconcile my grief left little time for journaling my dreams. The Nightmare was always in the back of my mind and figuring out how to survive each day was always on the forefront. I had grown accustomed to the fleeting images of the Nightmare. I was not as frightened by it anymore. In all honesty, I had become bored with the edited version that my mind insisted on replaying time after time. I grew frustrated that with all my dream work I had not had a dream that explained more of the Nightmare.

My dreamtime had become erratic now that my sleep cycle was disrupted by Megan's cries. One night I dreamed that I had walked by our old house. I saw Amber, Kevin, Stann and myself, playing in the yard of our old house. I knew I was watching a scene from my past and I so much wanted to be in it. I ran with my arms outstretched to hug Kevin, but instead, ran into a six-foot chain link fence. As I fought to get in, the fence became steel bars. Only my arms could fit between as I pulled Kevin toward me. We were both frustrated that the fence was keeping us apart and keeping me out.

When I awakened, I knew that everything I had ever wanted was on the other side of that fence. It was upsetting because this was the first dream where I was kept from touching Kevin. In examining the dream, I clearly understood that I was feeling imprisoned by some illusion about my past and my abilities to connect with Kevin. I wanted more from my dreams than wishful scenarios and revised editions of my memories. I wanted to know more about that Nightmare, and I wanted to see more of Kevin.

In my heart's desire to just be present with him in my dreams I had missed another important message in the Church Dream. Carrying Megan in the baby carrier into the church was a metaphor for the next step of the journey. The church represents the foundation of my faith and everything that has shaped it until now. The crying room (constant mourning), has been replaced by a wall (my self-imposed limitations and boundaries), that allows me to see over but still separates me from the front of the church (moving forward) I am not afraid to leave Megan (my new life), for a while to go to the restroom (to eliminate the fear that divides me). I see that Stann and Amber have not moved to pick up Megan (their chance for new life too). When I return, I discover that Megan is not where I left her, (my new life has been changed yet again), and now Kevin is taking care of her (Kevin will support me during this change)

I could not have imagined what was to come next. Kevin would become my spiritual coach and lead me in the opposite direction of my fears toward clarity and hope.

* * * * * * *

Dream Journal: September 4, 1992
Kevin and I are in a room. I am hugging and kissing him. I hold his face in my hands and look at every inch of him. He looks whole and healthy. I laugh at his cowlick and crazy hairline. His beautiful face is looking right at me and I feel his love for me. He hugs me tight, putting his arms around my neck. "I love you Kevin," I tell him. Next he wiggles away, but I am not ready to let him leave yet. He pretends to fuss at being coddled just as I remembered when he was with me. I look at him again, and say, "Oh Kevin, tell me what it's like in heaven? Where do you go?" As soon as I said it, he vanished. Instantly, I feel his energy rise above me. Next, I am kneeling under the window in Megan's room, beside Kevin's old bed. Again I ask, "Where do you go? What's it like in heaven?" I see that the mobile that hangs over her crib has been taken apart and is now laid out on the floor. As I think about picking them up, all the pieces rise, floating in the air. I become excited because I know it means that Kevin is right there but he is invisible. I gather my arms around the air hugging him. I feel him in the air. It is a glorious discovery! Then, he becomes visible to

me again. Overwhelmed, I kiss his face over and over and over. I want more.

Plodding down the dark hall to Megan's room I rubbed my eyes trying to rally myself for another two a.m. nursing. Sighing, I scooped her up from the crib and lay down on the day bed across the room. Her cries subsided as she sucked vigorously filling her empty tummy with warm milk. A few minutes ago, I had been kneeling beside this same bed hugging and kissing my Kevin. The two worlds were just a breath away and yet beyond my grasp.

What was it that enabled me to dream like this I wondered? I had a genuine heartfelt intention to see more and to see differently. How would I know when my intentions were truly without expectations? What happened in that space between dozing off to sleep and the dream world? Was I so afraid of losing my connection to my past that in my most vulnerable moments, that fear pushed the painful memories into my dream world? Was my desire to hold on to the past strong enough to keep me from moving to higher levels of consciousness? And worse, would it keep me separated from Kevin?

Why couldn't I be satisfied with dreams like these instead of obsessing over the Nightmare and the Blonde Woman? I felt so selfish. I had experienced the most profound dreams since Kevin's death. But, after eighteen months the Nightmare was still as real as any memory I had ever had. I had approached the Nightmare like a research project and it had evolved as more information was uncovered. I had continued to dissect every inch of it looking for one small clue that would tell me it was all a mistake. I should have let go of it long ago.

There was so much else that needed my attention in addition to recent motherhood. At ten years of age, Amber began to challenge me to loosen the rein I held so tightly. She wanted to be free to play as before instead of hearing my constant reminders about keeping herself safe from my imagined dangers. In the fall, Stann returned to school and his coaching position for football. Besieged by both schedules and the burden of grief, he had become distant, eventually shutting down his emotions. And, for me, this unceasing work of grieving felt like doing hard time in a prison. I only wanted my old life back with Megan in it.

I lay on Kevin's bed, now serving as a nursing berth covered with a pink spread and fluffy pillows. I sighed at the irony. What was the key? Why was I holding on to something that caused so much anxiety and pain? I had convinced myself that the dream was unfinished, short of the answers I expected to have at this point. If I could dream it all again would it be the same given what I understand now?

The Nightmare was filed away in my subconscious in its entirety. It was I who chose not to remember the details. If past memories could surface through dreams, meditations or hypnosis, then why couldn't the Nightmare surface again if my intentions to understand it were sincere? What if I could dream it all again? What if I could go back into the dream and see the sword of truth? What if I could go back into the dream armed with faith instead of fear?

30
"Mommy Come Find Me!"

"Mary, I want to go back into the Nightmare," I announced. "I'm ready to try hypnosis."

Accustomed to her silence, I waited. I knew she was assessing my motivation and I looked back with confidence. I sat up straight in the old oak chair, scooting in closer to the table to make my point.

"I am feeling stronger and I think I'm doing better. That's good isn't it?" I said, raising my eyebrows.

Mary leaned forward brushing her light brown hair over her shoulders. "Yes, it is, and Carla, you have come so far. I only suggested that the hypnosis might fill in the missing blanks. But, are you sure you want to delve into this again? What do you hope to accomplish?"

The afternoon sun pouring through the long rectangle window warmed the room. Orange and yellow leaves swirled across the lawn having been released from the broad arms of the tall cottonwood trees that shaded Mary's office. While the seasons changed so had my life but without the gracious transition given to nature. I had spent many hours looking out this window contemplating my existence. I wanted my life back or at least some semblance of one that would enable me to be productive again. Putting the Nightmare to rest might be the only way I could move on.

"Well, you said that hypnosis would help bring the dream images to the surface. Right? So, if I am relaxed and open enough my ego won't censor everything out of fear like it did the first time."

"Right. Your subconscious won't let you experience or see anything that you are not ready or willing to do. You will be in control. My job is to maintain a dialogue with you so I can help redirect you if you become frightened. You have the choice to stop whenever you want," she explained. I nodded, remembering our first discussion a few days ago.

"Mary, I was so afraid the first time. I didn't want to believe what I saw. I want another chance to see it without being fearful. I want to listen this time. I want to hear what the Blonde Woman was saying to me in the circle. Maybe she was telling me something that I was supposed to do?" I sighed, taking off my glasses to rub my tear-filled eyes. "I don't expect the hypnosis to bring an instant healing or alleviate my grief. It's just another tool and if I am willing to try, then why not?"

"I've always known you would never stop looking for answers," she said, cocking her head sideways.

"It makes me feel so incomplete. You're the only one who understands why I need to do this," I said tears spilling from my eyes.

"All right then, we will do it," she smiled. "I have spoken with my friend, Monte, a hypnotherapist. He said he would be very interested to assist us if you are comfortable with him. We can arrange a meeting and familiarize him with the Nightmare and talk more about your goals."

I felt a chill brush the hairs of my arms. It was exciting to think that in just a few days I might have some answers or at the very least more information to chew on. Recalling the scenes that had stirred feelings of anxiety and fear, I realized that my questions remained the same. Who were the cult people? Why did the black-handed woman grab Amber? Did they really want her instead? Was that a door behind the circle of women? What was the Blonde Woman saying to me? Why couldn't I find Kevin and where was he telling me to look for him?

****

I liked Monte the minute I met him. He was warm and friendly, open to my needs and supportive of my goals. He was a discerning individual who practiced a nurturing type of hypnosis that allowed the client to be in control. I appreciated his sensitivity to my situation and grew more excited as he expressed his enthusiasm to assist us. God had sent a strong team to walk this part of the journey with me. I was grateful to be in such capable hands.

A few days later, we met again in the African room, as I called it, a room Mary used for group counseling. Decorated with bamboo, baskets and tropical plants, the safari motif always suggested an adventure to me.

240

I lay down on the cane style couch covering myself with an afghan. The worn green, plaid cushions had seated many clients over the years as they too traveled to faraway places on the back roads of their minds.

Closing my eyes, I began breathing deeply to cleanse and renew myself. I had become quite adept with my meditation techniques and I relished any opportunity to float away on my cloud. With each breath, I prayed in the name of the Father, the Son and the Holy Spirit in thanksgiving for the loving assistance given to me. I prayed for the presence of God to surround us in white light, protecting and guiding us on my journey to the Dream Time. Soon, the whispered tones of my companions disappeared as I sunk deeper and deeper into my sacred world.....

I moved effortlessly toward my sanctuary, anticipating a place of peace that would envelope me in healing white light. It would be my place of refuge when I became frightened or uncertain about continuing the journey. Once I arrived, my celestial setting of fluffy white clouds soothed any doubts I had. Pleasantly surprised, I saw Kevin, waiting just for me. His eyes beamed with love as he looked deeply into mine. Feeling reassured, I smiled. I noticed that he was wearing his favorite white t-shirt with the #5 printed on the left pocket side.

Serene and composed, I wondered why I should leave this haven and bother with my subconscious at all. I felt Kevin's hand_in mine reminding me that he was my spiritual coach, the one who would encourage me to see differently. He would inspire me to see as he sees, without fear and in truth. Then, I heard Kevin's comforting voice inside my mind, "It's okay Mommy."

It was time. Hand in hand, we walked to the outer edges of the sanctuary. Leaving my body far behind, I left the threshold of my subconscious and sailed across the void...

"Carla, where are you?" a voice whispered behind me.

"I'm walking toward my house. Trees are in the neighbor's yard, to the left of our house. The people are on the grass and all around me....it's so green here. They are talking to me....he wants them...."

The children are on my right side, Amber first, and Kevin beside her, as we approach the sidewalk. I notice a majestic cottonwood tree in full bloom bordering the yard to the left of our driveway. Many men and women are gathered on the lawn, a velvet blanket of lush green grass. Their nondescript faces loom toward me in slow motion as we pass by. They are all talking at once and their words blend together creating a low humming sound.

One man moves in closer to talk to me as we walk down the sidewalk toward our home. Although he has a kind face, I become suspicious at his assumption to join us uninvited. My wariness to speak to him grows as I watch the others follow us forming a half circle. I am more nervous because they keep looking at the children. The man's proximity to me is distracting, and with growing concern, I realize the others are much closer to Kevin. Alarmed, I see that they are talking to Kevin and pretending that they know him. "Don't talk to them!" I caution, pulling the children closer. "Stay with me," I command. Kevin seems unafraid though and I worry that the brainwashing has begun. "Oh my God," I think to myself, "They are going to try to take them from me. I have to get us away from here. We're almost home....."

"I can't see their faces, but they are moving..."

The children and I huddle closely while I stare wide-eyed through the shadows. Shaking my head, I realize this isn't our house but someone else's house on the street. The room has wood floors and no furniture except a plain chair against the wall to my right. The humming noise fills the room becoming louder and louder. "They are here!" I gasp in terror. Someone brushes against my left arm and I shrink away. I can't see their faces. Through the shadows, I see they are all women wearing dark robes. They sway side to side moving us along in their circle.

Suddenly, the room begins to brighten as if a light has been turned on to feature the other side of the room. The Blonde Woman emerges from the shadows on the right, taking her place among the circle of women. Instantly, I know the children are not safe here, even with me. I am sure that she wants them.

I feel my chest tighten and it is difficult to breathe. I must do something to escape but the door is behind the Blonde Woman. How will I get past her? Frantic, I pull Amber and Kevin behind me, holding my position like a ferocious mother bear. But, the Blonde Woman does not move.

I inch forward hoping to force my way past her and through the door. To my surprise, the Blonde Woman is speaking to me. Her lips are moving but I cannot hear what she is saying. Wavy rays of light coming from the door behind illuminate her long blonde hair. Captivated by her striking eyes, they look deeply into mine, coaxing me to listen. I am not afraid of her. I only want to know. Holding out her right hand she nods and firmly says, "It has to be."

Her words slice open the scar across my heart slashing through the last thin layer of hope. In that moment, I perceive her message with such force that my body begins to tremble. Rattled by the truth and tortured by her compelling stare, I wince in agony.

242

I cannot bear it and I must look away. Glancing to my right, I realize for the first time that the circle is not closed. There is a space just in front of the chair between the Blonde Woman and Kevin. I gasp. The Blonde Woman and my son are the last link to complete the circle. She is from the door.

I have let my guard down and the shadowed woman beside me moves in closer! Throwing my arms across the children, I scream at the Blonde Woman, "No, because I am listening to YOU, she's getting closer! I won't listen anymore."

"The hand is coming...it's coming across my chest." I cried, my face contorted in agony.

Screaming obscenities at her, I slap the black hand away from my chest before it reaches Kevin. Summoning all my strength, I fight back harder with each blow. Over and over, I beat my fists upon the black handed woman as my inner battle rises to a fury. I grab her bony hands, twisting her fingers with all my power, until, I realize she is not fighting back. None of the women from the circle are fighting me. In the distance, the low humming noise returns, becoming louder now as the voices blend in unison. I drop her hands as if they are on fire. Taking my chance to run with the children. I am running so fast that I can feel the ground move with every pounding step.

"Run Kevin, run faster. Amber, we're almost there!" I yelled waving my arms wildly about.

"Carla, do you want to go to your sanctuary and rest?" Monte interjected.

"I have my hands on the back of the door," I answered, short of breath. "I can do anything now that I am in my house. There is light in my living room...open space."

"Where are the children?" Monte prodded.

"I don't see them anymore...they're probably playing." I said, relaxing into the cushions......

Leaning with my back against the door, I push hard to shut it closed. The children and I are safely inside away from harm. Catching my breath, I look around to discover that my living room is a bright, pristine and open space. It is airy and so light-filled that I cannot help but feel safe. Feeling relieved and much calmer now, I realize that the children have gone to play somewhere else in the house.

With this thought, I sense my consciousness moving backward as if I were inside a wide-angle lens of a camera. Now I see myself standing against the door. My inner lens broadens to include the whole house, but it looks like a doll-house with a pointed roof. I can see only two floors on the left side, while the rooms on the right side are obscured. The bottom floor is the living room with the entrance on the left wall, and above it is the kitchen. They are both lit up like a stage in a theater with darkness enveloping the outside of the dollhouse.

Once again, I sense my consciousness being pulled like a magnet to the second floor. The living room is unoccupied and the stage lights on that floor dim. Now, I see myself standing in the kitchen next to a counter, dressed in my red turtleneck sweater and denim jeans. The kitchen is bright, and everything in it is an immaculate white. There is nothing on the counters, no food, no appliances or knick-knacks. Alone still, I hear the kids playing in another room. Their laughter fills the air resounding through the house and touches my heart. I want to be with them!

"Mommy, come find me," Kevin calls playfully.

Turning toward their muffled giggles, I smile that I am "It" in their game of hide and seek. We've played this game before and I know all their hiding places. With that thought, Kevin's serene sweet face appears in my mind.

"Mommy, come find me," he calls again. I turn left toward his voice expecting to see him beside me. But, the kitchen light dims to total darkness. Bewildered, I look ahead of me to the left and sense that there are no floors to walk on! It is still too dark to see, but I know the space before me is as deep and wide as an abyss. I am too frightened to cross it. Next, I feel my consciousness being sucked up and away as if a vacuum hose were attached to the back of my head. Suspended in the void, I can see my dream self leap from the kitchen across the deep chasm to grasp a ladder.

"Mommy, come find me," Kevin calls louder, his voice becoming insistent, "Come find me."

"No!" I screamed in distress. "I see darkness...I'm afraid! I want to wake up... I want to wake up!"

****

It was several days before I could talk about what had transpired during the hypnosis. Now more than ever, I was certain that the dream was meant to prepare me for the catastrophic changes that were about to occur in my life. Clearly, it was I who had turned the dream into a nightmare. Reliving it allowed me to observe my fears distorting the truth with misperceptions that induced more guilt. I had often worried that the cult really wanted Amber and not Kevin at all. Like a script from a horror movie, I wondered if he had sacrificed himself for her by making a deal with the cult people?

244

If dreams reflect our fears from our waking life, then I must consider what was going on in our life at the time: Stann and I had been very concerned about Amber in the weeks before Kevin's death. We fretted over her struggle with academics and her lack of self-confidence, to the point of transferring her to another school. Kevin on the other hand was well adjusted in pre-kindergarten and was not a concern. Our anxiety about Amber grew, as did our need to protect her from being swallowed up in the school system. Amber's well-being had been on my mind throughout Christmas vacation until the first day back at school, the day of Kevin's death.

From the beginning of the dream, my sole purpose was to protect my children from any harm. Drawing from my pot of fears, my ego assumed that Amber would be the one in most need of protecting. As we walked together I had the children by my side, but it is Amber that is closest to me, rather than Kevin. How strange that I would let my youngest child be more exposed. Why were they not behind me? On some level, did I know that Amber would need more protecting because she would *not* be taken?

Furthermore, my ego had been trained to be suspicious of anyone who would attempt to take my children from me. How else could I keep them safe in this world without exercising my parental control? I was the only person they belonged to. In fact, my mother instincts ran so deep that I admitted I would not give them up, even to their own father. Any man, kind or otherwise, anyone trying to convince me to do so could only get them with brainwashing tactics. I was most afraid that the cult people in the dream would brainwash my kids.

With my fears in control, I missed a very important detail the first time, a detail that became buried in my subconscious. The cult people had moved right past me and made their way to Kevin. They only spoke to Kevin, *not to Amber*. And, typically, my Kevin was not afraid. My heart stung with disappointment as I remembered that my son was never afraid of strangers. He greeted almost everyone as if he had known them forever.

The cult people were not strangers to him. Kevin knew them and it showed on his face. He never flinched or shied away when I told him not to talk to them. I missed that detail the first time. As his mother, I assumed I had complete control over my son's life, I knew everyone he knew, I was involved in everything he did. How could he know these people and I did not? How could I have missed that crucial point?

I was not prepared for the emotion that I felt during the hypnosis. I did not expect to feel emotion as real as in my waking life or that it could be recalled with such intensity from the nightmare. When I pulled the leash in on my ego I could really listen. This time I clearly heard the Blonde Woman's message with my body, my heart, and my soul: *"It has to be. "* Her authority had come from the source of Light beyond the door. In that moment, I realized the circle would not be complete without Kevin.

Any sense of control I thought I had in my life was cut away, exposing my tattered soul. I had been foolishly living with a false sense of security that only served to deceive me and separate me from my God. The control over Kevin's life and death were out of my hands. It was not God's will that Kevin's body, the gift He had given to the world, be crushed and mangled. Nor was it Kevin's desire to throw himself behind a truck and be run over. Perhaps, it was only that God's world complied by giving Kevin an opportunity to exit. Unquestionably, Kevin's destiny had come full circle. I had not failed him.

Until the hypnosis, I felt that I had done nothing to stop him from being killed. Much of my guilt was about not being aware, not paying attention to what seemed like obvious clues only after the fact. That morning I had forgotten the Nightmare. I had buried it so deep that even moments of coincidence could not jar it loose from my memory. Thus, I believed I had given up my son without a fight.

The hypnosis proved otherwise as the replay allowed me to see again more clearly. I had already fought for him in the Dream Time. When I realized that the last link to complete the circle would be Kevin, my mother instincts took over, reneging on any agreements I might have made too. No one would take my son away from me. I would do everything humanly possible to stop it. I waged a ferocious battle with the black-handed woman, fighting a force that was stronger and more powerful than I imagined. I beat the woman with all my might, breaking her bony fingers in my hands.

However, the battlefield did not exist in this world, and the rules would be different. She did not raise her hand to me nor did the other women in the circle. They graciously allowed me my fight. I understand now that only evil forces would need to fight back and overpower me. Light and Truth stand alone.

My only disappointment was that the hypnosis ended when Kevin was calling to me and that our playtime ended so abruptly. It felt wonderful to play again and hear the children laughing. I would always cherish that moment of innocence. Returning to the Nightmare through hypnosis had given me moments of astounding clarity. I had come to a point of acceptance. I knew I had to complete the journey. I was headed back to the Dream Time.

****

246

The next hypnotherapy session took place in my living room. Lying down on the couch, I tucked myself in with a blanket. The high back cushions made me feel snug and secure. Mary and Monte sat beside the couch in chairs brought in from the dining table.

"This time I want you to view the dream on a screen, like a movie," Monte instructed. "It will remind you that you are an observer. If you get frightened, you can turn off your own movie. Mary and I will be here whenever you need us," he said reassuringly.

Smiling, I responded with a deep breath and closed my eyes. I offered my prayer for what I hoped would be the last time.

"I'm ready to begin," I said, taking one more cleansing breath. Just as before, Monte guided me through the relaxation steps one by one. Within minutes I was deep in trance and I made my way to the theater.....

I am sitting alone in the middle of the movie theater. I watch the black velvet curtains pull away from the screen. While the theater lights dim, my consciousness moves across the darkened room and into the screen.

I peer through the shadows, straining to see beyond the tips of my shoes. Again, there is no floor to walk on. Turning to my left, my energy seems to shift and I easily move around the corner. There is another room on the other side of the kitchen wall. I haven't been to this area of my house before. To my left are steps going up the side of the wall. Suddenly, I am climbing one of the many ladders that are propped next to the stairway.

"Mommy, come find me."

Abruptly, I stop to listen for the direction of Kevin's voice. Then, frantic, I keep climbing higher as Kevin's voice echoes through this obscure out of the way place. Again, I hear him calling, "Mommy, come find me. I'm in the.....

"Where are you Kevin?" I yell through the rungs of the ladder. I can only see the frame of an unfinished wall. I glance to my left and wonder why I am not taking the stairs. Determined to find him I climb even higher moving farther to the left, but always on the same ladder. I know something is wrong and I become more distressed.

"Mommy, come find me. I'm in the....."

"Kevin, I'm coming," I yell again, more frustrated than ever that I cannot hear more. I am moving so fast that my feet and hands barely touch the rungs. I can see the top of ladder. I grab the last rung and heave myself over the top landing in a heap on the attic floor.

With a sudden jolt, I sit up staring wide-eyed at the images still moving across my screen. Breathing hard and fast my chest feels as though it will explode. I cannot get my bearings. I'm not sure where I am.

I feel the soothing touch of soft fingers upon my arm gently pushing me back down.

"Where are you now?" Mary asks.

"I am standing before the door."

Do you want to open the door?" Monte interjected.

"I want to find Kevin. I can't see him," I cried. "The door is white and everything around me is dark. I can't bring myself to open the door."

"Is there something you should know about the other side?"

Confused by my own indecision, I bury my face in my trembling hands. "I'm finally here. What is wrong with me? Why can't I do it?" Grasping the knob in my left hand, I am unsure now that I should open it. Suddenly, my heart sinks deep to the pit of my stomach as if reminding me of something I already know. It circles my heart growing wider until it encompasses my whole being. I know then that I will find only death and darkness on the other side. I don't want to see it.

Pushing against the door with my right hand, I slowly release the knob from my bent fingers. I rest my head on the door shaking it back and forth. I know that I am fooling myself again. Could it be that the disappointment is because I have known all along it would end like this?

I twist my body around and push my back against the door, sliding down as my legs give way to this heavy burden. I cannot carry the illusion and misperceptions any longer. I lock my arms tightly around my knees, resting my weary head between them. I have seen so much pain and suffering. I cannot bear to relive that horrific moment again. I am tired of fighting this battle between my ego and my spirit. I want to be free and whole again, living a life of love and joy. In that moment, I finally concede to destiny.

The heaviness in my chest subsides and I breathe easier. I hear only the steady pounding of my heart echo in the stillness. Then, I sense a pulsating force vibrating higher and higher, as my awareness begins to expand.

Looking up, I am astonished that the dark and forbidding attic has disappeared and I am back in my light-filled sanctuary. Before my eyes have time to adjust, a dazzling shaft of light shines down encircling me in its ray. Tiny sparkles dance within the ray, swirling and whirling like dust particles exposed in the sunlight. Stretching my neck, I search above it to see the source. I squint and shade my eyes while the beam vibrates brighter than before. As I follow its path downward, I see that the base of this glimmering channel of light rests at my feet. And there, standing before me, is my precious son.

Suspended in a brilliant glow of effervescent light, Kevin has transcended time and space. He is dressed suitably in his blue jeans and the white shirt with the #5 emblazoned over his heart. Reaching through the beam, he tenderly holds my face in his warm hands. Mesmerized by his sparkling brown eyes, I cry, "I couldn't find you Boo Boo." Drawing me closer Kevin wraps his arms around my neck and embraces me.

"Mommy," he whispers sweetly in my ear, "I'm not on that side. I'm on this side of the door. "I'm in the Light."

Epilogue

In that moment, I finally understood. We had never been separated, not by the door, not by my illusions, and not by death. My beautiful son had come to comfort and assure me that we are still on the same side of the door. It was the most profound moment of my life. *"Mommy, come find me...I'm in the Light!"* Of course, I did not hear him say that in the Nightmare. There were no words that could adequately describe the mystery of his transition from this world to the next.

In dream after dream, Kevin revealed himself to me reflected in the glory of God. He appeared in a luminous golden light, in an awesome moon light, in an array of dazzling twinkling light, and now, in a beam of radiant white light. Our Father knew that in my brokenness, I would need convincing proof that Kevin had truly survived his death. Grief and mourning had taken up residence in my heart, and in my mind. Until I changed my perceptions, I could not see that the dreams were all the proof I would ever need. Time after time, Kevin showed me that the Light of God had enveloped his soul like a delicate tissue wrapped around a precious gift.

Together, we had begun to unmask my illusions by exposing my fears and bringing them to light. After the hypnosis, as pieces of the Nightmare became clearer, I realized that the last scene was more critical than I could have imagined. In the Nightmare, I was screaming "yyyancee" as I beat upon the shut door. I turned away to see a figure to my left, but I was so devastated by being shut out that I never looked further. I realize now that "yyyancee" was a primal cry for "I can't see."

251

My perception was that I could not see Kevin because I was refused entry to the attic. It was actually the illusions I held of suffering and death that would create more pain and separateness that would keep me blinded and stuck in my grief.

During the hypnosis, I chose not to open that door to see the darkness that represented my former state of unconsciousness. Returning to the attic door was symbolic of raising my consciousness to another level of understanding. The last thing I wanted was to be separated from my son. I did not realize that it also separated me from my God and closed the door to the healing power of the Holy Spirit. It was only in that vulnerable, receptive state that the Holy Spirit could work and heal those misperceptions.

Kevin proved to me that death is only a moment of transition for the soul to return home from its journey in the physical world. No matter how long or how short the trip, I am guaranteed new life. It is a place where fear cannot exist because God's love for me is more powerful and more enduring than any misperception that I could ever conceive. The key to my survival would be in choosing to live in light rather than in fear. It seemed like such a simple choice when I considered the alternative. I could have spent the next forty years yearning for my past. Instead, I could choose to create a future that would be remembered with love instead of pain. It has been the greatest challenge of my life, and I am continually presented with opportunities to practice this concept.

As my journey continues, Kevin has remained present, guiding, protecting, and inspiring me to see differently. Even now, given all that I have learned from this experience, I continue to have periods of unconsciousness that remove me from the presence of God. While preparing this manuscript for publication, I was plagued with self-doubt and uncertainty. One night, Kevin appeared to me in a dream and tenderly said, "Don't you know how important you are? Don't you know how important what you are doing is?" As God's humble servant, Kevin brought His unconditional love and encouragement to me. He helped me to see this project through when my self-esteem took a beating.

Kevin will always be my spiritual coach clothed in his special T-shirt stamped with the number five. A few years after the hypnosis session, I discovered a symbolic definition for the number five that appeared over Kevin's heart. The Buddhist tradition says: "The heart has four directions, which, with its center make five, and represents universality: the state of being present everywhere." Indeed.

And finally, what of destiny and agreements? It is now clear to me that we enter this life in a partnership with God. Our shared goal is based on agreements that we make to remain in the likeness and being of God's image, good and whole. Too often, once we are here living out that agreement, we have second thoughts and the agreements are perceived as a cross to bear! Long after the hypnosis session, I discovered an old dream journal, dated March 13, 1990. I was stunned when I came across a dream entry detailing my knowledge and acceptance of this plan less than nine months before the accident:

In the dream, I am seated at a big desk across from two priests that I know, the only two that I have ever shared my feelings with. In appreciation for doing something for the church, they give me two gifts (but before the meeting is over, I have forgotten what they are). The younger priest says he has one more gift for me. He reaches from behind the desk and hands me a long large object in leather case. I open the flap and pull out a huge, heavy, silver crucifix that is as long as the desk top. I hold it carefully, amazed that it is not as heavy as it looks. I am in awe and feel honored to possess such a gift. The priest and I shake hands, and he says, "Carla, a very special thing happened between us...you must not forget it." I tell him that I understand. We meet three more times to talk. On the last time I am very sad, but I know I will see my friend again. We say goodbye and kiss on the cheek as we embrace. I drive away with Stann feeling very secure with this sense of knowing.

Was the dream journal misplaced or did it surface at just the right time? In the early stages of this journey, would I have readily accepted this prophetic dream as the forerunner to the Nightmare? Was the silver cross I carried so carefully, the cross I would bear? Would I have ever accepted that with one handshake I had agreed to change the course of many lives? Surely, God knew that the mother in me would break our agreement and try to prevent Kevin's exit in any way I could. I had actually brainwashed myself with fears when it came time to carry out my part. Would not every mother change her mind? Did the end justify the means? That, of course, depends on whether you are asking my heart or my logic to respond.

As I searched for the meaning to this experience, the questions multiplied and harassed my sanity. Does destiny override choice, or does choice form destiny? Are the agreements discussed and refined until the best possible outcome can be achieved? What happens when souls stray from the goal and break their agreement? And, what about the other key players in this mystery? For after all, if I believe this concept to be sound and true, then must it not apply to everyone?

What kind of agreements did the Driver and the Neighbors make and why did they make the choices they did? After many years of contemplation, I realize that I cannot assume what the experience meant to the Driver and the Neighbors, or why they chose to participate, and I cannot judge whether it impacted their lives or not. Once I accepted the power of choosing with love or in fear, I understood that I held expectations of the way the Driver and the Neighbors *should respond*. When they did not, I felt disappointed and betrayed. It was unrealistic of me to expect them to respond in any other way than what they did. It is impossible to see clearly when our consciousness is clouded by fear.

I let go of any need to blame the Driver for what happened to Kevin and our family. I carried enough blame for my own participation and it required a lot of energy to do so. I hold no resentment for the Neighbors as well. Because of my faith, I live with the assurance that all of my questions have answers. When I make the transition from this life to the next, I will be granted the opportunity to understand this mystery from every perspective. I will see even more clearly.

I have also learned that I have a lot more to learn about the power of God's love for me! I have become less oriented to religious doctrine realizing that God is not confined to a set of rules that serve to keep our fears alive. Instead, I prefer to explore rituals, prayer and music that expand my awareness of God's presence and the working of the Holy Spirit in my life. Perhaps in God's desire for me to become all that I can be, there are things I must do without being privy to the plan. I must trust that together we have decided that there are certain things I must experience to complete this journey and that it is all for my highest good.

In Kevin's transition, I was given a gift, an opportunity to see beyond the door. I have experienced the presence of God, forever changing me to see differently. Dreaming Kevin gave me a chance to see my son the way God sees him, pure and good and whole. In those wondrous moments with Kevin, I was also allowed to touch him and to feel his spiritual body close to mine. I treasure those moments because as his mother I will always long to hold my son and kiss his sweet face. That desire will never cease for I am still human. The physical connection that I have with Kevin is deeply rooted in every cell of my body, available at a moment's notice. He is never more than a thought away.

My spiritual connection with my son and with my God is equally as strong, and everlasting. For long after Kevin's body has disintegrated to ashes and blown across the mountaintop, his soul lives on reaching out to me from beyond the door.

Acknowledgements

MARCH, 2002 ~ When I first heard the call to write *Dreaming Kevin: The Path to Healing*, my soul responded with a resounding yes that echoed all the way to the Somewhere. My gut knew it was time and my heart felt strong enough to bear those memories again. The rest of me panicked and fell in a crumpled heap on the floor. The excuses began to pile up beside me until I was covered by a blanket of doubt and fear. Where would I find the time to write my story when my hands were full with two small children and a budding teenager?

The more I resisted, the more the universe insisted with gentle yet firm nudges reminding me of my agreement to get to work. Frustrated that time did not seem to be cooperating by giving me more of itself so I could work freely, I finally collapsed in defeat. "All right God," I said defiantly, "This is your project not mine. If you want this to happen then you better send me help. I don't know how to do this!" With one final challenge I quipped, "I'll write the book, but it's up to you to make the rest happen". After all this time and through everything I had been shown, I still had the gall to demand God's attention with a tantrum. However, God heard my challenge and accepted it gracefully, sending me more help than I could have imagined.

Dreaming Kevin has been divinely guided and would not be in your hands without the assistance of some very special people in my life.

I thank my loving husband Stann, who made so many sacrifices during the five years I was consumed with writing this book and getting it published. In our twenty-three years together he has been an amazing model of love, trust and acceptance. I am blessed to call him my partner. I love you Stann, with all my heart.

I thank my precious daughter Amber, who has blessed me with her compassion and forgiveness, and who has become one of my greatest teachers. I am in awe of her inner beauty and the way it touches everyone she knows. You have blessed my life Amber Dear. I love you.

I thank my two youngest children, Megan and Jason, for choosing to come into our family despite the chaos and pain. Their positive energy and spontaneous spirits have recharged our family. They remind us daily that it is okay to play and laugh again! I am so blessed to be loved by them. I love you Miss Megan and Lovey Boy.

I thank God, who immediately answered my cry by sending the most supportive and loving people to walk this perilous path with me. I would not have survived without their unceasing love and support. I thank my Dad for the way he has modeled the spirit of giving, always there for me, never holding back. I thank my brother Paul for sharing my vision and creating the cover. Special thanks to my family, friends, acquaintances, and mere strangers who answered God's call and gracefully came to my side. I hope they find themselves among the pages of this book, and in my heart as well. You cannot imagine how much you have touched my life. I love you all.

I thank Mary, Chris, and Diana, three extraordinary women who opened their hearts and embraced me fully. Instead of mirroring my grief, they mirrored my strengths and helped me believe in myself again. I have been humbled by their presence in my life. Dear friends you have truly been my companions. I love you.

I also thank those companions who supported me while I was writing this book. Your pep talks, readings, revisions, insights, childcare, phone calls, emails, and prayers made my heart full. You lifted me with your faith and gave me the courage to continue writing when I doubted my abilities. I thank Steve my Mac Man for his perseverance in repairing my corrupted manuscript and for his patience with my limited computer skills. A special thanks to Kay for helping me listen to my angels and answer the call. Another special thanks to my Number One Book Buddy, Laura, for her encouragement and editing. And to my Bossanova, Judy, for reminding me to trust my intuition. I love you all.

Last, I thank my sweet Kevin, who helped me see beyond the door. I love you, Boo Boo. xxoo

Carla

PART V

Afterglow ~ 2014

"Let my love fill your heart with hope
like the afterglow of a sunset
illuminates the fullness of the day."
~Carla Blowey

JANUARY 2014 ~ When Kevin and I agreed to do the expanded edition of *Dreaming Kevin*, I knew the editor in me would insist on another proof reading. It would be tempting to play with the wording because as every writer knows, a piece is never really finished. My favorite part of my job as editor-in-chief for *Living With Loss Magazine*, was helping a writer find their voice to tell their story. Reading the book again with my editor skills, I was reminded that I had indeed found my authentic voice. My grieving soul cried out for understanding, balance and reconciliation, and ultimately gave voice to the unspeakable. The voice of grief can be harsh and unforgiving, and at times, even silent, but the impact of its truth is known only to the griever. In order for the healing to begin, I had to embrace the dream symbols and images that illustrated the indescribable.

As a result, dream work has raised my awareness to recognize the triggers that incite an uprising of undisclosed grief. Thankfully now, I can revisit my story without feeling traumatized. I have integrated the experience in my life, and I no longer live there...*it* lives within me, welcomed, and by *my* choice. I am no longer just surviving the experience; I am *thriving* beyond it because I choose to see it differently.

Dream work is an opportunity to embark on the spiritual path of individuation for healing and wholeness. For a bereaved parent, it is an excruciating process to become aware of oneself in grief as we reconcile the fears, conflicts and challenges of the perceived loss of the death of a child.

I've witnessed firsthand, the transformative power of dream work as a tool for healing. I've met so many courageous bereaved parents and families across the country (and beyond) who are willing to trudge through the murky waters of grief, dive in and do the depth work.

In my workshops, participants often confront me with narrowed eyes and crossed arms when I talk about healing. Their pained expressions scream, *"I'll NEVER get over this!"* I understand. In my early years, I would have stomped out of the room spitting fire at the mention of anything that implied I would be *healed*.

What does it really mean to heal? Webster's Online Dictionary defines healing as: *to make sound or whole; to restore to health; to rehabilitate; to cause and undesirable condition to be overcome.* The list goes on and yet there does not seem to be a definition sufficient for the newly bereaved or grievers in any phase. Do we take the word "healing" literally? Why does it trigger such volatile reactions of resistance in some of us? Where do we hurt the most? Where do we want that healing to occur? In our body? In our mind? In our spirit? Can it occur in one and not the other?

Every time I make that choice to see my dreams and my fears differently, I am in a state of *healing*. Healing the wounds of grief that reside in my body, in my mind, in my heart, and in my soul, can be achieved by changing the perception I have of death, loss, pain, and suffering. By setting an intention that I want healing to occur, I become open to it. By being open, ready and willing to change my perception of how that healing is going to occur I become receptive to it. Being receptive gives me the capacity to accept the presence of the Divine with humility and gratitude to make space for grace to move freely in my life and create healing. That healing brings my relationships with my family, friends, co-workers, my community, and my deceased loved ones, into balance.

My response then can be of nurturing and acceptance rather than reacting or defending. Then, *if I choose to reconcile* the death of my loved one, I can begin to integrate this present reality with a renewed sense of energy and confidence and I can find meaning and purpose in my life.

However you choose to perceive and define healing, remember this: the word "heal*ing*" expresses a mode of *being*, a process that is ongoing, lifelong. For those of us reconciling the death of a loved one there is no "ed". We cannot change the fact that our children or loved ones died but we can change our perception of the experience and see it differently. Perhaps, it is time we redefine healing.

We all have the opportunity to choose how we will react or respond in the aftermath of our children's or loved one's death. We also have a unique set of circumstances about the death that require different expressions. More importantly, *we always have choices* –sometimes not the choices we want or like –but we always have an opportunity to choose Love over fear in any given moment. If we are willing to see our grief and our dreams differently, we can release the narrow parameters of love and build a continuing relationship with our deceased child or loved one that will *celebrate them and bless our lives.*

I believe that Love overcomes virtually everything. Whatever the question, Love is the answer! I have not only survived this uncharted journey of more than twenty years, I *thrive* on Love. There is no other way. Love is the truth and the life we seek. *Love* is the way.

Dream work is a transformative tool for bringing our dreams of the night *and* our waking dreams of the day into the light to see them differently –making connections with personal and archetypal symbols from the inner world to develop creative solutions for our emotional, mental, physical and spiritual well-being in the outer world. I heard a calling from my interior world and responded. I believe you have a calling too.

After much soul-searching these past 23 years, I affirm that I am a dream worker –a seeker of light, truth, possibility, and hope; a facilitator for peace, grace and transformative healing.

I am passionate about encouraging more dialogue on how our dreams reveal the hidden issues that block the path of healing during a range of life transitions from birth to death. Projective feedback and discernment bring forth an "ah-ha" response –a reliable indicator that something must be true about the dream (or the nightmare) for the dreamer. The fact that the image or message is *remembered*, confirms that the dreamer is ready to confront it. Witnessing a shift of perspective on any level continues to affirm for me, the validity of the tool.

So, know that *my* story is my own and *your* story is your own, and we will recognize and embrace one another in each. Don't be blinded by someone else's extraordinary experiences and dreams or be intimidated by mine. Examine your own dreams for the extra-ordinary within! Bring your story from the inner world to the outer world where it can be illuminated, acknowledged and validated. In doing so, you give the community the gift of your experience, empowering yourself and others with insight and reflection to encourage personal change and spiritual growth. In turn, the potential for changing perceptions about death and loss also spread to the greater community. This raised consciousness enables us to explore creative approaches to grieving and model an authentic path of healing.

Dreams and Blessings,

Carla

Notes from the Children

"Pain that is not transformed, is transferred." ~ Richard Rohr

The death of our Kevin claimed not only the life of our son, but also the life of our family. Our vibrant family of four that played together, laughed together, and loved together became a family of three, in an instant. We became a family in crises and we began living the "nightmare".

In the years after Kevin's death, we experienced a warped sense of reality, blindly navigating through those vulnerable times. We questioned our decision-making abilities about our careers, finances, bills, illnesses, health issues, holidays, purchases, social engagements and raising our children.

We discovered again and again that the term, "stages of grief" was a misnomer! There were no stages of designated grief, just excruciating moments of vulnerability and loss.

Our worst nightmare had come true and we were living it – experiencing extreme emotions like shock, disillusionment, abandonment, fear, anger, rage, guilt, longing, despair, and sadness, in no particular order. We became physically ill, suffering from insomnia, listlessness, uncontrollable shaking, stomach distress, flu-like symptoms, surgeries and accidental injuries. Our mental state deteriorated and we suffered from memory loss, inattention, confusion and lack of concentration. Our productivity suffered at work and school. There were timely decisions to make but we were ill equipped to make them. Humiliated and embarrassed, we relied on others to pick up the slack. Thrust into the legal world, that included doctors, coroners, police, lawyers, and the court system, we were forced to learn their language.

Likewise, despite everything I learned from my dream world, I still questioned the unfairness of God's lack of intervention when we had "done all the right things". We had not yet integrated the amazing insights or gained enough perspective. We pleaded and bargained with hope that God would grant *us* a miracle. Our belief system crumbled around us and we plunged into *a spiritual* crisis.

These crises issues were not unique to my family. Many of these issues are typical of families who have experienced the death of a loved one, abuse, and other traumatic life-altering events. The word *crisis* literally means "a decisive moment" and is defined as such: *"an unstable or crucial time or state of affairs in which a decisive change is impending, especially one with the distinct possibility of a highly undesirable outcome."*

In our society, the acceptable path during a crisis is to flee from vulnerability to protection, rather than *"be"* with it to enter into the mystery and seek understanding, reconciliation, solutions, and personal growth. Addressing the cultural and spiritual needs of families in crises can only encourage and enhance healing. It isn't about "treating" or diagnosing the care receiver, it's about companioning them as they discover a holistic way of grieving. It is a "decisive moment" that can make or break the journey and grieving children are alone and unskilled to do so.

How can we as caregivers, facilitators, counselors, therapists, and parents *companion* children and their families as they grieve traumatic losses? First, we recognize that families in crises need assistance that supports the entire family –addressing bereavement issues from a holistic perspective, where caregivers understand the psycho-social, physiological, economic, cultural, and spiritual dynamics within the family. During the time of our crises in the 90's, the perception seemed to be that the children were flexible enough to deal with loss issues without intervention or assistance. "No worries –they'll get over it! They just need to get back to school and be with their friends and play! No need to drudge up all that sadness."

Thankfully, today there is a greater awareness about children's grief in the wake of the numerous and tragic school shootings in the past two decades. We now know that they experience the same feelings and issues as adults. It just looks different. Often, a child's grief is confused with normal developmental stages of growth. However, I also sense that society has hit the panic button with an expectation that sounds like this: *"now that we know this grief stuff needs our attention, bereaved children should be able to get over it in three counseling sessions and still make it to soccer practice!"*

For those of us who are doing the depth work, this perception is incongruous. We must recognize that healing is a life-long process. Reconciliation occurs on many levels, at a varying intensity, at unscheduled times, and only when the griever is ready. The most important thing for a grieving child to know is that they are supported and loved, and that they will be heard. The most common mistake we as adults make is to talk instead of listen. We are so focused on alleviating the pain, that in *our talking,* we actually rob the young griever of the opportunity to witness their inner world and express the unspeakable.

I believe we all need and appreciate someone to *be* with us in that vulnerable place, a brave companion to go deep and go the distance.

Seasoned grievers must avoid the rush to heal the newly bereaved and circumvent the process for the griever. It takes courage to companion a grieving person because most likely we will see a remnant of *our* story in *their* story. And, if *our* story is *unexamined*, we risk projecting our issues and agendas on them *–judging the griever's pain to mask our own*. As caregivers, we can assist the children best by first looking at our own grief and loss experiences. We must look at our perceptions about, death, loss, and grief *and our biases* about the healing tools that we find unacceptable or uncomfortable to work with, and in doing so we can work toward reconciling our own loss issues. We will be more present to a young grievers needs and less focused on our fears. We can be a conscious caregiver for a child who might be alone on his/her journey because the family is not ready or cannot do their grief work. Often times, the innocent children are the catalyst for the healing.

I first recognized the power of sharing our dreams, and our grief, when Stann and I spoke to a youth group at our Catholic church for a Confirmation retreat in 1994. Speaking together for the first time, we shared the risks we took in processing our grief, walking our faith, and living again. Later, inspired by a dream I had about the retreat, I realized our daughter, Amber, and other grieving children also needed a safe place to share their grief stories as well. I presented the idea to our parish priest and a core group of close friends who were also therapists, and their response was enthusiastic and supportive. I coordinated a local chapter of Rainbows, a national organization for children's grief support, in our town for the next three years. It was a powerful experience and our volunteer group served many grieving children. Amber was in the first group, and as a seventh grader, remembers feeling resentful that we were making her go to a support group!

Amber says: *"At first, I remember being really annoyed that you would make me go. Once I saw that there were other kids in the group that I went to school with, and they were experiencing some of the same things, I felt better. When we were there we were able to talk about things on a "kid" level and it was nice. Erik (our facilitator) was great, he had an awesome way of making us feel comfortable and allowed us to share (or not). I am sure we talked about confidentiality during our group, but I think that all of us were able to respect that outside of the group. I never felt like anybody broke that."*

I grieved deeply for the children who experienced Kevin's death. His sister, cousins and friends felt a void that no playmate could fill. It was painful to watch their social interactions but I felt too overwhelmed by my own daughter's needs to presume what the other children needed. I knew on some level that Amber would act out any unresolved grief at some point. Nearing adolescence, her needs, questions, and fears were different then at eight years of age.

I invited several of the parents who were still living nearby to consider the children's grief group for their own children. None of them pursued it. Some felt that too much time had passed. Why bring it up again? Others preferred to manage it privately at home or at church. I was disappointed but I knew it was ultimately up to each family to address Kevin's death from their own beliefs, perceptions, and religious affiliations.

Even so, I wanted the children to know that tears, sadness, confusion and anger are a normal response when a loved one has died. Remembering Kevin and talking about what happened was never off limits with me. I wanted to know how much they understood or accepted and I worried about how this would affect the children later.

In the first year, there was a spontaneous dialogue and compelling artwork. Amber, Kyle, Dillon, Mitchell, and Kevin's preschool class expressed their inner world in drawings and artwork, illustrating the mournful process of coming to terms with the permanence of death. For the youngest children, drawing was their only means of communicating the intuitive language they understood, just as it was for Kevin. I cherished their artwork and letters that gave me a glimpse of their inner world. It was an honor to be the recipient of such gifts.

Eventually, for many parents, the subject of their child's grief was replaced with reports of the family, sports, and school activities. For our family, Amber's grief remained front and center, sometimes obliterating the normal achievements and highlights of her childhood. I never stopped the dialogue with Amber –sometimes to a fault. I admit that during her adolescence I might have gone overboard in processing. I feared she would become unconscious and bury the pain, and we would lose her too, in a different way. It was a tenuous time never knowing just how much information and details to offer in answer to her questions.

My desire to companion Amber and provide resources for other grieving children was genuine but there was an underlying responsibility as well. As I began to accept the concept that Kevin's death was not accidental and his transition intentional, I struggled with an intense guilt over being a willing participant of a divine plan that would cause so much pain and suffering for my daughter and my husband. I so strongly identified with the archetype of the perfect mother that I mistakenly assumed sole responsibility for their pain and I believed it was up to me to ease their suffering.

As I matured spiritually, I realized each of us had made our own agreements, and that Amber had participated as well. We were in this together and we would learn from one another. Our parallel paths crossed often, and as she grieved, I grieved, embracing both my daughter, and my own grieving *inner* child. Amber actually became my greatest teacher, modeling the goodness of humanity, the resilience of the human spirit, and the blessing of forgiveness. Amber reminded me there was meaning and purpose in my life, and it all stemmed from her.

In the beginning, I needed to find a way to ease my guilt. I found the courage to join a support group for bereaved parents. Later on, I became a facilitator and coordinated support groups and grief camps for grieving children. I never imagined in those formative years that this journey would lead to writing and publishing our story, and ultimately, speaking and presenting workshops to the bereaved across the country about using dreams as a tool for healing through loss and transition.

This expanded edition of *Dreaming Kevin* is the result of guidance I received from a series of dreams in 2012. Earlier that year, I felt compelled to broaden my efforts in dream work beyond the bereavement field to include life transitions. I felt a resistance within me to move beyond the bereavement work because something about that notion felt incomplete. The dreams reminded me of three "projects" I had shelved years ago that needed my attention. The first one being to publish the expanded edition of *Dreaming Kevin* with an updated cover and an afterword section on healing; the second, a workbook dream journal for the bereaved; and the third, a children's book about Amber's dream visit with Kevin. I dove in, completed the first task, blessed it and moved down my list.

And, then, I heard Kevin's sweet voice whisper in my ear, *"Mom...what about the children? Don't you remember? We were going to write about them too."*

It took my breath away. I knew that *Dreaming Kevin* was complete as far as my story was concerned. The afterword on healing was actually the segue to the story of the silent, unseen grief of the children. I believed that the children who experienced Kevin's death first hand, and those who experienced it, through their parents or from a distance, shared a bond not only with Kevin, but also with one another.

How deep is the trauma after twenty-three years? What is their perspective of this life-changing event now that they are a young adult and/or parent of their own children? Would they be willing to share their memories of Kevin's death and the impact it had on their lives? Would they even remember? Would they *want* to?

In no time, I created a questionnaire and a list of names and sent out the first round of emails. A day later, their heartfelt responses poured in with more depth and insight than I could have imagined. With their permission, I share their memories –an unedited, spontaneous, and universal dialogue on children's grief.

"There is no greater agony than bearing
an untold story inside you." ~ Maya Angelo

1.) What do you remember most about Kevin? Describe him.

"Kevin was sweet, tender, funny, and loving. When we played together, he was always excited about creating new stories and was never afraid to be silly or be himself. Kevin had such a funny sense of humor and he could always make me laugh." **Amber: sister, age 8.5/31, autism-special education teacher**

"I remember Kevin being my other half, my partner in crime, my secret keeper, my best friend. I still believe I can hear his laugh even though it has been 22 years since we lost him. Most of all I remember his smile, and how it lit up a room, and more importantly the way it made everyone else smile."
Dillon: cousin, age 5.10/29, line operator in a carbon plant

"The thing that comes to mind most is his smile, he always had a huge smile on his face. Blonde hair, & bright sparkling eyes. I can't describe him any more than that, don't get me wrong I can see his face any time someone says his name or I read it even if they are not talking about him because they don't know him." **Dean: cousin, age 10/32, electrician**

"Kevin had a smile that was very contagious and was very warming."
Rex Lee: cousin age 12/34, heavy semi mechanic

"I don't remember Kevin as well as I would like. I have a few images of Kevin that will always be with me, and they usually involve Kevin making me laugh. My favorite memory is when my dad would take us to preschool in his Jeep with the roof taken off, and he would play Huey Lewis and News' album Sports. Kevin and I would dance as crazily and goofily as you could imagine; we would throw our arms and legs around and bang our heads like we were rock stars. I'm pretty sure we received some funny looks from passengers in other vehicles, but we didn't care. Though this final comment doesn't necessarily describe Kevin, I remember looking up to him (even though I was significantly taller). He had a confidence and a joy and a love for life that I wanted, and the thing that I find as I grow up is that I experience that same joy and love for life the more I spend time with Jesus." **Kyle: preschool and family friend, age 5.5/28, teacher**

"It's been 22 years and I don't remember much about Kevin. I do remember that he was my best friend. I remember us playing together. I remember us going to Montessori school together with Miss Sharon and chasing the dog at school. More than what he looked like, I remember my feelings of friendship, trust, and security with Kevin and his family. One random thing I do remember was the sponge like wedges in between his toes. I remember asking my mom why I did not have those on my feet. 'Why did Kevin get those and I didn't?'"
Michael: preschool and family friend, age 4.5/27, retail

"I remember his sweet face and playing with him in the back yard, I think it had a hill or was sloped? And that he was very kind and full of energy. I remember the tree that is decorated each holiday season, and how fast it seemed to grow. I remember that night at the Confirmation retreat at the cabin when you talked to us about Kevin and how sad and emotional I felt as though I'd never forgotten him or his death and how close I felt to you in that moment." **Morgan: preschool/church friend, age 5.5/28, athletic trainer**

"I remember such a beautiful boy. He always had immense energy and zest! I have one scene captured in my mind where he was running through the house with a yellow blanket tied around him as a cape. He was always roaring, running, and having such a great time imagining." **Whitney: family friend/Amber, age 8.5/30, marriage and family therapist intern**

"I remember his big brown eyes. I remember that he was funny he would make me and Amber laugh. I also remember Amber being annoyed when he would interrupt our playing dolls with his boy toys. I also remember a few times when he would be so bored that he would sometimes give in and play girl stuff with us. Like dress up." **Rachelle: Amber's friend, age 9/31, facility and property manager**

"I remember his blond hair and brown eyes. I remember Amber and I would always be playing together and Kevin would want to tag along. He would want to be a part of what we were doing. I think we would play house a lot. We were probably a bit bossy with him, but he would usually go along with our 'plans'. He was just very sweet and easy-going in that way. I'm thinking he must have been pretty well behaved, because I don't recall any memories of him getting in trouble. I also recall him wearing cowboy boots sometimes and playing 'cowboy' with his toy gun." **Nicole: family friend/Amber, age 7/30, teacher**

"I remember his light brown/blond hair and his cowlick in the front of his hair. I remember him in a blue coat with what feels like gray outlining of the hood. I remember him bothering the girls as all little boys would do during our family get-togethers and dinners." **Kori: family friend/Amber, age 9/31, banking**

"Brown wavy/curly hair, dark eyes, good smile. I have an image of playing with him in a tree. He was standing in between branches near the trunk of the tree. The tree leaves were yellow green and we were in the shade but there was sun hanging in the air. Amber and Josh were also there. That is probably the only direct memory I have of Kevin. Otherwise, most the memories I have I think are from looking at pictures of him and hearing stories. On a separate note I have a really cute picture of my son Jacob that looks similar to Carla's favorite picture of Kevin. I cannot use the picture because it is eerie to me. Almost like putting the picture up would be a bad omen." **Rachel P.M.: family friend, age 6/28**

"I remember the way he walked. He was very athletic for a five-year-old." **Katie: family friend, age 8.5/30, senior project coordinator for Vecenergy**

"Playing at get-togethers. He was always nice to me and we would play outside and run around." **Jessica: family friend, age 5.5/28, wedding coordinator (Mary's daughter)**

"I remember Kevin giggling a lot, running splashing in the waves and doing his little brother duty and pestering Amber and myself. He was with my little brother and the two of them together were a dynamic duo who always ran around and were filled with too much energy." **Rachel A.: cousin, age 8.5/30, special education teacher (Regina's daughter)**

"Laughing, great smile. Fun." **Tara: cousin, age 6/29, Corporate Education & Training Specialist (Regina's daughter)**

"I do not remember anything about Kevin other than what I had seen in pictures and heard from other family members." **Kate: cousin, age 5.5/28, financial analyst (Bunny's daughter)**

2.) Tell me about the last time you were with Kevin before he died.

"That last morning, I remember being anxious about starting at the new school. I was being bossy with him about making his bed before he could watch cartoons. Why I cared about that, who knows? I don't remember anything else about that day until I was standing on the corner waiting for you (Mom) to pick me up after school. I distinctly remember we were in the car on the way to gymnastics. He was teasing Rachelle and me with the bananas –being silly and laughing. I remember getting out of the car, saying goodbye and I love you, and then Rachelle and I laughing together as we went in to the gymnastic building. The weekend activities with the family are so blurry and for a long time I couldn't place the sequence of events. I do remember how much fun we had sledding at the hill and being with all the kids in the basement for sausage making day at the Woodruff's."
Amber: sister, age 8.5/31, autism-special education teacher

"With me being almost seven (six) at the time I do not recall the last time I was with my best friend." **Dillon: cousin, age 5.10/29, line operator in a carbon plant**

"All I can remember is that it was Christmas Day, the Christmas before he died." **Dean: cousin, age 10/32, electrician**

"I don't remember." **Rex Lee: cousin, age 12/34, heavy semi mechanic**

"Sadly, I have no recollection of the last time I was with Kevin. I get pictures in my mind when I read about our last time together in *Dreaming Kevin*, but they aren't really memories as much as some sort of familiarity that I don't know how to describe." **Kyle: preschool and family friend, age 5.5/28, teacher**
"The last memories I have of Kevin were on January 6th of that year. I truly don't remember if these are my memories or if they are fragments of the memories my family and I have shared since that date. It was a day like any other where our families had gotten together at our house in Woodgate. The kids played, ran around the house and ate food!"
Michael: preschool and family friend, age 4.5/27, retail

"It is a blur to me in my memories of different play dates at the house...But I'm unsure of my last time spent with him." **Whitney: family friend/Amber, age 8.5/30, marriage and family therapist intern**

"I was in the car with Amber and Kevin the day he died. You picked me up from school at Pomona Elementary and then we when to Johnson Elementary to get Amber then you took us to Gymnastics practice. I remember Kevin was making Amber and I laugh, I can't remember what he was saying but I remember it was funny. Then we went to the gym and started practice. Half way through practice someone came to pick up Amber. I was on bars. She ran over to the person they talked and then she came over to me and said that she had to go. I asked, "Why?" She said, "It was an emergency." I gave her a quick hug and she dashed out. I remember thinking, "That was weird what happened?" My mom was supposed to pick up Amber and me from practice and take Amber home and then me home. When practice was over, my mom came and she asked, "Where is Amber?" I told her that someone came and got her from practice about half way through. I told her Amber said it was an emergency. My mom asked "Did she know the person that came and got her?" I said, "I think so. I hope everything is ok." My mom said, "Me too." **Rachelle: Amber's friend, age 9/31, facility and property manager**

"Gosh, rusty memory. I believe we were with him the Sunday before he died. We were all at your house, I believe, or the Woodruffs. And, all the kids were downstairs. And, I remember the girls holding the door shut to a room in the basement and the boys kept trying to push it open. We didn't want them in because boys were not fun at that age and they got their laughs out of teasing us!" **Kori: family friend/Amber, age 9/31, banking**

"We were at our family vacation in Ocean City. I have one distinct memory of all of us cousins building sand creatures with Poppy Joe. it was Matthew's and Kevin's job to run down to the water and grab the wet sand. So back and forth, they went with their buckets collecting sand and dumping it in our massive mound to make our big creature. I remember myself being a little bossy and telling them to slow down because they were losing valuable wet sand from running so wildly! It was really a fun day and I treasure our beach memories." **Rachel A.: cousin, age 8.5/30, special education teacher (Regina's daughter)**

"Family Reunion in Ocean City, MD (when I was 4)." **Tara: cousin, age 6/29, Corporate Education & Training Specialist (Regina's daughter)**

Family Reunion in Ocean City, MD – **Excerpt from a school essay about Kevin; 12/18/2000.** "I remember playing in the sand with you and watching Poppy Joe make those great sand creatures. We thought we were helping but we really were in the way. Our sisters would chase us, and your dad would take us for rides on the boogie board. My dad took us fishing but we never caught anything. I still have some of the seashells we found together. I remember we would get all sandy and then run up to the shower on the boardwalk. By the time we got back to everyone on the beach we were covered with sand again and we would go back to the shower again and again. I thought that was pretty funny and we had everyone laughing at us too. I also remember when we went to the boardwalk at night and we could go on the rides. I think that was when you got lost. (usually people were looking for me) How about the train we rode after they found you? Your mom and dad stuck real close to you after that. Then I got lost after that ladybug ride! The best part was when we all went to the movie and saw " Batman". Wow! We were Batman and Robin the rest of the week. I still have three pictures of you and I on the beach just so I have something that we shared together. It's too bad we didn't get to spend any more great summers together. I know we would have been good buds. I really miss you Kevin. You were always like a big brother to me. You may be gone from us but I know you are in heaven. I also know you are probably laughing out loud at some of the stuff I try to get away with because if you were here you would be doing the same stuff.

271

We would have had them all in stitches. Once again you are missed not just by me but by everyone. Love your best bud and cousin. Matt." **Matt: cousin age 3.5/27, hotel services (Regina's son)**

"The last time I saw Kevin was the last reunion down the shore...where the infamous cousins beach picture was taken." **Kate: cousin, age 5.5/28, financial analyst (Bunny's daughter)**

3/4/5). Where were you when your parent(s) told you Kevin died? What did they tell you? Do you remember your first thought or feeling when you were told?

"I remember I was practicing my routine on the bars (at gymnastics) when my next-door neighbor walked in and told me that my mom couldn't pick me up. This neighbor's friend (who I didn't know) actually drove me to the hospital and I worried that something had happened to my mom. When we arrived there were people swarming everywhere and somebody took me into a small room to see my parents. I saw my dad and he lifted me on his lap and told me something horrible had happened. He said that Kevin had been hit by a car and died. My first thought was that we weren't ever going to play together again and that I would be an only child. But, I really didn't comprehend what he was saying. He was sobbing and I had never seen my dad cry before. I don't remember my mom being there at all." **Amber: sister, age 8.5/31, autism-special education teacher**

"I remember being on a stool in the kitchen of our place doing dishes when my mom, Sandra, got the call. Mom told me that Kevin was in a accident, and that he had passed away. I do not remember anything from that moment until the time at his funeral when we released the balloons. I just remember feeling like I lost part of myself." **Dillon: cousin, age 5.10/29, line operator in a carbon plant**

"I don't remember. I don't remember. Scared, How did it happen? Who would want to hurt a little boy?" **Dean: cousin, age 10/32, electrician"**

"I was in school, in Mr. Woodruff's class. I was very numb and upset."
Rex Lee: cousin, age 12/34, heavy semi mechanic

"I'm pretty sure I was in the living room on the first floor of my mom's apartment when she told me. I don't remember exactly what was said, but I think the words "run over" were used. I was confused. I saw my mom and older brother crying even before I heard the news, and even though this was my first taste of death, I recall understanding that I wouldn't be able to play with Kevin again. I'm pretty sure that when I was told, I went running up the stairs of my mom's apartment, stopped at the top step, curled up, and just wept. Eventually, I made it into my bedroom and continued crying on my bed."
Kyle: preschool and family friend, age 5.5/28, teacher

"According to my mom, we were at our house in Woodgate when she and my dad told me Kevin died. I did not understand what they were telling me. I just remember Mom kneeing down and sadly looking into my eyes. I was sad because she was sad. I cried because she cried. I do remember going to my room and hiding under my comforter. I did not want to get out of bed. Mom and Dad came in and stayed with me until I felt

better. I don't remember how I felt other than I think I was confused and so sad seeing my mom cry."
Michael: preschool and family friend, age 4.5/27, retail

"I just remember how scared and sad I felt. I cried a lot and remember thinking about how it happened and feeling immediate grief and fear."
Morgan: preschool/church friend, age 5.5/28, athletic trainer

"We were at home that evening and I actually don't remember hearing the words or explanation. I think it was something like, "Something terrible has happened. Kevin was hit by car and didn't make it, he died, honey." It sounded so hollow and unreal. My memory provides one scene I can recall: I was in the Blowey home within hours of Kevin's tragedy. I was among family members and deep mourning. It was the first time I'd witnessed adults in that much pain. I remembered only hearing deep loud wailing. I wanted someone to make it all stop. I hated how there was no fixing it. I had endless, yet unspoken questions." **Whitney: family and Amber's friend, age 8.5/30, marriage and family therapist intern**

"Later that same night at home after we had dinner, the phone rang. My mom answered then I just remember her crying. I ran over to her she was still on the phone. She was asking the person on the other line, "What happened?" and then she said, still crying "Oh no, no!" I knew something was really wrong. I don't remember what the rest of her conversation was but I remember feeling extreme worry and anxiety for my mom to tell me what was happening. After she hung up still crying she knelt down in front of me. I looked her right in the face and said, "What is wrong?" She said that Kevin was hit by a car when Amber and I were at practice and that he died and is in heaven. I just remember that my heart just started hearting so bad and we just stayed their hugging and crying. Such sadness and worry for my friend Amber."
Rachelle: Amber's friend, age 9/31, facility and property manager

"I was at home. My mom and I had gotten home from school before my dad. My mom received a phone call about the news. I think my mom told me, but I don't remember that specific part. I remember sitting on the couch in our living room, looking out our front window. I think we were both in stunned silence. I remember there was a bit of snow on the ground. I was staring out the window, waiting for my dad's truck to pull in, because I knew my mom would have to tell him the terrible news. I remember feeling very anxious for his arrival. My dad would always walk in the door so happy to see us, but this time he could tell right away, from the looks on our faces, that something was wrong. I remember him asking my mom what was wrong. I remember him reacting with disbelief and devastation. I don't remember the way in which I was told. I think my mom told me Kevin was in an accident, but I don't know if she told me right away that he had died. I mostly remember my mom explaining the accident to my dad, with me listening in. I also remember going to the hospital right after Kevin's death. I remember sitting in a little waiting room and seeing Stann and my dad talking. I remember them discussing whether or not to have Kevin's organs donated. I remember my dad saying that Kevin's little body had already been through enough trauma. I think this was probably my first experience with death; at least it is the first that I can recall. I remember feeling very sad

and in disbelief. It didn't make sense to me because I had just seen him. It didn't seem real that he could be gone. "We just saw him," I kept thinking to myself. I remember hoping that I would wake up the next morning and all of it would just go away, that this wouldn't be real.   In the days following his death, I remember wishing there was something I could have done to prevent what happened. It sounds a little silly to think about now, but I truly thought about if there was anything *I* could have done to 'save' Kevin. I imagined going back to that last night I had seen him and talking to him about bicycle/street safety. It haunted me that I had just seen Kevin. I wished so badly that I could rewind to that last night that I saw him and somehow help him."
Nicole: family friend/Amber, age 7/30, teacher

"I was at my Grandma's house. I used to walk there with other students from school and wait until my mom could pick me up. She took forever and I didn't know what was taking so long. Cell phones weren't invented so I just remember waiting and waiting for my mom to come get me. I would look at the clock every ten minutes. I remember my mom telling me that your neighbor had run over Kevin while he was riding his bike. I don't know if this was my mother's words or my own imagination but I remember thinking (either told or imagined) that the snow from the street had been pushed up along the sides of the road. And, Kevin, was biking down the sidewalk (again, for some reason, I feel he was riding downhill?) and the neighbor couldn't see him because of the snow alongside of the road, it made it impossible to see him and that is when he hit him. I don't feel like he died right away, I feel like it wasn't until the hospital. I remember my thought. I remember thinking of you, Carla, running furiously outside of your house when you would have found out he was hit. And, I remember thinking, Why? And, my parents told me that he was with God and that's better than this world and that God needed an angel and he needed Kevin. I remember thinking that is not fair. No, God doesn't need him. His mom does and his sister does. That is not what God should be doing. He should be watching over Kevin and make sure he is ok. I remember feeling mixed with anger and sadness about the guy that hit him. (I remember it being a guy but can't verify that is factual). I felt mad at him because I felt like he should have looked better. But, then I remember feeling sad. I remember feeling like he didn't have kids. I don't know if he did. I painted a picture of him in my mind. And, I remember feeling like he must feel like his life is over for having endured such a horrible accident. I remember thinking of you having to go into Kevin's room to clean it and my heart aching. I remember feeling like I wish I would have let the boys into the downstairs room we were holding them from (the family get together the night before) and we could have all played together. I remember feeling confused and so confused on why God would let this happen."
Kori: family friend/Amber, age 9/31, banking

"Cannot remember. I do not remember being told he died. I just somehow knew it happened as I grew up." **Rachel P.M.: family friend, age 6/28**

"I don't remember. I think my mom was picking me up from somewhere and she said that Kevin was in an accident."
Katie: family friend, age 8.5/30, senior project coordinator for Vecenergy

"I was at home. My mom was devastated. She said that Kevin was hit by a car and died and that he went to Heaven to be with God. I was sad and upset."
Jessica: family friend, age 5.5/28 wedding coordinator (Mary's daughter)

"I was at home, I had a friend over and we were running up stairs to go do something. I saw my mom in the corner on the phone crying and she said, "Kevin died". After my friend had left, Mom explained there was an accident and that he got hit on his bike and did not survive. I feel really guilty about this and I think this why the day was so clear in my head. When my mom first said, "Kevin died", I immediately thought she was talking about a kid in my class name Kevin. I didn't make the connection it was my cousin Kevin until my mom told the story and mentioned Amber. Then I remember being very sad, I thought about losing my little brother and then I thought about Amber. For some reason my memories all seem to include Amber and wanting to be with her."
Rachel A.: cousin, age 8.5/30 special education teacher (Regina's daughter)

"I don't have a memory of this." **Tara: cousin, age 6/29, Corporate Education & Training Specialist (Regina's daughter)**

"I don't remember. My dad said that my mom went to Colorado. I was not sure why. I don't remember actually being told. I remember my mom leaving, sleeping in my parent's bed with my Dad and brother, and eating takeout a lot that week. I don't remember when I put it all together that it was for my cousin." **Kate: cousin, age 5.5/28, financial analyst (Bunny's daughter)**

6.) If you lived nearby, describe what it was like for you when you came to Kevin's house for the first time after he died.

"It felt empty and quiet...even though it wasn't."
Amber: sister, age 8.5/31, special education teacher

"I don't remember." **Dillon: cousin, age 5.10/29, line operator in a carbon plant**

"Empty, like something was missing, which it was."
Dean: cousin, age 10/32, electrician

"Very empty. Kevin was the life of any family gathering. He could bring a smile to anyone's face at any given time, and he was gone and it was empty."
Rex Lee: cousin, age 12/34, heavy semi mechanic

"If I remember correctly, going back to Kevin's house was uncomfortable. I remember (indistinctly) thinking how strange it was to see Kevin's mom without a huge genuine smile on her face. I had always known her to be happy, and seeing her sad broke my heart even more. His mom told me that I could take one of Kevin's toys that we both loved to play with, and I was disappointed when I couldn't take a Batman toy, which understandably, his family held on to."
Kyle: preschool and family friend, age 5.5/28, teacher

"After Kevin's death, it was awhile till I went back to the Blowey's house. I saw Amber, but where was Kevin? It seemed I was always looking for him and did not quite understand that he was gone. I remember going to Bella's, Kevin and my daycare lady. She hugged me a lot trying to make me feel better but I don't remember ever feeling sad, Kevin was just not there."
Michael: preschool and family friend, age 4.5/27, retail

"I remember being in your kitchen with you and my mom and looking out of the window in the kitchen and it was a bright, sunny day and you and my mom were speaking quietly and I felt very confused and just wanted to play with my friend."
Morgan: preschool/church friend, age 5.5/28, athletic trainer

"After the first day visiting Amber and her family I really can't recall the next time...it seemed so long before I would see Amber again. I think I questioned if I ever would have her back in the way I'd known her before."
Whitney: family friend/Amber, age 8.5/30, marriage and family therapist intern

"I don't remember the exact day but I remember the days as a blur. It was sad for me because Amber would talk about Kevin and how much she missed him. We both missed him. We would talk about fun times we had with him and remember him. Sometimes Amber would just talk and I would be there for her and just listen because I didn't know what to say. I still had fun because I got to play with Amber."
Rachelle: Amber's friend, age 9/31, facility and property manager

"I don't remember." **Nicole: family friend/Amber, age 7/30, teacher**

"I remember walking in and I feel like the living room was to the left and the kitchen/dining room in front of me. I remember dim light. That's all I remember. Just dim light and people. What I do remember is leaving your house for the first time after we were there. I remember looking out the car of our station wagon, just looking with my brothers next to me, just sad and praying so hard and earnestly for all of your family. Praying so hard you would be okay. I felt so bad that you might feel sad or retrace your steps that day by letting him ride his bike outside. And, hoped you didn't ever feel bad."
Kori: family friend/Amber, age 9/31, banking

"I didn't know how to act. I knew that everyone was sad and I wanted to help Amber feel better. We played with her dolls and tried to act as though everything was normal. I remember Amber saying that Kevin didn't have a chance to play with his new toys."
Katie: family friend, age 8.5/30, senior project coordinator for Vecenergy

"I remember going to your house after it happened and it was filled with people and they were all sad, there was such a feeling of oppression/depression, and I remembered it bothered me and I just wanted to leave, but I didn't really get why."
Alexandra: family friend, age 6/29, teacher

"I don't remember exactly the first time but it was sad and too quiet."
Jessica: family friend, age 5.5/28 wedding coordinator (Mary's daughter)

"I didn't live nearby but I remember our first reunion without him. It was sad and deep down we all knew we were missing a cousin. Matthew was different too, his buddy was gone and he could tell he missed him because he hung around us more."
Rachel A.: cousin, age 8.5/30 special education teacher (Regina's daughter)

7.) Did you go to the rosary/viewing and/or the funeral? What do you remember?

"I remember everyone gathering in the living room for the rosary, but that's all. At the viewing, I remember standing at the casket and touching Kevin's face and thinking he felt so fake, like plastic. I remember the smell very distinctly; to the point it made me nauseous. He was wearing his Christmas outfit. I remember sitting in the front row, and different people came up to talk about Kevin. I don't remember specifically what anybody said, but I do remember that Rex Lee and Dean stood up to say something. I remember someone asking me if I wanted to say something but I couldn't even move from the seat. I remember thinking when it was over, that I just wanted to stay there and be with Kevin longer. I was upset that they (whoever that was) made me leave. At the funeral, I remember sitting in the pews at the Christian Church, and I remember watching all the people coming in. I remember thinking, how could all these people know who we were? I remember it feeling very long. I don't remember any of the songs or even who spoke. At the end, I remember releasing the balloons."
Amber: sister, age 8.5/31, autism-special education teacher

"I can only remember being outside holding a balloon over his casket, and then filling that balloon with every ounce of love I had for Kevin and sending it to God letting him know that Kevin meant a lot to me."
Dillon: cousin, age 5.10/29, line operator in a carbon plant

"Yes, I went to it all. I remember seeing him lying in the casket, I remember the preacher asking if anyone had anything to say about Kevin, I remember going up and talking about him but I don't remember what I said."
Dean: cousin, age 10/32, electrician

277

"Yes, once again pain mixed with numbness."
Rex Lee: cousin, age 12/34, heavy semi mechanic

"I only have one picture in my mind, and my guess is that it was about the funeral. I remember thinking that there were a lot of people there, and I'm pretty sure I convinced myself that none of them except his family were as close to Kevin as I was. My angry and jealous little heart wanted them to know that I was hurting more than they were. I was selfish, especially when it came to Kevin. My mom also told me that when I saw the casket, I asked if I could see him so that I could say goodbye."
Kyle: preschool and family friend, age 5.5/28, teacher"

"Mom and Dad told me that I went to the funeral but the only things I remember were the big, framed picture of him and the closed casket. I also remember Mom playing lullaby songs that were played at the funeral. I listened to them at night before bed."
Michael: preschool and family friend, age 4.5/27, retail

"I believe I did, but I can't pull ANY memory..."
Whitney: family friend/Amber, age 8.5/30, marriage and family therapist intern

"I remember sitting in the church. I know that it wasn't at St. Mary's. The church was very open and circular, with lots of seating. What I remember most was when Carla got up to speak about Kevin. I remember her holding up Kevin's little leg braces that he wore as a toddler. She told the story of how Kevin was born with clubbed feet, and that the doctors said he might never walk. She talked about how Kevin had overcome so many obstacles in his short life –that he had proven the doctors wrong."
Nicole: family friend/Amber, age 7/30, teacher

" I cannot remember" **Rachel P.M.: family friend, age 6/28**

"I remember not wanting to go to the funeral and I think this stems from my experience at my step grandfather's funeral from when I was younger. I wanted to avoid the sorrow that I knew I would see and experience."
Katie K.N: family friend, age 8.5/30, senior project coordinator for Vecenergy

"Yes but I don't remember much, just that everyone was sad and we let balloons off after the service." **Jessica: family friend, age 5.5/28, wedding coordinator (Mary's daughter)**

"I did not go, but I remember my mom leaving on the plane to go."
Rachel A.; cousin, age 8.5/30 special education teacher (Regina's daughter)

"No. ☹" **Tara: cousin, age 6/29, Corporate Education & Training Specialist (Regina's daughter)**

278

8.) Describe what it was like for you when you returned to school or to your child care home?

"It was lonely. Since I had just moved schools, I really didn't know a lot of the kids there. I know there were some kids that I knew, but I definitely didn't feel comfortable with them. I remember staying in from recess a lot. I also remember an older girl asked me in the hallway when I was on the way to the bathroom, if I had a brother. I said no, and then I was so upset that I said that I cried in the bathroom."
Amber: sister, age 8.5/31, autism-special education teacher

"I don't remember. It really frustrates me because I can't bring any of this back. I try but I only have a few select memories because I remember very little until I was in third grade when we moved from Montrose back to Idaho."
Dillon: cousin, age 5.10/29 , line operator in a carbon plant

"I was a lot older than Kevin, so school and daycare was not an option. After my parent's divorce, my mom, my brothers and I lived with Uncle Stann and Aunt Carla the year before Kevin died. **Rex Lee: cousin, age 12/34, heavy semi mechanic**

"I don't remember a single day of preschool after Kevin died, but my mom described that it was difficult for me." **Kyle: preschool and family friend, age 5.5/28, teacher**

9.) Did you talk to anyone about how you were feeling? What was their response?

"I honestly don't remember even one conversation with a friend about it. I am sure I did, probably to Whitney, Talia and Rachelle, but I have no idea what we talked about. I remember wanting to be around friends so I didn't have to be by myself. I talked to Mary Ann, my teacher (and our family friend), and the guidance counselor at school and they were comforting. I felt most comfortable talking to Mary (our grief counselor) because she made it a safe place to talk about Kevin and all the crazy stuff that was happening at school, the move, making new friends, and the new baby. I talked a lot with my parents about Kevin. I needed to remember him, but it wasn't until I was in middle school that I asked for more details about what happened."
Amber: sister, age 8.5/31, autism-special education teacher

"I don't remember talking to anyone then. I haven't talked to anyone but my wife and Aunt Carla about any of this (questionnaire)"
Dillon; cousin, age 5.10/29, line operator in a carbon plant

"I don't remember." **Dean: cousin, age 10/32, electrician**

"No, I didn't but I should have." **Rex Lee: cousin, age12/34, heavy semi mechanic**

"I don't remember talking with anyone soon after the accident. I've been told that I spoke with a psychologist. However, I do remember talking with Carla about it several times years later. I think we might have discussed it at their new house, maybe another time in Telluride (Is that right?), at Kevin's tree, and I think she once took me to the spot where he was hit. I remember our discussions helping quite a bit even though I don't remember the details. I was always amazed with how much Kevin's mom wanted to take care of me even though she was hurting more than I could imagine."
Kyle: preschool and family friend, age 5.5/28, teacher

"My parents were open to discussing Kevin's passing openly and even encouraged us to ask questions. I can't remember being able to articulate my pain. I do however, recall one night driving home from a party in the family car. My parents were in the front, and my brother Mitchell was laying in my lap on our drive home. I remember looking out at the moon and feeling so awestruck by the light of the moon, and it was then that a flooding of thought and feeling surrounding Kevin's death that I experienced a real quiet cry with tears streaming. It was somehow cathartic but I knew I wasn't able to articulate it in the moment to anyone in the car." **Whitney: family friend/Amber, age 8.5/30,**

"I don't recall any conversations I might have had afterward. I probably just kept most of my thoughts and feelings to myself. I still tend to be pretty private with my feelings."
Nicole: family friend/Amber, age 7/30, teacher

"I talked to my parents but I remember their answers not making sense to me."
Kori: family friend/Amber, age 9/31, banking

"Whenever I was sad I would just talk to my Mom and Dad. I remember asking why? Then they would talk about God and fate, and that God needed Kevin in heaven."
Rachelle: Amber's friend, age 9/31,

"Not at the time but since becoming a mother I have talked with Justin, my mom, and you about it more. Justin does not get how it affects me –so sad. My mom just shares info. Your conversation is the most helpful in getting a deeper understanding about how is death impacted your life and your family." **Rachel P.M.: family friend, age 6/28**

"I remember speaking with my third grade teacher, Mrs. Chenevert at school and having a conversation about how God could let something like that happen. I believe her answer was that we don't always know what God's plan is, but he always has His reason. No matter how hard it is for us to accept and understand."
Katie: family friend, age 8.5/30, senior project coordinator for Vecenergy

"Yes, my mom. She was comforting."
Jessica: family friend, age 5.5/28, wedding coordinator (Mary's daughter)

"I'm sure I told my friends but I don't remember how they reacted." **Rachel A.: cousin, age 8.5/30, special education teacher (Regina's daughter)**

"No, not that I can remember." **Tara: cousin, age 6/29, Corporate Education & Training Specialist (Regina's daughter)**

"I do not remember talking to anyone about how I was feeling. It did not affect me too much –I knew we were related and something tragic had happened to him but I had not spent much time with him or knew much about him to have a tremendous impact. If it did, I do not remember." **Kate: cousin, age 5.5/28, financial analyst (Bunny's daughter)**

10.) What did you observe in your parents?

"Crying lots of crying. I remember that you spent a lot of time the first few days in the bedroom. I remember that you kept trying to go outside to the driveway, and people would try to stop you. I remember Dad following you outside too. I really can't even place where Dad was those first few days. I do remember him answering the phone a few times though. There was definitely a change in their overall protectiveness of me. I had the sense that they wanted to make sure I was always okay and safe but it was too the point of smothering. It lessened when the younger children were born and it was more tolerable." **Amber: sister, age 8.5/31, autism-special education teacher**

"I don't remember." **Dillon: cousin, age 5.10/29, line operator in a carbon plant**

"I remember my mom crying a lot everybody did. The one I remember the most though was Uncle Stann. I remember people telling us that we needed to be strong not just for ourselves but for Mom and Kevin. All I could think though was seeing how hurt and sad Uncle Stann was and saying to myself, 'How are *we* supposed to be strong when someone as big and strong as Uncle Stann could barely move at times, and they want *us* to be strong?'" **Dean: cousin, age 10/32, electrician**

"Hurt and pain. My mother kept a very close eye on us three boys for a while." **Rex Lee: cousin, age 12/34, heavy semi mechanic**

" I don't remember." **Kyle: preschool and family friend, age 5.5/28, teacher**

"I don't remember how my dad was, but my mom was very sad and I remember when she would go talk with you how sad she would be." **Morgan: preschool/church friend, age 5.5/28, athletic trainer**

"I observed lots of sadness and anger. I couldn't help but wonder who they were angry with. I thought it was strange to be mad." **Whitney: family friend/Amber, age 8.5/30, marriage and family therapist intern**

"In the beginning, they were just very shocked and devastated. I just saw them hurting so badly for the two of you. One time my dad talked about how heart wrenching it was to see his good friend, one of the physically strongest men he knew, literally brought to his knees in agony. I know my parents, along with our other close friends, were there to give support, especially early on. That year, my mom took Amber into her third grade classroom." **Nicole: family friend/Amber, age 7/30, teacher**

"My mom was sad. She brought candy to church to give to you because she would usually have given it to Kevin during communion because he was too young to receive it." **Kori: family friend/Amber, age 9/31, banking**

"Hard to say how it affected them. They seemed protective and cautious but not excessively so. I think they would have been that way no matter what. Maybe the biggest thing we learned from our parents (my mom) was how to be sympathetic and considerate of others who have suffered such a loss. Like somehow watching Megan and Jason for the week you were gone was linked to Kevin's loss and taking Amber to Mexico with us was linked to Kevin's loss. So we learned that you should be there and really make grand gestures to try to help your friends when they are trying to recover not just for one week but for years. Also, we watched how you all talk about Kevin a lot and I think that shows that you do not have to bury everything." **Rachel: family friend, age 6/28**

"My dad avoided the situation and conversations. My mom was supportive although I think it was difficult for her. I don't think she felt like she could grieve. I remember when we went to your house not long after that we didn't stay long and that my mom was trying hard not to cry." **Katie: family friend, age 8.5/30, senior project coordinator for Vecenergy**

"Large amount of sadness. She prayed a lot and spent a lot of time with your family. She would not let me ride my bike for a long time and was very sensitive around cars." **Jessica: family friend, age 5.5/28, wedding coordinator (Mary's daughter)**

"I remember my parents being upset, especially my mom. As a child, you never see your parents upset. I knew something horrible had happened, I knew that it was because of Kevin's death. I remember my mom leaving for Colorado and wondering why we couldn't go; I wanted to see my family and be with my mom. I was sad I couldn't go." **Rachel A: cousin, age 8.5/30, special education teacher (Regina's daughter)**

"I do not recall observing anything in my parents." **Kate: cousin, age 5.5/28, financial analyst (Bunny's daughter)**

11.) Looking back, what do you think you needed most?
"I think that I got everything and more than I needed. I needed family, I needed friends, I needed company so I didn't feel alone (even though that was inevitable) I don't think could have been better cared for by you and Dad, our family and all our friends." **Amber: sister, age 8.5/31, autism-special education teacher**

282

"I can only remember wanting my best friend back."
Dillon: cousin, age 5.10/29, line operator in a carbon plant

"Comfort and answers that at the time I was probably too young for but now I don't remember what the questions were, other than 'Why? Why Kevin? Why a little boy that never had a chance?'" **Dean: cousin, age 10/32, electrician**

"I dealt with things differently than everyone else. I find that if I'm left alone and cry and get it out it's best for me, and I didn't get that."
Rex Lee: cousin, age 12/34, heavy semi mechanic

"I believe God gave me all the things I needed most. My mom and brother did everything they could to comfort and encourage me. Kevin's mom always had a way of helping me focus more on the fun I had with Kevin rather than time we no longer had with him. When I moved to South Dakota a couple of years after the accident, I became best friends with twins, and one of them was named Kevin. And though I knew they would never replace Kevin, God used them to help me move on and see that life was still definitely worth living."
Kyle: preschool and family friend, age 5.5/28, teacher

"I think I needed the normalcy of routine but maybe more opportunities to express through non-verbal means. I think I would have benefited from putting my feelings into art work or story. I felt like it would be 'trying to get attention' if I initiated any symbolic play or expression."
Whitney: family friend/Amber, age 8.5/30, marriage and family therapist intern

"Probably to be told that it was very sweet of me to want to go back and "help" Kevin, but that there was nothing I could have done differently to prevent what happened – that accidents happen sometimes, and it isn't anyone's fault. Also just to have a chance to share the happy memories we had of Kevin. I think sharing those memories would have helped them to remain with me longer."
Nicole: family friend/Amber, age 7/30, teacher

"I feel like I got what I needed. It was just to have people in my life that loved me and talked with me whenever I needed them."
Rachelle: Amber's friend, age 9/31, facility and property manager

"I needed for it to make sense but I don't think that was possible as accidents are not sensible." **Kori: family friend/Amber, age 9/31, banking**

"More/different information as time passes. I never really knew what happened to Kevin, your family, Amber, and how Megan and Jason came to be until just recently and it's still not as complete as I need. I think about the experience a lot but I do not feel peace with it so it is hard for me to find strength through the story when I apply it to my own life. I probably knew the appropriate amount of detail when I was young but my understanding

has not grown. Since my mom was involved so closely and I knew him, it was always just kind of assumed that I knew everything but I think what I needed was to understand more/differently as I grew up. Adults just assume that I understand as much as they do because I was 'around' for it all. But, as a kid I understood on a different level and it was never readdressed. I feel obligated to act like I know or just be quiet when I have questions. Trying to understand how to keep faith and move through the ups and downs of life is something I have not satisfactorily addressed with regard to the questions Kevin's death has raised. Having known someone who had a real tragedy in their life makes me wonder how to be strong and what answers about life did they/you learn. What wisdom do you have to share about living through grief, moving on, keeping faith, not being afraid, moving past anger, accepting that there is no answer to the question, "Why?". These are all things I would never have wondered as a child."
Rachel P.M.: family friend, age 6/28

"Just what I received, comfort, explanation, and tears." **Jessica: family friend, age 5.5/28, wedding coordinator (Mary's daughter)**

"At the time I was confused on what really happened. It wasn't until years later when I read *Dreaming Kevin* that the puzzle was put together. I think looking back it would have helped if I had known exactly what happened. Not that anyone held out on telling me but little details were missing and having those helped me process it as I got older. Especially on Jan 7th every year. I could imagine his last day in detail and it gave me a little peace."
Rachel A.: cousin, age 8.5/30, special education teacher (Regina's daughter)

"At the time, I needed more of an understanding of the situation. I knew what had happened. I knew Kevin had died. But I was so young at the time, it never really cut into me physically. I didn't have that physical pain that is brought on by the news of death when you get older; I only had what emotions I could provide on the surface."
Tara: cousin, age 6/29, Corporate Education & Training Specialist (Regina's daughter)

"I'm not sure. At that age I was too young to understand something like that.
Kate: cousin, age 5.5/28, financial analyst (Bunny's daughter)

12.) Did you have any dreams about Kevin when you were younger? If so, and if you are willing, please describe the dream.

"I don't remember the details of some of the early dreams. One of the first dreams that I remember was Kevin standing over me by my bed. He was in all white, and I remember that he told me that everything would be okay. I also dreamt that there were a pair of glasses on my bedroom floor and when I picked them up I could see Kevin in both lenses of the glasses. On one side was the hurt Kevin and the other side was the healed Kevin."
Amber: sister, age 8.5/31, autism-special education teacher

"I only have a recollection of one dream and it only sticks with me because I can't get it out of my mind and that is a picture of Kevin after the accident. I don't know if I ever actually looked at Kevin after the accident, but I've had this dream more than once that I see him in his casket, and I picture tread marks over his face and body. And, that pretty much is the only dream I've ever remembered." **Dillon: cousin, age 5.10/29, line operator in a carbon plant**

"Not that I can remember." **Dean: cousin, age 10/32, electrician**

"Not that I can remember." **Rex Lee: cousin, age 12/34, heavy semi mechanic**

"I'm sure I had dreams about Kevin, but I don't remember them." **Kyle: preschool and family friend, age 5.5/28, teacher (Kyle does not remember that his preschool teacher wrote down this dream that he shared with her:** *"The witch was going down the stairs trying to get to Kevin. The witch was running through people trying to get Kevin. Kevin was scared. They went down the stairs again. Carla was trying to save Kevin from the witch. The witch had a big nose, and ugly face, a black hat and a pink face. Kevin was falling and no one could catch him."*

"I don't really remember any dreams, but when I talked to my mom about Kevin after receiving this email, she jogged my memory about a picture that he made before he died that had your family members in it and him above as though he was in heaven looking down on you all. When she mentioned the picture I remembered it, but can't remember if I was there when he made the picture."
Morgan: preschool/church friend, age 5.5/28, athletic trainer

"I bet that I did (because I've always had very vivid dreams), but I can't remember."
Nicole: family friend/Amber, age 7/30, teacher

"Sometimes my memories seem to have a dream like quality. I wish I could turn up the volume and let the memory unfold more fully. I hate not having more to recall."
Whitney: family friend/Amber, age 8.5/30, marriage and family therapist intern

"I didn't have any dreams that I remember."
Rachelle: Amber's friend, age 9/31, facility and property manager

"No." **Rachel P.M.: family friend, age 6/28**

"No." **Katie: family friend, age 8.5/30, senior project coordinator for Vecenergy**

"Honestly, I bet I did but I cannot remember them."
Kori: family friend/Amber, age 9/31, banking

"I'm sorry I am not going to be much help, I have very few memories and they are very disjointed, the biggest one I have is that we are all camping at Ridgeway, and Kevin was following, Katie, Amber and I, and we didn't want him there so I think someone told him

to get lost. As little kids can be, we weren't nice. Then it was night and raining and Kevin was lost, he never came back to camp. I remember feeling guilty, like it was our fault. And my Mom telling us, "NO, no one could find him. He's gone, he won't be coming back." I just remember it was a sunny nice day, and we were walking around the camp, and you guys weren't worried about us, and then we told him to stop following us, and then we came back to camp, but he wasn't there, and everyone started looking, then it was night, after searching for him, and waiting, it was cold and I think snowing. To be quite honest I don't know if it was a dream, (as you know mine used to be vivid) or real or my memories are mixed with my dream. I don't even know if we went camping. To be honest when I think about it, even now, the parts that I remember are clear as day. Still disjointed as dreams often are, but the sights, sounds, feelings of us wandering around Ridgeway, the warmth of the sun, the type of pine trees there, the road, even the fact that we were wearing shorts and t-shirts –I can see it. Then, that night with the wind blowing in, the cold weather, my Mom, and going to sleep in the pop-up camper with my blue unicorn blanket. I can still see it. Dreams are interesting things, and some stick with you forever, I know you will never forget yours, and there are some I had as a kid that I still remember parts of that my Dad had to deal."
Alexandra K.: family friend, age 6/29, teacher

"Not that I can remember." **Jessica: family friend, age 5.5/28, wedding coordinator (Mary's daughter)**

"None that I can remember." **Rachel A.; cousin, age 8.5/30 special education teacher (Regina's daughter)**

"Not that I can remember, no." **Tara: cousin, age 6/29, Corporate Education & Training Specialist (Regina's daughter)**

"None that I can recall."
Kate: cousin, age 5.5/28, financial analyst (Bunny's daughter)

13.) How has Kevin's death and the ensuing experience impacted your life?

"It affected my life in every way. I don't know what or where I would even be without this devastating experience. I think it has made me value my relationships with others, I care about every moment we have together. I think it has made me compassionate of others situations, caring (almost to a fault) about their personal situations and wanting to make it better for them. I know how desperately I needed to be cared for and 'heard' during the time right after Kevin died. I feel like our friends and family did this so well, that I have to pay it forward. I think this carries over to my work in special education every day, with the students and the other teachers that I work with as well...at least I hope it does." **Amber: sister, age 8.5/31, autism-special education teacher**

"Every time I think about Kevin or my other cousin Kyle, I feel like I'm the last one standing from that year. I'm the only cousin from '85. I don't feel like I deserve it. That's kind of why it freaks me out. I think that both of my cousins were as deserving as I was to be here. Kevin was my rock when I lived in Montrose. My brothers did their own thing. But I always had Kevin. What I feel *even* now is that I'm still off kilter. Kevin was my best friend and I still consider him my best friend. It's always been hard because I don't have that person to turn to that rock, that guy that I could ask anything to. I can't remember a whole lot. I remember the day it happened, I remember one part of the funeral, and a there's a big gap between everything else for a couple of years. I have tried every day to live my life for two thinking that if Kevin was here we would be doing this together, but also I believe that I have lived my life better because I know that it could all be over at anytime. Kevin's passing has helped me live my life better, but I would take my cousin still alive so I can talk to him face to face. I don't think that we have ever gotten over the losses or my parent's divorce either, but I can say that all have made me a better person, husband, and father." **Dillon: cousin, age 5.10/29, line operator in a carbon plant**

"I never really thought about it. I mean he is always there in my mind but until my cousin Kyle's death I didn't realize what my mind was going through. It's made me a better person." **Rex Lee: cousin, age 12/34, heavy semi mechanic**

"Kevin's death taught me very early on that life is precious. For a while I was afraid of more accidents either taking the life of someone else I was close to or my own life, and that lead me to be scared of trying new things. But now I look at Kevin's death as more evidence for why Satan's lies about God and about how we should live are not worth listening to. Ever since the human family bought into Satan's lies, tragic events like Kevin's death have become common occurrences. I am so thankful God has done everything possible to restore this race, and to bring us back into peace with Him, so that when He returns, sin and its effects will never be felt or experienced again." **Kyle: preschool and family friend, age 5.5/28, teacher**

"When looking back at my childhood, almost all of my first memories include Kevin. We may have only been four and five-years-old but we definitely knew the meaning of friendship." **Michael: preschool and family friend, age 4.5/27, retail**

"Kevin's loss was the first traumatic loss for me and I have had quite a few since then that have also impacted my life. I am scared of death and I am very emotional when someone I know passes on and have a hard time getting over it. I feel happy when I hear that someone has experienced a connection with the deceased person because it helps me have faith that we are not alone, although I do tend to wish that someone would 'come to me' and let me know everything will be okay and not to be scared anymore." **Morgan: preschool/church friend, age 5.5/28, athletic trainer**

"When I think of Kevin's death it makes me realize how precious life is and how life can take unpredictable turns. There are times when I take a step back and tell myself that I shouldn't get so wrapped up in my work, responsibilities, and problems, that I forget to appreciate what is really important in life. Family and friends are the only things that truly matter in this life. Our jobs, homes, and possessions will not follow us in death, but the impact we make will live on in the hearts of those we love. So, when I think of Kevin and his death, it reminds me to focus on the important things in life and not take things for granted." **Nicole: family friend/Amber, age 7/30, teacher**

"Kevin's death was the first most impactful experience of death and dying I have had in my life. I believe because the nature and timing of his death was so foreign to my understanding of the world and order of things, it has forever shaped me. It changed my perception of "fairness" in the world. If I find myself defending a "rightness" in things or a natural order to things, I often drift back to Kevin's death as the first hard reality of things not making sense, and not being fair. Kevin's death has made me more hyper-aware of all the threats in everyday life. However, the MOST important way Kevin has shaped me is in the way I have interpreted his relationship with his family."
Whitney: family friend/Amber, age 8.5/30, marriage and family therapist intern

"Kevin's death impacted my life greatly. I think about him every time I back out of my drive way. Now as an adult, I live in the same neighborhood where Kevin lived. I always look at his tree around Christmas and think about him. Kevin's death helped me to have faith in God and not to fear death. It took a long time to really understand that.
tRachelle: Amber's friend, age 9/31, facility and property manager

"I talk about him at times because I remember the sadness I felt at that age. Such a different way that I would react now. I remember deep, unanswered sadness."
Kori: family friend/Amber, age 9/31 banking

"It seems to be the most personal experience that I compare my "bad" experiences to. Each time something really bad happens to me, I ultimately always compare it to you losing Kevin, and I say "this is not as bad, yet I feel like dying and hate the world...how did Carla survive?" I think my experience of Kevin's death has been more through pain for you and your family and wishing I could know all you know to maybe feel true peace."
Rachel P.M.: family friend, age 6/28

"I think it made me ask questions about God and His purpose earlier then I normally would have. I started to question faith, religion and God's existence at an early age."
Katie: family friend/Amber, age 8.5/30, senior project coordinator for Vecenergy

"It's made me very compassionate and took me on journey in my faith as well. I couldn't understand how God could take someone so small and so innocent. It didn't make sense, and as I've gotten older I still don't truly understand. It's definitely made us a stronger family. I'm so close with all my cousins that although we are miles and miles apart we see or talk to each other as much as possible. I have a way of offering support to those who are in need –it comes natural and I can only think it comes from earlier life experiences. It's Kevin's heartlight that shines through all of us."
Rachel A.: cousin, age 8.5/30, special education teacher (Regina's daughter)

288

"I wish I remembered more about my time with Kevin. It was so short and we were so young, but I do have one memory that is closely related to Kevin's death (i.e. besides family visits months or years later, etc). The memory doesn't involve a specific experience with Kevin himself, but whether he knew it or not, I felt like he was there during this time to help teach me and has since been one of the most vivid memories that I have.

I remember getting into a fight with my younger brother, Matthew. I have no idea what it was about now, I just remember that I got blamed for it and was sent to my parents' room to calm down. I'm a middle child and often felt that things were blamed on me, so naturally I went to the bedroom kicking and screaming because I didn't think anything was my fault. The anger was so intense because I was being punished and my brother wasn't that I remember screaming and wishing he were dead. I didn't want to deal with him and continue to take the blame for him. I was angry. I was emotional. I was a child. The next part of the memory I remember I'm lying on the bed looking at my mother crying in the doorway looking at me. As a child, you never see your parents cry and I feel like this was the first memory (and only one of a few in my lifetime) I have of my mother crying. Among her tears she managed to compose herself to get enough words out. She told me to think about what I had just said. She said Kevin was gone and Amber no longer had her brother and that I should be thankful I have mine. I remember it hitting me immediately that death was permanent. That my cousin, Amber, could no longer see her brother, Kevin again. That I would no longer see him again. And that I had just wished this very thing of my own brother. I'm stubborn, so I was still upset about the situation; but immediately felt compassion for my own brother. This memory reappears in my mind quite often. In some cases, it will come up weekly. Other times, just once a month. But it is there forever. In some way, I always felt like this was Kevin. Helping me hold onto a memory of more innocent times and reminding me of how important friends, family and especially siblings really are to us. I know this memory will never leave me, which comforts me because it makes me feel like a part of Kevin will always be there ensuring I never forget."

Tara: cousin, age 6/29, Corporate Education & Training Specialist (Regina's daughter)

"This one I can actually answer. Being that I was the same age as Kevin when he passed away, I often wondered as I grew up if family members looked at me and saw Kevin and either felt jealousy, envy, sadness or happiness. I think we were expected to be extremely close and it was a huge blow to the family. I found myself wondering what my place was in the family sometimes. I wondered if I needed to live my life for two people. It was odd because I barely knew Kevin and do not remember anything about him but his death affected my life a lot. I never talked to anyone about it and I don't remember anyone sitting down with me and talking about it either."

Kate: cousin, age 5.5/28, financial analyst (Bunny's daughter)

14.) How has Kevin's death impacted you as a parent of your own children?

"I think it has made me treasure every single moment that I have with my daughter, Carly, and my son, Andrew. I'm more aware of those random moments of hugging and kissing them and remembering how they smell, *every day*. I cherish even our smallest moments together, when I say goodbye, when they wake up in the morning or go to bed at night, and randomly throughout the day. I'm more conscious about saying "I love you" – I have to tell them several times, every day, no matter what and probably to an extreme at times. They'll probably think it over-bearing when they get older, but I don't want my children to ever doubt my undying love for them. I want Carly and Andrew to know how important they are to me. I try to pay attention to the little things throughout the day. It's those little things that I miss the most about Kevin. And, most especially, I want Carly and Andrew to love each other the way Kevin and I did, to be kind to each other and never ever take each other for granted." **Amber: sister, age 8.5/31, autism-special education teacher**

"It has helped me care for my children in a way that I didn't think I could. It also has made me a little paranoid about our surroundings that my children are in, and because of that I hold them a little tighter. I don't know if I would be a different parent if Kevin was still alive, but I feel better knowing that Kevin is watching over all of us."
Dillon: cousin, age 5.10/29, line operator in a carbon plant

"I pay attention really, really well when I'm backing out of anywhere especially on a street with a sidewalk, and make sure my kids are extra careful when riding their bikes and or walking on the sidewalk or next to a street."
Dean: cousin, age 10/32, electrician

"As a parent, you don't want your child to go through pain and suffering. But sometimes, you can't stop it. All you can do is be there for them, be a friend, be a parent and offer a shoulder or hug. It's something I had from only one parent."
Rex Lee: cousin, age 12/34, heavy semi mechanic

"I'm not a parent yet." **Kyle: preschool and family friend, age 5.5/28, teacher**

"I don't have any children, but I am very protective of my little cousins/my co-worker's children when they are playing in our work area and I am very attentive to young children." **Morgan: preschool/church friend, age 5.5/28, athletic trainer**

"I think about Kevin from time to time, and I let it be a reminder to appreciate every day that I have with my own children. Life is very fragile and unpredictable, and above all else, I need to make sure my children know how much they are loved. Thinking about Kevin also reminds me how fast time goes by. It's incredible to think that Kevin would be 25 years old now. This makes me want to enjoy every second of their childhood years. My son Eli is four years old right now, so that definitely makes me think of Kevin sometimes. It is such a precious age, that I wish would last longer. Time, when you're a

parent, just goes by too fast... In a practical sense, I am a little paranoid when my kids are near any streets or parking lots. There have been a couple instances that have given me a moment of panic. I've told them about what happened to a little boy that I knew, and how that is the reason why I try to keep them so safe."
Nicole: family friend/Amber, age 7/30, teacher

"It has made me attend to my own love and care for my young children, because there is a finite time on earth, and now more of me understands this. I catch myself looking at them and trying to imagine the profound grief and loss I might feel if they were to die. I am also a more hyper vigilant parent because of my experience." **Whitney: family friend/Amber, age 8.5/30, marriage and family therapist intern**

"We will have to wait and see I don't have children yet."
Rachelle: Amber's friend, age 9/31, facility and property manager

"No. I am not a parent so I am not sure." **Kori: family friend/Amber, age 9/31, banking**

"Just scared. I have a definite fear of trying to prevent bad things and a fear of turning away for a minute and something bad happening. A general awareness of your loss and wondering how I could ever carry on after a similar experience. Kevin's death is my motivation when I run out of energy to be vigilant because I never want to experience the same loss. Grateful for his gift and a reminder to cherish our time together and the little things in life. Afraid of my own dreams- how you said you always had a feeling that Kevin was never going to be with you for long- I get the same feelings and it scares me. Hopefully learning how to have faith that God's plan is better than mine and that I am here for God." **Rachel P.M.: family friend, age 6/28**

"It has brought the experience of losing a child closer to home. I think losing my child would be the most difficult thing to endure and I don't know how I would handle it. Carla, I admire Stann's and your strength." **Katie: family friend/Amber, age 8.5/30, senior project coordinator for Vecenergy**

"I am a mother of three (Michael 7, Ryan 3, and Kylie 18 months). It has affected me in the way I watch them. I am not comfortable with them playing outside without myself or my husband, I don't like them to ride their bikes, and am very uneasy in parking lots, streets, etc. I insist on them holding my hand at all times. I worry that they will be taken from me all the time. I cherish every moment with them."
Jessica: family friend, age 5.5/28, wedding coordinator (Mary's daughter)

"I don't have any children but I have a godchild (Carly, Amber's daughter) of whom I would do anything for. Right now, she is the closest I have to having my own child. It breaks my heart when I can't see her or that I live so far away. I try and see her as much as I possibly can and I just treasure our special moments together. Her spirit is so lively and loving that I could never imagine it not being around. The thought of something happening to her brings me to tears now as I type and makes my heart ache so hard. I

can't imagine it and I don't want too. The biggest thing I've learned throughout life about death is that they are still with you and you can always call upon them for love and support and in some ways that provides a knowing comfort even in some of the lowest of moments."
Rachel A.: cousin, age 8.5/30, special education teacher (Regina's daughter)

15) If you could ask Kevin anything at all what would that be?

The "little girl" in me would ask him why he left, but I would also ask, "Who would you be today? What would you be doing? Where would you live? What is heaven like?" There are endless questions but I would mostly just want to talk about his life in heaven and what I am doing here. **Amber: sister, age 8.5/31, autism-special education teacher**

"If he is proud of me, and what I have done so far."
Dillon: cousin, age 5.10/29, line operator in a carbon plant

"What did you want from life?"
Rex Lee: cousin, age 12/34, heavy semi mechanic

"Did you 'come to me' when I was first diagnosed with diabetes when I was 10?"
Morgan: preschool/church friend, age 5.5/28, athletic trainer

"I would want to ask what made his brief time on earth so wonderful? I feel that would lead me closer to what I want to instill in my children." **Whitney: family friend/Amber, age 8.5/30, marriage and family therapist intern**

"I would ask him why he had to leave this life so soon. I would ask him if he remained five-years-old in heaven, or if he grew up."
Nicole: family friend/Amber, age 7/30, teacher

"I feel like he would be wise now —not sure why. So I would ask him what he wanted to share with me." **Rachel P.M.: family friend, age 6/28**

"What is heaven like?"
Jessica: family friend, age 5.5/28, wedding coordinator (Mary's daughter)

"Were you scared and were you in a lot of pain?"
Rachel A.: cousin, age 8.5/30, special education teacher (Regina's daughter)

"What have you been up to? I often imagine what Kevin (and my sister, Larissa, who died at birth before I was born) would be like today if he were still alive. What would he be doing? What college would he have attended? It's every child's dream to grow up and I can only hope that God let him experience or feel that in heaven. So I would ask him what he did, what did he major in and what is he doing now to follow his own dreams?"

Tara: cousin, age 6/29, Corporate Education & Training Specialist (Regina's daughter)

"Probably, "How am I doing", and is there anything he'd want me to do on his behalf."
Kate: cousin, age 5.5/28, financial analyst (Bunny's daughter)

16.) If you could tell Kevin anything at all, what would that be?

"I love you. I miss you more than anything in the whole world. I wish you were here every day... *every day*." Amber: sister, age 8.5/31, autism-special education teacher

"I believe he knows everything because I tell him everything; he is with me all the time."
Dillon: cousin, age 5.10/29, line operator in a carbon plant

"First, is I love you, and miss you." Dean: cousin, age 10/32, electrician

"I miss your smile, your laugh, and I truly miss what a kind soul and person you are. I love you." Rex Lee: cousin, age 12/34, heavy semi mechanic

"I would tell him that I look forward to seeing him when Jesus returns."
Kyle: preschool and family friend, age 5.5/28, teacher

"You were and always will be loved, Kev. Continue to watch over your family, and please, tell Mitchell I'm sorry I never called him before he died."
Morgan: preschool/church friend, age 5.5/28, athletic trainer

"I would tell him that he was a beautiful little boy who made a huge impact on a lot of people's lives. I would tell him how much he is loved and thought about. I would thank him for helping me to be a better parent to my children."
Nicole: family friend/Amber, age 7/30, teacher

"He is so loved. He was such a special gift to so many people. Thank you for his life. He is missed." Rachel P.M.: family friend, age 6/28

"Your family is amazing." Katie: family friend/Amber, age 8.5/30, senior project coordinator for Vecenergy

"That his family and friends miss him dearly and we all love him so much." Jessica: family friend/Mary's daughter, age 5.5/28, wedding coordinator (Mary's daughter)

"I miss you and love you so much and think about your often." Rachel A.: cousin, age 8.5/30, special education teacher (Regina's daughter)

"Thank you. Thank you for your smile. Thank you for your laugh. Thank you for fun at the beach. Thank you for being my baby brother's beach buddy. Thank you for my memories of you. Thank you for helping me never let go of them. Thank you for carrying them with me every day. Thank You." **Tara: cousin, age 6/29, Corporate Education & Training Specialist (Regina's daughter)**

"I'm sorry that we never got to know each other."
Kate: cousin, age 5.5/28, financial analyst (Bunny's daughter)

17/18.) Have you experienced the death of a family member before or after Kevin's death, and what was their relationship to you? Did their death trigger any memories or experiences that you had when Kevin died? If so, how were you affected?

"Pop (maternal grandfather), Mitchell (Whitney's brother), Grandpa Blowey (paternal grandfather). Yes. When Mitch died, I saw myself in Whitney, just older. It was so painful to see my childhood best friend in such immense pain. I can't imagine how that felt for her as an eight-year-old to see that in a friend, because it was hard for me as an adult. It also brought up many of the feelings I had when Kevin died. It was hard at first to separate what was grief for Kevin, and what was grief for Mitch (and Pop and Grandpa)."
Amber: sister, age 8.5/31, autism-special education teacher

"I lost a good friend Derrick, a hero in my grandfather, Harry, and another first cousin, Kyle. I took each loss very hard, but I was more prepared for these losses because of losing Kevin. I also believe that Kevin as some more company. It was hard when Kyle died too because it triggered a lot of memories about Kevin. It was a little easier on my son, Cooper, because he was only three-years-old at the time. Cooper and Kyle were kind of close for that short time, and Cooper helped *me* get through Kyle's passing more than I helped Cooper get through it. I also had an experience this past year when a co-worker was injured at work and died. I got a lot of help from everybody that I've lost –Kevin, Kyle, Grandpa, my friend Derrick from high school. I felt every one of them with me when we were trying to save this guy. Trying to keep my head as clear as it could be. Afterward, while he was in the hospital fighting for his life I had kind of a calmness to me that I don't think I would have had if I had not of had such great help from the people who are watching over us every day." **Dillon: cousin, age 5.10/29, line operator in a carbon plant**

"I lost another cousin, Kyle, in 2011 and Grandpa Blowey in 2010. I was young when Kevin died so I don't remember much other than feeling like there was a big hole left when he died. Every time I go to a funeral I think about getting up and talking at Kevin's funeral. I don't remember what I said but I remember getting up there. I think Kevin's funeral was the first one I had ever gone to so it holds a dear place in my heart. No matter whose funeral I attend now, whether it be a family member, close friend or co-worker, my first thought is always of sitting in the pew at Kevin's funeral and seeing the casket at the front of the church. The one thing I did learn about funerals from being at Kevin's funeral is that, for me anyway, it is best to think about how they were and not about how they are when you look in the casket. Grandpa's funeral was different for me. For Grandpa, yes, I was sad about but I was glad to see his suffering was finally over. For the most part Grandpa had a long and happy life. Yes, we never want to let go of the ones we love, but it is a part of life, unfortunately. Call me crazy, but it's not as big a deal to me when older people who have lived as long as Grandpa did die, than it is to see someone as young as Kevin or my other cousin Kyle who haven't had a chance to live a full life. I guess it hits just a little closer to my heart. It makes me thank God for how lucky I am to be here today." **Dean: cousin, age 10/32, electrician**

"I lost my cousin Kyle on 9/25/12 and on my way to the hospital, I had thoughts of Kevin and how the two of them were a lot alike in a sense that they would always be there for you with a kind heart."
Rex Lee: cousin, age 12/34, heavy semi mechanic

"Yes, both family and friends after Kevin (my grandmother and Mitchell). I'm not sure if my experiences triggered anything from Kevin's death, but with the more traumatic deaths I certainly felt more emotional, scared, and confused as I'm sure I felt during Kevin's death." **Morgan: preschool/church friend, age 5.5/28, athletic trainer**

"Yes. A few family members and friends. Mitchell (my brother, age 22), a cousin, aunt, grandparents, and high school friend. Yes. The struggle of wondering why??? I felt much closer to God and yet more isolated from my old life and ways of relating to friends. I think over time the effects have been integrated into new meanings and I am much more at ease with people and the 'real world'."
Whitney: family friend/Amber, age 8.5/30, marriage and family therapist intern

"Kevin was my first experience with death, then my cousin, my grandfather, my grandmother and my dog. It was the same feeling, the stabbing pain in my heart at first. The same pain as when you get your heart broken. Then you just miss that person and you just wish that they were still around. It always helps to just remember that person and never forget. With each person my faith in God just grew and grew. And now as an adult I believe with all my heart that they are in at peace with God in heaven."
Rachelle: Amber's friend, age 9/31, facility and property manage

"Yes. Many friends and family and my father. The most recent and most difficult was the unexpected death of my father. 18.) No, it was unlike any other death I had experienced."
Jessica: family friend/Mary's daughter, age 5.5/28, wedding coordinator

"Larry, my Oma's husband, and I have weird memories about that also."
Alexandra K.: family friend, age 6/29, teacher

"Yes. My grandfather and grandmother both died, but it wasn't for at least 15 years after Kevin's death. At the times of their deaths, I was old enough to feel that physical pain that comes from losing a loved one. It was a horrible feeling and made me always think of Kevin, made me always think of my memory that he has never let me forget."
Tara: cousin, age 6/29, Corporate Education & Training Specialist (Regina's daughter)

"Yes, after. Both grandmothers, paternal grandfather, and a few friends. My closest relationship was with my maternal grandmother."

Kate: cousin, age 5.5/28, financial analyst (Bunny's daughter)

19.) Do you believe in life after death? If so, please elaborate.

"Yes, I believe there is something after death. I think that after people die, there is something for all of all of us."
Amber: sister, age 8.5/31, autism-special education teacher

"I believe that there is a great place for us after we die. I believe this with all my heart."
Dillon: cousin, age 5.10/29, line operator in a carbon plant

"Do I believe in life after death? To be honest, I don't know, but from reading the Bible I'm told there is a heaven. If this is true, then I hope I will have done enough good in my life to get there." **Dean: cousin, age 10/32, electrician**

"I believe that there is life after death. My perception of the after-life is that our spirit reconnects with loved ones and those who have touched us during our physical life and we walk amongst these angels, learning from them and watching over our loved ones on Earth, together. I believe that the after-life will reveal the deepest secrets that we could only imagine knowing in our life on Earth, and that we get to spend eternity learning from and loving God and all of His goodness."
Morgan: preschool/church friend, age 5.5/28, athletic trainer

"Absolutely. I believe the worldly experience is very brief compared to what came before and after this time on earth. I believe God has an overwhelming intricate fabric of plans for our souls to thrive within. I believe God has given us purpose in expanding love which reinforces this fabric with meaning, although this meaning may be incomprehensible in the human physical body...that's why *faith* tides us over."
Whitney: family friend/Amber, age 8.5/30, marriage and family therapist intern

"I believe that after death, our souls go to Heaven. I believe we meet Jesus and all of deceased family and friends. I believe we live pain free in happiness and watch over our family we have left behind. **Kori: family friend/Amber, age 9/31, banking. *From Ilene, Kori's mother:*** We were at my in-laws house after we left the Blowey's and Tyler (age 6.5) asked if we thought Kevin was in Heaven. Tanner his older brother (7.5) said that he thought Kevin was right 'up' there, the brightest star in the sky shining down on us. He pointed up to the sky and no lie, there was a huge star shining so bright all by itself! Tanner was the one with the most insight. Later, Kori mentioned in the car that she wondered if Kevin 'knew' about all the wonderful things people were doing for his family. Tanner answered so matter of factly, "Of course he knows." Kori said, "How do you know?" Tanner hit his chest and said, "because, I feel it right here in my heart."

"Yes, in a way, I believe in reincarnation, until we reach a point, or God comes and we no longer have things to learn." **Alexandra K.: family friend, age 6/29, teacher**

"Yes. I believe after we die we go to Heaven. I believe that HEAVEN is much like it is here with animals and nature. I believe that it is *perfect*. When we are in heaven, we have understanding and knowledge and wait for our loved ones." **Jessica: family friend/Mary's daughter, age 5.5/28, wedding coordinator**

"Yes, though my imagination of what life after death is like changes often. When I was young, it involved being above the clouds surrounded by golden sunlight in human form. Today, I feel like it is a combination of those pieces but more spiritual as well. Where your human form is gone, but your spirit and memories exist with those you love." **Tara: cousin, age 6/29, Corporate Education & Training Specialist (Regina's daughter)**

"I want to. The concept of the unknown is very scary to me. It's more the concept of the life as I know it ceasing to exist that is scary. I want to believe that there is something more (better) to this life afterwards. I hope to see my loved ones that have already passed on (or something like the movie, *The Five People You Meet in Heaven*). I refuse to believe in the notion that this is "it". That's the best way I can explain it." **Kate: cousin, age 5.5/28, financial analyst (Bunny's daughter)**

20.) Have you or anyone you know experienced an "after-death communication" with Kevin?

"When I was in college and we were at the Bereaved Parents of the USA Conference in Las Vegas. Dad and I went to the ADC workshop and you and Sandy Goodman were on the panel. You told your story about the pennies and Sandy told a story about receiving dimes from her son Jason. Later that night, I was sitting at the Black Jack table with my cousin. We were in between games and when I looked down there were two perfectly placed dimes right in front of me on the ledge of the table! I felt this incredibly calm, warm feeling come over my shoulders. I was overwhelmed with love. I knew at that moment that it was Kevin, there was *no other way* those dimes could have landed there other than it being Kevin (with some help from Jason!). I *knew* that Kevin was there with me." **Amber: sister, age 8.5/31, autism-special education teacher**

"I had a dream after my cousin Kyle passed away in 2011 that involved Kyle, Kevin, and Grandpa Blowey. All I can remember from it is laughter and smiles, like they were saying everything is okay." **Dillon: cousin, age 5.10/29, line operator in a carbon plant**

"No." **Dean: cousin, age 10/32, electrician**

"This is a hard question for me to answer especially in light of how important dreams are to Kevin's legacy and his family. However, in terms of an "after-death communication," I've never communicated with Kevin because I believe he cannot be communicated with right now. I believe he is (as Jesus described death) sleeping. I think his next moment of consciousness will be of seeing Jesus Second Coming.

Carla, I've been considering the questions that you posed about my thoughts on the perspective of Kevin's death being an agreement with God to further his spiritual growth and how I would explain your visits with Kevin. My first thought is how wonderful it is that we both have the hope of seeing Kevin again soon; I thank God for that hope. My second thought is how different our religious backgrounds are. We probably have different views on the meaning of "soul," we likely view the canonicity of the Apocrypha differently, and my guess is that we would have varying opinions on Ellen White and on the authority of the Pope. Many other factors like these can be attributed as reasons for our contrasting views about the state of the dead and why there is suffering on this earth, and so on. One of the things that Milty (my stepfather) reminded me of is that we may both be wrong or both be right at the same time on these subjects; my Western-thinking mindset has a hard time with that, but I'm glad Milty reminded me of it. My point for sharing these rambling thoughts is to let you know that *I* needed to realize that I should not respond to your questions with the intent to change your mind but so we could better understand each other. You appear to already be at this point; I'm just trying to catch up :)

In response to Kevin's death being an agreement with God to further his spiritual growth, let me first reiterate my view on why God allows suffering. With the experience I've had with the Bible apart from the Apocrypha and with Ellen White, **(1.)** I'm inclined to see God allowing suffering to remind mankind of just how terrible sin is and how horrible Satan's rule is and how we never want to come back to this sinful condition we are in. I personally think Kevin's death fits into this category, and God has used it to help me keep my eyes on Jesus who will come again and restore us to a sinless state (and reunite us with Kevin!). **(2)** I also think God allows suffering to help mankind understand that sins have consequences, and that living life apart from God is not worth it. I look at Adam and Eve getting kicked out of the Garden of Eden for eating the fruit of the Tree of Knowledge of Good and Evil as an example of this. I bet that every time Adam and Eve would see more and more wickedness on the earth or recall how Cain slew Abel, the sorrow they'd feel would remind them of how their sin in the garden had caused their separation from God. Just to be clear, I don't think Kevin died because of any of our specific sins but because we live in a world of sin. **(3)** I think God sometimes allows suffering to show the universe that Satan has lied about God's character and about God's servants. I see Job as a great example of this when Satan called God's and Job's character into question, and God allowed Satan to do his worst, but God ended up glorified when Job remained faithful and when God restored his blessings. I wonder if Kevin's death may fit in this category too, because I think you have remained faithful to God in spite of what Satan has done to your family. Now I'm sure there are other reasons for suffering, but that's all my human brain can think of right now.

The idea that God allowed Kevin to die so that he could grow spiritually definitely has one very bright perspective. It paints God as one who is very interested in our spiritual well-being, which I agree with fully. In fact, I think God is far more concerned for our spiritual growth then our physical growth (though He is certainly concerned about both.) However, I struggle with that perspective because of my belief about the state of the dead, which is that they are not conscious in any respect. I believe the Bible teaches this (of course the Parable of the Rich Man and Lazarus and references to dead souls under the altar of God in Revelation may sometimes hinder the matter from being clearly understood). Also, Ellen White's notes on this greatly speak to me, for she demonstrates how seeing death as a sleep really shows God as being very merciful and loving.

Now, the wisest answer I can give in response to how I'd explain your experience with Kevin since his death, is that I can't explain it. Any attempt to explain it would only emphasize how different our world view is on death and what happens to the "soul" when someone dies. What I do know is that your experiences have led you to become an important influence and support to those who endure similar tragedies, and that is amazing and admirable.

As far as a "coincidence" is concerned, to this day I always think of Kevin when I hear songs by *Huey Lewis and the News*."
Kyle: preschool and family friend, age 5.5/28, teacher

"I definitely am wondering if Kevin is the guardian angel that came to me when I was first diagnosed with diabetes. I would get low blood sugars in the middle of the night which my doctors would say were extremely dangerous. Most people with diabetes are unable to wake themselves up when they get that low while sleeping, causing emergency situations. I remember feeling tingling in my arms and once seeing someone standing in my doorway though I couldn't tell if it was a male or female figure. I would wake up and know immediately that I needed to test my blood sugar and get some juice! My mom told my doctors that I told her for close to a year after being diagnosed that I had a guardian angel and that's how I would wake up if I was low. Even to this day, I am lucky to be able to wake myself up. The tingling in my arms and lips, feels as though something electric is touching me, and it is the first sign. The strange part, is that when I get low during the day or even if it's while I'm laying down but not sleeping, I never feel that tingling sensation, it's only while I'm sleeping. That is why I asked that question because I do feel that someone has been watching over me in these situations."
Morgan: preschool/church friend, age 5.5/28, athletic trainer

"I do not recall such an experience." **Nicole: family friend/Amber, age 7/30, teacher**

"Not with Kevin as far as I remember. But I have had many dreams about my Grandpa Petersen and my dog Lady, so I believe that they happen."
Rachel P.M.: family friend, age 6/28

"Not in regards to Kevin that I know of. I've had some dreams and I've had a few penny moments but I can't figure out who it might have been."
Kate: cousin, age 5.5/28, financial analyst (Bunny's daughter)

******

This section would not be complete without the perspective of the two children who grew up in the shadow of Kevin's death –our beautiful children, Megan and Jason. Their perception of what it was like to come into a family that experienced the death of a child is quite insightful. Megan came to us thirteen months after Kevin's death (see Chapter 28, Endings and Beginnings, page 268) inviting us to acknowledge joy again. Jason joined us three years later giving us another opportunity to experience the exuberance of "boy" energy.

Feeling broken and far from whole or "healed", I felt unworthy of being entrusted with such precious gifts again. Megan and Jason's willingness to choose me as their mother in spite of my insecurity and fears was a testament of unconditional love. It challenged me to fully integrate and live the concept of spiritual agreements within a family unit and acknowledge yet another holy contract between my children and me. In my narrow focus prior to Kevin's death, I wasn't privy to the bigger picture –I learned that "contracts" and "agreements" become visible on a need to know basis. And, *they* would teach me so much more than I could ever teach them!

I know in my heart that our sincere intent as Megan and Jason's parents was to recognize and love them as individuals. There was never a comparison of either of them to Kevin. That said, I was stunned to realize the unconscious burden Jason carried as "the son who got to live". Growing up in the shadow of a big brother is difficult for most children, but for Jason, the "source" of this shadow was unknown and untouchable.

Each of the children experienced us in a different way because as we grew up, so did they. Amber and Kevin had the young and inexperienced parents; Megan and Jason had the older and mature version. I do wish I could have retained my spontaneity with the three of them but sometimes the grief was so intense and consuming that just being present was a challenge.

Overall, in spite of the grief, I hope Amber, Megan and Jason experienced a more "conscious" mother who promised to love them unconditionally –all the way to the moon and back...a bajillion times.

A Note from Megan & Jason

"To maintain a joyful family requires much from both the parents and the children. Each member of the family has to become, in a special way, the servant of the others." ~ Pope John Paul II

♡ I was born a year after my brother Kevin died and although I never knew him, his death has influenced my entire life. Growing up with parents who lost a child was definitely hard in many aspects throughout my childhood and into high school. It was always the little things, like when other kids could ride their bikes without helmets but I could not and I felt so "uncool" because I *had* to wear mine. Then as I grew older, it was about bigger issues like my curfew or my parents feeling uncomfortable about me riding in cars with older kids.

It wasn't until I went to college that I gained a different perspective on their parenting. In the past, I would have described my parents as strict, but looking back now, they were pretty laid back, considering! I understand now that it was never about them trying to control my life; they truly wanted the best for me and wanted to keep me safe. I feel lucky to have parents who care as deeply and intensely as they do. I received more understanding and support from my parents than I know some of my friends received from their parents. My parents were a team and did everything they possibly could to help me grow up to be a respectful, driven, passionate, and kind human being. They have always encouraged me to push myself to greater heights and live my life to the fullest.

Since I left home for college, I have had a huge reality check on what it is like to be an adult and live on my own! First, I realized how much love and support my parents have always given me no matter what choices I made, good or bad. Second, they have *always* had faith in me. I now have a deeper understanding of how lucky I am to be alive to make a difference in my lifetime and to help others do the same.

I believe with all my heart that things are meant to happen for a reason. I cannot imagine experiencing what my parents and sister did over Kevin's death and still staying true to that belief. However, I know that they do believe it as well, and because *they* do, *I know* it is true.

I am proud to be the daughter of Stann and Carla Blowey and without their love and support I would not be who I am today. My mom and dad and my sister are my rock; they are my heroes. They have helped me realize how precious our time is with one another, and the importance of family and relationships. Our passion, honesty, courage and perseverance make us stronger together. Our family is truly like no other, our love for one another runs so deep and true, and I believe it has a great deal to do with Kevin's death. It is the understanding we have that our souls are forever united, we are eternally bound to one another in this life and beyond. –Amore incondizionato (unconditional love)... *that is my family.*

Megan, age 21, photography student

♡ Being the brother of a son in my family who died used to affect me more as a child than as an adult. As a child, I thought about what kind of person Kevin was and what it would be like to have a brother. Some nights I would cry about Kevin, but I wasn't really sure why. As I got older, I thought less about my brother's death but there was one time when I was thinking more about Kevin and I was feeling sad. Curious, I finally decided to try and read my mom's book. I started the book but was only able to read to the part where my mother is describing the scene at the hospital. I could not read any further. I was only in middle school and just couldn't handle the detail or the pain I felt after I read only a small portion of it. Since then, I have never read the book. I guess the years have gone by and I haven't felt the right time to flip through those pages again.

In my middle school years and early high school years, I used to feel bad because I would think about how my father had a son and a different life before me. I would think about how his life used to be with Kevin, his first son, and I remember what a strange a feeling it was to think about that. I would always wonder what it would be like if he was alive and what he would look like at a certain age and how things would be.

When I was younger, and even now, Kevin appears in my head as a thought, something that I know is true but doesn't seem real. Whenever I would tell my friends about my brother I didn't feel as sad as I felt I should have been when they would respond by saying sorry or feeling bad for me. Their grief for me didn't mean anything to me because I didn't know what it was like to lose him. I was just born in the shadow of what I knew nothing about. I just didn't know. I never felt the pain and loss like Amber, my father and my mother did.

My father or mother never put any pressure on me and never made me feel like I had to fill Kevin's shoes or try to be what he once was. They

> Keven
> I wish my brother was alive because so I could see him when he is 19. And we can play together. Also so I could see him face to face. one more thing so my sister could say sorry because they had a fight before he died.

Jason age 9, 2004

302

raised me as my own person and they love me for who I was born to be. I am grateful for this, because even though at times I would make myself think that I needed to be the best son I could be like their memory of Kevin, *I* was their new son. I was a new beginning, a new memory for my mother and father's lives. I hope that one day soon I'll pick up the book and really find out the truth of what once used to be my parents' lives and how far they have come since then.

Jason, age 18, paramedic student

Jason Blowey
1/27/10

age 14.5

Kevin

I step into the only lamp alive in the street.
It is dim, with no life.
I look in the dark driveway ahead.
Flashing back as if I was there,
A slight chill runs from my feet up my spine to my head.
The air is cold and hard with lonelyness.
A boy rides his bike with glee,
The sidwalk is smooth on the bikes wheel.
Houses hide behind trees,
but one stands out with a moving car in th driveway.
The man in the truck peels out,
He clashes with the boy a bored the bike.
Slam! Aaahhh!
Everything happens so quickly there is no time to shout.
The Mother runs out in panic,
Trying to wake the tender child and cries and pouts.
In shock, there is nothing she can do for him.
Blood streams out of the face and head like a river.
Cries for help bring neighbors afoot,
Boys broken body lay like soot.
His face is as pale as snow,
Mothers face is drenched in Tears.
She can't help but cry her baby boys name,
So sudden for the boy to join his peers.
The man stands there empty minded
Finally, he calls the police.
I come back to reality,
More sensitive then ever I burst into tears
Feels like there is no gravity.
I walk a lonely road HOME.

—Jason
Blowey

303

A Note from Amber

"Time does not heal all wounds, but all wounds need the grace of time for any measure of healing to occur. " ~ Carla Blowey

January 2014 ~ I am so blessed for the opportunity to read all of your responses to the interview questionnaire that my mother sent to you. Reading what you all have so generously shared was both incredibly emotional as well as healing for me. I thank you all so much for being open and willing to share such amazing memories and intimate details of your grief experience from Kevin's death. I know that it must not have been easy to pull up all those memories after so many years.

It brought me to tears (happy ones) when I read that you remember Kevin as sweet, caring, and loving, and that for many of you he was your best friend. I have often wondered how all "the kids" remember Kevin, and it was so amazing to read that you all remember him the same way that I do! He truly was a best friend to many –a funny and ultimately loving little boy to all who knew him.

I was also so grateful to read that your last memories of Kevin were so happy and that you remember having fun. So many of your last memories involve me being with you as well, but my memory of so much of what happened in those days right before he died is a little blurry. I remember most of the activities that you described –sledding, playing at the Woodruff's house, spending Christmas day at Grandma and Grandpa's house –so many memories of having fun together and enjoying each other's company. I think what impacts me the most was reading Rachelle's last memory of Kevin. Rachelle, the way you remember that car ride is almost exactly as I remember it, and it is *my* last memory too. Kevin was being so silly in the car making us laugh and teasing us, just being himself. What a wonderful way to remember him!

As I continued to read (with tears still flowing) I was utterly amazed at the detail in which you remember receiving this horrible news; what it was like afterward; and your memories of the funeral. The days afterward are a blurry mess for me except for a few details of the funeral, and the overwhelming feelings of grief. All of your responses were stories that I had never heard before or at least I do not remember hearing them. One of the things that resonated most with me was the idea that how each and every one of us lost a piece of our innocence that day in losing a brother, a cousin, and a friend. Some of you mentioned you had experienced the death of another relative, but the loss of a peer, someone our own age, was just unimaginable. It's just not supposed to happen. We all witnessed the pain and grief that our parents and other adults were feeling, something that many of us had never seen before.

Life for my family was forever changed. We would never be the same. I know that I was not the "same" afterwards; our house was not the "same", *nothing* was the "same". The grief that I witnessed in my parents was so intense, I wondered if we would ever be happy again. I remember the sadness being all around me, especially with adults, and I wished things would go back to the way they were before Kevin died. In some way, even though it is 23 years later, it was oddly comforting to read what you observed in your parents and knowing that I was not the only one who experienced this extreme sadness among my parents and other adults.

While I remember being surrounded by the grief of so many others, I also remember the immense amount of support and caring that our friends, family, and community provided. I know my parents did everything in their power to make sure that I was taken care of during this time, but I always felt that our friends and family did the same as well. I know that my friends, their parents, and my teachers all wanted to make things better, and did their best to be supportive.

Your responses to the question, "Looking back what do you think you needed most" helped me realize that we were all searching for answers then, and even now, we want to know more. I still ask, "WHY?" "What could I have done differently?" "Could I have saved him if I was there" "Did I tell Kevin I loved him?" I know, for me, my questions have changed over as I've gotten older. I have different questions about what really happened. Rachel P.M. talk about how she needed more answers and different information, as she got older. As children we were only give pieces of "appropriate" information, but now, as adults many of us need more details to make sense of what we experienced as children.

It is overwhelming to me to read how Kevin's death has impacted you over the course of your lives. It is remarkable to me to know that my brother's life *and* his death have influenced how you live your lives today. I honestly can't express how much it means to me to know that because of Kevin, you cherish your siblings and families more than before; you appreciate your friendships and relationships with others; and, you care and love your own children with a heightened awareness. I am so grateful to each one of you.

I know that Kevin continues to watch over all of us, whether we have been aware of it or not. Coincidently, on the day that I began reading your responses, there was a bike/car accident involving a young girl that happened in my own neighborhood. On my way to pick up my husband at work, I had driven around the corner from our home when I came upon the accident. The girl was lying in the road and her bike was wedged underneath the car. My first instinct was to find her parents. Fortunately, the girl was able to tell me her phone number, and I called her parents just as the fire truck and paramedics arrived. I kept praying that she would be okay and thankfully, she was not badly injured.

What were the odds that I would encounter *a bike accident involving a child in my own neighborhood* when I had just been reading memories about my own past! I'm sure it was no coincidence that I was meant to be there. I know Kevin was guiding me in how to help this young girl.

I know that Kevin laughs and cries with us, and he has been there to guide us through all of our good and bad times, encouraging us to make the "right" choices as we grew up. He's been there as we've graduated school, gotten married and had children, continuing to bless our lives.

Thank you Dillon, Dean, Rex, Kyle, Michael, Morgan, Whitney, Rachelle, Nicole, Kori, Rachel M., Katie, Jessica, Rachel A., Tara, Matt, and Kate. I am grateful to each one of you for your support and friendship. Although it was overwhelmingly emotional at times, it was truly a gift to be able to read your stories and experiences. Each of our stories is unique and in sharing them, we not only help each other but other grieving children, their families and their caregivers. I hope this book brings us a little closer to Kevin, and brings us all a little more peace.

Amber Blowey Higgs, Littleton, CO

Notes from the Spirit

"The wound is the place where the Light enters you." ~ Rumi

In the ten years since the book was published and I began presenting dream workshops, I also became a dream work facilitator. I received my certification through the Marin Institute of Projective Dream Work with director, Jeremy Taylor. MIPD and the Association for the Study of Dreams emphasize that dream work is not a substitute for psychotherapy, or professional treatment and should not be used as such. While there are many valid approaches to dream work and art interpretation, I recognize that projective work respects the integrity of the dream without judgment and honors the dreamer's choice to participate at whatever level they choose to engage.

When I work a dream with the dreamer, the projective format invites me to make connections based on my experience or association with the images in the dream. I cannot see the dreamer's dream the way they dreamed it. I can only imagine it based on how they describe or express it. Carl Jung, psychoanalyst, philosopher and spiritual seeker believed that dreams are "a spontaneous self-portrayal, in symbolic form of the actual situation of the unconscious". Jung believed that the dream self uses physical experience and memories, and symbols, images and behavior patterns from the collective unconscious to relay an important message to the waking self about the status of the soul –the present condition of our emotional, mental, physical and spiritual well-being.

As an example, I present Jung's iceberg model to illustrate the point: imagine the tip of an iceberg representing the waking self –*the conscious or personal mind* –viewing, receiving and perceiving all that resides in the physical world. Just below the surface is the *personal unconscious* –your memory of all your physical experiences and those memories you have repressed. Beyond this is the *collective unconscious* –the universal memory of all human experience which includes your experiences as well. This is the source of all creative inspiration and is known as the spiritual realm.

I believe the same concept applies to drawings and art. The drawn images represent the words, feelings, attitudes and perceptions of the drawer from an unconscious level. Dreams and drawings have roots in the unconscious and reveal hidden issues and obstacles that cannot be grasped by the conscious mind. The images themselves are instruments of healing vying for the attention of the individual to raise its awareness and seek balance and healing.

My unconscious and conscious associations about the imagery come into clearer view using my intuition and discernment. I can form projections about a drawing (dream) using a.) my knowledge of the drawer or what was happening in their life at the time b.) my knowledge of and experience with my personal symbols and associations, and archetypal symbols and themes and, c.) diagnostic tools that art therapists use to interpret body image and awareness.

Just as I cannot view the dreamer's dream screen, I may not know where the drawer began drawing on the page. So, I begin with what I'm "drawn" to in the piece. What images am I familiar with in my waking or interior life? How does it make me feel? What emotional or physical response does it bring forth? What do I know about the dreamer that I relate to personally? Is there a repetitive use of shading or objects to underscore the importance of the message? What is *missing* or seems uncharacteristic of a universal image? What images speak to me? What strikes me at a gut level as a personal or universal truth?

My unconscious and conscious associations about the imagery come into clearer view using my intuition and discernment. Using symbolic sight will always unmask the truth, *if we are willing to see it differently.*

What follows is a collection of personal and universal truths as illustrated by some of the children you've just read about. I've included some of their comments and my own "projections".

I invite you to release your judgment and open your heart and "read" these sacred notes from the spiritual realm.

Figure 1

Amber: *"You have three bodies"*, (fig. 1 & 2) age 8.5

January 27, 1991 Although Amber says she didn't think much about God during this time, here is an example of the way she expressed what she intuitively knew. About three weeks after Kevin died, I was helping Amber get settled for bed. She had difficulty going to sleep and needed the comfort of someone staying with her for a while. Amber had been writing in her notebook and wanted to show me her drawing. Amber explained that she knew Kevin had gone to heaven. Confidently she said, "When Kevin came he had a body inside of you, then he had a body on Earth, and now he has a different body in heaven." Then, she wrote on the back of the page (fig. 2), "You have three bodies". Amber said that God, was both mother and father, illustrated in the one figure with short hair and long hair drawn around it. Next to God was a figure of my mother and below them, a line with clouds. Kevin is in the clouds rising, and she stated that Kevin is with them now. Note that the these three figures are drawn in the same style, and Kevin and I are clothed in earthly clothes.

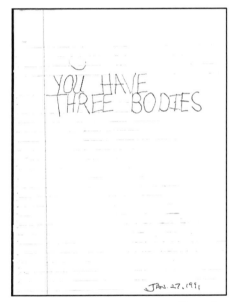

Figure 2

311

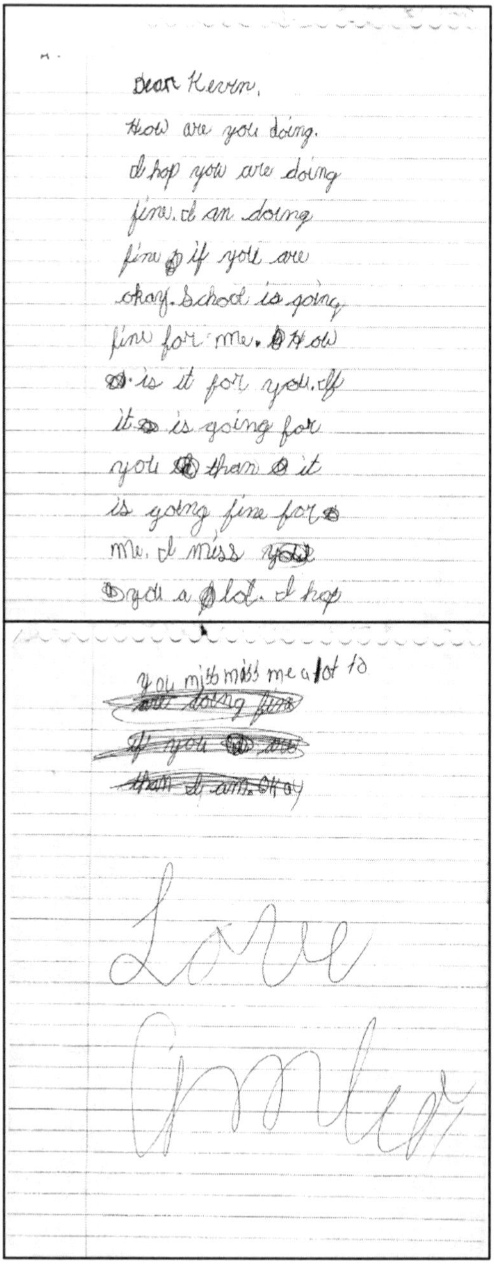

Dear Kevin,
How are you doing.
I hop you are doing
fine. I am doing
fine if you are
okay. School is going
fine for me. How
is it for you. If
it is going for
you than it
is going fine for
me. I miss you
you a lot. I hop

you miss miss me a lot to
am doing fine
If you are
than I am okay

Love

Carter

Figure 3

During Amber's grief counseling sessions, Mary (our counselor) would often give her a sheet of paper to doodle on while they talked. Sometimes, Amber would spontaneously write letters to Kevin as shown in these examples. (figures 3, 4 & 5)

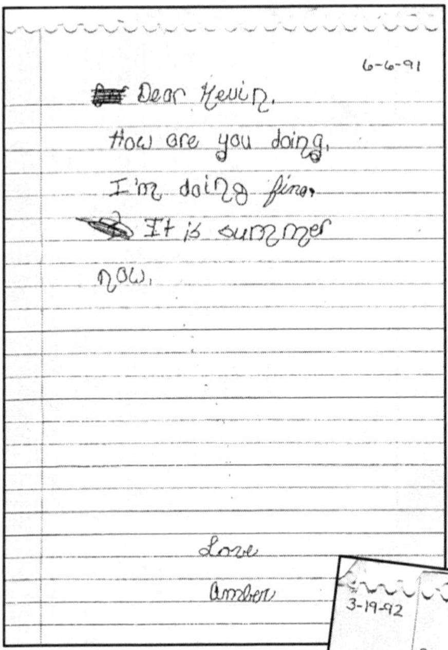

6-6-91

Dear Kevin,
How are you doing,
I'm doing fine.
It is summer now.

Love
Amber

Figure 4

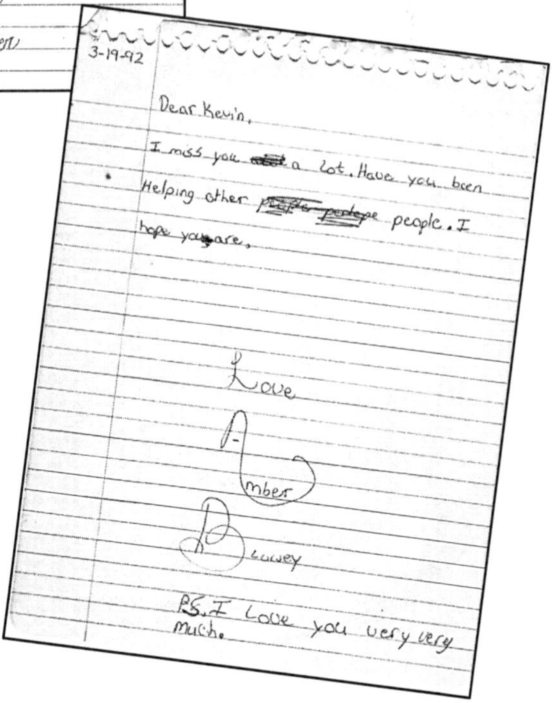

3-19-92

Dear Kevin,
I miss you a lot. Have you been Helping other people. I hope you are,

Love
Amber
Dewey

P.S. I Love you very very much.

Figure 5

Figure 6

Dillon: *"You had a lot of fun"*, (fig. 6) age 5.11

January 8-10, 1991 Upon seeing his drawing for the first time in 22 years, Dillon said: "I don't remember it, but my first impression is that we loved to have fun with each other. I wondered who the other person could be —maybe one of our friends, and I was confused as to who did it. Was it from me or from Kevin? I thought the cross meant it was something we did in church (but we didn't go to the same church together). I felt instantly happy and laughed out loud. It just made me feel good, then I really missed Kevin."

Carla: Dillon drew this drawing (fig. 6) with Grandpa Blowey in our living room during the week that Kevin died. Grandpa Blowey wrote the line at the bottom of the page (probably to show Dillon how to spell what he wanted to say) and at Dillon's request, taped the cross to the page. I don't remember who gave it to me only that Dillon wanted me to have it.

First, I feel so much love between the two figures I recognize as Kevin (left) and Dillon (right). The hearts centered on their chests illustrates this beautifully. Kevin's figure is aligned with the margin line suggesting he is a grounding or stable person in Dillon's life. Kevin's left leg is smaller and off the ground indicating that, the stability Dillon relied on was weakening and shrinking away. The positioning and the slant of Dillon suggest he is caught off balance. Neither figure has arms to catch the other −Kevin is not here to rely on, and Dillon is unable to support himself. The only connecting body part between them is Kevin's ear − Dillon does not have ears to hear. I wonder if the omission of ears is a defense mechanism that allowed Dillon to tune out the chaos and trauma around him and "tune in" to what he intuitively knew −that Kevin loved him. The third figure appears in the background, feet pointed as if moving forward . Again, another omission of arms and ears −but smiling −perhaps an unconscious depiction of his future self that will feel the love, as in the heart centered in the chest. The "way" or the "path" of the future is shown in the positioning of the cross just below Dillon's feet −his faith in God will show him the way.

The fourth figure is placed between Kevin's name, the word "you", and Kevin's figure. It feels small and alone, and insignificant. Perhaps how Dillon feels without his best friend −unable to reach out to Kevin or hear him at that moment as indicated by the omission of arms and ears again.

Look closely, on the faces of Kevin and Dillon and note the two faint circles around the noses. Dillon may have started to draw the heads and erased it to make them bigger. Nonetheless, it seems this area of the face is underscored. The nose is symbolic of the breath of life − in this case a life that was "snuffed out".

Lastly, Dillon's first response on seeing the drawing after 22 years was that it was addressed to him as if it were *from* Kevin. I believe that this was a joint effort −I believe that Kevin was communicating with Dillon through this drawing. Kevin was showing Dillon the way and the truth −"Listen to your heart Dillon −I'll always be with you, in your heart, loving you." What a gift!

Figure 7   Figure 8

Dillon: (fig. 7 & 8) 1991 "These drawing are all blanks in my mind which you might have guessed, but there are some things that I notice about them that caught my eye. First and most pronounced was the smiles. I made sure his teeth were showing, it was a must because Kevin's smiles were filled with teeth. Another thing that I noticed was neither one had arms I don't know what to say about that, just that it stood out to me. I also noticed both hearts, I think it might mean that he is always in my heart. Other than those couple of stand outs, the drawing make me happy, and also proud, because I am not sure if I could have done a drawing of anyone else I have lost. I just don't think I would have the courage to do such things as an adult. One last note on a funny side, I don't think my drawing skills are much better now then back then."

Carla: Months later, the descent into grief is evident *to me as I witnessed* it in Dillon. It is "masked" yet revealed in figures 7, 8, & 9. Although the figures drawn are supposed to be of Kevin, my sense is the images are actually symbolic of Dillon's fragile emotional state at that moment. For me, these drawings illustrate the inner turmoil of anxiety, insecurity, anger, confusion and helplessness surrounding the loss of his cousin and playmate. Through it all, Dillon is trying to remember Kevin's comforting smile as his unconscious brings forth the actual disfigurement Kevin suffered in the accident (perhaps a waking response to the dream –question #12). Figure 8 strikes me as bleary-eyed and battle weary boy who dons a shield of armor to protect his heart.

Carla: In May, 1992, I asked some of the children to draw an impromptu picture about Kevin. I invited them to draw anything they wanted, and when they were finished, I simply asked them to tell me about their drawing. When Dillon arrived he seemed eager and willing to do so until he began to draw. His mood changed quite abruptly when he started his first effort (fig. 9a). The result was the orange/red scribble. He pushed that aside, and on my invitation started again, this time only completing the black rectangle with lines (fig. 9b) His mood darkened and I asked him if he wanted to continue. In a painstakingly effort, he drew the face and stick body (fig. 9c).The raging chaos of the red scribble, the caged black lines of the rectangle and the icy blue eyes glaring from an absent body obliterated any memory of the previous heart images.

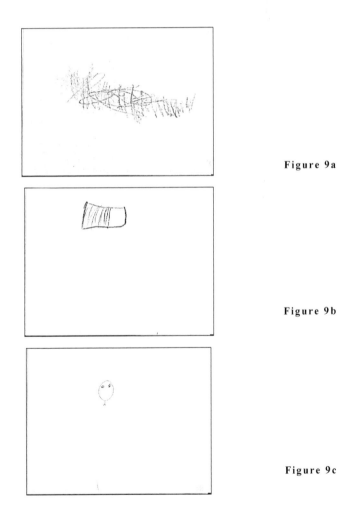

Figure 9a

Figure 9b

Figure 9c

317

Viewing the images individually was revealing enough, but when the sheets of paper are stacked in the order they were drawn (top to bottom), the images retain their original placement, but a more comprehensive message: an angry prisoner of grief. (fig. 9d)

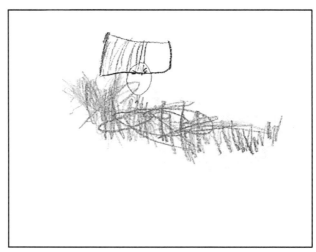

May 1992 Figure 9d

Insights aside, I realized that I was beyond my skill-set in my attempt to "help" Dillon or the other children express their grief in drawings. Admittedly, I was not equipped to handle him if this exercise triggered a break down. It was a sincere effort but not within my emotional means to tackle. However, I knew enough to save all of the children's drawings. My prayer is that sharing their artwork now might help them and other grieving families gain some insight and healing.

Kyle

Figures 10a and 10b

Carla: Kyle drew this drawing (figures 10a, 10b, 10c) within the first week after Kevin died. Although he wanted me to have it, the drawing was intended for Kevin, not me. He folded the paper, addressed it on the back side and placed it in an envelope addressed to Kevin. I assumed the

Figure 10c

rectangle on the right half of the paper was the driveway and that Kyle tried to draw the accident. The advantage of today's technology allowed me to scan the paper and zoom in on a computer screen. I see a figure (Kevin?) lying in the crumpled mess at the top. As I write this, I am reminded o f Kyle's response to question #3 and consider another layer of meaning: "...when I was told, I went running up the stairs of my mom's apartment, stopped at the top step, curled up, and just wept."

Just as heart-wrenching , is what is visible from the backside through the front side of the paper. After he folded the drawing, he made two attempts to address it. On the front, upper left side of the paper, Kyle drew a rectangle (my symbolic sight sees a doorway) and Kevin's name appears faintly behind it. Was it an unconscious understanding of Kevin being "on the other side"? Ah...the risk of projection, we will never really know.

Figure 11

Carla: Figures 11, 12, 13 were drawn during the remainder of the school year. I believe it was a brave effort in processing the details he heard (or unconsciously knew) about the accident in images and words. Figure 11 was the first drawing at preschool, drawn in an aqua blue color crayon. I've enhanced the contrast in the drawing for printing purposes because the crayon lines are so light it is barely visible. What stands out in the original is this: The letter "T" is traced in black and the "v" in Kevin is traced in aqua blue. Kevin's face is shaded darker and the eyes are void of pupils as if to suggest he didn't see the truck. However, note that he draws Kevin riding directly in the path of the oncoming truck rather than being run over from behind. In another projection, there is a strong red line separating the word "over" from "Kevin", as if to underscore Kyle's anger about the finality of the accident. Subsequent drawings (fig. 12 & 13) focus on cars and trucks as he continued to process what he was told happened at the accident.

320

Figure 12

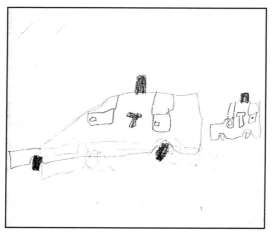

Figure 13

321

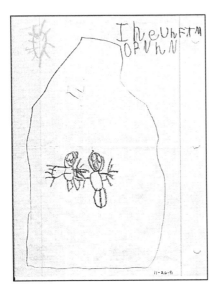

The final two drawings, were drawn after Kyle moved out of state later that year. On first sight, I'm glad to see the two boys are smiling and holding hands (fig. 14). Overall the drawing is unsettling because the two figures are encapsulated and drawn in red floating above the ground. I sense containment and a feeling of being ungrounded. The use of the color red can also be symbolic of love as well as anger. I'm hoping for Kyle's sake that he was holding on to the love inside him while life continued outside.

Figure 14

In figure 15, Kyle dictated what he wanted to say about the drawing to his kindergarten teacher at the new school. He moved to an area where eagles are common and it became one of his favorite animals. In an unabashed projection, I've titled Kyle's drawing, **"Eagle's Wings"** (fig. 15) because of my personal association with eagles and the hymn, *"On Eagle's Wings"* (by Fr. Michael Joncas which was sung by our friend Pati at Kevin's funeral). With a keen vantage point of a higher spiritual perspective above the physical world, the eagle (symbolic of the spirit) flies under the emotional storm clouds as a protector above Kyle in the car. Kyle states that he and Kevin have seen

Figure 15

an "eagle". In their short time together, I believe they have witnessed a spiritual truth between them. The yellow car feels symbolic of a means of transportation of that truth that will carry Kyle through life.

Figure 16

Mitchell : "Catch it, Carla", (fig. 16) May 1992

Carla: I was visiting Mitchell's family at their home, when I asked Mitchell to draw a picture of himself and Kevin. Mitchell's eyes lit up and he said he would do it for me. As soon as I left, he began drawing this picture. He wanted to take it to me that evening when he finished. By then it was too late and he was disappointed that he could not bring it to me.

I wrote my impressions immediately after I spoke briefly with Mitch. He told me it was about the boys playing football and that the cloud was a happy cloud yelling catch it. The cloud image feels much more aggressive than Mitchell's explanation and the bared teeth contradict a sense of happiness. Although they did play football, I expected Mitchell to draw them playing "guns" because it was one of their favorite games. The football game could have represented his current interest or a desire to share that activity with Kevin. Nevertheless, my first impression was that it was representative of their playfulness as very active boys.

I do not know if Mitchell had any other writing tools available at the time but he uses red for the entire drawing except for black in addressing it to me. His mother said he began the drawing immediately after I left and picked up whatever was at hand. (Dad is an architect and mom is creative so I know that crayons, art supplies, etc would have been available if requested.) My initial projection on the red was his sense of danger for himself, and for Kevin; vulnerability; and a consuming state of angry emotion or a burning problem on his mind. As "happy" as this drawing is *supposed to be* I didn't feel that sentiment.

In 1992, I first viewed the page by dividing it into quarters as suggested by an art therapist.

The upper right quadrant = the present: Cloud speaking - "Catch it"
Why is the cloud humanized to speak the message "Catch it"? Why isn't Mitchell saying, "Catch it"? The cloud image feels much more aggressive than Mitchell's explanation that it is a happy cloud, and the bared teeth contradict any sense of happiness. The eye of the cloud is looking directly at my name. The outlined lettering suggests my importance to Mitch and that he wants *me* to catch the message. I'm presuming that the drawing was completed in red and he addressed it to me as a last effort, using the black pen. The cloud is the *only* figure that has black coloring, suggesting its importance —a storm cloud, a chaotic storm of confusion in my head. Noteworthy is that this is a *third* emphasis on a *head* —the black wavy line feels like a tight band of barbed wire around the cloud's head —Mitchell feeling trapped in his own mind? The cloud has one nostril, a seeming after thought drawn in black ink. The nose is symbolic of the breath of life. Mitchell had no known allergies, respiratory issues, or recent illness.

The lower right quadrant = the immediate past: Kevin diving to catch the ball
Kevin is diving to catch the ball but in reality, he would be diving to catch a ball that is in front of him rather than behind him. The football is pointing to the back of Kevin's head and has three dashes. Kevin's head is distorted, colored red on the back, top, and down over the eyes. He faces to the right. Kevin's eyes are covered but one eye is barely visible through the red. He has a nose and mouth but no ear. He might be wearing a shirt but there is no neckline —the arms seem to be bound or wrapped (vulnerable and exposed). Kevin's name is written on his stomach but the letters are split in half. The bottom half illustrates that he is grounded in the reality/memory of this relationship but hitting my friend in the back of the head suggests anger about my friend dying. Is this Mitchell's "understanding" of the accident? (Kevin could not see or hear what was coming from behind him) Is this Mitchell's "guess" at how Kevin died? How much did Mitchell know or hear about the details of the accident? (1992 notes: Caroline says they have never directly discussed Kevin's injuries but he may have overheard conversations. She also said she insists for Mitchell to wear his bike helmet but he refuses.) The bottom half illustrates that Mitchell is grounded in the reality/memory of this relationship but hitting his friend in the back of the head suggests anger about his friend dying.

The lower left quadrant = the unknown; darkness: Mitchell throwing the ball
Mitchell faces the right and with his left arm throws the ball to Kevin. However, note that the left arm is actually pointing to the message *"Catch it"*. Mitchell's arms feel "locked", unbendable and away from his body. Mitchell's face is missing a nose all other figures have noses (absence of the breath of life?). Only

324

Mitchell and the cloud have bared teeth (aggression; anger). There are 11 lines creating 11 teeth –the same number of teeth in the cloud. The cap seems "bulbous" as if that area of Mitchell's head is swollen –there are three lines within the cap as there are three lines within the football. Both figures have objects associated with their heads –the football draws attention to Kevin's head injury. Why is Mitchell's head "swollen" or appearing injured as well? Mitchell is shirtless and the letters in his name are "split" as well. There is a shading emphasis on the letter "h". Perhaps, a feeling of being exposed and vulnerable like his peer Kevin? I can't shake the sense that the naming feels like being labeled or marked.

I'm disturbed rather than comforted that both figures "share" similar items –red pants, no shirt, objects on head, the split letters and naming, "winged" shoes (shoelace loops). I am struck by the detail of the shoelaces on the shoes, which to me look like tiny wings helping Kevin fly to catch the ball. (Kevin has taken flight –died.) Interesting that Mitchell has the same kind of "winged" shoes on the ground. Again, this feels like a labeling or "sameness".

The door of the house is also disturbing. It's not inviting. It feels blocked and is shaded and dark as if it is impassable. It would be natural to assume that this is Mitchell's family home. By outward appearances, the family is sociable, warm and inviting. They are a very emotional and feeling family but his mother admits that expressing emotions and staying with those feelings to go deeper was not typical at that time. Looking on the bright side was a more typical response to stress or problems and so the grief was not discussed. In dream work, a house or dwelling is symbolic of the self. I believe the house is representative of Mitchell, and the shaded door does not allow anyone access to the inside –he is actually standing in front of the doorway blocking anyone from gaining entry to his interior world.

Upper left hand quadrant = the future: Good Toss Sun
Note the height of the house –it reaches the sun –the roof of the house being the higher mind; the windows are symbolic of the eyes of my house. What can be seen from this higher perspective? If this were my house and I looked out that window, I would see the sun, not the cloud. Why is the sun humanized? I notice that it is the only "head" that is depicted facing outward rather than sideways and to the right. The sun doesn't feel all that welcoming either as if its tongue is hanging out. Why is the Sun saying "Good toss" to Mitchell? Why is that important to him? Why isn't Kevin, who is trying to catch the ball, saying, "Good toss"? Why doesn't Mitchell as the artist place the dialogue with the appropriate characters?

It can be noted that objects are often repeated in drawings, and some art therapists suggest it is significant of units of time pertaining to events in the past, present or future. Mitchell has drawn 16 rays around the sun. I've noted the date of the drawing is May 1992, 16 months *after* Kevin's death. However, if this quadrant represents the *future* (as in art therapy interpretation), I also note that at the time of the drawing, Mitchell is age seven. If I consider numerology as a projective tool and reduce the number 16 to seven, then, what

325

is coming **seven** years later? Mitchell would be 14-years-old, in high school, at the beginning of his chaotic and troubled high school years. What was happening then?

I also can't shake a nagging feeling that this drawing actually places Mitchell engaged in an activity *in the past, at the age of six.* Keeping that in mind, and as uncomfortable as it is for me to consider, I'm drawn to the notion of what is coming **16** years later. Is this drawing validating, the beginning of Mitchell's post-traumatic stress (as the family suspects) and the course it will take?

The rooftop of the house (Mitchell's higher mind) reaches the sky – windows as the eyes of the soul connect with heaven and earth. Can I see hope? Are sunny days ahead? In projective dream work, we pay attention to puns and metaphor. The sun is speaking as an authority –my projection would suggest "sun" as "son". I perceive "a good toss" as "a good try". Is this message from the Sun, saying, "Good try, Son"?

It feels like an acknowledgment of how I am coping or how I am supposed to cope. I'm thinking of the song lyrics, "grey skies are gonna clear up put on a happy face..." Typically, it's the way the family addressed pain –look on the bright side. Perhaps it is Mitchell's perception of the behavior that was expected of him but the storm within his mind is so strong that it needs to be contained or bound. He literally places himself as the cloud between the sun and me (my name) to get my attention. There is so much emphasis on these looming contrasting figures and their competition with each other in dialogue. If this were my "dream", I'm feeling split, experiencing extreme emotions that I can't reconcile.

****

Mitchell and his family have held a special place in our family for 35 years. I first met Caroline, his mother, at my dentist office where she was my hygienist. Although we were never in the same social or professional circles, we had a special connection and became good friends during our first pregnancies. Those precious babies, our daughters, Amber and Whitney, shared the same special connection from birth, as did our boys, Kevin and Mitchell. Ten years later, our youngest daughters, Megan and Hayden followed suit. Play dates and activities often included the girls and the boys. Amber and Whitney played house and babies, and Mitch and Kev played superheroes and football. They were adorable but pesky little brothers always scheming to crash the girls playtime. Kevin's death fractured their tight foursome and permanently wounded Mitchell deeper than anyone realized.

Caroline remembers Mitchell's reaction to Kevin's death:

"The one visual that I have is when we drove over to your house that night after we heard Kevin died. Mitchell had put himself in the very back of the van, as far away as he could get. When we arrived, he did not want to get out of the van and he wouldn't move. We didn't want to force him and so we went inside to be with you all, leaving Mitchell in the van for a short time. But now, looking back over all these years, Mitchell was what I would call, comatose. He

326

couldn't move, he was totally shut down. I am identifying it now, as the way Mitchell responded to trauma after that. If I don't move, breathe or talk I can isolate myself so I don't have to feel this pain.

Unbelievably, within the next two years, Mitchell witnessed a harrowing house trailer fire involving the rescue of three toddlers; the death of a man from a heart attack in an airport; the death of a man who washed ashore on the beach from a heart attack; and the death of a classmate who drowned in a public pool during a field trip. Each time, Mitchell stuffed his feelings, and "Pollyanna" here (*me*, Caroline) didn't see this. I didn't have any experience with this kind of trauma! I was working, remodeling the house, taking care of the children, trying to keep up the "perfect" life. Even when Mitchell developed shingles, I never connected it with any of this. And so, we learned later in therapy, that Mitchell's response to Kevin's death, was actually the beginning of a post-traumatic stress syndrome for him.

Mitchell believed early on that life was *not fair* and it went on throughout high school. He even started a petition in 8th grade because he believed the teacher showed favoritism to another student and was unfair to him. He wrote, *"How can this unfairness be fixed?"* And, he got all the students in his class to sign it! He used to always say, "Life is not fair", and the anxiety piece didn't get better, and so he found drugs and alcohol to numb him from feeling.

Later, during an intense rehab program, Mitchell's therapist used Carla's book to help him resolve that initial grief. Unfortunately, he taught himself at an early age to not go there...and he never would. I specifically remember how hard it was for him to read it. He is a beautiful reader, he read at least 50 books when he was there in therapy. But, there again reading out loud about Kevin was unbearable. So, the therapist read it out loud in group. He would put his head down and cover his head with his arms. She bought him a sterling necklace of a monkey —"see no evil, hear no evil, speak no evil" — symbolizing his skill of *not* "going there".

So, it was a lifelong issue for him. Maybe if he had made it through his early twenties he might have been able to work through it. Instead, he didn't stay to face it, and took his life. He took the easy way, it's *not* that easy, technically he took he took the *harder way*, because *you can't repair it if you don't go through it.* You have to do the grief work. Mitchell gave up there's no question.

A dear friend once said to me that perhaps, Mitchell was only supposed to be here those 22 years. It helps me to remember that every time I start doing what I'm doing now, questioning that maybe he could have worked through this. But, he *didn't*, and he wasn't supposed to be here any longer, and I don't know why. *Mitchell was here for 22 years,* and I have to accept that.

One last thing I want to share is that after he died I went up to his bedroom and found a notebook he had written a poem in on the floor next to his bed. He wasn't even living there anymore because he'd been in Florida, having a rough time, and wanted to come home. So, we rescued him and brought him back home that summer and he started college again that August. Why the tablet was even there or open to this page I don't know.

Category 5
By Mitchell Davis

The news said a storm was coming.
I assumed it was severe.
Impulsively, I packed my bags and got ~~the hell~~ out of there,
So I felt safe for a while.
I knew I'd be alright
But that's just because I was away.
I should have stayed to fight.
Later on that week, from a distance I watched tv
And all of the survivors said they could make it through anything.
It made me remember all the great times I had
And recovering from a hurricane really isn't that bad
So I tried to make it up, and to come back and repair.
But, the house that I had lived in was stronger than before
You looked at me from the window,
I hung my head in shame.
I should have stayed to fight and help rebuild again.
©2006 Mitchell Davis

The longer I read this, the more I felt, "Oh Mitchell, you *didn't* stay to fight!" He wrote it before he died! But, he didn't stay to fight the battle. So, I go back to Kevin's death and our talks about grief —you have to go through it! You can't go around it, and people that go around it don't get better. He didn't know how to go through it.

'You looked at me from the window —I hung my head in shame, I should have stayed to fight and help rebuild again.' I felt like maybe he was saying, "I'm sorry" to us after he died. It still breaks my heart. All the years will never take away the pain. I still want him back, of course."

Carla: Mitchell took his life on September 20, 2006, one week before his 22nd birthday. His parents were traveling out of the country, his younger sister was staying with friends, and his oldest sister lived out of state. Stann, Megan and I immediately went to stay with Hayden until Whitney arrived. It was uncanny how our roles had reversed…it was our turn to embrace them in *their nightmare.*

Mitchell's story has many layers. It would be presumptuous of me to assume that I understand or fully know Mitchell's story. Projection is based on hindsight, personal and archetypal associations, and intuition.

Just as Kevin's story continues to evolve, we see that Mitchell's story evolves as well.

For me, *Category 5* is the evolution of the storm cloud from the football drawing. In projective dream work, we use the format "in *my* imagined version of your dream, I sense...". I use this to demonstrate my projection of Mitchell's poem and give voice to the dream (poem) as I perceive it. In my imagined version of Mitchell's dream (poem), I understand that my first experience with death, the death of my playmate, Kevin, at age five, was equal to a "Category 5" storm. Although my present situation might be unrelated, as I am writing this poem I am feeling the depth of the pain and grief I experienced with the trauma from my childhood. Only this time, I can't do it anymore. The news said a storm was coming and I assume from my past experiences that it will be severe again. I must get the "hell" out of there –get this hell *out of me*! I know I should stay and fight but I feel safe when I shut down. I've survived these storms before by impulsively packing my bags and getting the hell out of there, but somehow, this storm is different. I tried to come back and repair the damage but the house I lived in (my fortress against pain) was stronger than before.

My sense is that this house is the same house in the football drawing – a fortress looming high, its red door blocked and impassable. And if this were my house (self), I feel such shame for not being able to meet society's expectation that everybody else can do it, so I should as well. "Good try, son, but you should have tried to rebuild again."

That last sentence speaks to the excruciating pain from the storm wreaking havoc within this beautiful young man.

Mitchell's storm has ended, and I believe he *is* rebuilding again...with a little help from an old friend.

Love Notes from Companions on the Journey

♡ For obvious reasons, I find it difficult to talk or write about the period of time when Kevin died. It is always hard to discuss things that are painful. In my attempt to recall what happened to me personally, and as the director of my preschool during that time, I continually find myself involved in something else. Perhaps this is a natural tendency for it is much easier to walk around a painful memory than work through it.

As I look back on the school days before Kevin's death, I remember a fun-loving group of children from a variety of lifestyles, all eagerly learning how to get along. I recall having a rather large group of boys that year. This boy-girl ratio presented its own set of challenges. The good news was that this particular group had an uncanny ability to get along and to work things out among themselves without my intervention.

The holidays were especially enjoyable that school year before we lost Kevin. At Halloween, I had two Ninjas, two Batmen, a Spiderman, and a cowboy! They were all quite pleased with their world of make believe. During Christmas time our class participated in the Holiday Parade of Lights. We had no idea during those carefree days that we would embark upon a first-hand experience with death. It was beyond our imagination to dare think of such pain when our world was filled with so much happiness.

We had only one school day together following the winter break. One day to renew our friendships. One day to share all of our holiday and vacation experiences. One day to say hello…and goodbye. It all seems so unfair, even today. I often say to myself, "If I had only known that it was to be my last day to spend with Kevin, I would have been so much more attentive to his needs." I'm sure many of us have said the "if only's. I do know that this loss has changed me. I certainly pay more attention. And, I value the day more than ever before.

Kevin's death was a "first" experience for me as a preschool teacher. I muddled along in my own misery while trying to help the children deal with their loss and pain. My staff had always encouraged creative writing and creative art. We did a lot of dictation, writing the children's story explanations verbatim. After the accident, school did not close and life did not stop for us. We had to carry on. Our first attempt to help the children understand Kevin's death *and* the permanence of it, was through writing. It was an activity that they were used to but also an outlet for their emotions. Unfortunately, some children still had very primitive drawing experiences and vocabulary but we encouraged the activity anyway.

Our assignment was for them to draw a picture of what they remembered about Kevin. As the children began their projects, it was very clear who were Kevin's closest friends. It was difficult to motivate them for they were so sad. It was also clear that many of the children did not understand that Kevin was not coming back to school anymore. Some of the children could only express their feelings in present tense. "I like Kevin" or " This is Kevin chasing Nana" seemed to express their feelings of love, but not of loss.

Theses first simple remarks remind me of my fondest memories of our last school year with Kevin. The children engaged in what seemed like endless chases around the yard. The boys discovered that if they would chase our dog, Nana, she would run from them, grabbing anything she could find to carry as her keep-away prize. The boys would spend their entire recess and a great deal of energy chasing Nana from one end of the yard to another. Around and around they would go until they would drop to their knees laughing, trying to catch their breath for the another round! This memory must have been special to the children because many of our conversations with the class about Kevin after he died involved their outside experiences with Kevin and Nana.

After that day, friendships changed. Social groups in the classroom were forced to readjust. It took some time for the children to learn to play with one another minus one. We would attempt to have group discussions about loss, accidents and injuries, and all the changes that could occur with such events, including learning how to get along without our classmate. A few children mentioned the loss of a cat or dog, maybe even a grandparent, and others mentioned seeing car accidents.

What surprised me about the children's response to Kevin's death was their inability to understand the finality of it. I had only dealt with the loss of a child when they had moved away. Many of the children appeared to think of Kevin's absence as him moving to another place. After several weeks, the classroom appeared to have returned to "normal". I found the group discussions of Kevin's death were no longer necessary. For fear that I could possibly create unnecessary anxiety, I chose to refrain from our discussions on the accident.

I found the children that were most affected by the loss were those children who had connections with Kevin and his family outside of our classroom. These children experienced Kevin's death through their parents as well. They saws their mother's tears and their father's sadness. They went to the funeral and experienced many days of sadness with Kevin's family. I continued to open conversations with those particular children who appeared to be struggling and grasping for some means to cope with the pain and sadness.

I recall having several conversations with Kevin's closest friends. They talked about how sad they felt and how much they missed him. I wanted so much for them to work through their pain. I encouraged them to talk about Kevin – what they liked to do when they played together. They shared stories of playing guns and going to each other's houses. But after sometime, perhaps due to my need to move forward, I found myself rejoicing over "normal" days – days when the children were working and playing together as they had before Kevin died.

I am surprised by my daughter's inability to recall the sadness of those days. She lived through great sadness as I struggled through each day. She saw my tears. She visited Kevin's tree with me year after year. She browsed through old photos of happier days with Kevin. Yet, her memories of him are very vague. I suppose each child had his or her own method of mourning. Perhaps she was too young. They were all so young.

Enough time has passed now that I am able to see the blessings that Kevin's short life had on me. Kevin was and always will be a positive and powerful spirit in my life. He lives on in my memory, of course, but he also lives in my passion to live each day, one moment at a time. My memories of Kevin constantly remind me of the joy that each moment brings. I truly value my time spent with each in my life, more than ever before. And, I try to pay attention. I don't want to miss anything. I don't know how much any one of us have before it is our time to move on.

Sharon Penasa, Montrose Montessori Preschool, Montrose, CO

♡ "Kevin is gone". The time leading up to, and after, are personal blurs for me. But, I still remember Sandy's words to me, and my inability to process what she was saying. Gone? Gone, where?! Through her emotion, she explained what had happened and that we had lost Kevin. I don't remember my reaction other than being dumbfounded. The next thing I remember is hearing my father sobbing, when I drove to give him the news. It's there that I remember my breaking down, sobbing with my father, as I saw the depth of his pain.

Our drive out to Montrose to be with Carla, Stann and Amber, was near silent. They were emotionally and physically spent from the tragedy by the time we arrived. We cried together. But what struck me was my level of grief. I felt guilty that I was not experiencing the depth of grief that everyone else was feeling. It's hard to explain. Yes, I was deeply, deeply sorrowful and emotional for the loss of Kevin, but the bottom level of my grief was for Carla and my father – feeling their hurt.

I can attribute some of my response to what was happening in my life at that time. I was on the front side of recovery, so my ability to 'feel" was dulled by years of drug abuse, starting just before and continuing through my mother's illness and our loss of her to cancer. I honestly wouldn't "feel" their loss, until many years later when my own daughter, Kailee was born, and I immediately felt the bond of parent and child. After Kailee was born, I remember crying many times –thinking of Kevin and finally knowing how empty and lost Carla, Stann, Amber and my father felt with his death.

The next few days were amazing as our relatives arrived from out of state. The deep, deep, sorrow was still present, but very slowly, we turned a corner as we began to remember and be grateful for the short time we had with Kevin. Together, we shared stories, looked at photographs and laughed. It's one of the most valuable lessons that I've learned –that even in death, we celebrate the life. I've practiced it many times, more recently with the passing of our father a few years ago. In each instance, I remember that I learned this lesson from my nephew, Kevin. I have been fortunate enough for Carla to trust me to help execute her vision for the cover of the book. It's an honor to play a very small part in helping Carla give voice to her journey. I could not be more proud of her, and her efforts to help others experiencing their own losses. She continues to amaze.
Paul S. Frocchi, photographer, www.stillsthatmove.com, Burbank, CA

♡ I was at work when I received a phone call from the Hospital informing me that my nephew Kevin was in an accident. I really didn't know what to expect, but I do know I was filled with dread on my way to the hospital. When I got there and saw my brother Stann and my sister-in-law Carla, I knew it wasn't good. Never in a million years could I have prepared for what had happened.

I will never forget going into the exam room and seeing Kevin's poor little body. His life forever taken from him in a totally senseless act. Stann and Carla were beside themselves with grief as any parent would have been. I most certainly would have been if it were one of my children. While at the hospital, I called my parents in Grand Junction, and Carla's father in Denver and told them the horrible news. I have three boys of my own (Rex Lee, Dean and Dillon) and honestly, I couldn't tell you where they were while all of this was going on. I believe they were at home, but I honestly do not remember.

At some point, we left the hospital and went to Stann and Carla's house. Family and friends started to show up, and phone calls were made to inform other family members about Kevin's death, although again, I don't remember who made them. Sometime that night I went home to be with my boys to explain to them what had happened. Of course, they didn't understand it any more than I did. I just thanked God that they were all alive and well, even though I was filled with sorrow at what had happened. I know it had to be very hard for Stann and Carla to have my boys around during this time. Especially my son, Dillon, who is four months older than Kevin. It had to be a constant reminder of what I still had and they no longer did.

I remember going to the private family viewing at the funeral home. Some members of the family got up and talked. I don't remember who all talked or what was said, or even if I did or not. It was all a haze. The church for Kevin's funeral was packed. I couldn't believe all of the people that came. It was very touching to know there were so many people who cared about Kevin whether they knew him or not. I remember sobbing with grief during the service especially during the songs. The song "Heartlight" will always have a special place in my heart. Releasing the balloons after the service by the family members was an especially hard but touching thing to do. It was a way of saying goodbye to someone we shouldn't have had to say goodbye to.

One day, after Kevin's funeral, Dillon and I were riding in the car and he said, "Look, Mommy! I see Kevin up in the clouds!" I burst into tears and said, "Yes Dillon, I believe you do!" It was such an innocent but truly believable statement for Dillon truly believed he could see his cousin.

An especially hard time was during the trial. I couldn't believe that the man who had caused this terrible injustice, could act as cold and heartless as he and his family did during the trial. It was unbelievable that the jury could not be informed that Kevin was dead. It wasn't that I felt that the man responsible should be in jail, but I felt he should be held accountable for his actions. Unfortunately, that didn't happen. It was a grave injustice to the memory of a little boy. The court system didn't do what I believe it is there for, not by a long shot.

It is hard to believe that 23 years have passed since that horrible accident took Kevin's life. I think of Kevin often and I wonder what he would be doing today at the age of 28; would he be married, would he have kids, what would his career be? It seems as if there has always been a hole in our family since he passed away.

Kevin and Dillon, used to dress up and be superheroes when they played together. One time Carla took a picture of them. I still have that picture of those two superheroes frozen in time. The only difference is, is that one of those superheroes isn't wearing a cape any more. He is wearing the wings of an angel. I love you Kevin.

Sandra Blowey-Curry, church office manager, Cory, Colorado

♡ Twenty-three years has passed since Kevin's death and I am so grateful for God's Love that has blessed and protected each one of us through the years. We were all traumatized by this experience –a senseless and careless act by another person that shattered the hearts of so many lives.

I just remember asking God to *help me* help the Blowey family. I had not ever been through anything like this before, personally or professionally. When I got the word about Kevin's accident, I was in Lubbock, Texas at Texas Tech University Medical School, speaking at my dear friend's funeral. I flew back to Montrose, Colorado not realizing how this was going to change all of our lives. There were times when nothing made sense. I do know that God put his loving arms around us all, and He carried some of us daily. As time went by, we knew we had to help each other heal from this horrible tragedy.

Healing is an acceptance of our brokenness. We can claim to do all kinds of therapeutic techniques that will help fix us or make us feel better, but the truth is, only through the healing power of God's Love do we cope with the loss and pain, and begin to live again. *Loving one another* through this is what we did. God did the rest. Looking back, I realize that God gave us spiritual ears, spiritual eyes and spiritual feelings in order to cope with each other's reactions every day. God also gave Carla "spiritual dreams". Carla's dreams helped heal her heart, and God showed her how she could help others by sharing her dreams. Ultimately, we are healed by healing others.

We are all children of God. He loves us and promises that He will never leave us. As parents, we never want to leave our children, either. Kevin was so precious and special, and he was loved dearly by his family. Leaving Kevin behind was never an option for Carla, but being able to join him in her spiritual dreams was her pathway to healing. Oh, to dream about those whom you love –that is a very special gift from God.

So, "Love was the answer" and it was the only thing that brought us through those challenging times. Loving people and having to let go of them through death, before we are ready, is one of the hardest experiences in our lives no matter what our age or place in life. This past year, when my daughter's father died, we loved him and held him through the process, and then, finally had to let him go...but do we really let go? It is a lifelong journey when you lose someone you love.

My life has never been the same, since this experience. Like many of the parents, my reaction was that I never wanted my children to be too far away from me. I have had to learn to trust God and realize that everything belongs to God. I know Kevin is with God and he is looking forward to the day of joining his family again...but until then he will always be in their hearts and dreams.

Love & Peace,
Mary Zahasky, M.A., Panama Beach City, FL

♡ I was still at school when I heard the news of Kevin's accident and passing. I knew Stann, Carla's husband, quite well from working together at the middle school where we were employed and sometimes we went on runs together. I was a school counselor and a licensed professional counselor. I had only talked with Carla a few times, but I could see that she had a strong intuitive side. I knew that side of her was communicated in hunches, visions, and dreams. It was communicated in dreams when she was blocking.

My first reaction upon hearing the news was disbelief. Then, as the reality dawned, it was if all energy immediately left me. I felt confusion. I knew that if I was to be helpful at all I needed to center and restore my own energy. I was used to having a strong sense of guidance that I fully trusted.

By the time the three of us first met alone, my guidance was restored. I just asked that I be open and say what was needed. During that meeting it was obvious that Carla was very fragile and making a supreme effort to hold herself together. Stann was naturally a very tough-minded man, but the confusion, like what I felt initially, was just below a controlled surface.

The meeting was miraculous in many ways. Carla revealed to me her dreams just before Kevin's passing and one or two just afterwards. It was obvious that her dreams foretold the accident, and that Kevin was aware of it. After hearing the dreams, I asked her, "Are you ready to see this differently?"

Carla later told me that my question initially shocked her. I could see at the time that it jarred her psyche into a different place. She could not fully accept the question at first, but she was just too spiritual a being not to see it and begin to open to it. As time went on my relationship with Carla grew closer in friendship. Kevin's passing had allowed for spiritual growth on the part of both of us.

The major lesson I learned around Kevin's passing with both Stann and Carla was that love does indeed go on and on, and so do our loved ones. We do not ever have to feel separate from them. It also taught that we are all born to learn lessons that make us a more aware person and to make this world a better place. We see in action that our unconditional love does conquer all and bring us all closer together. Even now, I feel gratitude for Kevin and his lessons.

Harry McDonald, M.A. retired licensed school and professional counselor and author of *Touched By Love: A Parable for Today*, Grand Junction, CO

♡ Carla came into my life 31 years ago traveling a parallel path. We were born in the same year, we were married in the same year and we had our first child in the same year. We met at a La Leche League support group as new moms, and our lives would never be the same. Today, we are grandmothers together having welcomed our first born grandchildren into this world in the same year. But, this is not a story about when we met or where we are today.

This is a story about a profound event that blinded us both in the darkest night and the love it took to help us see again in the brilliant light of truth. Kevin's fearless truth, as told through his mother's transcendent love, brought us each through the darkness and into the light of God's great love. For my part, paragraph by paragraph, sentence by sentence and

336

word by word, I followed my friend's courageous lead through the painful process of editing a truth I didn't want to live. Together we came through the darkness as "sisters" for life, and I will be forever grateful for the journey.

My later involvement in bringing the promise of wholeness to grieving young children through Carla's vision of *Rainbows for Children* support groups in Montrose was supposed to bring healing to a child's broken heart. In the end, it was the children of *Rainbows* who brought healing to my broken spirit. Once again, traveling through the darkness of a truth I didn't want to live, I found the light of God's great love living in us and through us. In the eyes of a wounded child, I saw the light of God and it changed everything. In their innocence and their faith, the grieving children I worked with shared a profound wisdom that can only come from real knowing and complete trust. And, in that knowing, I rediscovered the innocence and the healing power of a child's love in me.
Laura D. Pearsall, Ed.D., Bodega Bay, CA

♥ *People like us, who believe in physics, know that distinctions between past, present and future are only stubbornly persistent illusions.* (Albert Einstein) ~When I first met Carla in 1995, her pain was still palpable. We worked together for the local hospice, doing different tasks and I got the opportunity to watch her closely as she worked with other's suffering as well as her own.

When Carla wrote *Dreaming Kevin* and published it, even though I had *heard* the story, the reading of it moved me in deep ways. I dreamed of her dreams for a long time. The images and messages of my own healing were again catalyzed by the intrepid nature of Carla's pilgrimage towards healing and wholeness.

Now, nearly 20 years after I first met this brave heart, and even though our physical paths rarely cross, my heart is entwined with hers. The work that she did inspired in me to do some of my own deeper grief work and has continued unabated. I have done some exploration into quantum physics as it relates to dream work, near death experiences and altered consciousness.

The experience of Carla's healing seems to be related to the *morphogenic field* formed by the spiritual DNA that both she and Kevin are part of. Spiritual DNA can be defined, if far from being understood, as the blueprint for the morphogenesis, the creation of shape, of our spiritual nature, our longings, depth, intent and the ultimate flowering of our spiritual selves.

In this perspective we literally are formed in the memory bank or pooled memory of our ancestors. A developing embryo or seedling "tunes in" to the form of past members of the same species through a process sometimes called *morphic resonance.* Where fields of experience transmit forms and behavior that are not necessarily just biological. This I have come to believe, includes our spiritual heritage, our spiritual ancestral wisdom.

Carla and Kevin, and the rest of his family have become part of the blueprint for morphogenesis of a new level of healing from trauma and the resulting grief. Kevin and Carla have grown together past Kevin's physical passage. It seems that once any of us have been connected to another's spiritual DNA, their resonance, we are never again far from it. In fact this resonance moves out in unweakened ripples into the world.

Such is this story of Carla's, and I believe Kevin's, healing. And because of the nature of healing and love, it is the healing of me, those touched by me.

And now you too are being called to become part of this resonance. My deepest prayer is that you will let this story heal you in places and dimensions you haven't even realized that healing was needed.
Beth Patterson, M.A. in Religion, www.findingground.com, Bend, OR

♡ My husband Dave and I, and our children are longtime friends of the Blowey's. After Kevin's death, Stann and Carla were concerned about the Amber's emotional well-being in dealing with Kevin's death. Coincidently, I was teaching third grade at another elementary school in Montrose and the decision was made to transfer Amber into my classroom. I wanted to provide comfort and security, not only for Amber but also for Stann and Carla as well, as they were dealing with a tremendous amount of grief.

Before Amber arrived, I knew that I would need to make her comfortable and watch for any signs that she needed an extra hug, and be available to talk to her. When Amber arrived in my class, she was nervous. I assured her I was there if she needed anything. Having been close friends with Amber's family reassured her that I knew what she was going through. In the beginning, she seemed sad, but as the year went on, she began to smile more. She made several friendships in our class. On a few occasions, I noticed her by herself at recess, so I went to her to offer comfort. I did notice at times that Amber would drift off in thought. Amber talked about the death of her brother with other students and answered questions other students were curious about. We did have a class discussion about loss, where students shared deaths they had experienced in their own families. It was important to me that Amber found our class to be a secure and caring environment.
Mary Ann Arellano, retired elementary school teacher, Montrose, CO

♡ As an elementary school teacher, there are few honors or compliments that come our way. Early in my career, a great compliment did come along, when Amber was enrolled into our fourth grade classroom, by her parents request. I thought at the time, the honor was mine, as the classroom teacher. After all, I was entrusted to offer a secure, gentle, loving and enriching environment to a young girl grieving the loss of her five-year-old brother. It soon became clear that the honor belonged to the entire class.

Lead by Amber's courage and quiet, (seemingly) confident ways, she accomplished her vision that she receive no special treatment or stand out because of her current circumstances. With her grief not evident, she was just like everyone else...except, she was not. None of us is, thank goodness. We are all unique individuals whose identities are shaped by our experiences. Rather than treating Amber alone as exceptional, we treated everyone exceptionally. Together, we created that secure, gentle, loving, and enriching environment for us all. One cannot do that alone. At a young age, Amber taught us how much an individual offers a friend, a class, a group or a community when we share the richness of ourselves, and go on with the experience we call life.

Linda Becker, retired elementary school teacher, Montrose, CO

♡ I moved to Montrose with my wife, Leslie, in 1992, where I joined a counseling practice as a marriage and family therapist. As newcomers to town, Leslie's father introduced us to Carla, who was his hairdresser. We became not only her hairdressing clients but good friends as well, and our friendship spans over 20 years.

I remember feeling so honored when she asked me to be a facilitator for Rainbows (the children's grief support program). I was a very young therapist just getting started and honestly, I was kind of going through it blindly with my "text book" experience. I remember feeling like a kid when I joined the facilitator group because they were all experienced therapists. Looking back, it ended up being such a significant point in my career. I just jumped in and learned very quickly that being "Mr. Therapist" (what *I thought* a therapist should be) was not going to work with this group of 12 and 13-year-old teens! I remember getting that raised eyebrow look from the kids that said, "Seriously, you said what?!". It was my first lesson in being authentic. The kids challenged me *to be real*, to be "me", and not play the role. Truly, it was a wonderful lesson because it happened on the front end of my career and I learned to walk a more authentic path from the beginning.

Working with the children's grief group taught me that there really is magic in silence. I didn't have to talk all the time! It just hit me profoundly when I was quiet while they talked or when we were all working in silence on our art projects. I remember thinking this is powerful stuff! I was *witnessing the process and we were all being present to that moment.*

I remember growing up in my family, we had a Jewish expression that says, "God is closest to those with broken hearts." I didn't know how to describe it but I felt that when we were in group. *I could feel God in the midst of us* and it was such an empowering and fulfilling feeling. I was so young back then, I didn't have many experiences where I felt touched like that.

It is not something we are taught in school –we learn about textbook grief rather than the value of the process. It taught me that there are no cycles to grief –it's not a cookie cutter process. Everyone has a different twist in the way they do it. So, it taught me to meet the client wherever they are in their process with the perspective that they are going to *teach me* about how they are doing it. It turned my whole head and heart around about how to facilitate as a therapist.

The timing was especially significant because when I first moved to Montrose, my good friend, David, was killed in a motorcycle accident. I was going through my own grief and although I had "learned" about it, I didn't know what to do with it. So facilitating the group helped me go through my own grief process as well. I didn't see the therapeutic relationship like that because it was supposed to be me giving to the kids –saying and doing the right things for them. I didn't see it was going to be this incredible exchange of giving between us.

I'm grateful for that now because I've learned to be comfortable talking about death both personally and with my clients where I might not have been before. By and large, most people (therapists included) don't want to talk about death, they don't know what to say or they stumble around it. I've recognized that the easier time I have talking about it the easier it will be for my clients. And, it's *okay* for us to talk about how difficult it is to talk about death! It allows humility around the fact that we don't know how to articulate grief but we can allow ourselves to be vulnerable to do so if we make it safe for one another. I would encourage any therapist or facilitator working with the bereaved to do their own grief work first before they take on a family or a group. At the very least, be as clean as you can be because it is going to take you doing your own work and knowing yourself before you can reach your clients.

One of the things that affected me deeply was listening to the children talk about the person they were grieving. I listened to what they focused on as they shared their memories –both positive and negative remarks. It made me think about the cliché of what would people say about me if I had died. It was profound to have that as a reminder through the years in all my relationships, especially with my daughters. What kind of an impact am I having on them? It made me impress upon my girls the sacredness of being present and the sacredness of time –that we don't go to bed angry or leave the house without hugging and kissing each other and saying "I love you". Now, even as teenagers, they come and find us before they leave to give a hug and kiss goodbye. I think it's really special because now that I've seen lots of families in therapy I realize it's not something that every family does naturally.

The older I get the more I am embracing the idea that everything that happens moves me to something greater. My incredible experience with the grieving children in Rainbows absolutely has moved me to something greater. I am so grateful and so honored that Carla asked me to be a part of it.

Erik Cooper, M.A. marriage and family therapist, author of *Shall We Dance: A guide to happiness (2014)*, Montrose, CO

♡ Oscar Wilde once said, "Yes: I am a dreamer. For a dreamer is one who can only find his way by moonlight, and his punishment is that he sees the dawn before the rest of the world." When I think of Carla Blowey, I think of this quote. Carla is an advanced soul who has such keen insights to life.

I met Carla shortly after the death of her son Kevin. I remember how fragile life felt then for her and Stann, trying to put the pieces of life back together after losing their very young son. I could see that this was going to be a powerful journey for both of them. I wondered how it would unfold because many couples who experience the loss of child often end up in divorce. I invited Carla and Stann to speak at a high school confirmation retreat I was leading for our church youth group. On the Saturday evening of the retreat, Carla and Stann shared their story and gave a talk on unconditional love and risking the walk of faith in grief. Afterward, the teens received love letters from their parents and friends. Carla and Stann's talk transformed and opened up so many teenagers. I knew at that point that their journey was destined for greatness.

Carla made a decision early on that Kevin's life was instrumental in her own. Through really tough personal and spiritual work, Carla is one of the few people I know who used the grief of her son's death to gain insight into her own life. We had many conversations as she continued to work through the pain, and I saw her embrace forgiveness. The dream that predicted Kevin's death was also the tool that would lead to her wholeness. I knew that the dream was not simply a dream but rather an invitation to something much greater. And, that is exactly what happened. Through her dream work, I've watched Carla continue to heal and help others in that healing journey as well. She touches so many lives because of the work she continues to do in personal development. A conversation with Carla is never simply about the weather. A conversation with Carla always feels like you have been heard and that there is a great Divine life unfolding.

A very beautiful friendship has developed over the years between us. She is a soul sister and each time we visit, it is always powerful. Carla is a true seeker and managed to use her grief journey to pull herself forward in consciousness to live a powerful life. Over the years, I have watched Carla grow and seen her heart and mind continue to be open to her next "yet to be". She also possesses a gift to help you get to the heart of the matter for whatever is going on in your life. I often call Carla with my dreams and she always seems to pull forth such wisdom with her questions, insight and projections. As the quote said in the beginning, Carla sees the world in clarity before many do and that is the gift that she brings to the world.

Rev. Norman L. Bouchard, M.Div., senior minister at Center for Spiritual Living and author of *29 Questions for the Ordinary Life* (2011), www.normanbouchard.com, Colorado Springs, CO

♡ I met Carla a few years after she lost her son Kevin. We worked together briefly in the same hair salon and then moved on to different careers. We reconnected several years later and our friendship grew even closer. Neither of us imagined that we would be working together again and I realized that there was a reason why Carla came back into my life. In 2012, I lost my 32-year-old brother, Cody, in a dirt bike accident and Carla held my hand, my heart, and my sanity in her heart. She helped me honor my journey and validated my grief.

We've had many tearful and insightful conversations about grief and dreams since then (yes, I am a life-long dreamer too). I have to bear so many roles in my family –as a grieving daughter, a sister-in-law and an aunt –and yet, my relationship as a grieving sibling often takes last place. I'm learning that I have to take care of myself and that my relationship with Cody was just as significant. We've talked a lot about my grief dreams and my wonderful dream visits from Cody. I'm not so afraid of my dreams anymore now that I understand they are designed to get my attention about a grief issue or open a path of communication with Cody.

I'm beginning to understand that our loss as siblings (Amber, myself, and countless others) is largely uncharted. It's misunderstood as an "easier" loss, which is so sad. I don't think a majority of the world understands the pressures of what we deal with as a sibling. I'm not saying our loss is worse or sadder but our siblings make up a lot of who we are, how we deal in life and our personality, and they are our first and last best friends. I honestly felt like I lost my left arm after Cody died. I'm frustrated and sometimes I feel no one gets what a sibling goes through. Society would have us believe that we have to pick up the pieces for the whole family; the pressure to TRY to make your parents happy again, and take care of the family who is left behind.

Recently, I dreamed that I was on a stage in a large conference room and Amber and I were getting ready to speak to a crowd of people. There was a screen behind us with a backdrop of a mountain scene with a

342

photo of Kevin and a photo of Cody. It was the cover of our book about sibling loss from the perspective of a younger sibling and an adult sibling. I looked older in the dream. Amber and I were holding hands. We were smiling, looking at each other and crying but crying with a sense of understanding and joy about what we knew.

My dream made me have a passion for Amber and myself that I never felt before. I also have wondered so often about Megan and Jason and their feelings. I've felt strangled and I want to help other people who feel this way. I'm so far away from being able to give to anyone right now but I believe it's my path to help someone else someday. Cody would expect no less of me and I want to honor him to the fullest. I would never feel I truly grasped my purpose in life, if I didn't help at least one person. It's not about telling them what to do but giving them space and understanding and letting them know their grief as a sibling is just as valid.
Laura Browning Rattan, Montrose, CO

♡ It was July 2005, and I was in Boston as a first time presenter at The Compassionate Friends National Conference, an art therapist and as a bereaved mother, whose seventeen-year-old daughter Kristin, ended her own life. I was facilitating my collage workshop, *"The Art of Healing...loss, grief and grace,"* that introduced participants to a creative approach to healing. On my arrival, I checked out the TCF bookstore, offering hundreds of books on grief and bereavement. I was drawn to one book and finally bought it. I tucked *Dreaming Kevin: The Path to Healing* into my suitcase, knowing I'd read it in the coming days.

On the first morning of the conference, I spotted the one person I knew in a sea of fifteen-hundred attendees. I made my way toward Mitch, hoping there would be an empty seat for me. I sat down as he introduced me to his friend, Carla Blowey, author of *Dreaming Kevin*. I sensed my movement toward Carla from the night before when I unknowingly bought her book. That moment changed us forever for it set us on a path of friendship, as professionals and as mothers committed to our unique healing journeys. Carla and I sat, we talked, we laughed, we cried. We attended each other's workshops. I was captivated by the journeys we shared, for Carla's dreams and my collage images intermingled, as healing modalities that beckoned us into the depths and back into the light. Carla engaged the elements of her dreams while I engaged the fragments and elements of my collage creations. In the end there was healing.

When I met Carla, I was at a crossroads with my professional work as an art therapist. As the Compassionate Friends National Conference came to a close, Carla urged me to consider a synthesis of the various ways I was exploring my own healing as a template for my work with others. As a dream worker, she urged me to combine my creative process of collage with my meditation and dream work. I listened and felt

343

the winds of change blowing through me. When I returned home to Baltimore, I sat in my garden under the shade of our maple tree, and read *Dreaming Kevin*. "I was overcome by her prophetic dream alerting her to her son's death, and the spirited transmission that would occur for both mother and son. She shared her story with passion." (Strouse, 2013) I was transfixed by this real and honest description of grief, which "involved finding her way into all the elements of her dream so that she could free herself from the guilt she harbored over Kevin's death." (Strouse, 2013)

Carla and I see each other at national and regional conferences, where we continue to offer our individual workshops, along with workshops we have developed as co-facilitators. We take particular pleasure, combining dream work and image making, which serve as powerful and transformational experiences for participants. I am blessed to have met Carla, and to have picked up *Dreaming Kevin*, which introduced me to dream work as a way through grief. I sense Kevin and Kristin's part in bringing us together, and I am grateful.

Sharon Strouse, MA, ATR, art therapist, author of *Artful Grief: A diary of healing*, www.attherefuge.com, Cockeysville, MD

And lastly, from my greatest companion and love of my life...

A Note from Stann

♡ The publication of this expanded edition of Carla's book will mark 23 years since the loss of our son Kevin. Part of my healing process was being able to love and support my lovely wife, Carla, and beautiful daughter, Amber these past years. However, I admit there were many times when I neglected my own grief. Most men and women don't grieve in the same way. I was overwhelmed by the pressures of having to return to work and support the family. I was not comfortable talking about my feelings with many people, except Carla, and then I was worried about how my pain would affect her. So, as many men do, I did not recognize that my pain was just as important and valid.

Dreaming Kevin has given me a better understanding of Carla's inner world and the grieving process from a mother's perspective. It was very difficult not being able to relate to her dream world. I wanted so much to experience those kinds of dreams and have the same relationship with Kevin that she had. Thankfully, Kevin was persistent and found a way to come to me too. So, Carla's book helped me with my own grief issues and enabled me to heal some of my wounds. I encourage all bereaved fathers to take the risk to read our story and recognize that although as fathers our grief journeys may be different than the grief of our deceased child's mother, our feelings of loss are just as valid. What is most important is that we loved.

Even after all this time, I still think of Kevin and miss him very much. There is always something or someone to remind me of him, like a song or seeing his classmates and friends. Sometimes, people are afraid to talk about Kevin fearing it will bring back bad memories for me. I tell them they had just made my day because they remembered and I can talk about him once again. It brings me happy memories. There are also times people want to know about Carla's book or they ask for advice because they know someone else who has lost a loved one or a child. I've learned how to help other bereaved parents with the direction and guidance of my wonderful wife through her dream work, her professional consulting, national conferences and workshops, as editor of *Living With Loss* magazine and most of all through her book.

It seems like such a long time ago since Kevin's accident. I've retired from teaching after 34 years. Carla has written a book and developed her dream workshop program. Amber has grown to be a wonderful wife, loving mother, and an excellent special education teacher (and, she made me a granddad!). I've been blessed with two more children, Megan and Jason, who have become responsible young adults pursuing their education and careers. They have all made me a very proud husband and father.

My journey has been up and down, but I do know Kevin has been with me every step of the way. I've never been very good with words, so if I had to describe how I really feel about Kevin, listen to the song by Diamond Rio called "I Believe". I love you Kevin.

Stann Blowey, Montrose, CO

For Amber
With Love, Mom

"Never lose hope my heart.
Miracles dwell in the invisible."
~ Rumi

Dreaming Kevin was written for Amber
so that she would know and understand our story.
With the publication of this expanded edition,
we come full circle.

A Note from Kevin

While I was editing the final draft of the *Notes from the Children* section, I received an email from Mary (our grief counselor) saying that she had found several pages that Amber had written during their counseling sessions. Mary thought that perhaps the papers might be helpful for the children's section on grief. In the file were several letters Amber had written to Kevin and some Q&A responses (letters are featured on page 358 & 359). Mary would give Amber a sheet of paper during their sessions and Amber would "doodle" while they talked. In figure 17a., Mary only remembers that Amber was talking about Kevin during the session.

Amber recalls that she always liked to "doodle" her name using different styles of the letter "A". You can see Mary's handwriting to the left of the margin, and to the right of the margin how Amber tried to duplicate the small letter "a" style that Mary uses in her name. Across the top of the page she wrote her name three times in different script. Just below the first *"Amber"*, on the left, she begins the first attempt at writing Kevin's name.

Note how controlled Amber's penmanship is when writing her own name compared to when she is writing Kevin's name, which looks more childish. Then note that *one* of the *"Kevin's"* is smaller, and *its style matches* her previous *"Amber"* style above. Below that, she pens a somewhat controlled cursive *"Amber"* but digresses with the last three letters. Both of these are sandwiched between the two bold *"Kevin's"* in the childish style.

When I reached this point in my "scan" of the paper, I had to catch my breath. My sense was that Kevin was writing through Amber! I compared a sample of Kevin's handwriting (fig.17b) to what Amber had written. It is a perfect match.

I then scanned both pages to the computer to examine it more closely. When I zoomed in on my computer screen, the zoom went to the center of the page bringing into focus the small *"Kevin"* (in Amber's handwriting) and the scribbled cursive *"Amber"* name. At once, I saw: *"I am"*.

Non-believers, naysayers and skeptics would say I'm reaching but my intuition tells me that Kevin was communicating with her. This sacred page has been tucked away in Mary's file for 22 years…an unopened gift until now.

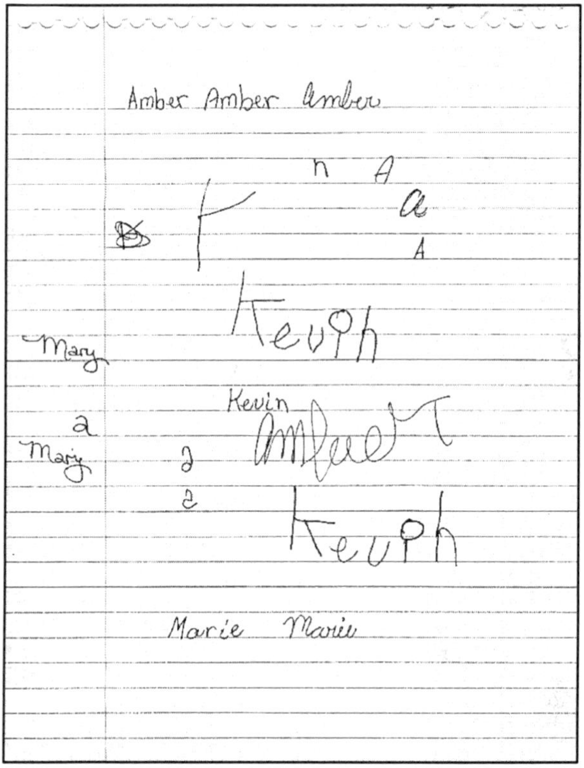

Figure 17a

Amber: (fig 17a) "First this kind of makes me laugh because even now when I "doodle", I still write and rewrite my name and others names using different kinds of letters. What I think is interesting about this is the way I wrote Kevin's name in comparison to my own. It looks like someone much younger wrote his name, almost like the way he would have written it. " (fig. 17b)

Kevin's handwriting sample - Figure 17b

Amber: "I Am" - April 1991 (fig. 17c)

When my mom opened up the file, and it zoomed in to the middle of the page focusing on the "i" in Kevin's name and the "Am" in my name, she had the realization that Kevin was "writing through me". I was stunned, but it made sense! It took me a bit to let this information sink in. While I don't have any memory of writing this, the more I looked at the doodling and the way Kevin's name is written, I know I never would have written his name in that way. I liked writing the names of my family in a way that was fun and different, and I didn't try to "copy" the way they would write it. I can't deny that Kevin was with me that day! It made my heart race, and I knew it was true.

Figure 17c

350

351

With Gratitude and Love

Once again, I am indebted to my wonderful husband, my children, and my companions on the journey! Your essay contributions became unexpected "love notes" reminding me that giving and receiving is the same. I extend my heartfelt gratitude to all my companions near and far who supported this project with your loving thoughts, generosity and prayers. I love you.

To my brother Paul for accepting my invitation to redesign the cover – your exceptional skills have truly transformed this sacred image from my inner world to the outer world. I love you, Po.

To my Ya-Ya's, Laurita and Patita –I love you. We've hiked our San Juan mountains, falling into 7-1-1- formation with laughter and tears, changing places to suit whoever is in need most that day. We've toasted our 30+ year friendship with goblets of wine, flutes of champagne and morsels of chocolate. How blessed am I to have you both by my side on this ever changing journey!

To my professional colleagues for supporting my dream work with the bereaved. When two or more of us gather, a sacred space is created by our desire to invite the bereaved to see their grief differently and choose Love. It's been an honor to work with you *and* call you my friends. I love you all.

To my friend and fellow dream worker Jeremy, for your exquisite insight, candid projections, and gentle nudges in our dream work sessions. I've learned so much from you about upholding the integrity of the dream and creating a non-judgmental space for the dreamer. The depth of the unconscious waters no longer overwhelms me. I breathe freely and swim deep, ultimately bringing my dreams to the surface light. I couldn't have asked for a more generous or committed diving companion than you.

To the *Children of Dreaming Kevin*...I am so grateful for your willingness to participate in our project. I commend all of you for your courage in taking the risk to revisit a very emotional time in your life. I hope "talking" about it in written form brought you a measure of healing. My prayer is that in sharing your stories, together, we will bring a greater awareness of children's grief to caregivers, parents, facilitators and counselors and enable them to better companion their children toward reconciliation and healing.

And, finally...thank you my sweet Kevin for encouraging me to dream big. I love you Boo-Boo. XOXOXOX

Carla

Bibliography

Bach, Richard, *One*, Bantam Doubleday Dell Publishing Group, 1989

Cooper, J.C. *An Illustrated Encyclopaedia of Traditional Symbols*, Thames and Hudson, 1978

Furth, Gregg M., *The Secret World of Drawings: A Jungian approach to healing through art*, Inner City Books, 2002

Gaskell, G.A. *Dictionary of Scripture and Myth*, Dorsett Press, 1988

Rohr, Richard, *Center for Action and Contemplation*, www.cac.org

Sanford, John A. *Dreams and Healing*, Paulist Press, 1978.

Taylor, Jeremy, *Where People Fly and Water Runs Uphill: Using dreams to tap the wisdom of the unconscious*, Warner Books, 1992

The Lockman Foundation *The New American Standard Bible*, Nashville: Holman Bible Publisher, 1977

Skeie, Eyvind, *Summerland: A Story About Death and Hope*, Brethren Press, 1989

Carla Blowey has gained insight, guidance and healing from her dreams for more than 25 years. In 1991, at age 33, the death of her five-year-old son, Kevin, and the prophetic dream that predicted it, forced Carla to re-examine her perceptions about death, grief and the afterlife. Using her dream journal with much discernment and prayer, she uncovered the personal symbols, metaphors and archetypes that led to forgiveness, healing, spiritual growth, and new life.

Carla recognized the power of sharing our dreams and grief experiences when she and her husband were invited to speak at their church for a Catholic Confirmation youth group retreat in 1994. Speaking together for the first time, they shared the risks they took in processing their grief, walking their faith and living again. Later, inspired by a dream she had about the retreat, Carla realized her daughter and other grieving children needed a safe place to share their grief stories as well, and coordinated the first children's grief support group in Montrose, Colorado. Carla coordinated and facilitated bereavement support groups, camps, workshops and volunteer training for children and adults.

In 1997, Carla retired from hairdressing to be present for her growing family. In the midst of changing diapers and teaching her oldest daughter to drive, she answered the call to write *Dreaming Kevin*. The success of the book is due in part to her ability to write from the heart, exposing her inner world so others might see differently too. *Dreaming Kevin* has been divinely guided to serve by inviting the bereaved to see their perceptions about death, grief and the after-life in a new light.

Carla is a certified Dream Work Facilitator through the Marin Institute for Projective Dream Work with director, Dr. Jeremy Taylor. She is a trained Stephen Minister and a past member of the advisory board for Hospice of the Uncompahgre Valley in Montrose, CO. Carla is a trained facilitator in Attitudinal Healing peer support from the Center for Attitudinal Healing. She is a member of the International Association for the Study of Dreams. As editor-in-chief for *Living With Loss Magazine* from 2006-2009, Carla's columns included *Reflections from the Editor, The Heartlight Connection*, and *The Dream Connection*.

An exceptional speaker, Carla has presented programs and workshops on dreams, grief, healing and after-death phenomena, writing a memoir and self-publishing. In her workshops and speaking programs, based on *Dreams: A Blessing Disguise©*, Carla offers group participants an opportunity to see beyond the illusions of death, bringing their dreams, their deceased loved ones and ultimately themselves, into the Light. Nationally, Carla presented *Dreams: A Blessing in Disguise for Grieving Parents* at The Bereaved Parents of the USA National Gathering; The Compassionate Friends National and Regional Conferences; TAPS, and The Afterlife Awareness Conference.

As an MIPD certified dream work facilitator, Carla believes *"all dreams come to us in service of health and wholeness, and only the dreamer knows for certain what his/her dream means." (Jeremy Taylor, D.Min.)* Using the projective format, we share our "imagined version" of the dream offering the dreamer another perspective to see it differently, leaving the analysis and interpretation to the dreamer. Weaving the values of spirituality with personal loss and transition for psychological and spiritual growth, Carla invites the dream images to speak their truth, thus creating a space for grace to nourish...and Love to flourish.

Carla says: "Sharing our dreams is an opportunity to see our grief journey *and* our life journey from a different perspective. I believe that when *we see our grief and our dreams differently, we are in a mode of healing* –letting go of perceptions that inhibit our emotional and spiritual growth. With each insight, we can examine the diverse issues that complicate living with loss, illuminating the imagery from the inner world to manifest creative solutions in the outer world. I am a dream worker –a seeker of light, truth, possibility, and peace; a facilitator for peace, grace and transformative healing."

Carla lives and dreams in beautiful southwestern Colorado with her family. Kevin continues to be her spiritual coach, inspiring and guiding her on this incredible journey.

For more information about her book, speaking,
dream workshops, dream groups and online programs, visit
www.dreamingkevin.com or **email: carla@dreamingkevin.com**